Hedge Fund Structure, Regulation, and Performance around the World

Hedge Fund Structure, Regulation, and Performance around the World

DOUGLAS CUMMING
NA DAI
SOFIA A. JOHAN

OXFORD
UNIVERSITY PRESS

OXFORD
UNIVERSITY PRESS

Oxford University Press is a department of the University of Oxford.
It furthers the University's objective of excellence in research, scholarship,
and education by publishing worldwide.

Oxford   New York
Auckland   Cape Town   Dar es Salaam   Hong Kong   Karachi
Kuala Lumpur   Madrid   Melbourne   Mexico City   Nairobi
New Delhi   Shanghai   Taipei   Toronto

With offices in
Argentina   Austria   Brazil   Chile   Czech Republic   France   Greece
Guatemala   Hungary   Italy   Japan   Poland   Portugal   Singapore
South Korea   Switzerland   Thailand   Turkey   Ukraine   Vietnam

Oxford is a registered trademark of Oxford University Press
in the UK and certain other countries.

Published in the United States of America by
Oxford University Press
198 Madison Avenue, New York, NY 10016

© Oxford University Press 2013

All rights reserved. No part of this publication may be reproduced, stored in a
retrieval system, or transmitted, in any form or by any means, without the prior
permission in writing of Oxford University Press, or as expressly permitted by law,
by license, or under terms agreed with the appropriate reproduction rights organization.
Inquiries concerning reproduction outside the scope of the above should be sent to the
Rights Department, Oxford University Press, at the address above.

You must not circulate this work in any other form
and you must impose this same condition on any acquirer.

Library of Congress Cataloging-in-Publication Data
Cumming, Douglas.
Hedge Fund Structure, Regulation, and Performance around the World / Douglas J. Cumming,
Na Dai, Sofia A. Johan.
pages cm
Includes index.
ISBN 978-0-19-986256-6 (cloth: alk. paper) — ISBN 978-0-19-975723-7 (alk. paper)
1. Hedge funds.   I. Dai, Na.   II. Johan, Sofia A.   III. Title.
HG4530.C8296 2013
332.64'524—dc23
2012026863

ISBN 978-0-19-986256-6

9 8 7 6 5 4 3 2 1
Printed in the United States of America
on acid-free paper

For

Sasha Adeline and Dylan Jedi

Kangguo Cheng and Michael Cheng

CONTENTS

Preface ix

CHAPTER 1. Introduction to Hedge Funds 1

CHAPTER 2. Agency Problems in Delegated Portfolio Management 21

CHAPTER 3. International Differences in Hedge Fund Regulation 37

CHAPTER 4. Overview of Empirical Finance Methods to Study Hedge Funds 69

CHAPTER 5. Hedge Fund Forum Shopping 94

CHAPTER 6. Hedge Fund Capital Raising 122

CHAPTER 7. Hedge Fund Performance and Compensation 157

CHAPTER 8. Hedge Fund Regulation and Misreported Returns 199

CHAPTER 9. Regulatory Induced Performance Persistence 227

CHAPTER 10. Hedge Fund Liquidation and Hedge Fund Influence on the General Market 265

CHAPTER 11. Conclusion 278

References 281
Index 289

PREFACE

This book is intended for advanced undergraduate and graduate students in business, economics, law, and management. It is also directed at practitioners with an interest in alternative investments in general and the hedge fund industry in particular as we consider a number of different countries around the world.

Hedge funds are pooled investment vehicles that typically source capital from institutional investors and are best characterized by their relative lack of regulatory oversight in most countries and their fee structures. Although media reports frequently suggest that hedge funds are unregulated, they are in fact regulated at least to some degree in every country in the world, although these regulations will differ from country to country. These differences are central to this book, as they enable an assessment of the impact of regulation on fund structure, governance, and performance. Regarding fund structures, it is often said that the best way to characterize a hedge fund is by fees. Hedge funds often follow the "2–20" rule whereby fund managers receive a 2% fixed fee and a 20% performance fee.

Broadly framed questions addressed in this book include the following:

- Why might hedge fund regulations be needed, and what are the problems that arise with delegated portfolio management?
- What are the existing regulations that affect hedge funds, and how do these regulations differ across countries?
- What are sources of hedge fund data, and what are the empirical tools that are useful in studying hedge funds?
- Do hedge funds move to jurisdictions that regulate less strictly?
- How does regulation affect a hedge fund's ability to raise capital relative to the fund's performance?
- How does hedge fund regulation affect a fund's fee structures?
- How does hedge fund regulation affect fund performance?

- How does hedge fund regulation affect fund survival and performance persistence?
- How do hedge funds affect the overall market?

By considering hedge funds in an international setting, this book offers an explanation of how hedge fund regulation influences fund structure, capital flows, governance, and performance.

It is important to review data to show how regulation is central to actual hedge fund structure, capital flows, governance, and performance. Without analyzing data, we would be limited to our best guesses, which is not the intention here. Like the data used in most academic hedge fund papers, the ones in this book are derived from data vendors that provide international datasets. The data considered in this book are international in scope, drawn from most regions of the world, including onshore and offshore funds. However, different from most studies, we examine international differences in hedge fund regulation from country to country. We believe it is important and worthwhile to consider such differences in legal and institutional settings across countries as they directly affect the structure, governance, and performance of hedge funds, as documented herein. It is important to consider data from a multitude of countries to understand how and why hedge funds markets differ around the world. As well, idiosyncratic features of certain countries may distort our understanding of how hedge funds work in practice.

In short, by considering international datasets, and not data from just one country such as the United States, we are able to gain a significant amount of insight into how hedge funds operate in relation to their legal and institutional environment. Each chapter in this book, where possible and appropriate, will refer to and analyze data. Note however that hedge funds are not compelled to publicly report data, nor are they always willing to voluntarily report information. As such, there are always more data that can be collected. It is the authors' hope that this book will not only provide an understanding of how hedge funds operate but also that it will inspire further empirical work in the field so that we may better understand the nature and evolution of hedge fund markets in years to come.

Selected chapters in this book are based, in part, on previously published material:

Chapter 3:
Cumming, D., S. A. Johan, and D. Li, 2011. "Exchange Trading Rules and Stock Market Liquidity." *Journal of Financial Economics* 99(3), 651–671.

Chapter 5:
Cumming, D., and S. A. Johan. 2008. "Hedge Fund Forum Shopping." *University of Pennsylvania Journal of Business Law* 10(4), 783–831.

Chapter 6:
Cumming, D., and N. Dai. 2009. "Capital Flows and Hedge Fund Regulation." *Journal of Empirical Legal Studies* 6, 848–873.

Chapter 7:
Cumming, D., and N. Dai. 2010. "A Law and Finance Analysis of Hedge Funds." *Financial Management* 39, 997–1026.

Chapter 8:
Cumming, D., and N. Dai. 2010. "Hedge Fund Regulation and Misreported Returns." *European Financial Management* 16, 829–867.

Chapter 9:
Cumming, D., N. Dai, L. H. Haß, and D. Schweizer. 2012. "Regulatory Induced Performance Persistence: Evidence from Hedge Funds. *Journal of Corporate Finance* 18, 1005–1022.

We are indebted to Dan Li, Lars Haß, and Denis Schweizer for their generosity in allowing us to use some of the material upon which Chapters 3 and 9 are based, as that work was developed jointly with these excellent coauthors. We are very grateful to Terry Vaughn and Catherine Rae at Oxford University Press for their helpful comments and feedback in preparing this book. Moreover, we have benefited from comments by Jerry Cao, Bill Christie, William C. Gerken, Michael Hutchinson, Michael King, Andrew Karolyi, Kate Litvak, Jeffry Netter, Melvyn Teo, and the seminar participants at the following: American Law and Economics Association Annual Conference at Harvard Law School (2007); Canadian Law and Economics Association Annual Conference, University of Toronto (2011); the Conference on Empirical Legal Studies (Cornell, 2008; Northwestern University, 2011); Singapore Management University (2011); Eastern Finance Association Annual Meeting, Boston (2012); the EFM Symposium on Risk Management at the Audencia School of Management, Nantes (2008); the EFM Annual Conference at Bocconi University, Milan (2008); the EFM Symposium at the University of Cambridge Judge Institute of Management (2008); the Financial Management Association, New York (2010); Hofstra University (2007); the Western Finance Association Annual Conference (2007); the Northern Finance Association Conference (2007); the DeGroote Conference on Market Structure and Market Integrity (2007); the Financial Intermediation Research Society Conference (2008); the Amsterdam Conference on Financial Intermediation at the Crossroads (2008); Queen's University International Finance Conference (2008); Université Catholique de Louvain (2009); University of Pennsylvania Law School (2008); Vanderbilt Law School (2007); and York University (2007). Douglas Cumming and Sofia Johan owe thanks to the Social Sciences and Humanities Research Council of Canada for generous financial support.

Each chapter of the book begins by describing the issues and learning objectives. As well, each chapter ends with a list of key terms and a number of discussion questions. PowerPoint lecture slides, course syllabi, and exam questions for each chapter are available from the authors, and any comments or questions about the book can be sent to the authors. The authors are easiest to reach by email at dcumming@schulich.yorku.ca (Douglas Cumming), ndai@albany.edu (Na Dai), and sjohan@schulich.yorku.ca (Sofia Johan).

CHAPTER 1

Introduction to Hedge Funds

1.1. Introduction

Hedge funds have been the subject of media attention in the United States and around the world since the Bernard Madoff scandal and the more recent allegations against the Galleon Group. Given the pronounced growth of the hedge fund sector in recent years and the comparative dearth of regulations faced by hedge fund managers, this attention is probably appropriate. One concern shared by market participants and many regulators worldwide is that the size of the hedge fund industry coupled with potential agency problems, activist investment practices, and herding behavior exacerbates financial instability. By 2005, hedge funds collectively had accumulated over a trillion dollars in assets, while at the peak in the summer of 2008, industry estimates suggest that the market had more than US$2.5 trillion in assets (Ineichen and Silberstein, 2008). This amount, while not trivial, is comparatively small compared to the size of worldwide mutual fund capital, which is estimated at US$24.32 trillion by the Investment Company Institute. There is, however, significant scope for the industry to move markets. For example, in the week of August 6, 2007, hedge funds following long/short equity strategies experienced massive losses. Empirical evidence on this event shows significant and growing systematic risk in the hedge fund industry (see Khandani and Lo, 2007, and Getmansky et al., 2004).

Hedge funds are not prohibited from employing a variety of investment instruments in pursuing their investment strategies (i.e., the primary mandate of a hedge fund), many of which would not be permitted by other funds such as mutual funds and private equity funds. This is possible by compromising on the extent to which their products or funds can be offered to the public. In the United States and the United Kingdom, for example, hedge funds can only be distributed by private placements. Hedge funds may utilize derivative instruments and may short sell and leverage rather highly to achieve their investment goals. Commonly observed hedge fund strategies include investment in distressed companies, commodity trading advisers/managed futures, short biased and small/micro capitalization (hereafter "micro cap") focused strategies, among numerous other strategies identified here.

In this chapter we first describe what hedge funds are in Section 1.2. We explain their investor base, investment strategies and use of leverage, transparency, valuation, liquidity, pricing, regulatory oversight, and fees. Also, in Section 1.2 we compare and contrast hedge with other asset classes such as venture capital, private equity, and mutual funds. In Section 1.3 we provide some descriptive statistics of the size of the hedge fund market over time and make some size comparisons with other asset classes. Finally, in Section 1.4 we outline some of the main issues relevant to the analysis of hedge funds and thereby provide an outline for the scope of material that comprises the subsequent chapters of this book.

1.2. What Are Hedge Funds?

What are hedge funds? Financial regulators in the United States and the United Kingdom have yet to promulgate a legal definition of hedge fund (see Garbaravicius and Diereck, 2005). In the United States, relative to other managed funds, hedge funds do not have their investment activities as restricted by the Investment Company Act's (1940) restrictions on leverage, short-selling, cross-holding, 10% limits, incentive compensation, and derivatives positions; however, this is because the hedge funds prefer to adhere to the limitations on number of US investors (99 maximum), solicitation of US investors, and public advertising and disclosure. Other jurisdictions have differing views on what hedge funds are, and by taking into account the investment strategies used, they have specified such funds as Sophisticated Alternative Investment Vehicles, Highly Leveraged Institutions, and Leveraged Investment Funds (see Donaldson, 2003). In view of the fact that highly competent regulatory bodies have themselves been unable to define the term "hedge fund," we will not attempt to do so in this book. Therefore, for the purposes of this chapter, when reference is made to the term hedge fund, we will use the description provided by Hodder and Jackworth (2007): "a compensation scheme for a pool of money to be collectively managed and invested on behalf of the capital providers."

Hedge funds are essentially financial intermediaries, as illustrated in Exhibit 1.1. Hedge funds are pools of capital that are typically sourced from institutional investors. Institutional investors include pension funds, university endowments, foundations, banks, and insurance companies. High net worth individuals may also invest in hedge funds. The scope of investors that may invest in a hedge fund depends on the regulatory landscape in which the fund is registered, as explained in Chapter 3 of this book. While hedge funds most commonly trade in liquid securities, the scope of investments and trading activities that a hedge fund can undertake is typically wider than that of other types of funds. Hedge funds often make use of leverage and short selling. Hedge funds seek to provide their investors with returns that significantly exceed benchmark market index returns, and in turn, charge significant fees. The typical fee structure is the "2 and

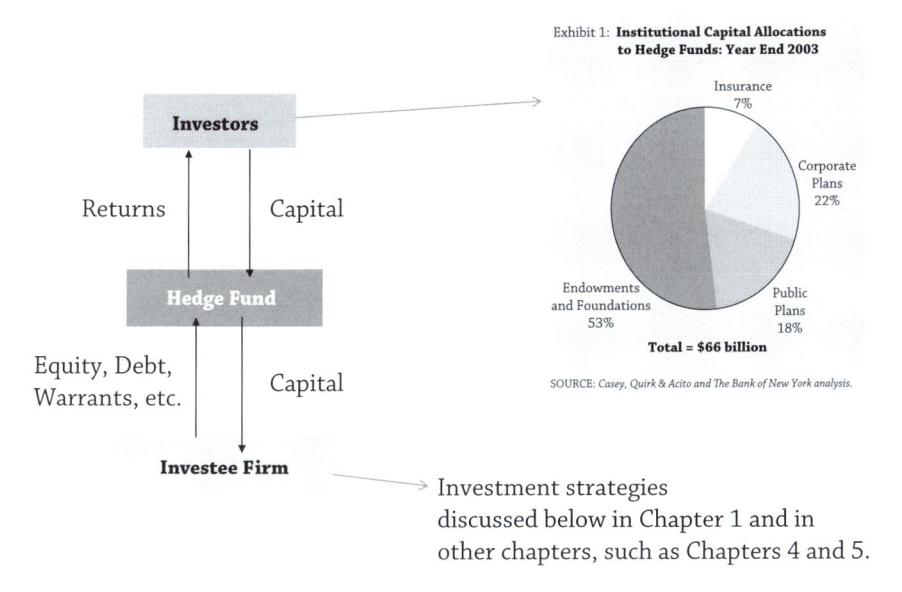

Exhibit 1: **Institutional Capital Allocations to Hedge Funds: Year End 2003**

- Insurance 7%
- Corporate Plans 22%
- Public Plans 18%
- Endowments and Foundations 53%

Total = $66 billion

SOURCE: *Casey, Quirk & Acito and The Bank of New York analysis.*

Investment strategies discussed below in Chapter 1 and in other chapters, such as Chapters 4 and 5.

Exhibit 1.1 Hedge Fund Financial Intermediation

20" model which means 2% of committed capital as a "fixed fee" and 20% of profits as a "carried interest fee." Hedge funds often follow strategies that make their returns less correlated with the market than other asset classes.

It is said that no man is an island, and that holds true for hedge fund managers. Hedge fund investment strategies are facilitated by various external (and increasingly internal) service providers, as depicted in Exhibit 1.2. A hedge fund itself has no employees and no assets other than its investments. The portfolio is managed by the investment manager, a separate entity which is the actual business and has employees. The hedge fund managers, rather obviously, have overall authority over the functions of the fund and determine the investment strategies. If they are successful, they may manage a few funds in tandem. They may have assisting them other investment and professional advisers such as lawyers, accountants, consultants, and tax and audit specialists.

As well as the investment manager, the functions of a hedge fund are delegated to a number of other service providers. The most common service providers are administrators, registrar, prime brokers, custodians, and distributors. The *administrators* assist the fund managers in providing administrative and accounting services for the fund, including record keeping, making independent valuation of investments, and meeting disclosure requirements. The administrator typically deals with the issue of shares and performs related back office functions. In some funds, particularly in the United States, some of these functions are performed by the investment manager, a practice that gives rise to a potential conflict of interest inherent in having the investment manager both determine the net asset value and

4   Hedge Fund Structure

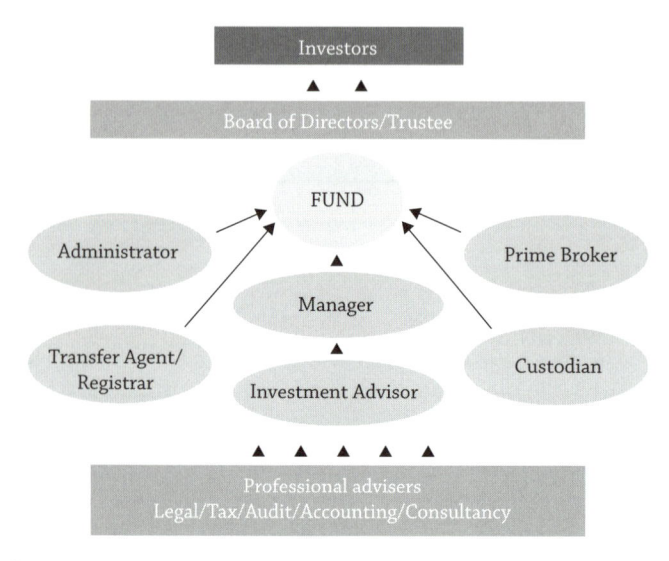

Exhibit 1.2 Typical Parties Appointed to Operate a Hedge Fund

Notes to Exhibit 1.2:
Administrator: records and does bookkeeping and independently verifies asset value of the fund
Registrar / Transfer Agent: processes subscriptions and redemptions and maintains registrar of shareholders
Custodian: charged with safe-keeping of assets
Prime Broker: provides access to stock and loan financing as well as a host of value-added services
Source: PriceWaterhouseCoopers www.pwchk.com/home/eng/hedge_fund_operation_jul2005.html.

benefit from its increase through performance fees. Outside the United States, regulations often require this role to be taken by a third party. The *registrar* or *transfer agent* may assist the fund manager in processing subscriptions and redemptions and in maintaining the register of shareholders. Sometimes, depending on the structure of the fund and the human resources of the manager, these duties may be carried out internally by the fund manager. The actual financing arrangements and execution of investments are more often than not carried out by external *prime brokers*, which can be either securities firms or banks. Occasionally, the prime brokers themselves decide to set up their own fund, and they therefore also become hedge fund managers. Prime brokerage services include lending money, acting as counterparty to derivative contracts, lending securities for the purpose of short selling, trade execution, clearing, and settlement. Many prime brokers also provide custody services. Prime brokers are typically parts of large investment banks. There is of course another service provider, the *custodian* that has custody over the fund assets. Again, this duty may sometimes be carried out internally by the prime broker. Finally, the *distributor* is responsible for marketing the fund to potential investors. Frequently, this role is taken by the investment manager.

Hedge funds differ from traditional investment funds in a variety of ways. The main differences are management style, investment purpose, return targets, fees, economies of scale, investor base, and legal structure. These differences are summarized in Table 1.1 and explained in greater detail thereafter below.

Table 1.1 **Hedge Funds versus Traditional Investment Funds**

	Traditional Investment Funds	Hedge Funds
Management style	Active / passive	Active
Investment policy	Heavily restricted by mandate and regulations, usually cannot use leverage	Very flexible; leverage is key tool
Return targets	Normally small annual % above benchmark (active), or identical to benchmark	Target absolute % return with aim of achieving this, regardless of market conditions
Fees	Based on funds under management (rarely performance related component)	Based on funds under management and performance related component
Economies of scale	The bigger the funds, the larger the fees	Nature of activity means often an optimal fund size
Liquidity	Normally investors can enter / leave funds at any time	Highly restricted and hence enabling funds to invest in highly illiquid markets
Investor base	All	High net worth individual, institutional investor
Legal structure	Usually subject to raft of financial market regulations. High degrees of transparency	Organized to reduce obligations. Poor degree of transparency

A hedge fund manager is essentially just another financial intermediary, just as mutual fund managers or private equity (and venture capital) fund managers are. Mutual funds invest in publicly traded companies with severe restrictions that fit with their retail client base. Venture capital funds invest in private start-up companies often with a 30%–50% ownership stake. Private equity funds use significant leverage to fully purchase companies for the purpose of changing their structure or operations. Hedge funds cover many different investment styles and invest with shorter durations than venture capital and private equity funds. There are of course other significant differences among types of financial intermediaries, and we will very briefly set out the most obvious differences, including but not limited to their investor base; transparency, liquidity and pricing; strategies and leverage; regulatory oversight; and fees. These differences are summarized in Table 1.2 and explained in greater detail below.

Table 1.2 **Differences across Mutual, Hedge, Private Equity, and Venture Capital Funds**

	Mutual Fund	Hedge Fund	Private Equity Fund	Venture Capital Fund
Strategy	Directional strategy	Directional, arbitrage, and spread strategies	Long-term buy (acquisition), hold, exit, includes public to private	Long-term investment in private start-ups
Securities, asset classes	Stocks, bonds	Stocks, bonds, currencies, commodities	Common, preferred, convertible preferred, convertible debt, straight debt, warrants	Common, preferred, convertible preferred, convertible debt, straight debt, warrants
Long or short	Long only or short only (dedicated)	Both long and short	Long only	Long only
Correlations	Return is correlated to market averages	Return has low correlation to market averages	Return has low correlation to market, stage of investment countercyclical to initial public offering volume	Return has low correlation to market, stage of investment countercyclical to initial public offering volume
Duration	Investor mentality (buy and hold)	Trader mentality (opportunistic)	Very long term (3–7 years) illiquidity	Very long term (3–7 years) illiquidity
Benchmark	Focus on beating a benchmark	Focus on absolute return with low volatility	Valuation of private assets, benchmarking very difficult	Valuation of private assets, benchmarking very difficult
Leverage	Typically unleveraged	Use of leverage	Use of leverage	Typically unleveraged
Risk management	Low degree of risk management	High degree of risk management	Risk management in due diligence and mitigating idiosyncratic risk	Risk management in due diligence and mitigating idiosyncratic risk

Table 1.2 (Continued)

	Mutual Fund	Hedge Fund	Private Equity Fund	Venture Capital Fund
Personnel	Low sensitivity to personnel	High sensitivity to personnel	High sensitivity to personnel	High sensitivity to personnel
Compensation	Salary-based compensation of staff	Performance-based compensation of staff	Performance-based compensation of staff	Performance-based compensation of staff
Analysis	Fundamental analysis (financial accounting)	Fundamental, statistical and technical analysis	Due diligence—scientific merits of technology and personnel quality	Due diligence—scientific merits of technology and personnel quality
Price entry and exit	Low sensitivity to price entry and exit point	High sensitivity to price entry and exit point	High sensitivity to price entry and exit point	High sensitivity to price entry and exit point
Speed	Decision and execution of ideas relatively slow	Decision and execution of ideas relatively fast	Decision and execution of ideas relatively slow	Decision and execution of ideas relatively slow
Assets under management and returns to scale	Low sensitivity to increasing assets under management	High sensitivity to increasing assets under management	High sensitivity to increasing assets under management	High sensitivity to increasing assets under management
Regulation	Heavy	Less regulated, but limited to accredited investors	Less regulated, but limited to accredited investors	Less regulated, but limited to accredited investors
Other constraints (limited partnership contract is applicable)	Investment memorandum and scope for style drift	Investment memorandum and scope for style drift	Formal limited partnership agreement, serious if style drift	Formal limited partnership agreement, serious if style drift

1.2.1. INVESTOR BASE

Generally speaking, mutual funds, hedge funds, and private equity funds could be categorized as public investment companies or pooled investment vehicles. What inevitably exempts hedge funds and private equity funds from the legal and regulatory requirements and ensuing oversight of public investment companies or pooled investment vehicles are the characteristics of their typical investors. Unlike mutual funds, hedge funds and private equity funds limit the number of investors, as required by the relevant regulatory authorities. For example, in the United States, hedge funds utilize the exemptions in Section 3(c)(1) of the Investment Company Act 1940 and do not exceed the number of 99 investors to avoid regulatory oversight (see 15 U.S.C. § 80a-3(c)(1)). Hedge fund investors also are primarily institutional investors and high net-worth or wealthy individuals. Taking the US example again, to take advantage of the exemption under the Investment Company Act, hedge funds would not likely market their services to the retail public with assets below US$5 million (see 15 U.S.C. § 80a-3(c)(7)).

The minimum investment in a hedge fund varies from fund to fund, and sometimes fund managers waive minimum investment amounts at their discretion. Funds commonly require US$250,000 to $500,000, but some funds have minimums as low as US$10,000, while established funds may require as much as US$10,000,000. Many funds have lockup periods (the time period over which an investor in the fund cannot remove invested capital, or at least not without paying a penalty) which can last a year or more depending on the contracts associated with the fund.

1.2.2. TRANSPARENCY, LIQUIDITY, VALUATION, AND PRICING

Mutual funds, as a result of their investor base, have to meet stringent disclosure requirements, are obliged to implement established valuation principles, and have to price their portfolios on a daily basis. Private equity funds are not bound by similar stringent disclosure requirements as they do not have retail investors, although some private equity funds are required by their public institutional investors to disclose performance data such as internal rate of return as the investor itself is required to provide such information by law. In response, many private equity funds have excluded such investors. Hedge funds are extremely opaque with regard to the reporting of their operations and the valuation of their portfolio and limit their exposure to investors that require more transparency. With regard to liquidity, hedge funds are more liquid than private equity funds as private equity funds require their investors to commit their capital for up to 10 years while hedge funds at most have lockup periods of up to 25 months. Mutual funds are also the most liquid of the three funds.

1.2.3. STRATEGIES AND LEVERAGE

Among hedge funds, mutual funds, and private equity funds, hedge funds are the most autonomous in their ability to implement their rather innovative investment strategies. Mutual funds are usually, to a certain extent, constrained legally and by regulation in their asset choices, and have to disclose to their investors the anticipated allocations in such asset classes. Private equity funds are equally constrained by contract as they are required at the outset to specify the maximum amount of capital to be invested in any one company, and also the industry and stages of development of investee companies. Hedge funds in contrast are able to use a variety of investment strategies that ironically have far less to do with hedging, and these strategies include the use of facilities not normally accessible to mutual funds and private equity funds, which are short-selling and derivatives. While it is not possible to perfectly classify different hedge fund strategies, it is possible to carry out a rather rough grouping of strategies, and for the purposes of this book we will refer to the following strategies: convertible arbitrage, fixed income arbitrage, merger/risk arbitrage, capital structure arbitrage, statistical arbitrage, long/short equity, multi-strategy, CTA/Managed futures, emerging markets, technology sector, macro, event driven, distressed securities, Regulation D, and high yield low grade fixed income securities, short bias, small/micro cap, special situations, energy sector and country specific.

Another rather significant difference is that both mutual funds and private equity funds are constrained in their ability to leverage. In an investment context, *leverage* refers to borrowing to invest. Leverage constraints are usually legal and regulatory in form for mutual funds, and contractual for private equity funds. In contrast, hedge funds are "leveraging" creatures in that they "sell securities short and buy securities on leverage" (see House Committee on Banking and Financial Services, 1999). They are however not leveraged in the more traditional sense of taking on more debt capital. They leverage themselves by the innovative use of derivatives instruments, the use of margin financing in lieu of trading in the case of securities that require full payment, and short selling. Most hedge fund trades involve leverage because leverage amplifies the profits (but also the losses) from the trade. Leverage is carried out by borrowing external funds to invest more or sell short more than the equity capital the hedge fund puts in. Borrowing is done through a brokerage margin account.

The "hedge" in hedge funds is a strategy to offset investment risk. A *perfect hedge* in theory enables gains and losses to be offset fully, which results in a completely neutral outcome. In practice, most hedges are *partial hedges* for which outcomes depend on the expected versus actual gains and losses. A *direct hedge* refers to hedging with another asset that exhibits a similar price movement, such as a common stock with its call option. A *cross hedge* refers to hedging with a dissimilar asset, such as preferred stocks and interest rate-driven treasury futures.

A *dynamic hedge* refers to changes in strategies over time depending on market conditions while a *static hedge* does not vary with market conditions over time.

A *market neutral hedge fund strategy* is an arbitrage in expectations, as graphically illustrated in Exhibit 1.3. The short position's exposure matches the long position's exposure. The short position finances the long position.

Long-short hedge fund strategies involve hedge funds buying one undervalued stock, say Stock A, and selling another overvalued stock, say Stock B. Long-short strategies can make money for hedge funds in a number of ways. For example, the fund can short sell Stock B since it is overvalued, and then when it goes back to a normal price the hedge fund can buy back Stock B at the lower price and pay back the Stock B loan. As another example, the hedge fund can borrow to buy the undervalued Stock A at the low price, and then when Stock A is at a fair value it can sell Stock A and repay the loan.

Event driven hedge fund strategies focus on unusual corporate activity. For example, unusual events of interest include public to private buyouts, mergers and acquisitions, share buy-backs, reorganization following bankruptcy, and debt/equity capital restructuring. In view of the possibility of news leaks and insider trading following news announcements, media and regulators are often very critical of hedge fund activity around these events. As well, hedge funds that are activist investors may use their voting power to influence the outcome of these events, and at times this activity generates criticism of target corporations.

Event driven merger arbitrage hedge fund strategies involve the hedge fund taking a position based upon assessment of likelihood of success of merger/takeover activity. Pre-announcement, hedge funds use statistical models to assess the likelihood of takeover targets. Post-announcement, hedge funds buy the stock of

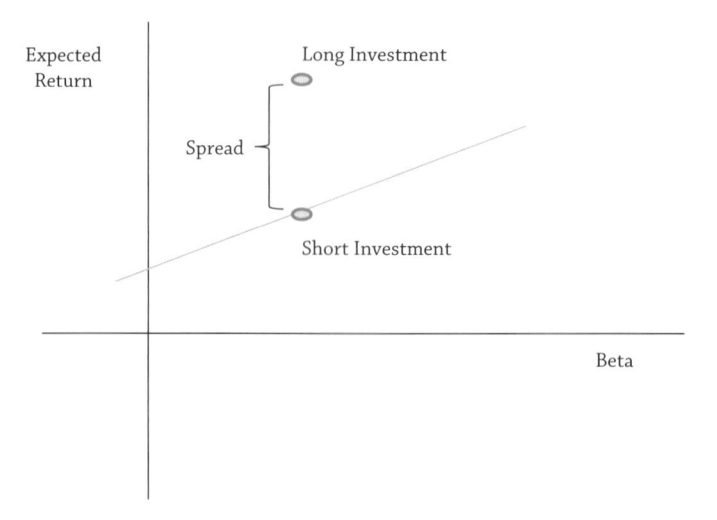

Exhibit 1.3. Market Neutral Hedge Fund Strategy

target companies and sell the stock of acquirer companies, since acquirer stocks typically fall in price upon announcement (Cumming and Li, 2011). The risk of event driven merger arbitrage strategies is that the deal does not materialize or evolve as predicted.

Directional hedge fund strategies are strategies that do not use hedging but instead use significant leverage to benefit from broad market movements. Examples include global macro funds (e.g., George Soros's fund) and emerging market funds, and sector funds such as commodities, technology, and energy.

Hedge fund managers earn their returns through manager skill (opportunity identification, activist investment, knowledge of market imperfections, and modeling techniques). There is a variety of different hedge fund strategies. Different strategies to varying degrees will employ leverage and short selling. Specific strategies have low correlation, enhanced diversification, and potential for superior returns. The different sources of strategies generate returns based on different sources of alpha and beta, so it is important for investors in hedge funds to know what they are investing in. It is possible for funds to drift in the sense that they do not always follow the strategy that they claimed they would follow, so it is important for investors in hedge funds to monitor their investments. Fund managers may also earn returns through illegal activity, including fraud, insider trading, and market manipulation. Therefore it is potentially important for regulators to have oversight over hedge fund activities.

1.2.4. REGULATORY OVERSIGHT

Due to their accessibility to the retail public and their investment strategies, mutual funds are subject to rather strict legal and regulatory oversight. In the United States, for example, the Securities and Exchange Commission (SEC) requires mutual fund managers to be registered. In addition, they are also subject to various regulations under the Investment Advisers Act of 1940, the Securities Act of 1933, the Investment Company Act of 1934, and the Securities Exchange Act of 1933. Hedge funds and private equity funds are not as strictly regulated as they are enabled by their structure and investment strategies to meet the relevant requirements to be exempt from the laws and regulations that could limit their operational freedom. They essentially avoid regulation by following the letter of the law.

Hedge funds are not obligated to register in the jurisdiction in which they are physically based. Many funds are registered "offshore" in a tax haven country. In fact, offshore registrations comprise a substantial portion of the hedge fund industry. For example, the Eurekahedge Database contains an approximate 50/50 North American onshore/offshore split, and our non-North American coverage has an approximate 30/70 onshore/offshore split. In Chapter 3 we provide statistics for the offshore/onshore registrants in the the Center for International Securities and Derivatives Markets (CISDM) database.

12   Hedge Fund Structure

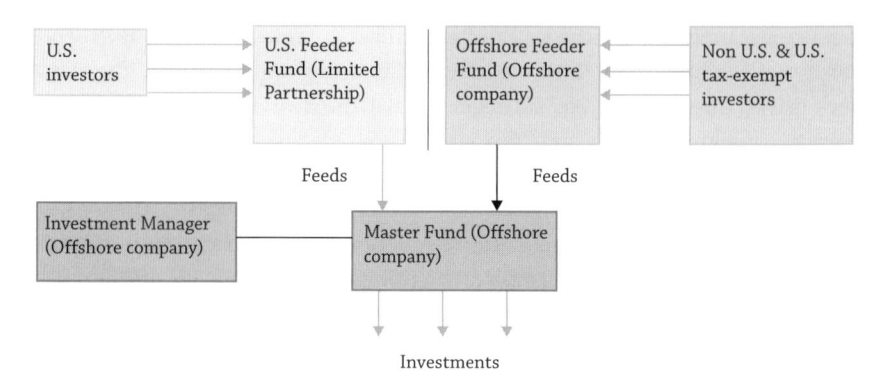

Exhibit 1.4. Master-Feeder Hedge Fund Structure

Source: http://richard-wilson.blogspot.com/2008/01/master-feeder-fund-structure.html

The *master-feeder hedge fund structure* is a common way that hedge funds are set up to accept assets from both foreign and domestic investors in the most tax and trading efficient manner possible. The "master" or central fund is usually located offshore. The structure helps fund managers to market a fund to both offshore and onshore investors, each with different tax exempt status. The fund manager typically sets up one "master" company and two "feeders": one feeder for onshore investors and the other feeder for offshore investors. The two feeders share the same underlying asset portfolio and the investment decision is made at the master company level. The master-feeder structure is illustrated in Exhibit 1.4.

The differing sets of regulations and taxation of hedge funds around the world is explained in greater detail in Chapter 3 of this book.

1.2.5. FEES AND PROPRIETARY INVESTMENT

Mutual funds are usually constrained in their ability to arbitrarily impose fees or sales charges, and they are more often than not required to disclose their fees to their potential investors. In contrast, hedge fund and private equity fund managers impose a management fee based on the size of fund managed (usually 2.5% for private equity funds and 1.5% for hedge funds), and a performance fee that is usually 20% of the profits. For most hedge funds, the management fee is collected in 25% quarterly trenches, in advance, while the performance fee is calculated annually. Private equity fund managers and hedge fund managers are usually required to put their money where their mouths are, or pay to play. This is not the case for mutual fund managers. Private equity fund managers, however, only really invest a minimal amount in the fund partnership to meet the requirements of general partnership, and they are for the most part restricted from co-investment in investee companies. Hedge fund managers in contrast are not restricted in the amount of proprietary capital they may invest in the hedge funds they manage.

Most hedge funds have *highwatermark fees*. In other words, the hedge fund manager will only receive performance fees on that particular pool of invested money when its value is greater than its previous greatest value. For example, if the value of the fund is $100,000 in 2010 and $150,000 in 2012, then the performance fee is paid on ($150,000–$100,000) only. In the event that the investment drops in value, the manager must bring it back above the previous greatest value before performance fees are paid again. The rationale of highwatermark fees is that they avoid agency problems whereby a fund manager could deflate the value of the fund temporarily to subsequently restore value only for the purpose of collecting a performance fee without generating value for the investors into the hedge fund.

Most hedge fund managers report their returns from prior years "net of all fees," including management and performance fees, but there are differences in reporting across funds so that investors need to understand their investment reports. Most hedge funds promise returns in the form of alpha (return in excess of market expected return for the given level of systematic risk) and promise alphas greater than 5%. With over US$1 trillion in capital under management among hedge funds, this implies that hedge funds are able to earn more than US$50 billion in excess returns that are not picked up by market participants. Unfortunately, not all funds actually achieve these returns, as we will see in Chapter 7 of this book. Moreover, as we will see in Chapter 8, many funds misreport their investment returns in various ways. For instance, with voluntary reporting to hedge data vendors such as CISDM or TASS, hedge funds typically report only after they have achieved 12–18 months of superior performance (otherwise known as a *backfilling bias*). As well, fund managers tend to smooth returns to avoid the appearance of negative returns (or down months) and report unusually high returns at the end of the year for the purpose of obtaining performance bonuses.

While there are significant differences among hedge funds, private equity funds, and mutual funds, what is strikingly similar among them is that all three types of fund managers owe their funds and fund investors a fiduciary duty to act in the best interest of the fund and fund investors. The duties of good faith and fair dealing, loyalty, and care have to be upheld by all hedge fund managers as well as his counterparts, and they are prohibited against fraudulent activities as are other financial intermediaries. However, as with any form of financial intermediation, there will inevitably be conflicts of interest or agency problems. Such agency problems are exacerbated by the characteristics of the hedge fund we listed earlier. In the next section we will list the potential agency problems encountered in hedge fund management, how they are connected to the characteristics of hedge funds, and how regulatory measures have sought to mitigate such problems.

1.3. How Large Is the Hedge Fund Market?

The first hedge fund was established in 1949 by Alfred Winslow Jones, which followed strategies of buying and shorting publicly traded securities. In 1966 it was reported that this "hedge" fund outperformed the best mutual funds, even

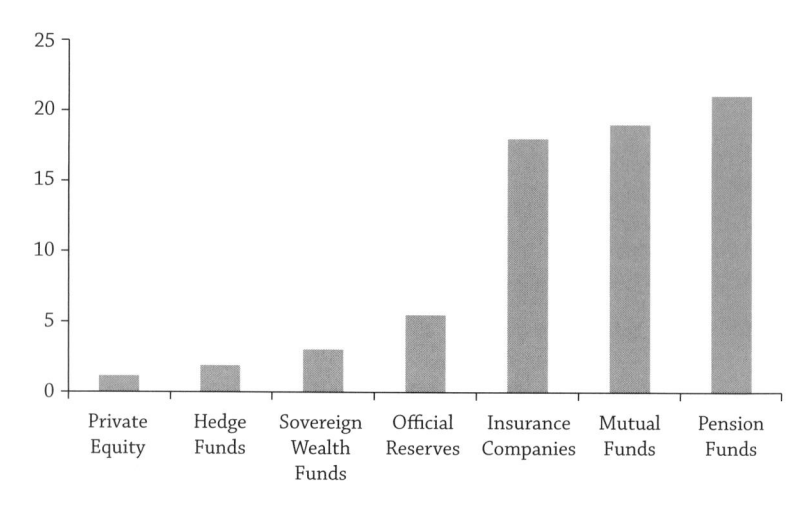

Exhibit 1.5. Capital under Management by Asset Class in US$ Billion

Source: Fotak, Bortolotti, and Megginson (2008)

after the 20% performance fee. By 1968 there were 200 hedge funds and in 1969 there was the first fund of hedge funds.

As of 2011, the hedge fund market worldwide has capital under management in the range of US$1.5–2 billion. Estimates vary because hedge funds typically do not have registration or reporting requirements. Hedge funds collectively manage more capital than private equity funds, but less capital than sovereign wealth funds, official reserves, insurance companies, mutual funds, and pension funds. See Exhibit 1.5.

Exhibit 1.6 presents capital under management and the number of funds worldwide by year. According to Eurekahedge, as of 2011, there are nearly 10,000 funds and US$1.8 trillion in capital under management. Some estimates put hedge fund capital under management in excess of US$2 trillion in 2007 prior to the financial crisis. Most hedge funds source their capital from the United States, Switzerland, and Japan, as shown in Exhibit 1.7.

These preliminary statistics provide some guidance about the relative size of the hedge fund industry worldwide. In Chapter 4, we provide a number of additional statistics on hedge fund size, location, structure, and performance.

1.4. What Issues Are Relevant to the Study of Hedge Funds?

In this subsection we outline some of the main issues pertinent to hedge funds. In doing so, we explain the topics addressed in the subsequent chapters of this book.

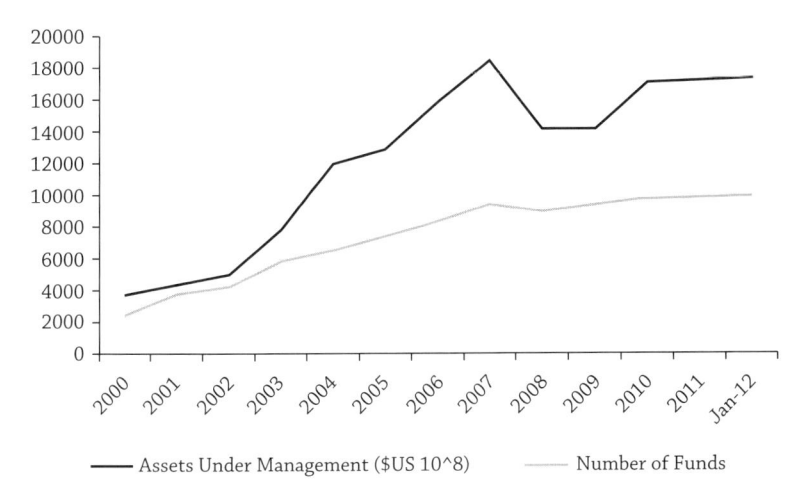

Exhibit 1.6. Hedge Fund Capital under Management and Number of Hedge Funds by Year

Source: Euerkahedge, www.scribd.com/doc/86151002/Eurekahedge-March-2012–2011-Key-Trends-in-Global-Hedge-Funds

1.4.1. AGENCY COSTS AND INFORMATION ASYMMETRIES

As with any form of financial intermediation, there are inevitable agency problems associated with hedge fund management. While these specific agency problems are described in more detail in Chapter 2, here we briefly outline the extent to which potential agency problems may arise. First, in a more direct manner, hedge

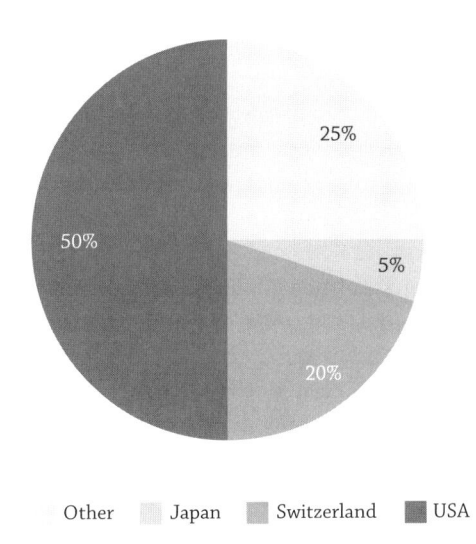

Exhibit 1.7. Source of Hedge Fund Assets by Country, Directly and Indirectly

Source: Harcourt Estimates (2007)

funds might pursue investment strategies and/or prepare financial reports that benefit the hedge fund manager at the expense of their investors. For example, hedge funds are much more likely to report marginally positive monthly returns than returns that are marginally negative, and this type of return manipulation significantly aids capital raising efforts of hedge fund managers (see, e.g., Bollen and Pool, 2008, 2009, 2006, and Cumming and Dai, 2009). Second, in a more oblique manner, hedge funds' investment strategies might be counter to the interests of the other shareholders of portfolio companies in which hedge funds invest (see Kahan and Rock, 2007, for examples of this category of agency problem). For example, hedge funds that acquire significant voting rights in a company may seek to act in ways that primarily bring about financial benefit to the fund (and therefore its investors) at the expense of the company's other shareholders (see, e.g., Hu and Black, 2006). Such active participation in portfolio companies by hedge funds has been labeled (in a flattering manner) hedge fund activism and (in a more critical manner) vulture fund activity.

In short, agency costs and information asymmetries play a central role in shaping the structure and governance of hedge funds. Agency problems thereby provide a context for the data that are presented and analyzed in the subsequent chapters. Chapter 2 of this book provides an overview of the potential agency problems associated with managing a hedge fund, and thereby the associated rationales for hedge fund regulation.

1.4.2. INTERNATIONAL INSTITUTIONAL AND LEGAL CONTEXT, AND EMPIRICAL METHODS

The data considered in this book are international in scope. Consideration of data from just one country might potentially lead to inferences that are not generalizable to other contexts. Chapter 3 therefore provides an overview of international differences in institutional and legal settings for different countries discussed here.

While hedge funds are hardly regulated in the United States, other jurisdictions outside this country implement different and sometimes more onerous sets of regulatory requirements. As explained in Chapter 3 of this book, international differences in hedge fund regulation include but are not limited to minimum capitalization requirements, restrictions on the location of key service providers, and different permissible distribution channels via private placements, banks, other regulated or non-regulated financial intermediaries, wrappers, investment managers, and fund distribution companies.

We also discuss recent legal debates over the past few years pertaining to the taxation of fund managers. The carried interest compensation of fund managers has been taxed at lower capital gains tax rates, but there has been a push in the United States and the United Kingdom, among other countries, to change this to a higher income tax rate.

It is important to review data to show how regulation is central to actual hedge fund structure, capital flows, governance, and performance. Without analyzing data, we would be limited to our best guesses, which is not the intention here. Therefore, in Chapter 4 we provide an overview of empirical methods to study hedge funds in an international setting. The discussion of the statistical and econometric methods in Chapter 4 of this book enables a reader to follow all of the chapters, regardless of prior training. It is important to consider data from a multitude of countries to understand how and why hedge funds markets differ around the world. As well, idiosyncratic features of certain countries may distort our understanding of how hedge funds work in practice.

1.4.3. DO HEDGE FUNDS REGISTER IN JURISDICTIONS WITH THE LEAST STRICT REGULATION?

Chapters 5–8 of this book provide empirical analyses of hedge fund strategies, structure, fund flows, performance, and misreporting behavior in the context of international differences in hedge fund regulation. One argument consistently put forward in opposition to more onerous regulation of hedge funds is the threat of regulatory arbitrage—that hedge funds will move from one jurisdiction to another less regulated to avoid regulatory oversight. Hedge funds are free to seek the most favorable climate by registering in many different countries around the world subject to meeting the requirements of jurisdiction. A central issue considered in Chapter 5 is therefore whether hedge funds that are pursuing riskier strategies are also practicing regulatory arbitrage to facilitate such strategies. If hedge funds pursuing risky investment strategies select more highly regulated jurisdictions, then it is possible to infer that hedge fund managers seek to signal their interest in mitigating potential agency conflicts associated with fund management, thus increasing their ability to raise more capital. If hedge fund managers pursuing riskier strategies select less regulated jurisdictions, then it may be possible to infer that the managers are practicing regulatory arbitrage potentially at the expense of investors. If hedge fund strategies are invariant to international differences in regulation then we may infer that regulatory differences provide little or no information to a fund's investors.

The data presented in Chapter 5 offer little support for the view that hedge fund managers pursuing riskier strategies or strategies with potentially more pronounced agency problems systematically select jurisdictions with less stringent regulations. In fact, to the extent that there is evidence of forum shopping, it is for the most part suggestive that funds pursuing riskier strategies or strategies with greater potential agency problems select jurisdictions with more stringent regulations (for examples of consistent empirical evidence found in other unrelated contexts, see Romano, 1985, and Cumming and MacIntosh, 2000). We may infer from the evidence that forum shopping by fund managers in relation to the strategic focus of the fund is not consistent with regulatory arbitrage where funds select jurisdictions with limited regulation so that regulators have incentives to curtail regulation. Rather, the data suggest that hedge funds select jurisdictions that are in the interest of the funds' investors in order to facilitate capital raising by the hedge fund.

1.4.4. HOW TO ATTRACT INSTITUTIONAL INVESTORS?

Chapter 6 focuses on the issue of the flow-performance relationship in hedge funds, or the ability of hedge funds to attract capital from their investors in response to changes in prior returns. Among other things, Chapter 6 shows that hedge funds registered in countries that have larger minimum capitalization requirements tend to have higher levels of inflows. This suggests that minimum capitalization enhances investor confidence in terms of greater stability with larger funds. This finding holds even after controlling for minimum investment amounts per transaction. Chapter 6 also shows that hedge funds registered in countries that restrict the location of key service providers also have lower levels of inflows. This latter result is consistent with the view that locational restrictions are perceived by investors to mitigate human resource quality, and this perceived reduction in human resource quality is more pronounced than any associated perceived improvement in regulatory oversight. Also, country-specific regulations related to distribution channels tend to impact fund flow-performance sensitivity.

1.4.5. HOW WELL DO HEDGE FUNDS PERFORM, AND HOW ARE FUND MANAGERS COMPENSATED?

Chapter 7 explains the different ways to measure hedge fund performance, including raw returns, alphas, Sharpe ratios, and manipulation proof performance measures. We present data consistent with the view that restrictions on the location of key service providers and permissible distributions via wrappers are associated with lower fund alphas, lower average monthly returns, and higher fixed fees. Further, restrictions on the location of key service providers are associated with lower manipulation-proof performance measures, while wrapper distributions are associated with lower performance fees. As well, the data show that standard deviations of monthly returns are lower among jurisdictions with restrictions on the location of key service providers and higher minimum capitalization requirements. Chapter 7 also shows how fund performance and managerial compensation differ depending on legal conditions, economic conditions, institutional investor characteristics, fund characteristics, and fund manager education and experience, among other things.

1.4.6. DO FUND MANAGERS MISREPORT INFORMATION?

Chapter 8 of this book addresses the issue of hedge fund misreporting of monthly returns to institutional investors. Among other things, we show evidence that international differences in hedge fund regulation are significantly associated with the propensity of fund managers to misreport monthly returns. We find a positive association between wrappers and misreporting, particularly for funds that do not have a lockup provision. Also, we find some evidence that misreporting is less common among funds in jurisdictions with minimum capitalization requirements and restrictions on the location of key service providers. We assess the robustness of our finds to a number of specifications, including different specifications of misreporting bin widths, subsets of the data by fund type, specifications controlling for collinearity and selection effects, and other robustness checks. We show that misreporting significantly affects capital allocation; we calculate the wealth transfer effects of misreporting and relate this wealth transfer to differences in hedge fund regulation.

1.4.7. WHAT INFLUENCES HEDGE FUND SURVIVAL AND PERFORMANCE PERSISTENCE, AND DO HEDGE FUNDS AFFECT MACRO-FINANCIAL OUTCOMES IN A COUNTRY?

Chapter 9 of this book considers hedge fund performance persistence and assesses, among other things, whether or not hedge fund regulation affects persistence. The data show evidence of three types of regulation influencing performance persistence: (1) minimum capital restrictions, which restrict lower quality funds and hence increase the likelihood of performance persistence; (2) restrictions on location of key service providers, which restrict human capital choices and hence tend to mitigate performance persistence; and (3) distribution channels, which make fund performance more opaque and thus decrease the likelihood of performance persistence. Furthermore, in Chapter 9 we show differences in the effect of such regulations on persistence by fund quartile ranking.

Chapter 10 of this book assesses the determinants of hedge fund survival. Among other things, we consider whether regulation plays a role in fund survival. Finally, we examine arguments regarding the interplay between the hedge fund industry and the stability of financial systems and consider whether hedge funds affect macro-financial outcomes in a country or the reverse causality regarding the affect of macro-financial conditions on the stability and survival of hedge funds. Other questions are similarly considered.

In summary, hedge funds are distinct investment vehicles relative to other financial intermediaries with distinct investment strategies. The asset class is very large in terms of its size and scope, and it offers investors significant possibilities for enhancing returns. But hedge funds also present specific issues of agency and other problems that arguably give rise to the importance for regulation. Hence, it is worthwhile to consider evidence-based policy making by examining worldwide data on the interplay between hedge fund regulation and hedge fund structure, governance, and performance. We hope the chapters of this book provide some initial guidance for understanding these interrelationships to students, academics, practitioners, and policy makers alike. Also, we hope that this work will inspire further work on the topic as the structure and regulatory landscape of the hedge fund industry around the world evolves over time.

Keywords

Administrator
Carried Interest Performance Fee
Custodian
Cross Hedge
Direct Hedge
Directional Hedge Fund Strategy
Distributor
Dynamic Hedge
Event Driven Hedge Fund Strategy
Event Driven Merger Arbitrage Hedge Fund Strategy
Hedge Fund
Liquidity
Long-Short Hedge Fund Strategy
Management Fee
Market Neutral Hedge Fund Strategy
Master-Feeder Hedge Fund Structure
Mutual Fund
Partial Hedge
Perfect Hedge
Prime Broker
Private Equity Fund
Registrar/Transfer Agent
Static Hedge
Transparency
Venture Capital Fund

Discussion Questions

1.1 What is a hedge fund? How do hedge funds differ from private equity, venture capital, and mutual funds? Are hedge funds regulated?
1.2 What factors might influence the size of the hedge fund industry across countries and over time? How common are onshore versus offshore funds?
1.3 What are some of the common hedge fund strategies?
1.4 Do all hedge fund strategies involve the use of short selling and leverage?
1.5 What is a master-feeder hedge fund structure, and where/why is it employed?
1.6 How do hedge fund managers ensure fund opacity?

CHAPTER 2

Agency Problems in Delegated Portfolio Management

In the modern era of fund-based asset management, most investment decisions are delegated to agents (fund managers) whose behavior and character are imperfectly observed and known. Agency conflicts have long been a concern with delegated portfolio management. While the agency relation in the delegated portfolio management shares many features with a traditional principal-agent model, it also presents its own challenges. In this section, we describe the standard principal-agent problem, then in Section 2.2. we discuss theoretical and empirical works on the agency problems in traditional institutions such as mutual funds. In Section 2.3, we discuss the agency problems and the mechanisms to mitigate such problems in the hedge fund industry.

2.1. Classic Principal-Agent Problem

Most economics studies of agency problems adopt, implicitly or explicitly, the framework of Jensen and Meckling (1976). In their framework, an agency relationship is defined as a contract under which one or more persons (the principal(s)) engage another person (the agent) to perform some service on their behalf that involves delegating some decision-making authority to the agent. Agents will not necessarily act in the best interests of the principal as their objective is to maximize their own utility. In the face of such inconsistency in their interests—those of the principal and the agent—the principal can limit divergences by the agent by providing appropriate incentives for the agent and by employing monitoring mechanisms that will alert the principal if the agent takes certain actions that would harm the principal's benefits. However, these mechanisms are costly to design and enforce and are employed only to the extent that their benefits outweigh their costs. Therefore, in most agency relationships, the principal and agent will incur monitoring and bonding costs. Furthermore, the agency problem can only be alleviated; it cannot be eliminated. The cost of using incentive and monitoring mechanisms to reduce agency conflicts and the reduction in firm valuation as a result of the agency problem is called agency cost in Jensen and Meckling (1976).

Although Jensen and Meckling (1976) focus on the agency problem in the setting of corporation, they do point out that the agency problem is quite general. It exists in all organizations and in all cooperative efforts, including the delegated portfolio management industry.

2.2. Agency Problems in Delegated Portfolio Management

In a delegated portfolio management setting, the principal delegates the management of her capital to an agent. The agent is better informed about her own quality than the principal before the contract is signed, which is the so-called adverse selection problem. Further, the effort made by the agent to deliver the best result is not observable to the principal; thus, there is a moral hazard problem. Nonetheless, the outcome depends not only on the agent's effort but also on environmental factors outside the agent's control. The problem is that the investor cannot distinguish the effect of the manager's effort from the effect of the randomly determined environmental factors, nor can the investor costlessly observe the manager's choice of risk level. Agency problems arise as to whether the managers' choices (both effort and risk) are optimal from the investor's perspective. Therefore, the task of the investor is to design a contract that encourages the best fund managers to participate and, at the same time, gives the fund managers the right incentives to work hard to achieve the desired result after the contract is signed.

Both the theoretical and empirical works in this area have explored the existence of various agency problems in the delegated portfolio management and have evaluated the effectiveness of some mechanisms designed with the aim of reducing agency problems.

2.2.1. EVIDENCES OF AGENCY PROBLEMS

The literature examines various dimensions of agency conflicts in delegated portfolio management. Examples include window-dressing, risk taking, market timing, and cross subsidization, which is certainly not a complete list. The following are a few representative studies on these issues.

Window Dressing
Lakonishok, Shleifer, Thaler, and Vishny (1991) studied window-dressing behavior among pension fund managers and found that pension funds tend to oversell stocks that have performed poorly, especially in the fourth quarter, in order to impress sponsors about their portfolio holdings. Sias and Starks (1997) examined the trading activity of individual and institutional investors at

year-end and show that institutions are more inclined to buy recent winners, which is also consistent with window dressing. Carhart et al. (2002) found that mutual fund managers inflate quarter-end portfolio prices with last-minute purchases of stocks already held. Meier and Schaumburg (2004) provided additional evidence on the prevalence of window dressing in the mutual fund industry by documenting the significantly increased turnover during the last days of the quarter.

Risk Taking

Theoretical and empirical work on risk taking by US fund managers includes Brown, Harlow, and Starks (1996); Chevalier and Ellison (1997a); Goriaev, Palomino and Prat (2001); Busse (2001); and more recently Basak, Pavlova, and Shapiro (2007).

Brown et al. (1996) view the mutual fund industry as a tournament in which all funds having comparable investment objectives compete with one another. Assuming such a framework, these authors show that relative losers during the interim performance assessment period increase the portfolio risk to a greater degree than the relative winners. The implication of their finding is that it is possible that this tournament structure provides adverse incentives to fund managers to choose a risk level that is not necessarily optimal from investors' perspective. That is, fund managers may focus on the short-term performance that is consistent with their own best interest but not necessarily that of their investors.

Chevalier and Ellison (1997a) define risk-taking incentive as the sensitivity of a fund's value to its volatility and examine the portfolio holdings of mutual funds in September and December. Similar to Brown et al. (1996), they show that mutual fund managers do alter the riskiness of their portfolios at the end of the year as a response to their compensation incentives.

Goriaev, Palomino, and Prat (2001), on the other hand, theoretically proposed and empirically confirmed that a good (top decile) interim performance generates strong incentives to take on more, rather than less, risk in order to end the year ranked first. So, if performance is defined in terms of relative ranking and if this creates a "winner take all" situation, the mutual funds with the highest chance of being the interim winner, and not the interim loser, will take on the most risk.

Busse (2001) found that using monthly returns and daily returns generates different results regarding how fund managers choose risk level. When daily returns are used, there is no evidence that underperformers are more likely to increase their risk relative to better performing funds. The author attributes the differences in the results from monthly and daily returns to the biases in the monthly volatility estimates given the autocorrelation in returns.

Instead of measuring risk-taking as the sensitivity of the managers' payoff to volatility as used by Chevalier and Ellison (1997a), Basak, Pavlova, and Shapiro (2007) define risk taking as the fraction of the fund optimally invested in the risky asset. They theoretically proposed and empirically confirmed that underperforming managers boost the deviation of their portfolio from the benchmark, that is, they increase the tracking error variance, but not the volatility of their portfolios. Furthermore, the authors argue that mangers' risk-taking behavior is conditional on their risk tolerance and the extent of underperforming as compared with the benchmark. Specifically, they find risk-averse managers are more likely to decrease their portfolio betas when underperforming. In addition, they find that funds increase risk when moderately behind the benchmark but cease to do so when they have fallen far behind.

Market Timing
Zitzewitz (2003, 2006) showed that mutual funds use pricing policies that allow market timers to earn large trading profits at the expense of long-term shareholders even though this arbitrage opportunity has been understood by the industry for 20 years. The author finds that the speed and efficacy of a fund's actions in market-updating their prices are negatively correlated with its expense ratios and the share of insiders on its board, suggesting the agency problem may be the fundamental cause of the arbitrage problem.

Cross Subsidization
Gaspar et al. (2006) found that mutual fund families strategically transfer performance across member funds to favor those more likely to increase overall family profits. This family strategy of "favoritism" is also the result of the divergence of interests between fund management companies and shareholders.

2.2.2. MECHANISMS DESIGNED TO ALLEVIATE
AGENCY PROBLEMS

A second strand of literature examines whether and how incentive contracts (both explicit and implicit) and disclosure requirement mitigate the agency conflicts as discussed.

Explicit Incentives: Compensation
The traditional and dominant form of compensation for mutual fund investment advisers has been a basic percentage of the market value of the assets managed. In the late 1960s, mutual funds began rapidly adopting symmetric and asymmetric performance fee contracts. In 1970, on the recommendation of the SEC, Congress prohibited the use of asymmetric performance fee contracts, ruling that if investment companies used performance-based compensation contracts, the contracts had to be symmetric. More recently, the SEC has allowed asymmetric performance fees for investment advisors of wealthy clients. Hedge funds and commodity trading advisors commonly employ these types of fee schedules (see, e.g., Brown et al., 2001; Fung and Hsieh, 1999; Ackermann et al., 1999). In addition, the Labor Department has allowed their use for corporate pension

funds, which now commonly use performance-based fees for their investment managers. Despite the increased usage of asymmetric performance fee structure by other types of investment managers, mutual funds in the United States servicing small investors are still not allowed to use asymmetric performance fees.

Modigliani and Pogue (1975), Starks (1987), Grinblatt and Titman (1989), and Admati and Pfleiderer (1997) have considered the incentive effects of explicit performance contracts between a mutual fund manager and mutual fund investors. Theoretically, incentive fees should elicit more effort on the part of the portfolio managers, or attract better managers, thus reducing the agency conflict in delegated portfolio management. Empirical evidences are fairly mixed. Starks (1987) showed that the "symmetric" contract dominates the "bonus" contract in aligning the managers' interests with those of the investor, where the symmetric contract penalizes managers if the performance falls short of the benchmark while a bonus contract does not. Golec and Starks (2004) examined how mutual fund managers changed their portfolio risk around the 1970s when Congress and the SEC prohibited mutual funds from employing asymmetric performance fee schedules. They showed that mutual funds have increased their portfolio risk when forced to change their performance fee schedules. However, their results also suggest that, without the contract changes, managers would have increased risk even more. Blake, Elton, and Gruber (2003) found that funds with incentive fees do better than funds without incentive fee structures. At least part of the outperformance can be explained by the better stock selection ability of fund managers with incentive fees. However, they also found that incentive-fee funds take on more risk than non-incentive-fee funds and they increase risk after a period of poor performance.

Implicit Incentives: Reputation and Career Concern
There is an adage in the delegated portfolio management industry that "the real business of money management is not managing money; it is getting money to manage." In this situation, the concern of raising new funds in the future may motivate fund managers to undertake costly efforts. Thus, reputation provides implicit incentives to fund managers (in addition to the explicit incentives provided by performance-based compensation) in delegated portfolio management.

Berkowitz and Kotowitz (1993) and Huddart (1999) discussed the incentive effects of the flow-performance relationship theoretically. Chevalier and Ellison (1997b) showed that career concerns of mutual fund managers play a significant role in their decision about risk taking. They showed that fund managers are frequently terminated (or quit) and they frequently reappear later, managing other funds. Both the systematic and the unsystematic risk they choose for their fund appear to impact their future ability to secure employment in the industry.

Several studies indicated that there seems to be an asymmetry in the payoffs related to reputation concerns. Sirri and Tufano (1998), among others, have documented that net investment flows are much less sensitive to past returns when these are bad, and they are more sensitive when these are good. Lynch and

Musto (2003) claimed that this is so because funds respond to bad performance by replacing the personnel or techniques that produces it. Thus a good outcome may be more informative for the future performance than a bad outcome.

The asymmetry of implicit incentives might trigger possible excessive risk taking by portfolio managers. The fact that fund managers compete with each other for reputation and future fund-raising might encourage portfolio managers to discard their private information and herd with the market. These tendencies do not necessarily benefit investors or the overall efficiency of the financial market.

Disclosure Requirement

Edelen et al. (2011) studied the transparency of operating expenditures in mutual funds. They found that greater transparency in fund operating expenditures results in lower agency costs and better return performance. Kacperczyk, Sialm, and Zheng (2008) showed that despite extensive disclosure requirements in the mutual fund industry, investors do not observe all actions of fund managers, and this has performance implications. The authors documented that unobserved actions of some funds persistently create value, while such actions of other funds destroy value, indicating the existence of agency cost.

2.3. Agency Problems in Hedge Fund Management

The debate with regard to the regulation of hedge funds probably began in earnest with the Long Term Capital Management debacle in 1998 and will probably continue as capital increasingly floods into the industry. The systemic risks such funds pose to the stability of the financial industry as a whole is becoming more apparent. While being demonized in the popular media, it would, however, be incorrect to say that hedge funds are wholly unregulated, rogue entities. Across the globe, the activities of hedge funds are constrained to certain extents by various laws and regulations that aim to protect investors and the stability of the financial market or economy within a given jurisdiction. However, even in the United States and the United Kingdom, which are considered the strictest regulatory regimes, such laws and regulations have been deemed insufficient in view of the potential systemic damage, and there is a call by policy makers for this "regulation-lite" environment to be reviewed.

The agency problems that may arise within a hedge fund manager and client relationship comprise conflicts of interest between any of the parties involved in the management of the hedge fund. Depending on the structure, size, and jurisdictional base of the hedge fund, the duties carried out by the manager, its advisers, administrator, registrar or transfer agent, prime broker, and custodian may be carried out partly or wholly internally or partly or wholly outsourced. There will therefore be an endless list of potential conflicts of interest that may arise between the parties depending on the nature and extent of their relationship. We will for the purposes of this book limit our discussion of conflicts to those that are more common and readily recognizable among the parties and regulatory bodies and how they relate to the characteristics unique to hedge funds. We will also provide a brief description of the nature of the conflicts, whether they are operational in nature, related to the marketing process, or a legal conflict. These types of conflicts may also overlap. For example, the business conflict of the manager using his proprietary assets to allocate securities to his own account before implementing his investment strategy may be a business conflict, a legal conflict of insider trading, and a breach of fiduciary duty.

2.3.1. POTENTIAL CONFLICTS ARISING FROM INVESTOR BASE

Hedge funds comprise institutional investors, endowments, and high net worth individuals. While the argument against the regulation of hedge funds may center around the fact that its investors are sophisticated investors, it can also be argued that of the different types of investors, the least sophisticated of the purported sophisticated lot may be the high net worth individual. For a person to be considered a high net worth individual, or a sophisticated investor, the threshold might require assets of US$1 to $5 million and above. If we take an example of an average person with a home in an established US city, other recreational property, investments and retirement savings, it is possible that the threshold of US$1 million could easily be reached. The average age of a US-based investor with more than US$5 million is 67 and with US$1 million is 62. In 2009 in the United States alone, the number of families with a net worth of more than US$1 million (excluding primary residence) numbered 7.8 million, and there were more than 790,000 households with a net worth of more than US$5 million (see Leondis, 2010). Would these investors be as sophisticated in investing as the managers of an endowment fund? Unfortunately, we do not believe this would be likely. Neither would a hedge fund manager. The hedge fund manager is aware that the level of due diligence carried out prior to investment by a high net worth investor will be different from that done by an endowment fund manager. The high net worth individual may have neither the technical capabilities nor the desire to incur the added expense of hiring experts to carry out the due diligence. The institutional investor, however, has a fiduciary duty to its own clients and will therefore carry out a thorough search for appropriate fund managers and carry out a due diligence exercise. The hedge fund manager may therefore have the incentive to provide different levels of information during the marketing exercise to different types of investors. The hedge fund manager also aims not only to attract new investors to a fund but also to retain existing investors as potential investors in other hedge funds he will inevitably establish. The potential for conflicts to arise as a result of his preference to retain specific investors over others may result in preferential disclosure in different marketing efforts and preferential investment and preferential redemption terms among others. Such agency problems may give rise to a legal conflict with regard to allocation issues, breach of fiduciary duty, and disclosure issues (see Bollen and Pool, 2006). A potential business conflict is that the high net worth individual will be given less favorable investment terms in the fund than other more sophisticated investors.

2.3.2. POTENTIAL CONFLICTS ARISING FROM FEES AND PROPRIETARY INVESTMENT BY HEDGE FUND MANAGERS

The fee structure for hedge fund managers may also bring about potential agency problems as the hedge fund manager may be encouraged to take unnecessary risks. The manager essentially has a 20% share of unlimited upside potential but will not have share of any losses. Unlike the investor, the manager in essence has an option-like compensation structure, unless he invests his own proprietary capital. That said, as he has total control over the investment strategies, he may be able to protect his share of the fund from the additional risks to which he is exposing the rest of the fund. This total control over the investment of the fund also follows through to the fees to be paid to support service providers.

We mentioned earlier that some successful hedge fund managers manage several funds, sometimes concurrently. There are also instances when prime broker banks that already manage a few mutual funds establish their own hedge funds. What is increasingly obvious is other financial intermediaries joining the fray so to speak and establishing hedge funds alongside other types of funds, such as mutual fund managers and private equity fund managers. This is also the case for the support service providers such as prime brokers who may not have their own hedge funds to manage but provide services to both hedge funds and mutual funds. In these situations, where one institution wears two hats, or where one party has to act in the interests of various side-by-side clients, there is the potential for agency problems to arise. This is especially the case where levels of fees acquired from different clients, or different types of clients, differ in that some funds or managers are willing to pay higher transaction fees for "special" services. Some managers and prime brokers therefore may provide additional information regarding an investment, carry out preferential allocations, confer liquidity preferences, or provide other preferential treatments in favor of a specific hedge fund either due to higher fees paid or the level of proprietary investment made in that specific fund. Specific hedge funds may also be favored over other mutual funds, again due to the higher fees or the institution's dependency on the execution business of the hedge fund. It has been indicated that more prime brokers are becoming dependent on the income stream garnered from hedge funds, to the point of such income comprising an eighth of total revenue in one case (Bollen and Pool, 2006). Such agency problems may give rise to a legal conflict with regard to allocation issues, breach of fiduciary duty, disclosure issues, and insider trading. A potential business conflict is the competition of allocations and investment opportunities between an institution (or manager), on a proprietary basis, and the hedge fund.

2.3.3. POTENTIAL CONFLICTS ARISING FROM LACK OF REGULATORY OVERSIGHT

We mentioned earlier that in many jurisdictions, hedge funds are not as strictly regulated as mutual funds, for example, as they are enabled by their structure and investment strategies to meet the relevant requirements to be exempt from the laws and regulations that could limit their operational freedom. This ability to operate freely may give rise to a gamut of potential agency problems. Lord Acton once said that "Power tends to corrupt, and absolute power corrupts absolutely" (see Hirsch et al., 2002).

Agency problems in hedge fund management often take a more basic form of simple fraud. Bollen and Pool (2009) made a recent study of hedge fund litigation cases and found that the most common type of offense involved misappropriation whereby a fund manager diverts investor capital for personal expenses.

While it is true that regulatory oversight may not totally remove agency problems, proper regulation might mitigate the potential for them to arise if all parties involved know that deviation from proper rules of behavior and procedures to be adhered to carries the threat of civil or criminal penalties. An interesting note is that just as hedge funds have utilized the letter of the law to be exempted from regulatory oversight, they are also using the law to protect themselves in the event that they or any of their support service providers become "corrupted absolutely." In some private placement memoranda, the instrument with which they market their fund to sophisticated investors, they include a section specifically addressing a range of potential conflicts of interest or activities that could be construed as such, including but not limited to proprietary trading, managing side-by-side funds, and managing competing funds. With this disclosure, investors are then given notice and will have to agree that the disclosed potential activities will not be actionable, thereby protecting the fund and the manager from potential lawsuits or disciplinary measures. The lack of regulatory oversight may provide the hedge fund manager and other support service providers with the necessary latitude to undertake behavior that may be improper, if not illegal but for the lack of regulation. On the other hand, this perception of the hedge fund industry as comprising wholly unregulated, rogue financial intermediaries may be detrimental to the participants and therefore the lack of formal regulation may be made up by self-regulating actions.

2.3.4. POTENTIAL CONFLICTS ARISING FROM LACK OF TRANSPARENCY, LIQUIDITY, INDEPENDENT VALUATION, AND PRICING

Hedge funds are known for their opaqueness, illiquidity, highly subjective valuation methods, and inability (or rather unwillingness) to price themselves. If the investors in hedge funds find it difficult to obtain a full picture of the investment, they will find it almost impossible to determine the full extent of the related party transactions among the external support service providers and the fund itself. It is not difficult to see how agency problems may arise in this case. Also, note that even if most of the support services are provided internally, they will be provided by different departments or agents and therefore there is still the potential for conflicts of interest to arise. Take for example the simple valuation of investments carried out by the hedge fund. This is not usually carried out independently by an external agent, and this subjective valuation process gives rise to the potential for managers to over-value certain investments, under-value losses, and generally sugar coat fund performance (see Bollen and Pool, 2009). Even where such valuation is carried out independently, the valuer is essentially carrying out the instructions of its client, the hedge fund manager, and valuations and disclosures are made on the basis of information that is in turn disclosed to the valuer or justified by the hedge fund manager. Conflict may also arise when all support services are provided internally as different business units within an institution do not act in alignment and against the interest of the fund the institution is managing. For example, some banks have units that carry out mergers and acquisitions (M&A) advising, underwriting activities, and advising to distressed companies. These activities may have an effect on the companies in which a hedge fund unit of the bank is investing. Conversely, where all business units do act in concert, conflict may also arise. For example, where a custodian acts in concert with the manager and against the interest of the fund, there is a potential for the manager to misuse the fund capital at the expense of fund investors. Such agency problems may give rise to a legal conflict with regard to disclosure issues, breach of fiduciary duty, insider trading or improper related party transactions, and allocation issues. A potential business conflict is the provision of such fee-generating services as M&A advising, underwriting activities, and advising of distressed companies by a unit of the bank at the expense of the investments made in such companies by the hedge fund unit of the same bank.

2.3.5. POTENTIAL CONFLICTS ARISING FROM STRATEGIES AND LEVERAGE

Hedge funds in contrast to mutual funds or private equity funds are able to use a variety of investment strategies that ironically have far less to do with hedging. These strategies include the use of facilities not normally accessible to mutual funds and private equity funds: short-selling and derivatives. Contrary to popular belief, hedge funds no longer primarily hedge nor do they utilize uniform investment strategies or investment instruments. Roel Campos, a commissioner of the US SEC once remarked, "The complexity of the strategies employed by hedge funds as they aim for absolute returns adds to the barrier of understanding regarding the specific risk posed by the investments." Fund managers may even pursue offsetting strategies that are disguised by marketing materials. For example, a fund manager might invest long in one index and short the same index within the same fund or with two different funds. Such a fund manager would collect management fees on both funds and performance fees on one of the two funds, at the expense of the investors. Further, hedge fund managers might "style drift" and invest in a strategy that is different from the strategy that was stated to their investors (see Bollen and Pool, 2009).

Different hedge fund strategies may pose conflicts of interest with the other shareholders or debt holders in the companies in which the fund invests (see Kahan and Rock, 2007). For example, for micro cap investments, while the hedge fund investors are very large, the investee companies themselves are very small and illiquid, and it is relatively easy to manipulate trading activity and returns among such investments. As another example, hedge funds can innovatively take advantage of derivatives instruments, margin financing, and short-selling to make both debt and equity investments in financially distressed companies and thereby profit by investing in ways that are counter to the interests of the company's other shareholders and/or debt holders. Further, hedge funds may engage in "empty voting" when they acquire voting rights that are divergent from their ownership interests and thereby vote in a way that is counter to the interests of the other shareholders and solely at a financial gain to the fund (see Hu and Black, 2006). More generally, it is possible that hedge fund interests are much more short term than those of the other shareholders, thereby leading to investment strategies and voting decisions by the hedge fund that are to the detriment of their investee companies and such companies' other shareholders (see Kahan and Rock, 2007). Such practices, however, have not been prevalent or severe enough for legal analysts to conclude that a case for legal intervention has been made.

Hedge fund investment horizons also tend to be more short term than the horizons of banks. For instance, hedge funds may pursue strategies in which they trigger bankruptcy in a financially distressed company and then buy the debt of the company in the secondary loan market. Banks, for instance, face regulations that impose a "Chinese Wall" to separate commercial and investment banking activities within the institution, and these restrictions were strengthened by the Sarbanes-Oxley Act of 2002 (Pub. L. No. 107–204, 116 Stat. 745). Hedge funds face a comparative dearth of oversight and are nevertheless able to lend and hold equity in the same company.

2.3.6. MITIGATING AGENCY PROBLEMS IN THE HEDGE FUND INDUSTRY

The agency conflicts in the hedge fund industry are amplified because of the severe information asymmetry between investors and fund managers given the very limited disclosure requirement. In the United States prior to the Dodd-Frank Act of 2010, hedge funds registered with the Securities and Exchange Commission on a voluntary basis only. Information about funds is available only to qualified investors who review the fund offering memoranda or the narrow, voluntarily provided information in public databases. Given the lack of government oversight and disclosure requirements, the mechanisms for alleviating the agency problems in hedge fund industries have historically been relying on the design of the organizational structure and compensation contracts.

Ackermann et al. (1999) showed that a few mechanisms are at place to address the principal-agent conflict in the hedge fund industry. For instance, hedge funds often combine considerable managerial investment with strong bonus fees, which potentially help align the interests of managers and investors. They show that these features are related to the better performance of hedge funds in comparison to mutual funds. Goetzmann et al. (2003) studied the inclusion of a highwatermark provision in hedge funds' performance-based incentive contracts. The highwatermark requires the manager to make up past deficits before earning the incentive portion of the fee. They showed that this option-like compensation structure can encourage managers to undertake greater efforts.

On the other hand, the option-like compensation contracts in the hedge fund industry may at the same time encourage managers to take greater risks. Brown, Goetzmann, and Park (2001) found that hedge funds with below average performance during the first half of a year tend to increase volatility. However, they further showed that fund managers' concern with their reputations to some extent offsets this risk-taking behavior. They collected data on individual hedge fund managers active in the offshore fund industry from 1989 through 1995 and found that once a hedge fund manager is fired (the fund is terminated), the chances of his reappearing as a money manager are very small. This lends support to the idea that career concerns or a manager's performance relative to his peers is an important motivation for hedge fund managers when choosing investment risks.

Another mechanism at place in hedge funds to mitigate agency cost is the internal control system. Cassar and Gerakos (2009) examines several internal controls in hedge funds, including the independent pricing of investment positions, signature protocols for transferring funds from bank and prime brokerage accounts, and the use of reputable service providers, such as auditors and administrators. They found that funds with stronger internal control earn higher incentive fees and are less likely to commit fraud or misreport financial data.

Brown et al. (2008, 2009, 2011) studied the operational risk of hedge funds (measured by the ω-Score) that is related to the strength of internal control. They found that operational risk is more important than financial risk in explaining fund failure and there is significant and positive interaction between operational and financial risk. These findings are consistent with rogue trading anecdotes suggesting that fund failure associated with excessive risk taking occurs when operational controls and oversight are weak. Their studies on "problem funds" showed that operational risks are highly related to the funds' external and internal conflicts of interest (see Table 2.1). Problem funds are those whose management companies answered "yes" in the SEC Form ADV to any of the questions on Item 11 while non-problem funds answered "no" to all questions on Item 11

Table 2.1 **External and Internal Conflicts of "Problem Funds"**

| | Panel A. External Conflicting Relationships ||||||
| | "Problem" || "Non-Problem" ||| |
With:	N	% Yes	N	% Yes	Diff	p-value
Broker/Dealer	368	73.1	1929	23.7	49.4	0.00**
Investment Company	368	50.3	1929	15.8	34.5	0.00**
Investment Adviser	368	73.9	1929	41.6	32.3	0.00**
Commodities Broker	368	53.5	1929	20.7	32.8	0.00**
Bank	368	40.5	1929	9.8	30.7	0.00**
Insurance	368	39.9	1929	8.3	31.6	0.00**
Sponsor of LLP	368	56.8	1929	21.5	35.3	0.00**

| | Panel B. Internal Conflicts ||||||
| | "Problem" || "Non-Problem" ||| |
	N	% Yes	N	% Yes	Diff	p-value
BuySellYourOwn	368	30.7	1929	8.3	22.4	0.00**
BuySellYourselfClients	368	84.8	1929	69.3	15.5	0.00**
RecSecYouOwn	368	75.5	1929	50.4	25.1	0.00**
AgencyCrossTrans	368	30.7	1929	2.3	28.4	0.00**
RecUnderwriter	368	69.0	1929	47.0	22.0	0.00**
RecSalesInterest	368	22.6	1929	15.7	6.9	0.00**
RecBrokers	368	46.7	1929	38.0	8.7	0.00**
OtherResearch	368	81.0	1929	70.5	10.5	0.00**

Table 2.1 *(Continued)*

| | Panel C. Ownership / Capital Structure ||||||||
| | "Problem" ||| "Non-Problem" ||| | |
	N	Mean	Median	N	Mean	Median	Diff	p-value
Direct Owners	368	9.96	9	1929	7.33	6	2.63	0.00**
Controlling	368	8.28	7	1929	5.97	5	2.31	0.00**
75% Ownership	366	0.73	1	1929	0.5	0.5	0.23	0.00**
Domestic Direct Corporation	368	0.8	1	1929	0.49	0	0.31	0.00**
Indirect Owners	368	2.33	1	1929	1.37	0	0.96	0.00**
Leveraged	367	0.51	1	1929	0.57	1	−0.06	0.03*
Margin	280	0.35	0	1451	0.49	0	−0.14	0.00**
Personal Capital ($mm)	109	1.26	0	622	2.62	0	−1.36	0.02*

(*Source*: Brown et al., 2008)

This table reports cross-sectional means, medians, and the difference in means of descriptive statistics for both problem and non-problem funds in our population of hedge funds filing Form ADV. Problem funds are any TASS fund whose management company answered "Yes" to any of the questions on Item 11 of Form ADV. Non-problem funds are all other TASS funds that filed Form ADV. Panel A reports results for performance statistics. Average return, standard deviation, 1st-Order AC, Sharpe ratio, and Appraisal Ratio are the average return of the fund, the standard deviation, the first-order autocorrelation, Sharpe ratio, and appraisal ratio of the fund over its life. Panel B reports results for external conflicts of interest, while Panel C breaks down internal conflict data. Broker/Dealer is one if the fund has a related broker/dealer. Investment Company is one if the fund has a related investment company. Investment Adviser, Commodities Broker, Bank, Insurance, and Sponsor of LLP are one if the fund is related to one of these respective companies. BuySellYourOwn is one if the company buys and sells between itself and clients. BuySellYourselfClients is one if a related party buys and sells securities also recommended to the fund. RecSecYouOwn is one if the fund recommends securities in which a related party has an ownership interest. AgencyCrossTrans is one if the fund performs agency cross-transactions. RecUnderwriter is one if a related party recommends securities to clients for which they are the underwriter. RecSalesInterest is one if a related party recommends securities with a sales interest. OtherResearch is one if the fund uses external research. Panel D looks at fund/manager characteristics and governance/ownership variables, respectively. High water mark, leveraged, and margin are one if the fund has a high water mark, uses leverage, or uses margin. Direct Owners represents the number of direct owners. Controlling is the number of controlling owners; 75% ownership is the percentage of owners who own at least 75% of the fund. Domestic direct corporation gives the number of domestic corporations listed as direct owners. Indirect owners represents the number of indirect owners. **, * indicate significance at the 1% and 5% level, respectively.

(such as past felony or finance-related misdemeanor charges or convictions).[1] Brown et al. showed that problem funds exhibit significantly more external and internal conflicts. For instance, problem funds are more likely to have an investment adviser who has a relationship to the fund, to recommend securities to clients in which a related party has some ownership interest, and to allow their personnel to buy and sell securities owned by the fund. These findings suggest there is a strong relationship between legal and regulatory problems and various measures of internal and external conflicts of interest. They also suggest that the potential for conflicts of interest can lead to operational risk events, as measured by legal and regulatory problems. This may be due to a higher incidence of fraudulent activity by managers of problem funds, or alternatively, it may be that the simple presence of apparent conflicts of interest attracts more regulatory scrutiny and litigation. Another important finding from the Brown et al. studies of problem funds is that problem funds have a higher number of direct and controlling owners; also, the number of direct owners in the form of non-individual domestic entities is higher for problem funds than it is for non-problem funds. This implies that problem funds have a more concentrated ownership structure and are more likely to be structured as a venture or partnership with another institution. These studies suggest that more disclosure of hedge funds' internal control and operational risk are potentially beneficial to investors.

Cassar and Gerakos (2009) also found some evidence that monitoring and screening provided by leverage providers is negatively related to hedge fund misconduct, indicating that outside monitors such as leverage providers also help mitigate agency conflict between investors and managers.

2.4. Conclusions

Given the prevalence of agency problems and the material scandals and frauds in the hedge fund industry, an important question is whether we should rely more on regulatory oversight on hedge funds to mitigate agency cost. If so, what are the potential benefits and costs? In Chapter 5 of this book we consider alternative fund strategies in more detail. Specifically, we address the question of whether differences in hedge fund strategies encourage managers to carry out

---

[1] Form ADV is the uniform form used by investment advisers to register with both the Securities and Exchange Commission (SEC) and state securities authorities. The form consists of two parts. Part 1 requires information about the investment adviser's business, ownership, clients, employees, business practices, affiliations, and any disciplinary events of the adviser or its employees. Beginning in 2011, Part 2 requires investment advisers to prepare narrative brochures written in plain English that contain information such as the types of advisory services offered, the adviser's fee schedule, disciplinary information, conflicts of interest, and the educational and business background of management and key advisory personnel of the adviser.

regulatory arbitrage or are associated with hedge fund forum shopping. That is, because hedge funds may register in different jurisdictions, it is possible that funds pursuing strategies with more pronounced agency costs select jurisdictions with comparatively less regulatory oversight. Before we turn to that question, we first explain international differences in hedge fund regulation in Chapter 3 and empirical methods to study hedge funds in Chapter 4.

Keywords

Cross Subsidization
Explicit Incentives
Implicit Incentives
Market Timing

Operational Risk
Principal-Agent Problem
Risk Taking
Window Dressing

Discussion Questions

1. What is a classic principal-agent problem?
2. Give an example of agency problems in delegated portfolio management. Explain how the benefits of the "principal" are at risk given the rise of such agency problem.
3. How can explicit incentives help mitigate agency problems in delegated portfolio management? What are the potential problems?
4. How can implicit incentives help mitigate agency problems in delegated portfolio management? What are the potential problems?
5. How are agency problems in the hedge fund industry different from those in traditional delegated portfolio management such as mutual funds?
6. What is operational risk? How is it related to the agency problems in the hedge fund industry?
7. What would you suggest to address agency problems in the hedge fund industry from the perspectives of external oversight and internal governance of the hedge fund?

CHAPTER 3

International Differences in Hedge Fund Regulation

Hedge funds are not, should not be, and will not be unregulated!!
 – Christopher Cox (Chairman of SEC) in testimony before the Senate Banking Committee
 – *Wall Street Journal,* June 23, 2006

When a fight breaks out in a bar, you don't hit the man who started it. You clobber the person you don't like instead.
 – Anonymous, "Finance and Economics: Payback Time; Fund Management"
 The Economist, November 21, 2009, 393(8658), 77–78

3.1. Introduction

There is significant scope for potential agency problems in hedge fund management, as discussed in Chapter 2. Moreover, some have argued that hedge funds exacerbate the systemic risk of financial markets, as discussed further in Chapter 9. For these two reasons, regulators in many countries around the world have been calling for additional hedge fund regulation in recent years.

It has been conjectured in the media (see, e.g., Mackintosh, 2008) that major players in the hedge fund industry sought to avoid a growing regulatory burden by agreeing to higher voluntary standards of disclosure. That is, with greater voluntary disclosure they sought to mitigate the possibility of more onerous regulatory standards being imposed in the future. For example, on January 23, 2008, 14 of the largest hedge funds in the United Kingdom agreed to greater voluntary disclosure standards. The disclosure standards are designed to produce more information about investment strategies, risks, and asset valuation. The possibility for more onerous regulation, however, has become a reality as regulatory burdens have grown over time, particularly after the financial crisis of 2008. Indeed, the colorful epigraphs that began the chapter indicate that the United States

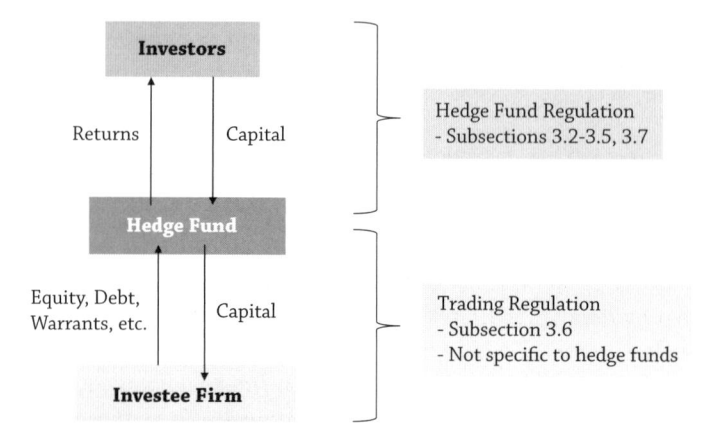

Exhibit 3.1. Hedge Fund Financial Intermediation and Regulation

has aggressively pursued greater hedge fund regulations since 2006. And the *Economist* quote in particular refers to the fact that even though hedge funds did not start the financial crisis, regulators have used the 2008 financial crisis as a rationale to impose stricter regulations on the hedge fund industry. By contrast, even though the famous hedge fund failure of Long Term Capital Management[1] in 1998 sparked calls for tougher regulatory scrutiny of the industry by Brooksley Born at the Commodity Futures Trading Commission,[2] none were implemented. Alan Greenspan (at that time chairman of the Federal Reserve Board), Robert Rubin (at that time secretary of the Treasury), and Larry Summers (then deputy secretary of the Treasury) prevailed upon Congress to stop Born, and they succeeded in limiting future regulation at that time.

In this chapter we begin in Section 3.2 by outlining the primary ways in which hedge funds have been regulated around the world prior to the financial crisis. These primary differences include permissible distribution channels, minimum size, and restrictions on the location of key service providers. Thereafter in Section 3.3 we explain international differences in hedge fund taxation. In Section 3.4, we explain the recent regulatory changes in the United States, particularly in reference to the Dodd-Frank Act. Section 3.5 explains hedge fund regulatory developments in Europe, particularly with reference to the Undertakings for Collective Investment in Transferable Securities Directive ("UCITS"). Section 3.6 explains the regulation of trading activities, which includes but is not limited to the trading activities of hedge funds. In other words, hedge funds do not (and should not) face a separate set of regulations regarding market manipulation and conduct. The regulatory structure and reference to Sections in this chapter is illustrated in Exhibit 3.1. Finally, in Section 3.7 we make conjectures about future

---

[1] http://en.wikipedia.org/wiki/Long-Term_Capital_Management
[2] See, e.g., www.pbs.org/wgbh/pages/frontline/warning/interviews/born.html.

developments in the regulation of hedge funds and provide a brief summary and concluding remarks.

3.2. Permissible Distribution Channels, Minimum Size, and Restrictions on Location

As discussed in Chapter 1, hedge funds operate in conjunction with a number of service providers to facilitate fund operations and distributions. Some of the key players are represented in Exhibit 3.2. The fact that hedge funds operate in conjunction with these key players in Exhibit 3.2 means that the most important international differences in hedge fund regulation are those that are outlined in Table 3.1. In particular, international differences in hedge fund regulation fall within three primary categories: (1) minimum capital to operate as a hedge fund, (2) permissible marketing channels, and (3) restrictions on the location of key service providers, as indicated in Table 3.1. Also, Table 3.1 highlights international differences in legal origin (La Porta et al., 1998) and economic conditions and shows the number of hedge funds by country that are in the CISDM dataset (both live and defunct funds as of 2008). Chapter 4 discusses the CISDM dataset in further detail. Specific elements of these differences across countries are reviewed in PriceWaterhouseCoopers (2006, 2007) and briefly summarized later in the chapter.

Hedge Fund Major Players

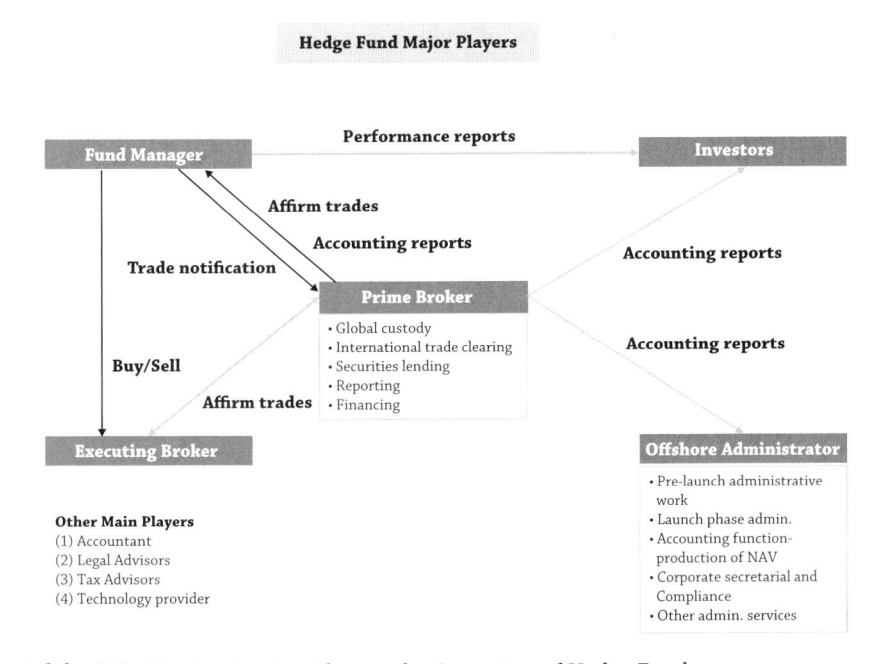

Fund Manager — Performance reports → Investors

Fund Manager ↔ Prime Broker
- Affirm trades
- Accounting reports
- Trade notification

Prime Broker:
- Global custody
- International trade clearing
- Securities lending
- Reporting
- Financing

Prime Broker → Investors: Accounting reports
Prime Broker → Offshore Administrator: Accounting reports

Fund Manager → Executing Broker: Buy/Sell
Executing Broker → Prime Broker: Affirm trades

Other Main Players
(1) Accountant
(2) Legal Advisors
(3) Tax Advisors
(4) Technology provider

Offshore Administrator:
- Pre-launch administrative work
- Launch phase admin.
- Accounting function-production of NAV
- Corporate secretarial and Compliance
- Other admin. services

Exhibit 3.2. Key Service Providers in the Operation of Hedge Funds

Table 3.1 Regulation of Hedge Funds by Country

Fund Domicile	# Funds in CISDM Dataset	Proxy for minimum capital requirement to operate as hedge fund manager (2005 US$)	Banks	Fund distribution compa-nies	Via wrap-pers	Private place-ments	Invest-ment manag-ers	Other regulated financial services institutions	Non-regu-lated finan-cial inter-mediar-ies	Total number of mar-keting channels	Restric-tions on location of key service provid-ers?	English	French	German	Scandi-navian	GDP per Capita (2009 US$)
Algeria	1	0	0	0	0	0	0	0	0	0	0	0	1	0	0	8100
Anguilla	23	500000	1	0	0	1	1	0	0	3	1	1	0	0	0	8800
Australia	15	0	1	1	1	1	1	1	0	6	0	1	0	0	0	37500
Austria	3	0	1	1	1	1	1	1	0	6	0	0	0	1	0	39000
Bahamas	169	25000	0	0	0	1	1	0	0	2	1	1	0	0	0	22700
Barbados	1	0	0	0	0	0	0	0	0	0	0	0	0	0	0	19700
Bermuda	547	0	1	0	0	1	1	0	0	3	1	1	0	0	0	69900
Brazil	18	362000	1	1	0	1	1	1	0	5	1	0	1	0	0	9700
Canada	53	0	1	1	1	1	1	1	0	6	0	1	0	0	0	38200
Canary Islands	2	0	0	0	0	0	0	0	0	0	0	0	1	0	0	29600
Cayman Islands	2696	500000	1	0	0	1	1	0	0	3	1	1	0	0	0	43800

Chile, Rep. of	4	0	0	0	0	0	0	0	0	0	0	14400
Curacao	2	0	0	0	0	1	0	1	1	0	0	11400
Cyprus	1	0	0	0	0	0	0	0	0	1	0	27100
Denmark	3	4658000	1	0	0	1	0	3	0	0	1	37100
Dominican Rep.	1	0	0	0	0	1	0	0	0	1	0	9200
Estonia	1	0	0	0	0	0	0	0	0	0	0	21800
Finland	1	183750	1	1	0	1	0	4	0	0	1	35500
France	70	183750	1	1	1	1	0	5	0	1	0	33800
Germany	10	441000	1	1	1	1	1	7	1	0	0	34400
Gibraltar	6	46750	1	0	0	1	0	3	1	0	0	38200
Guernsey	192	46750	1	1	1	1	1	7	0	1	0	44600
Hong Kong	2	360000	1	1	0	1	1	5	0	1	0	42000
Ireland	265	933450	1	0	0	1	1	4	1	1	0	45600
Isle of Man	46	140250	1	1	1	1	1	7	1	1	0	35000
Israel	2	0	0	0	0	0	0	0	0	1	0	20800
Italy	35	1470000	0	0	1	0	0	1	1	0	0	31000

(Continued)

Table 3.1 (Continued)

Fund Domicile	# Funds in CISDM Dataset	Proxy for minimum capital requirement to operate as hedge fund manager (2005 US$)	Banks	Fund distribution companies	Via wrappers	Private placements	Investment managers	Other regulated financial services institutions	Non-regulated financial intermediaries	Total number of marketing channels	Restrictions on location of key service providers?	English	French	German	Scandinavian	GDP per Capita (2009 US$)
Japan	2	0	0	0	0	0	0	0	0	0	0	0	0	1	0	33800
Jersey	62	46750	1	1	1	1	1	1	1	7	0	0	1	0	0	57000
Liechtenstein	5	0	1	0	0	0	1	1	0	3	0	0	0	1	0	25000
Luxembourg	380	183750	1	0	0	0	0	1	0	2	0	0	1	0	0	80800
Macedonia	1	0	0	0	0	0	0	0	0	0	0	0	0	1	0	8400
Malta	9	183750	1	1	0	1	1	1	0	5	1	0	1	0	0	23200
Mauritius	15	0	0	0	0	1	0	0	0	1	1	1	0	0	0	11900
Netherlands	15	183750	1	1	1	1	1	1	0	6	1	0	1	0	0	38600
Netherlands Antilles	68	0	0	0	0	1	0	0	0	1	1	0	1	0	0	16000
New Zealand	1	0	1	1	1	1	1	1	0	6	0	1	0	0	0	27300

Panama	2	0	0	0	0	0	0	0	0	1	0	7100
South Africa	10	0	1	0	1	1	0	4	1	0	0	10600
St. Kitts & Nevis	3	0	0	0	0	0	0	0	0	0	0	8200
St. Vincent & the Grenadines	3	0	0	0	0	0	0	0	0	0	0	3600
Sweden	8	183750	1	1	1	1	1	6	1	0	0	36900
Switzerland	81	184000	1	1	1	1	0	6	1	0	1	39800
United Arab Emirates	1	0	0	0	0	0	0	0	0	1	0	55200
United Kingdom	19	73500	1	0	1	1	1	4	0	1	0	35300
United States	2755	0	0	0	1	0	0	1	0	1	0	46000
Virgin Islands, British	1077	500000	1	0	1	1	0	3	1	1	0	38500
Virgin Islands, US	4	500000	1	0	1	1	0	3	1	1	0	14500

This table summarizes by country the regulation of hedge funds across 48 countries, including the minimum capital requirements, permissible marketing channels, and whether there are restrictions on the location of key service providers. The minimum capital requirements to operate as a hedge fund manager vary from country to country depending on fund characteristics and as such are proxied, as summarized in this table, for the purpose of empirical analyses in the subsequent tables (and the results are robust to alternative proxies). Most regulation variables are rather stable over years; however, some of them do change over time. In this case, we report the most recent (2008) regulation data for each country. Source: PricewaterhouseCoopers (2008). Operational Risk: An Alternative Challenge.

Some jurisdictions require hedge funds to maintain minimum capitalization to remain in operation. One rationale is that greater minimum capitalization facilitates financial stability by mitigating the risk of fund failure. An additional rationale for minimum capitalization requirements is that lower quality and less reputable fund managers will have difficulty establishing funds in jurisdictions with higher minimum capitalization requirements. In view of the sophisticated investor base, it is perceived that the funds that are able to attract enough investors and pass their due diligence exercises to raise the minimum amount of capital required should be allowed to operate. Also, as the fees charged by the hedge fund managers are dependent on the capital raised, there needs to be sufficient capital to meet overhead costs of managing a fund and meeting relevant administrative, disclosure, and regulatory requirements. Minimum capitalization also indirectly ensures that investors in hedge funds will be limited to high net worth individuals and institutional investors. Funds are restricted in the number of investors they may have; therefore each investor has to invest a rather substantial sum. The larger the amount an investor invests, the better his bargaining power with regard to seeking more transparency from the hedge fund, obtaining better liquidity terms, and ensuring that proper valuation and pricing methods are used. However, minimum capitalization amounts indicated in Table 3.1 are comparatively small relative to potential losses. For some countries, minimum capitalization depends on fund operating costs and other things specific to the fund; as such, the values indicated in Table 3.1 are proxies. For details, see PriceWaterhouseCoopers (2006). Among the 48 countries enumerated in Table 3.1 Austria has the greatest minimum capitalization requirement at US$6.75 million. Many jurisdictions such as Bermuda, Canada, New Zealand, and the United States currently have no minimum capitalization requirements.

Different countries also have different permissible distribution channels. In the hedge fund industry, capital is most often sought through private placements. Jurisdictions limit the hedge funds' distribution channels to mainly private placements as it precludes them from direct access to retail investors and thereby limit potential conflicts of interests that might arise with unsophisticated retail based investors (see, e.g., Barclay et al., 2007). In view of their aim to limit their investor base to sophisticated institutional and high net worth individuals, this limitation on their distribution channels cannot be said to be overly detrimental. In fact, this limitation may enable hedge funds to be less transparent with their initial disclosures, such as their fee structure and liquidity terms. Their private placement memoranda (and ensuing negotiations) may be tailored to meet the requirements of different types of investors; therefore, the investors may not be playing on a level playing field. Private placements are the only permitted distribution channel in some jurisdictions, such as Italy, the Netherlands Antilles, and the United States.

In many countries outside the United States, there are additional distribution channels through which funds may gain greater access to a wider range of investors. For example, 14 of the 48 countries in the sample permit distributions via wrappers. Wrapper products are typically insurance policies or structured products, purportedly used by investors for tax deferral (see Fink, 2005). For example, with insurance policies, the insurance company will be treated as owning the assets being managed by the hedge fund in order to meet its obligations under the policy, and the investor will obtain the tax benefits of owning an insurance contract. Some jurisdictions such as the Isle of Man and South Africa permit wrappers distributions via insurance companies only (see PriceWaterhouseCoopers, 2006). Legal practitioners have noted potential conflicts of interest with respect to disclosures in the wrapper (see Gerstein, 2006), and generally wrappers are used to overcome regulatory barriers in distributions to high net worth individuals (see Fink, 2005). While it is possible that unsophisticated retail investors may take advantage of this potential access to a hedge fund via wrapper products, these products are most probably characterized as higher risk products within the institutions that create them. As these institutions themselves are highly regulated and will have more stringent risk disclosure requirements, it is unlikely that the products would be marketed to, and included in, an unsophisticated retail investor's portfolio.

Distributions via banks are permitted in 28 of the 48 countries enumerated in Table 3.1. Many (albeit not all) of these jurisdictions that permit distributions via banks also permit distributions via other regulated financial services institutions. Twenty-eight of the 23 jurisdictions permit distributions via investment managers and 16 of the jurisdictions permit distributions via fund distribution companies. These additional channels of distribution may be deemed by regulators to be appropriate in view of the strict regulatory oversight over these institutions themselves. Also, it is in the interests of the hedge fund themselves to avoid the inclusion of potentially unsophisticated investors to ensure the continuity of their ability to operate rather free of regulation. Therefore, the hedge fund managers will themselves ensure that investment managers market the product appropriately.

The final type of regulation we address in this section is the restriction on the use of key service providers based outside the jurisdiction. Twenty of the 48 jurisdictions impose restrictions on the location of key service providers. Restrictions on location of key service providers typically require the presence of a local agent (PriceWaterhouseCoopers, 2006, 2007). For example, the Isle of Man requires local residency for day-to-day operators for Professional Investor Funds and Experienced Investor Funds. For Germany, the investment manager and custodian bank are required to be based in and regulated by Germany. Additional details on the restrictions of location are provided by PriceWaterhouseCoopers (2006). It is most probably the view of the regulatory authorities that the existing regulatory oversight of the key service providers providing support services to the hedge fund will suffice. Even if these services are carried out internally within an institution, the provision of such services by the specific department will be regulated by the relevant regulatory body or authority. Unlike the two previous types of restrictions mentioned earlier, which are somewhat related to the mitigation of exposure of the hedge fund to unsophisticated retail investors, this restriction is more in line with ensuring that the hedge fund utilizes only recognized (thus potentially regulated) service providers. For example, the higher fees the hedge funds pay may not be that much of an incentive for service providers to act in concert with hedge fund managers contrary to the interest of hedge fund investors if there is a threat of disciplinary action or loss of reputation. The reputational concerns among service providers may urge them to ensure that the hedge funds meet certain transparency, disclosure, liquidity, and valuation method benchmarks. Also, as hedge funds seek to build up their own reputations for professionalism to seek further capital, they will align themselves to the more reputable and professional service providers.

Practitioners often warn against using low quality service providers as it increases risk while reducing investor confidence. The recent failure of hedge funds affiliated with Lehman Brothers, Bear Sterns, and Madoff has been attributable to low quality, unreliable service providers. Service providers are vitally important because they provide due diligence services for the fund, provide research on counterparty risk, and generally facilitate the execution of the fund's activities. A fund's relationship with its service providers involves substantial human capital and asset specificity. Local or lower cost service providers can save on fees by up to 20%, but such cost savings can drastically hurt fund performance due to the reduction in auditor timing and support, inaccurate auditing services, enhanced counterparty risk, slower execution, delayed custody services, and conflicts of interest in marketing the fund.

Suffice it to say that the international differences in hedge fund regulation broadly depicted in Table 3.1 do not capture all of the nuances of the differences across countries. For additional details, see PricewaterhouseCoopers (2006, 2007). They do, however, enable broad levels of comparison that can be used in our empirical analyses of the effect of such regulations, which are carried out in Chapters 5–9 of this book.

3.3. International Differences in Taxation of Hedge Funds

Just as there are nuanced hedge fund regulatory differences, the nuances associated with taxation are even more pronounced. Taxation is very much dependent on the types of investments that a fund makes, as well as the characteristics of a fund's investors. As such, it is not possible to provide much more than an overview description of taxation differences across countries here. Some further details are available from PricewaterhouseCoopers (2006, 2007). Practitioners interested in learning more about hedge fund taxation issues are advised to consult a tax specialist.

Table 3.2 Taxation of Hedge Funds and Hedge Fund Managers by Country

Country	Single-Strategy Fund	Funds-of-Hedge Funds	Hedge Fund Manager
Austria	Fund is tax transparent.		Subject to corporate income tax at the rate of 25%.
Australia	Resident fund is tax transparent.		Subject to corporate income tax at the rate of 30%. However, if Offshore Banking Unit concession applies, tax rate is 10%.
Bahamas	0%		0%
Belgium	N/A		N/A
Bermuda	0%		0%
Canada	Domestic funds are generally not subject to tax as long as they are structured as such. However, the investors are subject to tax on any amounts paid or payable to them. Assuming that the foreign fund meets Canada's Safe Harbour rules (i.e., it does not have a nexus in Canada) and is excluded from the proposed non-resident trust rules, foreign funds are generally subject to a 25% withholding tax on investment income paid by Canadians, which can be reduced if the foreign fund is eligible for treaty benefits. Interest paid from a non-related Canadian to a non-resident is not subject to withholding tax, with some exceptions. Non-residents are subject to Canadian income taxes on disposition of "Taxable Canadian Property," which can be reduced if the foreign fund is eligible for treaty benefits.		A Canadian-domiciled hedge fund manager in the legal form of a corporation is taxed at a federal corporate income tax at the rate of 19.5% plus the applicable provincial rate (i.e., 14% for an Ontario resident corporation). A foreign-domiciled hedge fund manager without any permanent establishment that does not carry on business in Canada is generally not subject to Canadian income taxes.
Cayman Islands	0%		0%

(Continued)

Table 3.2 (Continued)

Country	Single-Strategy Fund	Funds-of-Hedge Funds	Hedge Fund Manager
Denmark	Tax exempt. Subject to a final withholding tax of 15% on dividends received on shares in Danish companies.		Taxed at corporate rates.
Finland	Finnish common funds within the meaning of the Finnish law are tax exempt.		Subject to corporate income tax at the rate of 26%.
France	Fund is tax transparent.		Taxed at standard rates.
Germany	Tax-exempt.		A German-domiciled hedge fund manager in the legal form of a corporation is taxed at a flat rate of 15% corporate tax plus trade tax (trade tax rate is applicable according to regional laws) and solidarity surcharge.
Gibraltar	Any Gibraltar fund approved by the Commissioner of Income Tax will be exempt from tax.		0% (tax-exempt companies) or 30% for tax year 2008/09 for income accrued in or derived in Gibraltar (there is a small company's rate of 20%, which rises to 30% once taxable profits have exceeded £95,665).
Greece	25%		25%
Guernsey	5% (20% on Guernsey income excluding bank interest).		0% to 20%
Hong Kong	0% if tax exempted; otherwise 16.5% subject to legislative enactment.		16.5% subject to legislative enactment.
Ireland	Tax exempt assuming declarations are in place for all non-resident investors.		12.5% on trading profits; 25% on non-trading income.

Isle of Man	0%	Taxed at 0%.
Italy	12.5%/0% (only foreign qualified investors).	27.5% (corporate income tax) and 3.9% / 4.82% (regional tax on productive activities).
Japan	0%/30%/42% depending upon the income and whether the Fund has a PE in Japan.	A Japanese resident corporate fund manager, and non-resident corporate fund managers deemed to have a PE in Japan, would be subject to corporate income tax at an effective rate of 42%.
Jersey	0%	20%, falling to 0% from 2009.
Liechtenstein	0%	Profits are taxed under normal corporate tax regime from 7.5% to 15% (up to 20% if a distribution with a sum bigger than 8% of the capital of the company is made). Capital of the company is taxed at 0.2%. Additional withholding tax of 4% must be paid on distributions of corporations.
Luxembourg	Tax-exempt, but registration duty of €1,250 and annual subscription tax of 0.01% (for Specialized Investment Funds or sub-funds, the shares of which are dedicated to institutional investors) or 0.05% on funds net asset value. For fund of hedge funds, no subscription tax is levied in respect of Luxembourg-domiciled underlying funds. An exemption can also be granted for funds the securities of which are reserved for institutions for occupational retirement provision, or similar investment vehicles set up on one or several employers' initiative for the benefit of their employees and companies of one or several employers investing the funds they own, in order to provide their employees with retirement benefits.	Profits are taxed under normal corporate tax regime at 29.63% plus annual 0.5% Net Wealth Tax (on unitary value of the company). Capital duty of 1% is levied upon incorporation. The management company of a sole FCP could benefit from an exemption from income tax and net wealth tax.

(Continued)

Table 3.2 (Continued)

Country	Single-Strategy Fund	Funds-of-Hedge Funds	Hedge Fund Manager
Malta	Maltese licensed hedge funds would typically have more than 15% of their investments situated overseas. Such funds are not taxed in Malta on their income or capital gains. Separate rules apply for funds having at least 85% of their investments situated in Malta.		Fund managers managing non-resident funds and/or local funds are subject to tax at the normal corporate rate of 35% (although effective tax leakage upon distributions to non-resident shareholders could be minimal due to a local imputation system that would result in a refund of most of the tax paid on distributed profits).
Netherlands	Dutch funds are either transparent or subject to a special tax regime (0% corporate income tax and profits distributions are subject to 15% dividend withholding tax). As per October 2007 a new special regime came into force for investment funds. This regime provides for a full exemption from corporate income tax, capital gains tax, and dividend withholding tax.		Income and capital gains are taxed at normal corporate rates (25.5%; 2008 rate).
Netherlands Antilles	0%		Taxed at 34.5%.
Norway	N/A		Subject to corporate income tax at the rate of 28%.
Portugal	Domestic hedge funds that qualify as mutual funds are subject to taxation at rates that vary from 10% to 25% depending on type of income received by the fund.	Domestic hedge funds that qualify as mutual funds are exempt on distributions or redemption from underlying funds. Other income is subject to taxation at rates that vary from 10% to 25% depending on type of income received by the fund.	Taxed at normal corporate rate of 25% plus 1.5% (maximum) municipal surcharge on taxable income.

Singapore	0% or 18%	10% or 18%
South Africa	Fund is tax transparent.	Corporate managers taxed at 28%.
Spain	Corporate Tax on net profits at a 1% rate (for Collective Investment Institutions incorporated under Law 35/2003 – Real Estate funds have to comply with additional tax rules).	Corporate Tax on net profits at 30% rate in 2008.
Sweden	Realized income is taxed with the exception of capital gains on shares and share-based derivatives. Profit distributions to shareholders are deductible. Any excess income is taxed at 30%.	Taxed at 28% on an accrued income/loss basis.
Switzerland	Can be either tax transparent or opaque depending on form. If opaque, taxed as a corporate and if transparent, no tax at fund level.	13–25% taxed on income depending on the canton in which the Hedge Fund Manager is domiciled.
Taiwan	Fund is tax transparent.	Subject to corporate income tax at the rate of 25%.
Turkey	i. Taxation of Turkish hedge funds (FIFs): There is no clear and specific regulatory guidance. However, it is widely accepted in practice that analogous to other types of investment funds, effective rate of taxation at the FIF level is 0%. ii. Taxation of Foreign Hedge Funds: Generally, the taxation of portfolio investment income (e.g., capital gains, interest and dividends) derived in Turkey by foreign hedge funds changes depending on various factors, such as the residence status of the fund, the legal status of the hedge fund in its country of domicile, whether the foreign hedge fund has a permanent establishment (fixed place of business or a representative) in Turkey, type of income, the type of assets and the specifications of the assets (e.g., for securities, the issuance date, date of acquisition, type). Moreover, Turkish sourcing rules, which determine when an income of a non-resident is subject to Turkish taxation rules, set out different standards for various sources of income (e.g., income from real property, securities, etc.).	Turkish resident fund manager is subject to ordinary corporate income taxation at the rate of 20%. In addition, certain transactional taxes may apply as a result of the operational activities (such as Banking and Insurance Transactions Tax (BITT) at the rate of 5% over management income).

(Continued)

Table 3.2 (Continued)

Country	Single-Strategy Fund	Funds-of-Hedge Funds	Hedge Fund Manager
United Kingdom		Funds organized as open-ended investment companies / authorised unit trusts are taxed on income at 20% with capital gains exempt from tax. Unauthorized unit trusts are taxed at 22%.	Corporate managers are taxed at 30%. Fund (28% from 1 April 2008) managers organized as Limited Liability Partnerships are tax transparent. Income tax at Partner's marginal tax rate (up to 40% plus self-employed National insurance) are paid by partners.
United States	Hedge funds marketed to US investors are structured through a parallel or master-feeder structure. Under a parallel structure, a separate fund in the form of an offshore (e.g., Cayman or British Virgin Islands corporation) is set up for US tax-exempt investors such as pension funds and not-for-profit entities and a US limited partnership (LP) or a US limited liability company (LLC) fund is set up for US taxable investors, such as US individuals and corporations. Under the master-feeder structure the two funds invest in an offshore corporate vehicle (the "master fund") that holds the investments and that makes an election to be treated as a partnership for US tax purposes. While the parallel structure normally allows for more flexibility with respect to structuring the investments, a master-feeder structure can reduce administration costs as all the investments are held through a single vehicle.		

This table summarizes the taxation issues for hedge funds in 36 countries. Not all taxation issues can be highlighted in a single table or even a single document; therefore, only select salient tax issues are highlighted here. Source: PricewaterhouseCoopers (2008). *Operational Risk: An Alternative Challenge.*

Table 3.3 **Tax Barriers to the Distribution of Hedge Funds**

	High Net Worth Individuals	Pension Fund	Corporate	Bank	Life Insurance Company
Austria	5	5	4	4	4
Bahamas	5	5	5	5	5
Belgium	3	3	3	3	3
Bermuda	5	5	5	5	5
Cayman Islands	5	5	5	5	5
Denmark	5	5	5	5	5
Finland	4	4	4	4	4
France	4	4	4	4	4
Germany	4	4	4	4	4
Gibraltar	5	5	5	5	5
Greece	3	3	3	3	3
Guernsey	5	5	5	5	5
Ireland	2	5	2	5	5
Isle of Man	5	5	5	5	5
Italy	2	2	2	2	2
Jersey	5	5	5	5	5
Luxembourg	5	5	5	1	1
Malta	5	5	5	5	5
Netherlands	5	5	1	1	1
Netherlands Antilles	5	5	5	5	5
Norway	3	3	3	3	3
Portugal	2	5	4	4	4
Russia	3	3	3	3	3
Spain	4	5	4	4	4
Sweden	5	5	5	5	5
Switzerland	5	5	1	1	1

(Continued)

Table 3.3 (Continued)

	High Net Worth Individuals	Pension Fund	Corporate	Bank	Life Insurance Company
United Kingdom	4	5	4	4	4
United States	5	5	5	5	5

1 = More favorable treatment for foreign hedge fund
2 = Direct tax discrimination against foreign hedge fund
3 = Not likely to be a significant investor class; investment in hedge funds not permitted; or there are no domestic hedge funds
4 = Indirect tax discrimination against foreign hedge fund
5 = No tax discrimination against foreign hedge fund
Source: PricewaterhouseCoopers (2008). *Operational Risk: An Alternative Challenge.*

Tables 3.2 and 3.3 summarize some of the main differences in hedge fund taxation around the world. Table 3.2 shows that tax rates across countries vary depending on the type of fund (single-strategy versus fund-of-hedge funds) and vary for the hedge fund manager. In some countries the rate is 0%. In other countries the rates are the same as the corporate or capital gains tax rate. Some countries tax domestic and foreign funds differently.

Taxation can have implications for the distribution of hedge funds depending on the type of institutional investor. These differences are summarized in Table 3.3 in terms of rankings. The barriers include dissimilar tax treatment for foreign investors, as well as tax reporting requirements for investors, including capital gains tax treatment on the disposal of an investment. Specific details on these barriers are provided by PricewaterhouseCoopers. In some cases these barriers reduce the probability that a fund will be marketed in a particular jurisdiction if the benefits of a distribution in terms of the assets that might be raised are outweighed by the taxation and other regulatory costs.

Finally, it is worth noting that the tax treatment of income from hedge funds, as well as other alternative investment funds such as private equity and venture capital funds, is very likely to change in coming years. In the past, the 20% carried interest fee of private equity and hedge funds has been taxed as capital gains in most countries, including the United States. Fleischer (2008) argued that the rationale for the lower capital gains taxation was meant to apply to investors who risk their own capital and that rationale does not apply to private equity and hedge fund managers who risk other people's capital; therefore, such fund managers should pay the regular income tax rate.

3.4. Recent Changes to Hedge Fund Regulation in the United States: From Goldstein to Dodd-Frank

3.4.1. GOLDSTEIN

In 2006, the US SEC chairman, Christopher Cox, expressly indicated that hedge funds should not remain unregulated (see also Goldschmid, 2004). Prior to the Dodd-Frank Act, most hedge funds were largely unregulated irrespective of SEC initiatives (See Brown et al., 2008).

As stated in Chapter 1, in the United States, hedge funds have been generally exempt from the Investment Company Act of 1940 and the Investment Advisers Act of 1940 as long as they operate pursuant to an exemption under the Investment Company act that they have 100 or fewer beneficial owners or all investors are qualified high net-worth individuals or institutions.

If hedge funds are required to register under the Investment Advisers Act, they would be required to (Peter and Kinsman, 2007) (1) prepare and file a registration form, (2) refrain from charging performance fees to investors that do not qualify as "qualified clients," (3) adopt written compliance procedures and appoint a chief compliance officer, (4) adopt a written code of ethics, (5) make certain disclosures regarding payment of a cash referral fee to third party placement agents, (6) enhance record retention, (7) comply with additional reporting and audit requirements, and (8) submit to periodic inspections by the SEC. The SEC argued the advantages of this registration would be that it would (1) enable the SEC to compile census information about hedge fund advisers, (2) deter fraud by hedge fund advisers, (3) remove unfit persons from advising hedge funds, (4) encourage hedge fund advisers to adopt compliance controls, and (5) limit ordinary investors' exposure to hedge fund investments. One of the main problems with these regulations and reporting requirements, however, is that the costs are relatively the same regardless of the size of the fund; consequently, such regulations are relatively more costly to smaller funds.

An SEC Staff Report (2003) concluded that hedge fund regulation was necessary due to (1) the growth in hedge fund assets under management, (2) the growth in exposure of hedge funds to ordinary investors, and (3) the growth in hedge fund fraud actions. Critics of the SEC regulation of hedge funds argued that registration and disclosure may enable competitors to replicate fund strategies, thereby making it difficult for funds to develop proprietary trading tactics. Also, it would slow down a hedge fund's ability to take advantage of arbitrage opportunities due to the time costs of the regulatory burden. Moreover, the SEC oversight would not be very effective anyway since hedge fund trading positions frequently change and would more than likely change by the time SEC staff reviewed the disclosed fund activities.

As a result of the SEC Staff Report (2003), the SEC introduced a number of rule changes known as the "Hedge Fund Rule." One of these changes ensured that

56 Hedge Fund Structure

hedge funds fell within the definition of the Investment Company Act. Another one of these changes pertained to the private adviser exemption of the Investment Advisers Act that exempts advisers with fewer than 15 clients. Prior to 2006, hedge funds counted groups of investors to which it provided advice as one client, up to the 14 client limit. The SEC rule change effective February 1, 2006, required funds to count as clients the shareholders, limited partners, members, or beneficiaries of the fund for the purposes of complying with the investor quantity limitations. In other words, the term "client" would now be interpreted to mean "investor." In effect, no hedge fund could meet the private issuers exemption under the 15 client rule, and as such, each hedge fund would be required to register with the SEC by February 1, 2006.

The "Hedge Fund Rule" was challenged in *Phillip Goldstein et al. v. SEC*.[3] In particular, Goldstein challenged the part of the rule that equated "client" with "investor." The United States Circuit Court for the District of Columbia unanimously agreed with Phillip Goldstein that the SEC misinterpreted the word "client," and that the Hedge Fund Rule was arbitrary in extending the meaning of the term to include investors in hedge funds.

3.4.2. DODD-FRANK

On July 21, 2010, President Obama signed the Dodd-Frank Act,[4] which brought about changes to the regulation of hedge funds that became effective July 21, 2011. A number of changes were introduced, as discussed in the following sections.

Registration of Advisers to Hedge Funds
Effective until July 2011, investment advisers managing US$30 million or more were generally required to register with the SEC, but there were two important exemptions: (1) if the hedge fund has fewer than 15 clients during the preceding 12 months and (2) if the hedge fund does not present itself to the public as investment advisers (the "private adviser exemption"). For the registration exemption, one hedge fund is generally considered one client, and as such, most hedge fund advisers were exempt from registering because they have less than 15 clients.

Effective July 2011, Dodd-Frank eliminated the private investment adviser exemption under Section 203(b)(3). As well, under Dodd-Frank certain smaller advisers (less than US$100 million in general) had to deregister with the SEC and

---

[3] *Goldstein v. SEC*, No. 04-1434, DC Ct. App (June 23, 2006).

[4] Dodd–Frank Wall Street Reform and Consumer Protection Act (Pub.L. 111–203, H.R. 4173). A number of webpages provide overviews, summaries, and analyses of Dodd-Frank, including www.hedgeco.net/ and http://en.wikipedia.org/wiki/Dodd%E2%80%93Frank_Wall_Street_Reform_and_Consumer_Protection_Act.

register instead with the states. This change shifts the monitoring function to the states so that the SEC may focus examination resources on larger investment advisers. Moreover, registered advisers are subject to not only the anti-fraud provisions of the Advisers Act, but also new additional compliance obligations and periodic SEC inspection: appoint a chief compliance officer, establish a compliance program and a code of ethics, and comply with custody and recordkeeping requirements. Exemptions from the Dodd-Frank registration requirement include Venture Capital Fund Advisers, certain Private Fund Advisers (with less than US$150 million assets under management), Foreign Private Advisers, Commodity Futures Trading Commission Registered Advisers that advise private funds, and family offices. In addition, funds may need to register with the National Futures Association as a Commodity Pool Operator if they buy commodities and are defined as a "major swap participant."

Reporting
Reporting requirements to the SEC have increased. Reports must include a description of funds' amount of assets under management, on- and off-balance sheet leverage, counterparty credit risk exposure, trading and investment positions, valuation policies and procedures, types of assets held, side letters, trading practices, and any other information that the SEC deems to be "necessary or appropriate." The Form ADV comprises amendments to the Firm Brochure (Form ADV Part 2A), requiring information about advisers' services, fees, business practices, and conflicts of interest, as well as the Brochure Supplement (Form ADV Part 2B), requiring individualized information about advisory personnel on whom clients rely for investment advice. Additional proposed form ADV reporting requirements about the adviser and its advisory business have included information about the adviser's clients and employees, expanded list of reportable advisory activities, types of investments the adviser manages, security rating or pricing services, business practices that may present conflicts of interest (e.g., use of affiliated brokers, soft dollar arrangement, payments for client referrals), information about the adviser's related persons and certain non-advisory financial activities, new disclosures about private funds, substantial reporting requirements about private funds (such as census data, number and types of investors, investment strategy, net asset value), reporting of private fund service providers (auditors, prime brokers, custodians, administrators, and marketers), and fair value reporting of private fund assets (including illiquid securities).

Investor Certifications
Dodd-Frank increased the "accredited investor" and "qualified client" standards. First, accredited investors' net worth no longer can be calculated by including the primary residence of the investor, and the net worth threshold is for natural persons to be in excess of $1 million. This standard is subject to period review

to adjust for inflation and other things that might warrant changes over time. Moreover, Dodd-Frank implemented a uniform fiduciary standard of conduct and supervision of broker-dealers and investment advisers regarding the provision of advice to retail customers.

Custody of Client Assets
Under the Dodd-Frank Act (Rules 204–2 (maintenance of books and records) and 206(4)-2 (the "Custody Rule")), the SEC has discretionary rule-making authority to require registered investment advisers to take steps to safeguard client assets in their custody. Investment advisers with custody of client assets are required to undergo an annual surprise examination. This surprise audit requirement will *not* apply to an adviser who is deemed to have custody of client assets *solely* because a related person of the adviser has custody of them; certain conditions must be satisfied for an adviser to be "operationally independent" of a related adviser (subsection (b)(6) of the Custody Rule relating to "operational independence").

The "Volcker" Rule
The Volcker Rule brings about amendments to the restrictions on proprietary trading in the Bank Holding Company Act. In particular, if you are affiliated with a bank, you generally must not engage in proprietary trading activities or sponsor or invest in a hedge fund, private equity fund, or similar entity. Subject to certain limitations, a banking entity may "organize and offer" a hedge fund or private equity fund, including sponsoring such a fund, if certain conditions are satisfied. Exemptions include certain cases of "trading on behalf of customers," "risk-mitigating hedging activity," and "underwriting and market-making activities." The activities and investments of banking entities must comply with the sponsoring and investing prohibition by July 2014 (there are possibilities of three one-year extensions and an additional extension of up to five years for investments in illiquid funds).

Transparency, Disclosure, and Systemically Important Financial Companies
The SEC may adopt rules designed to raise transparency and disclosure and possibly impose restrictions on securities lending and shorting. Reporting could facilitate assessing and complying with margin and capital requirements and position limits. Further the SEC may adopt rules and regulations restricting or prohibiting the use of mandatory arbitration agreements by advisers.

The Dodd-Frank Act attempts to identify systemically important financial companies and impose stricter prudential standards on them. Hedge funds and other non-bank financial companies may be designated systemically important by the Financial Stability Oversight Council. The Council may request information from hedge fund managers even if they are not designated as systemically important if they are candidates for designation. For systemically important institutions, the

Federal Reserve is the systemic risk supervisor of the designated fund or adviser and may impose heightened (to be determined) standards. Heightened regulation must include enhanced risk-based capital, leverage, liquidity and reporting requirements, enhanced risk-management requirements, resolution plans, credit exposure reports, concentration limits, and early remediation steps. The Federal Reserve may establish additional prudential standards, including contingent capital requirements. For "covered financial institutions" (>US$1 billion of assets), Dodd-Frank requires regulations that prohibit incentive-based compensation that is excessive or that could exacerbate risk taking and potentially lead to material losses. "Large covered financial institutions" (>US$50 billion of assets) are subject to more substantial incentive-based compensation restrictions.

3.5. Recent Changes to Hedge Fund Regulation in Europe: Undertakings for Collective Investment in Transferable Securities Directive (UCITS) and Alternative Investment Fund Managers Directive (AIFMD)

3.5.1. UCITS

UCITS are funds that comply with the Undertakings for Collective Investment in Transferable Securities Directive[5], the European Directive for retail open-ended investment funds. UCITS are incorporated and authorized by the regulator in a European Union (EU) member state. UCITS are essentially mutual funds designed for retail investor consumption. UCITS is a framework to standardize rules for the authorization, supervision, structure, and activities of collective investment undertakings. As summarized by Cumming, Imad'Eddine, and Schwienbacher (2012a,b), UCITS rules apply to funds marketed to retail investors, and a number of its important provisions ensure investor protection. The competent authorities of home Member States carry out the supervision of fund management companies. For example, the authorities in a home Member State supervise each fund and require that each fund management company (UCITS III, Article 5f)

> (a) has sound administrative and accounting procedures, control and safeguard arrangements for electronic data processing and adequate internal control mechanisms including, in particular, rules for personal transactions by its employees or for the holding or management of investments in financial instruments in order to invest own funds and ensuring, inter alia, that each transaction involving the fund may

[5] 2001/107/EC and 2001/108/EC.

be reconstructed according to its origin, the parties to it, its nature, and the time and place at which it was effected and that the assets of the unit trusts/common funds or of the investment companies managed by the management company are invested according to the fund rules or the instruments of incorporation and the legal provisions in force;

(b) is structured and organised in such a way as to minimise the risk of UCITS' or clients' interests being prejudiced by conflicts of interest between the company and its clients, between one of its clients and another, between one of its clients and a UCITS or between two UCITS.

At the end of August 2011, Eurekahedge estimated that there were 740 unique UCITS hedge fund managers with assets under management of nearly US$200 billion.[6] UCITS can be distributed throughout the European Economic Area and beyond. Managers who are able to offer their strategies in UCITS format will be able to access a large universe of investors attracted by the UCITS brand in Europe, globally and particularly in Asia. The transparency, liquidity, and regulatory oversight required in a UCITS addresses investor concerns that arose after widely reported cases of hedge fund fraud and after the recent financial crisis. For the hedge fund manager, UCITS enables distribution to a different (retail) investor base, thereby diversifying business risk.

UCITS is designed for liquid strategies and for low to moderate leverage strategies. The Sophisticated Fund classification measures leverage in terms of value at risk. Nominal exposure is not an appropriate measure of leverage admission as a UCITS. UCITS is designed for portfolios of eligible liquid assets that are eligible by virtue of their price discovery and transparency. UCITS portfolios enable accurate and representative valuation of assets. To be UCITS a fund must be open-ended, liquid, well diversified, invest only in certain "eligible" assets (namely, quoted securities, money market instruments, deposits, certain derivatives and units in other UCITS) and can only employ limited leverage. The following strategies are feasible under UCITS: long short equity, long short credit—liquid markets only, convertible arbitrage, global macro, fixed income arbitrage, commodity index funds (only commodity indices are eligible), commodity trading advisers and managed futures, event driven, funds of UCITS funds, structured and guaranteed products, and exchange traded funds. The following are not recommended for UCITS and fall foul of UCITS liquidity and valuation requirements: less liquid credit strategies, distressed debt, mezzanine, private equity strategies, small and micro cap strategies. Detailed provisions within UCITS for hedge funds are summarized by, for example, Bryan Goh.[7]

---

[6] www.eurekahedge.com/news/11_oct_UCITS_Hedge_Funds_Key_Trends.asp
[7] http://hedged.biz/tenseconds/2010/05/11/ucits-iii-for-hedge-fund-strategies-a-brief-guide/

3.5.2. AIFMD

UCITS lies outside the scope of the European draft Alternative Investment Fund Managers Directive (AIFMD),[8] and as such UCITS provides a potential means of dodging the AIFMD. AIFMD generally prohibits any AIFM not authorized by a Member State of the EU from providing management services to any AIF domiciled in the EU. Also, AIFMD prohibits a non-EU domiciled AIFM from soliciting or distributing to EU investors. The AIFMD focuses on the AIFM and not the AIF itself, similar to the US registration requirement under Dodd-Frank discussed earlier.

AIFMD imposes a number of business requirements on AIFMs including, without limitation, a duty to[9] (1) act honestly, with due care, skill, and diligence and fairly in conducting its activities; (2) act in the best interests of the AIF it manages, its investors, and the integrity of the market; (3) act in a manner that treats investors fairly; (4) identify the conflicts and manage those conflicts; (5) operate its organization effectively; and (6) structure its internal organization such that risk and portfolio management are separated.

AIFMD imposes a number of standards:[10]

1. Risk management. The Directive mandates that there be a separation between risk management and portfolio management.
2. Short sales. There is a specific concern with and focus on short selling. The EU Commission is to set forth rules with regard to short sales.
3. Liquidity management. The AIFM must adopt procedures and implement appropriate liquidity management policies to ensure that its liquidity profile is consistent with its investment strategies.
    a. Regular stress testing is required.
    b. AIF redemption policies need to be consistent with liquidity management policies and vice versa.
4. Leverage. Disclosure to investors and regulators on a quarterly basis. The EU Commission is authorized to establish standards.
5. Independent valuator required.

---

[8] DIRECTIVE 2011/61/EU OF THE EUROPEAN PARLIAMENT AND OF THE COUNCIL of 8 June 2011 on Alternative Investment Fund Managers and amending Directives 2003/41/EC and 2009/65/EC and Regulations (EC) No 1060/2009 and (EU) No 1095/2010. A directive is a set of guidelines decided at the European level by all EU Member States. Each Member State has a certain time to implement the directives into local law. The European Commission verifies the conformity of the local law to the directives implemented ex post.

[9] www.hedgeco.net/blogs/2009/10/28/proposed-eu-directive-on-alternative-investment-fund-managers-michael-g-tannenbaum/

[10] More details on AIFMD requirements are described at the hedgeco.net URL in n. 9. See also www.kpmg.com/ie/en/whatwedo/market-sectors/fs/investment-management/pages/aifmd.aspx. Other related material on compliance in different environments can be found at www.hedgefundmatrix.com/en/.

6. Independent administrator required.
7. Independent depositary required; must be a credit institution authorized in the EU.

AIFMD does not directly apply to trading activities of hedge funds in regard to potentially manipulative practices. Instead, there are specific trading rules in different countries, as discussed next.

3.6. Regulating Trading Activity: Exchange Trading Rules

Hedge funds are frequently accused of insider trading and market manipulation. Scandals involving funds like Galleon[11] and Madoff[12] feed the opinion that hedge funds ought to be more heavily regulated. However, in practice, trading by hedge funds is appropriately regulated in exactly the same way that trading of other market participants is regulated.[13] In this section, we briefly explain such regulations. More detail can be found in Cumming, Johan, and Li (2011) and Cumming and Johan (2008).

Stock exchanges around the world invest considerable manpower, technological effort, and financial resources to curb market manipulation and promote market efficiency and integrity (Aitken and Siow, 2003; Avgouleas, 2005; Comerton-Forde and Rydge, 2006). It is widely believed that securities law (La Porta et al., 1998, 2002, 2006; Jackson and Roe, 2009) and market microstructure (Harris, 2002; Harris et al., 2008) play an important role in the development of stock markets around the world. In this section, we explain forms of market manipulation, insider trading, and broker-agency conflict and build indices for stock exchange trading rules. Rules can be broken down into three types: rules designed to mitigate insider trading, rules designed to limit market manipulation, and rules designed to limit broker-agent conflicts. Each is described immediately following.

3.6.1. INSIDER TRADING

Insider trading refers to a market participant who acts on material non-public information. Although rules prohibiting insider trading in general are

---

[11] http://en.wikipedia.org/wiki/Galleon_Group

[12] http://en.wikipedia.org/wiki/Bernard_Madoff

[13] If different market participants in the same market faced different sets of regulations, there would be an unlevel playing field; this would distort the ways in which trades are carried out, obscure the avenues in which trades were executed, distort and mitigate the level of trading activity as investors would need to know the identity of the counterparty, and make surveillance and enforcement extremely difficult if not impossible.

commonplace around the world, specific regulations governing market participants with respect to insider trading differ significantly across exchanges.

Insider trading can take many different forms, two of which involve brokers using the information of a client order: client precedence and front-running. Client precedence refers to brokers violating the time priority of client orders. A client precedence rule is violated during insider trading when a broker initiates a trade on his own account shortly ahead of the execution of a client's order, with the client's trade being executed at a worse price. Front-running likewise refers to brokers trading ahead of clients' orders. In the case of front-running, upon receipt of a large client order, a broker trades shortly before placing a client's order with the expectation that the client's order will move the price. Front-running can also involve brokers who, after receiving a client's order, take the opposite position to the client's order in the market without the client's knowledge and then, immediately thereafter, the same broker crosses with the same client off-market at a profit.

Other forms of insider trading can involve the use of material non-public information about the company being traded. Trading rules can mitigate the presence of this form of insider trading by prohibiting trading ahead of the public release of research reports created by brokerages and the separation of research and trading departments at brokerages (separations commonly referred to as "Chinese Walls"). As well, rules that limit affiliation between exchange members and member companies, or between members and their investment company securities, mitigate the flow of information that might be material and non-public. Rules can also provide details with respect to the nature of communication between brokerages and the public by regulating how the flow of material non-public information is released. Further, trading rules sometimes limit brokerage ownership, the extent to which brokerages can influence or reward employees of others, or ban anti-intimidation and/or coordination activities (e.g., to stop people from reporting illegal activities). These restrictions can have the effect of limiting the flow of material non-public information.

3.6.2. MARKET MANIPULATION RULES

Market manipulation rules encompass price manipulation, volume manipulation, spoofing, and disclosure manipulation.

Price Manipulation Rules
Price manipulation can be carried out in many different ways and take many forms. One common way is for one broker (or colluding brokers) to enter purchase orders at successively higher prices to create the appearance of active interest in a security, which is also termed ramping/gouging. This can also take the form of pump and dump schemes whereby exchange participants generate a significant increase in price and volume for a security, carry out a quick flip, and then sell the securities (often to retail customers) at the higher prices. Another similar

type of price manipulation takes the form of pre-arranged trading. Pre-arranged trades involve colluding parties simultaneously entering orders at an identical price and volume. Because pre-arranged trades avoid the order queue, they can influence the price of a security.

Price manipulation can be carried out through domination and control and take the forms of corners or squeezes in cross-market activity. Corners and squeezes involve shortages in one market that can affect the price of a cross-market security. A corner involves securing control of the bid- or demand-side of both the derivative and the underlying asset, and the dominant position can be exploited to manipulate the price of either. A squeeze involves taking advantage of a shortage in an asset by controlling the demand-side and exploiting market congestion during such shortages in a way that creates artificial prices. Another related form of manipulation includes mini-manipulations whereby trading in the underlying security of an option is carried out in order to manipulate its price so that the options will become in-the-money, or the option is worth exercising. (Merrick et al., 2005).

Price manipulation can also be carried out to take advantage of market setting whereby brokers cross-order at the short-term high or low to effect the volume weighted average price, or to set the price in one market for the purpose of a cross in another market.

Three different forms of price manipulations refer to a specific time period: marking the open with regard to the opening of the market, marking the close with regard the closing of the market, and trading to manipulate prices at the end of the month/quarter/year. The opening session can be subject to particular types of manipulation subject to the rules for entering bids and asks in the pre-opening session. Similarly, end-of-day trades may be geared toward manipulating the closing market price of the security, and exchanges often specifically prohibit this type of act. Financial record keeping among companies provides incentives to manipulate share prices around the end of the month/quarter/year that depend on the governance specific to the company.

Volume Manipulation Rules

Volume manipulation can take two primary forms: churning and wash trading. Churning refers to the excessive trading of a stock to inflate its volume thereby giving rise to the false impression that there is positive investor sentiment for the stock. While the churning of client accounts may be carried out by traders and/or brokers to generate commission fees, given that the end result of churning is to manipulate markets and that the central motivation of traders and/or brokers in churning both house accounts and client accounts is to manipulate the appearance of volume, Cumming, Johan, and Li (2011) consider churning a form of volume manipulation.

Wash trading, another form of volume manipulation, means having the same client reference on both sides of a trade. While there is no beneficial change in ownership, wash trades have the effect of creating a misleading appearance of an active interest in a stock. Wash trades can indirectly affect price, but wash trades more directly and significantly affect volume, and as such, this kind of trading is categorized as a type of volume manipulation.

Spoofing Manipulation Rules
Spoofing, also known as "painting the tape," is a form of market manipulation that involves actions taken by market participants to give an improper or false impression of unusual activity or price movement in a security. Some trading rules have very general statements of prohibition toward actions that give rise to a false appearance. Other exchanges more explicitly indicate ways in which false appearance might be created, which includes fictitious orders, giving up priority, layering of bids-asks, and switches. The more general act of entering fictitious orders involves entering orders on one side of the market, then completing orders on the other side of the market and deleting the original order after the trade occurs. Giving up priority refers to deleting orders on one side of the market as they approach priority and then entering the order again on the same side of the market. Layering of bids-asks refers to traders or brokers staggering orders from the same client reference at different price and volume levels to give the misleading impression that there is greater interest in the security from a more diverse set of exchange participants; it might be viewed as being carried out for the purpose of manipulation. Switches involve deleting orders on one side of the market as they approach priority and then entering the order again on the opposite side of the market. These distinctions are somewhat subtle but nevertheless these different scenarios are explained in detail in some exchange trading rules.

False Disclosure Rules
Distinct from insider trading rules, some rulebooks include information pertaining to false disclosure. For instance, market participants might actively distribute false or misleading information that has the effect of distorting the marketplace. Alternatively, there can be a failure to disclose information such as the mandatory disclosure of ownership interests when they reach threshold level. This latter form of manipulation is commonly known as parking or warehousing.

Overall, we refer to trading rules pertaining to price manipulation, volume manipulation, spoofing, and false disclosure as market manipulation rules. In Cumming, Johan and Li (2011) these rules are aggregated to form separate indices for each, which they refer to as subcomponent indices. They then combine them in their sum total to form the Market Manipulation Rules Index, one of three primary legal indices created in Cumming, Johan and Li (2011). These indices are considered separately from insider trading rules and broker-agency conflict rules, which form the other two primary indices.

3.6.3. BROKER-AGENCY CONFLICT RULES

Brokers act on behalf of clients, but they can do so in ways that are against client interests. This type of principal-agent problem may arise from the failure of the broker to obtain the best price for a client (commonly known as a breach of a trade through obligation), the broker charging excessive fees, or acting in ways that are generally detrimental to client interests such as by investing in securities that do not match the risk/return profile of the client (referred to as breach of the "know-your-client rule"). As well, brokers might use the exchange's name improperly in marketing their services, or carry out other forms of improper or unethical sales and marketing efforts.

3.6.4. IMPACT OF EXCHANGE TRADING RULES ON FINANCIAL MARKETS

The trading rules for a stock exchange are drafted with varying degrees of specificity as they outline the exchange membership requirements, listing requirements, trading rules and regulations, and especially trading practices that are prohibited. The Markets in Financial Instruments Directive (MiFiD) was introduced on November 1, 2007. MiFID is a European-wide harmonization directive. An earlier directive, the Market Abuse Directive (MAD), was introduced in 2004, but the appropriate measures were not in place in 2004 across Member States for a number of reasons. First, surveillance data from Cumming and Johan (2008) indicate exchanges in 2004 and 2005 did not adopt/implement the provisions in MAD in a meaningful way. Second, articles in MiFID cover many aspects of MAD and state that provisions are needed to ensure that MAD principles are in place by November 1, 2007 (see, for example, Article 25 in MiFID). The draft provisions in MiFID in 2004 even made this point, so investors in 2004 would expect adoption of MAD at the time of MiFID. Third, principles in MAD were added to/clarified in MiFID for the implementation and definition of conduct to ensure that MAD was legally effective. Hence, while the legal situation in Europe is not perfectly delineated over time, one can argue that the market adoption of these principles was best reflected (and best perceived by the market to have been reflected) with the November 1, 2007, change.

We would expect that substantial details in rules across countries and over time enhance investor protection and facilitate liquidity. In other words, explicit rules pertaining to insider trading, market manipulation, and broker-agency conflict enhance investor confidence, mitigate abuse, and thereby facilitate trading activity. Cumming, Johan, and Li (2011) provide trading rule indices that can be used in studying market quality across countries and over time. More detailed trading rules have been shown to enhance liquidity (i.e., lower bid-ask spreads, higher velocity, and lower volatility; Cumming, Johan, and Li, 2011), influence where cross-listed stocks are traded (Cumming, Humphery-Jenner, and

Wu, 2012), and lower the degree of insider trading (Cumming, Zhan, and Aitken, 2012).

3.7. Conclusions

As noted in the introduction to this chapter, the media frequently discuss the lack of regulation of hedge funds. In fact, however, as we saw in Section 3.2, hedge funds face very different sets of regulatory restrictions in different countries around the world, including but not limited to differences in minimum size restrictions, restrictions on the location of key service providers, and different marketing channels. These differences across countries and over time enable assessment of the impact of hedge fund regulation on the structure, governance, and performance of hedge funds, as analyzed in Chapters 5–8 of this book. More recently, Dodd-Frank has brought about big regulatory changes for the US hedge fund industry, as has the AIFMD in Europe.

At the time of this writing, these regulatory developments are too new for researchers to test their impact empirically, but future work will be able to use these regulatory experiments to better assess the economics of hedge fund regulation and the costs and benefits of regulation and ideally better understand the form of optimal regulation: Is a registration requirement enough? What kind of disclosure, if any, makes sense? And what kind of transparency is needed? Certainly, commentary from reputable publications such as *The Economist* highlight the fact that regulations such as AIFMD were introduced because of the financial crisis, even though hedge funds and private equity funds had nothing to do with the crisis.[14] With the passage of time we will eventually have enough data and enough regulatory changes to better assess the optimal design of hedge fund regulation.

Keywords

AIFMD
Broker-Agency Conflict
Client Precedence
Dodd-Frank Act
Churning
Corner
Cross Order

Market Manipulation
Marking the Close
Marking the Open
Painting the Tape
Pre-arranged Trading
Price Manipulation
Private Placement

---

[14] See, e.g., "The Alternative Investment Fund Managers Directive: The Wrong Targets. A Pointless Tussle over Regulating Hedge Funds and Private Equity," *The Economist*, May 20, 2010, Berlin, www.economist.com/node/16168086.

Custody of Client Assets
Phillip Goldstein et al. v. SEC
Distribution Channel
Domination and Control
False Disclosure
Front-running
Insider Trading
Key Service Provider

Pump and Dump
Ramping / Gouging
Squeeze
UCITS
Volcker Rule
Volume Manipulation
Wash Trades
Wrapper

Discussion Questions

1. Have the increased regulatory standards for hedge funds in the United States and Europe been warranted in the aftermath of the 2008 financial crisis, even though hedge funds did not cause the 2008 financial crisis?
2. Why might it be appropriate for different financial intermediaries to be subject to different types of regulations, while different stock exchange equity market participants are not subject to different types of regulations?
3. Identify the major types of differences in hedge fund regulation around the world prior to 2006.
4. Identify the broad major differences in hedge fund taxation.
5. Compare and contrast AIFMD with UCITS. Which approach do you think is more appropriate for hedge funds?
6. How will the Dodd-Frank Act affect the hedge fund industry and strength of US stock markets in coming years?

CHAPTER 4

Overview of Empirical Finance Methods to Study Hedge Funds

4.1. Introduction to Hedge Fund Databases

In this chapter, we discuss the popular hedge fund databases, the biases with the databases, and the empirical measures of hedge fund return and risk.

The returns of individual hedge funds are available through a number of commercial databases such as CISDM, Lipper TASS, Hedge Fund Research (HFR), HedgeFund.net, and Altvest. In this chapter, we use the Center for International Securities and Derivatives Markets (CISDM) database (between January 1994 to December 2008) as the main sources for examples.

The CISDM database consists of monthly returns, assets under management, and other fund-specific information for both hedge fund and fund of funds.[1] As of December 2008, there were 6,634 hedge funds and 3,395 funds of funds. Some funds are dropped out of the database for various reasons. Ackermann et al (1999) argue that this causes survivorship bias in the data. Following their methodology, we identify funds that stopped reporting by December 2008 and report the statistics of these funds separately. Specifically, as of December 2008, there were 4,882 extant funds and 5,147 disappearing funds.

The CISDM database classifies hedge funds into one of 22 different investment strategies. Panel A of Table 4.1 reports the number of hedge funds in each category. As shown in this table, the distribution is not even across investment styles, but rather concentrated in the following categories: Equity Long/Short (2,557), Emerging Markets (564), Sector (465), Multi-Strategy (367), Global Macro (365), and Equity Market Neutral (358). Together, these six categories account for 70% of all the hedge funds. The CISDM database classifies fund of funds into one of six strategies. Most of the funds of funds fall into Multi-Strategy (2,426) and Single Strategy (655).

---

[1] Unlike other databases such as TASS, where fund of funds is treated as one investment strategy, fund of funds is treated as a different fund type from hedge funds in CISDM. CISDM also covers Commodity Trading Advisor and Commodity Pool Operator, which are not included in the analysis of this book.

Table 4.1 **Number of Funds in the CISDM Database (January 1994– December 2008)**

Panel A: Hedge Funds			
Strategy	Extant Funds	Disappearing Funds	Total
Capital Structure Arbitrage	2	23	25
Convertible Arbitrage	42	181	223
Distressed Securities	60	128	188
Emerging Markets	247	317	564
Equity Long Only	114	115	229
Equity Long/Short	1,039	1,518	2,557
Equity Market Neutral	124	234	358
Event Driven Multi-Strategy	113	147	260
Fixed Income	85	109	194
Fixed Income – MBS	31	66	97
Fixed Income Arbitrage	61	148	209
Global Macro	118	247	365
Market Timing	2	1	3
Merger Arbitrage	14	110	124
Multi-Strategy	227	140	367
Option Arbitrage	25	21	46
Other Relative Value	15	18	33
Regulation D	3	15	18
Relative Value Multi-Strategy	46	60	106
Sector	167	298	465
Short Bias	11	45	56
Single Strategy	85	62	147
Total	2,631	4,003	6,634

Table 4.1 (Continued)

	Panel B: Funds of Funds		
Strategy	Extant Funds	Disappearing Funds	Total
Conservative	29	2	31
Invest Funds in Parent Company	38	26	64
Market Neutral	105	57	162
Multi-Strategy	1606	820	2426
Opportunistic	44	13	57
Single Strategy	226	429	655
Total	2,048	1,347	3,395

4.2. Measures of Hedge Fund Performance

In this section, we introduce the commonly used measures of hedge fund performance in the literature, including average monthly excess returns, Sharpe ratio, information ratio, Treynor ratio, Fung and Hsieh (2004) multi-factor alpha, Goetzmann et al. (2007) manipulation-proof performance measure (MPPM).

4.2.1. AVERAGE ANNUALIZED RETURNS

Table 4.2 contains basic summary statistics (sample size, mean, and standard deviation) of annualized returns for the funds in the CISDM database. The sample is winsorized at the 99% level.[2] There is a great deal of variation in mean returns and volatilities across fund types and investment categories and between active and non-active funds. The mean and median of annualized return of all hedge funds during the period from 1994 to 2008 is 8.13% and 7.58%, respectively. On the other hand, the mean annualized return of all funds of funds is 0.40%, with a median of 3.04%. There are 2,557 Equity Long/Short Funds (both active and non-active). The mean annualized return is 9.31%, with a median of 8.35%. In contrast, the mean annualized return of the 209 Fixed Income Arbitrage funds is 4.38%, with median of 5.35%. In addition, the annualized returns of the disappearing funds appear to be higher than those of extant funds, which reflects the effect of survivorship bias due to both termination and self-selection of the funds.

---

[2] Winsorizing or winsorization is the transformation of statistics by limiting extreme values in the statistical data to reduce the effect of possibly spurious outliers. A typical strategy is to set all outliers to a specified percentile of the data; for example, a 90% winsorization would see all data below the 5th percentile set to the 5th percentile, and data above the 95th percentile set to the 95th percentile.

Table 4.2 **Mean and Median of Annualized Return by Fund Type and Investment Strategy**

| | **Panel A: Hedge Funds** ||||||||||
| | *Full Sample* ||| *Extant Funds* ||| *Disappearing Funds* |||
Strategy	Sample Size	Mean	Median	Sample Size	Mean	Median	Sample Size	Mean	Median
Capital Structure Arbitrage	25	10.28%	7.19%	2	5.41%	5.41%	23	10.70%	7.19%
Convertible Arbitrage	223	6.71%	7.26%	42	−0.27%	3.13%	181	8.33%	8.08%
Distressed Securities	188	8.02%	9.45%	60	4.87%	7.23%	128	9.51%	10.33%
Emerging Markets	564	5.70%	7.26%	247	0.73%	5.63%	317	9.57%	9.73%
Equity Long Only	229	0.44%	2.56%	114	−3.25%	0.26%	115	4.10%	5.21%
Equity Long/Short	2557	9.31%	8.35%	1039	6.17%	7.05%	1518	11.47%	9.33%
Equity Market Neutral	358	5.78%	5.38%	124	6.50%	6.99%	234	5.40%	4.77%
Event Driven Multi-Strategy	260	8.78%	8.28%	113	5.91%	6.62%	147	10.99%	10.02%
Fixed Income	194	6.03%	4.91%	85	4.09%	4.63%	109	7.55%	5.34%
Fixed Income – MBS	97	10.79%	9.43%	31	8.96%	6.52%	66	11.65%	10.27%
Fixed Income Arbitrage	209	4.38%	5.35%	61	4.02%	3.50%	148	4.53%	5.61%
Global Macro	365	9.52%	8.33%	118	12.53%	11.66%	247	8.07%	6.13%
Market Timing	3	8.36%	8.01%	2	6.75%	6.75%	1	11.57%	11.57%
Merger Arbitrage	124	9.01%	7.45%	14	7.07%	7.79%	110	9.26%	7.39%

Table 4.2 (Continued)

Panel A: Hedge Funds

Strategy	Full Sample Size	Mean	Median	Extant Funds Size	Mean	Median	Disappearing Funds Size	Mean	Median
Multi-Strategy	367	6.88%	5.11%	227	4.19%	3.27%	140	11.22%	7.12%
Option Arbitrage	46	10.03%	9.59%	25	10.61%	8.39%	21	9.33%	11.06%
Other Relative Value	33	11.25%	6.79%	15	12.56%	3.04%	18	10.15%	6.97%
Regulation D	18	22.36%	16.00%	3	26.53%	16.66%	15	21.52%	15.33%
Relative Value Multi-Strategy	106	7.99%	7.60%	46	7.26%	8.41%	60	8.55%	7.28%
Sector	465	11.48%	10.29%	167	4.25%	6.31%	298	15.54%	13.70%
Short Bias	56	9.22%	5.21%	11	28.34%	16.80%	45	4.54%	4.73%
Single Strategy	147	6.43%	9.19%	85	4.35%	4.80%	62	9.30%	10.46%
Total	6634	8.13%	7.58%	2631	5.20%	6.48%	4003	10.06%	8.46%

Panel B: Fund of Funds

Strategy	Full Sample Size	Mean	Median	Extant Funds Size	Mean	Median	Disappearing Funds Size	Mean	Median
Conservative	31	−0.96%	1.06%	29	−1.17%	0.30%	2	2.08%	2.08%
Invest Funds in Parent Company	64	2.21%	2.43%	38	−4.18%	−1.39%	26	11.55%	6.70%
Market Neutral	162	−3.35%	0.92%	105	−7.38%	−2.07%	57	4.09%	5.14%
Multi-Strategy	2426	1.48%	3.38%	1606	−0.30%	2.34%	820	4.96%	5.56%
Opportunistic	57	−5.53%	−0.80%	44	−7.95%	−3.16%	13	2.65%	3.48%
Single Strategy	655	−2.24%	2.19%	429	−4.49%	1.07%	226	2.04%	3.75%
Total	3395	0.40%	3.04%	2251	−1.65%	1.96%	1144	4.45%	5.24%

4.2.2. AVERAGE EXCESS RETURNS

Using the CRSP market index return as a benchmark, the monthly excess return of an individual hedge fund is

$$\text{Equation 1: } ER_{it} = R_{it} - R_{mt}$$

Where ER_{it} represents the excess return of an individual hedge fund i in year t; R_{it} represents the annual return of an individual hedge fund i in year t; R_{mt} represents the monthly market return in year t.

Average excess return of an individual hedge fund is calculated as

$$\text{Equation 2: } \overline{ER_i} = \frac{1}{N}\sum_{t=1}^{N} ER_{it}$$

Where $\overline{ER_i}$ represents the average excess return of an individual hedge fund.

In Table 4.3, we calculate the average annualized excess returns of funds in the CISDM database relative to the Standard and Poor (S&P) 500 during the period from 1994 to 2008. Consistent with Table 4.2, there is a great deal of variation in excess returns across fund types and investment categories and across extant versus disappearing funds. However, since our returns are not net of fees, the positive excess returns do not necessarily suggest that hedge funds outperform the S&P 500.

4.2.3. SHARPE RATIO, TREYNOR RATIO, AND INFORMATION RATIO

The Sharpe ratio was introduced in Sharpe (1966) and is calculated as the ratio of the average excess return and the return standard deviation of the fund that is being evaluated.

$$\text{Equation 3: Sharpe Ratio} = \frac{E(R_{pt}) - R_f}{\sigma_p}$$

where $E(R_{pt})$ represent the average return of a fund, R_f is the risk-free rate, and σ_p is the standard deviation of the fund return. The use of the Sharpe ratio to measure hedge fund performance, nevertheless, is a subject of intense criticism because hedge fund returns do not display a normal distribution (see Kao, 2002; Amin and Kat, 2003; Gregoriou and Gueyie, 2003). Table 4.4 contains the mean and median of the Sharpe ratio by fund types and investment categories.

The Treynor ratio is similar to the Sharpe ratio. However, it relates excess return to market risk instead of total risk. It is calculated as the ratio of the average excess return and the systematic risk or market risk.

$$\text{Equation 4: Treynor Ratio} = \frac{E(R_{pt}) - R_f}{\beta_p}$$

where $E(R_{pt})$ represents the average return of a fund, R_f is the risk-free rate, and β_p represents the fund's systematic risk, which is estimated with the following regression:

Table 4.3 **Mean and Median of Annualized Excess Return by Fund Type and Investment Strategy**

	Panel A: Hedge Funds								
	Full Sample			Extant Funds			Disappearing Funds		
Strategy	Sample Size	Mean	Median	Sample Size	Mean	Median	Sample Size	Mean	Median
Capital Structure Arbitrage	25	9.33%	−2.58%	2	43.18%	43.18%	23	6.38%	−2.58%
Convertible Arbitrage	223	2.65%	1.53%	42	7.72%	5.19%	181	1.47%	0.71%
Distressed Securities	188	6.74%	6.00%	60	16.73%	10.48%	128	2.05%	2.74%
Emerging Markets	564	7.50%	7.21%	247	15.31%	13.97%	317	1.42%	1.09%
Equity Long Only	229	8.03%	6.10%	114	13.97%	8.96%	115	2.17%	1.55%
Equity Long/Short	2557	10.20%	7.20%	1039	18.49%	12.43%	1518	4.52%	2.72%
Equity Market Neutral	358	6.73%	4.88%	124	16.96%	12.42%	234	1.31%	0.61%
Event Driven Multi-Strategy	260	10.83%	6.64%	113	18.78%	10.14%	147	4.72%	3.71%
Fixed Income	194	12.05%	4.65%	85	23.45%	10.60%	109	3.17%	−0.15%
Fixed Income – MBS	97	16.06%	6.31%	31	29.99%	13.06%	66	9.51%	4.21%
Fixed Income Arbitrage	209	0.50%	−1.10%	61	13.86%	4.94%	148	−5.00%	−3.92%
Global Macro	365	8.96%	3.56%	118	26.96%	15.10%	247	0.36%	−2.19%
Market Timing	3	28.30%	34.68%	2	41.15%	41.15%	1	2.59%	2.59%
Merger Arbitrage	124	3.17%	2.75%	14	8.44%	9.21%	110	2.50%	0.97%
Multi-Strategy	367	18.20%	9.70%	227	23.31%	14.40%	140	9.92%	5.72%

(Continued)

Table 4.3 *(Continued)*

Panel A: Hedge Funds

	Full Sample			Extant Funds			Disappearing Funds		
Strategy	Sample Size	Mean	Median	Sample Size	Mean	Median	Sample Size	Mean	Median
Option Arbitrage	46	21.72%	12.29%	25	33.84%	16.35%	21	7.28%	9.28%
Other Relative Value	33	28.36%	13.17%	15	52.27%	34.03%	18	8.43%	4.93%
Regulation D	18	22.90%	13.11%	3	26.71%	15.39%	15	21.55%	11.46%
Relative Value Multi-Strategy	106	14.63%	8.14%	46	16.39%	11.97%	60	5.36%	3.49%
Sector	465	13.11%	9.63%	167	16.40%	11.97%	298	11.26%	8.44%
Short Bias	56	8.90%	1.79%	11	56.29%	45.42%	45	−2.69%	−0.71%
Single Strategy	147	1.71%	11.69%	85	23.41%	17.58%	62	8.53%	7.80%
Total	6634	10.08%	11.69%	2631	19.37%	12.13%	4003	3.98%	2.14%

Panel B: Fund of Funds

	Full Sample			Extant Funds			Disappearing Funds		
Strategy	Sample Size	Mean	Median	Sample Size	Mean	Median	Sample Size	Mean	Median
Conservative	31	12.51%	6.56%	29	13.58%	6.97%	2	−2.93%	−2.93%
Invest Funds in Parent Company	64	8.67%	5.61%	38	11.70%	7.43%	26	4.26%	1.15%
Market Neutral	162	5.99%	4.09%	105	9.38%	6.05%	57	−0.26%	−1.44%
Multi-Strategy	2426	7.89%	5.52%	1606	10.05%	6.92%	820	3.67%	1.64%
Opportunistic	57	9.30%	5.25%	44	10.59%	5.76%	13	4.93%	3.85%
Single Strategy	655	7.12%	4.93%	429	10.21%	6.72%	226	1.24%	0.25%
Total	3395	7.74%	5.38%	2251	10.14%	6.89%	1144	3.01%	1.22%

Table 4.4 Mean and Median of Sharpe Ratio by Fund Type and Investment Strategy

| | **Panel A: Hedge Funds** ||||||||
| | Full Sample ||| Extant Funds ||| Disappearing Funds |||
Strategy	Sample Size	Mean	Median	Sample Size	Mean	Median	Sample Size	Mean	Median
Capital Structure Arbitrage	25	0.46	0.39	2	0.28	0.28	23	0.47	0.49
Convertible Arbitrage	223	0.23	0.16	42	0.01	0.01	181	0.28	0.20
Distressed Securities	188	0.18	0.16	60	0.11	0.08	128	0.22	0.22
Emerging Markets	564	0.06	0.06	247	0.01	0.04	317	0.10	0.08
Equity Long Only	229	−0.07	−0.01	114	−0.11	−0.03	115	−0.02	0.02
Equity Long/Short	2557	0.10	0.11	1039	0.07	0.09	1518	0.12	0.13
Equity Market Neutral	358	0.11	0.09	124	0.15	0.12	234	0.09	0.07
Event Driven Multi-Strategy	260	0.17	0.16	113	0.08	0.10	147	0.23	0.23
Fixed Income	194	0.29	0.10	85	0.18	0.10	109	0.36	0.11
Fixed Income – MBS	97	0.34	0.26	31	0.14	0.15	66	0.44	0.33
Fixed Income Arbitrage	209	0.19	0.08	61	0.15	−0.02	148	0.20	0.12
Global Macro	365	0.10	0.12	118	0.16	0.18	247	0.07	0.08
Market Timing	3	0.17	0.21	2	0.15	0.15	1	0.21	0.21
Merger Arbitrage	124	0.19	0.19	14	0.24	0.21	110	0.19	0.19
Multi-Strategy	367	0.11	0.06	227	0.04	0.00	140	0.23	0.16

(Continued)

Table 4.4 (Continued)

Panel A: Hedge Funds

Strategy	Full Sample Size	Mean	Median	Extant Funds Size	Mean	Median	Disappearing Funds Size	Mean	Median
Option Arbitrage	46	0.24	0.21	25	0.32	0.22	21	0.14	0.17
Other Relative Value	33	0.20	0.11	15	0.22	0.10	18	0.19	0.15
Regulation D	18	0.50	0.47	3	0.29	0.28	15	0.54	0.47
Relative Value Multi-Strategy	106	0.22	0.20	46	0.20	0.18	60	0.23	0.22
Sector	465	0.11	0.11	167	0.04	0.05	298	0.15	0.14
Short Bias	56	0.01	0.03	11	0.25	0.24	45	−0.05	0.02
Single Strategy	147	0.27	0.20	85	0.20	0.05	62	0.36	0.24
Total	6634	0.12	0.11	2631	0.08	0.08	4003	0.15	0.13

Panel B: Fund of Funds

Strategy	Full Sample Size	Mean	Median	Extant Funds Size	Mean	Median	Disappearing Funds Size	Mean	Median
Conservative	31	−0.12	−0.14	29	−0.12	−0.09	2	−0.15	−0.15
Invest Funds in Parent Company	64	0.07	−0.02	38	−0.18	−0.16	26	0.47	0.16
Market Neutral	162	−0.12	−0.08	105	−0.25	−0.18	57	0.14	0.11
Multi-Strategy	2426	−0.01	0.01	1606	−0.07	−0.02	820	0.12	0.11
Opportunistic	57	−0.18	−0.13	44	−0.22	−0.17	13	−0.04	0.03
Single Strategy	655	−0.08	−0.03	429	−0.14	−0.07	226	0.01	0.02
Total	3395	−0.03	0.00	2251	−0.10	−0.03	1144	0.10	0.10

Equation 5: $R_{pt} - R_f = a_p + \beta_p(R_{mt} - R_f) + \epsilon_{pt}$

where R_{mt} is the market return. Table 4.5 reports the Treynor ratio of hedge funds over the 1994–2008 period by fund types and investment categories.

The Information ratio is the ratio of excepted active return and tracking error. Specifically, we can measure information ratio as follows:

Equation 6: $\text{Information Ratio} = \dfrac{\alpha_p}{\sigma(\epsilon_{pt})}$

where α_p is the intercept from equation 5 and $\sigma(\epsilon_{pt})$ is the standard deviation of the residuals from Equation 5. Table 4.6 reports the information ratio of hedge funds and funds of funds across investment categories. Overall, information ratios of hedge funds are much higher than those of funds of funds.

4.2.4. GOETZMANN ET AL. (2007) MPPM

The MPPM is analogous to the Sharpe ratio. However, it is now widely known that the Sharpe ratio and other reward-to-risk measures may be manipulated with option-like strategies (Goetzmann et al., 2007). This type of manipulation may reasonably be expected to be commonplace among hedge funds. The MPPM proposed by Goetzmann et al. (2007) is defined as follows:

Equation 7: $\hat{\theta} = \dfrac{1}{(1-r)\Delta t} \ln\left(\dfrac{1}{T}\left(\dfrac{1+r_t}{1+r_{ft}}\right)^{1-r} \right)$

where r_{ft} and x_t is the per period (not annualized) risk-free rate and the excess return of the fund over period t. The parameter ρ is the relative risk aversion; historically, this number ranges from two to four for the CRSP value-weighted market portfolio depending on the time and frequency of data used. T is the total number of observations. Δt is the time duration between observations. For instance, if using monthly returns, Δt is 1/12. The $\hat{\Theta}$ can be interpreted as the annualized continuously compounded excess return of the portfolio (Goetzmann et al., 2007). The MPPM is interpreted as the average per period welfare of a power utility investor in the portfolio over the time period in question.

Following the Goetzmann et al. (2007) methodology, we calculate MPPM for the hedge funds in Table 4.7.

4.2.5. FUNG AND HSIEH (2004) 7-FACTOR ALPHA

Following the single-factor models, a variety of multi-factor models have been developed and applied in the research of hedge funds (Fung and Hsieh, 1997, 2004; Getmansky et al., 2004; Lo, 2006). The multi-factor models could be expressed in a general form as follows:

Table 4.5 **Mean and Median of Treynor Ratio by Fund Type and Investment Strategy**

| | **Panel A: Hedge Funds** ||||||||
| | Full Sample ||| Extant Funds ||| Disappearing Funds |||
Strategy	Sample Size	Mean	Median	Sample Size	Mean	Median	Sample Size	Mean	Median
Capital Structure Arbitrage	25	0.10	0.02	2	0.03	0.03	23	0.10	0.01
Convertible Arbitrage	223	0.07	0.01	42	0.04	0.00	181	0.08	0.02
Distressed Securities	188	0.05	0.01	60	0.00	0.01	128	0.07	0.02
Emerging Markets	564	0.01	0.01	247	0.00	0.00	317	0.02	0.01
Equity Long Only	229	−0.02	0.00	114	−0.02	0.00	115	0.00	0.00
Equity Long/Short	2557	0.01	0.01	1039	0.01	0.00	1518	0.02	0.01
Equity Market Neutral	358	0.03	0.01	124	0.05	0.01	234	0.01	0.00
Event Driven Multi-Strategy	260	0.03	0.01	113	0.02	0.01	147	0.03	0.02
Fixed Income	194	0.01	0.00	85	0.03	−0.01	109	0.00	0.01
Fixed Income – MBS	97	−0.02	−0.04	31	−0.09	−0.02	66	0.02	−0.04
Fixed Income Arbitrage	209	0.03	0.00	61	0.05	−0.01	148	0.02	0.01
Global Macro	365	0.02	0.00	118	0.05	0.00	247	0.01	0.01
Market Timing	3	−0.01	0.01	2	−0.02	−0.02	1	0.01	0.01
Merger Arbitrage	124	0.03	0.03	14	0.03	0.02	110	0.03	0.03
Multi-Strategy	367	0.04	0.00	227	0.01	0.00	140	0.07	0.01

Table 4.5 (Continued)

Panel A: Hedge Funds

	Full Sample			Extant Funds			Disappearing Funds		
Strategy	Sample Size	Mean	Median	Sample Size	Mean	Median	Sample Size	Mean	Median
Option Arbitrage	46	−0.05	0.00	25	−0.11	−0.06	21	0.02	0.02
Other Relative Value	33	0.01	0.00	15	0.00	0.00	18	0.02	0.01
Regulation D	18	0.08	0.06	3	0.11	0.05	15	0.07	0.06
Relative Value Multi-Strategy	106	0.03	0.02	46	0.10	0.02	60	−0.02	0.02
Sector	465	0.02	0.01	167	0.00	0.00	298	0.02	0.01
Short Bias	56	0.01	0.00	11	−0.02	−0.02	45	0.02	0.00
Single Strategy	147	−0.02	0.00	85	−0.04	0.00	62	0.02	0.01
Total	6634	0.02	0.01	2631	0.01	0	4003	0.02	0.01

Panel B: Fund of Funds

	Full Sample			Extant Funds			Disappearing Funds		
Strategy	Sample Size	Mean	Median	Sample Size	Mean	Median	Sample Size	Mean	Median
Conservative	31	0.03	−0.01	29	0.04	0.00	2	−0.02	−0.01
Invest Funds in Parent Company	64	0.00	0.00	38	−0.01	−0.01	26	0.01	0.01
Market Neutral	162	−0.02	−0.01	105	−0.03	−0.01	57	−0.01	0.00
Multi-Strategy	2426	0.00	0.00	1606	−0.01	0.00	820	0.02	0.01
Opportunistic	57	−0.02	−0.02	44	−0.02	−0.02	13	−0.03	−0.01
Single Strategy	655	−0.01	0.00	429	−0.01	−0.01	226	0.00	0.00
Total	3395	0.00	0.00	2251	−0.01	0.00	1144	0.01	0.00

Table 4.6 **Mean and Median of Information Ratio by Fund Type and Investment Strategy**

	Panel A: Hedge Funds								
	Full Sample			Extant Funds			Disappearing Funds		
Strategy	Sample Size	Mean	Median	Sample Size	Mean	Median	Sample Size	Mean	Median
Capital Structure Arbitrage	25	0.42	0.47	2	0.57	0.57	23	0.41	0.47
Convertible Arbitrage	223	0.25	0.16	42	0.13	0.05	181	0.28	0.19
Distressed Securities	188	0.21	0.14	60	0.24	0.12	128	0.20	0.17
Emerging Markets	564	0.11	0.09	247	0.17	0.13	317	0.05	0.02
Equity Long Only	229	0.01	0.06	114	0.07	0.09	115	–0.04	–0.04
Equity Long/Short	2557	0.11	0.12	1039	0.16	0.15	1518	0.08	0.08
Equity Market Neutral	358	0.10	0.09	124	0.17	0.14	234	0.07	0.05
Event Driven Multi-Strategy	260	0.19	0.17	113	0.19	0.17	147	0.18	0.17
Fixed Income	194	0.42	0.08	85	0.34	0.09	109	0.47	0.07
Fixed Income – MBS	97	0.45	0.26	31	0.24	0.12	66	0.54	0.33
Fixed Income Arbitrage	209	0.19	0.07	61	0.21	–0.01	148	0.18	0.08
Global Macro	365	0.11	0.10	118	0.23	0.18	247	0.06	0.02
Market Timing	3	0.20	0.18	2	0.20	0.20	1	0.18	0.18
Merger Arbitrage	124	0.20	0.21	14	0.33	0.28	110	0.18	0.19
Multi-Strategy	367	0.17	0.12	227	0.11	0.10	140	0.28	0.15
Option Arbitrage	46	0.41	0.26	25	0.62	0.31	21	0.16	0.17

Table 4.6 (Continued)

Panel A: Hedge Funds

Strategy	Full Sample Sample Size	Mean	Median	Extant Funds Sample Size	Mean	Median	Disappearing Funds Sample Size	Mean	Median
Other Relative Value	33	0.36	0.22	15	0.47	0.37	18	0.26	0.16
Regulation D	18	0.48	0.48	3	0.31	0.32	15	0.52	0.50
Relative Value Multi-Strategy	106	0.25	0.27	46	0.29	0.35	60	0.22	0.21
Sector	465	0.13	0.11	167	0.13	0.11	298	0.12	0.12
Short Bias	56	−0.02	0.06	11	−0.08	0.05	45	0.00	0.10
Single Strategy	147	0.41	0.19	85	0.30	0.17	62	0.55	0.20
Total	6634	0.15	0.12	2631	0.18	0.14	4003	0.14	0.09

Panel B: Fund of Funds

Strategy	Full Sample Sample Size	Mean	Median	Extant Funds Sample Size	Mean	Median	Disappearing Funds Sample Size	Mean	Median
Conservative	31	−0.03	0.02	29	−0.02	0.02	2	−0.25	−0.25
Invest Funds in Parent Company	64	0.15	−0.03	38	−0.05	−0.08	26	0.47	0.03
Market Neutral	162	−0.09	−0.09	105	−0.17	−0.14	57	0.08	0.03
Multi-Strategy	2426	0.03	0.04	1606	0.00	0.03	820	0.08	0.06
Opportunistic	57	−0.08	−0.09	44	−0.09	−0.10	13	−0.03	−0.02
Single Strategy	655	−0.04	−0.02	429	−0.06	−0.01	226	−0.01	−0.03
Total	3395	0.01	0.02	2251	−0.02	0.01	1144	0.07	0.05

Table 4.7 **Mean and Median of MPPM by Fund Type and Investment Strategy**

Panel A: Hedge Funds

Strategy	Full Sample Sample Size	Mean	Median	Extant Funds Sample Size	Mean	Median	Disappearing Funds Sample Size	Mean	Median
Capital Structure Arbitrage	25	0.05	0.04	2	0.03	0.03	23	0.06	0.04
Convertible Arbitrage	223	0.01	0.02	42	−0.05	−0.01	181	0.03	0.04
Distressed Securities	188	0.01	0.04	60	−0.01	0.02	128	0.02	0.05
Emerging Markets	564	−0.10	−0.01	247	−0.13	−0.02	317	−0.07	0.00
Equity Long Only	229	−0.01	−0.04	114	−0.18	−0.06	115	−0.09	−0.02
Equity Long/Short	2557	0.00	0.03	1039	−0.02	0.02	1518	0.01	0.03
Equity Market Neutral	358	0.01	0.02	124	0.02	0.03	234	0.00	0.01
Event Driven Multi-Strategy	260	0.03	0.04	113	−0.01	0.02	147	0.05	0.06
Fixed Income	194	0.01	0.02	85	−0.02	0.01	109	0.03	0.02
Fixed Income – MBS	97	0.03	0.05	31	−0.01	0.02	66	0.05	0.05
Fixed Income Arbitrage	209	−0.02	0.01	61	−0.02	−0.01	148	−0.02	0.01
Global Macro	365	0.01	0.03	118	0.04	0.06	247	0.00	0.01
Market Timing	3	0.04	0.04	2	0.03	0.03	1	0.06	0.06
Merger Arbitrage	124	0.03	0.03	14	0.03	0.04	110	0.03	0.03
Multi-Strategy	367	−0.02	0.01	227	−0.06	−0.01	140	0.05	0.03

Table 4.7 (Continued)

Panel A: Hedge Funds

Strategy	Full Sample Sample Size	Mean	Median	Extant Funds Sample Size	Mean	Median	Disappearing Funds Sample Size	Mean	Median
Option Arbitrage	46	0.04	0.05	25	0.05	0.05	21	0.04	0.07
Other Relative Value	33	0.04	0.02	15	0.05	0.00	18	0.03	0.03
Regulation D	18	0.14	0.10	3	0.16	0.10	15	0.14	0.10
Relative Value Multi-Strategy	106	0.03	0.04	46	0.03	0.04	60	0.04	0.04
Sector	465	−0.04	0.02	167	−0.10	0.00	298	−0.01	0.04
Short Bias	56	−0.05	−0.03	11	0.16	0.10	45	−0.09	−0.04
Single Strategy	147	−0.03	0.04	85	−0.07	0.00	62	0.03	0.05
Total	6634	−0.01	0.02	2631	−0.04	0.01	4003	0.00	0.03

Panel B: Fund of Funds

Strategy	Full Sample Sample Size	Mean	Median	Extant Funds Sample Size	Mean	Median	Disappearing Funds Sample Size	Mean	Median
Conservative	31	−0.05	−0.03	29	−0.06	−0.03	2	−0.02	−0.02
Invest Funds in Parent Company	64	−0.03	−0.01	38	−0.09	−0.05	26	0.07	0.03
Market Neutral	162	−0.09	−0.02	105	−0.14	−0.06	57	0.00	0.01
Multi-Strategy	2426	−0.04	0.00	1606	−0.05	−0.01	820	0.00	0.02
Opportunistic	57	−0.14	−0.05	44	−0.18	−0.05	13	−0.02	0.00
Single Strategy	655	−0.08	−0.02	429	−0.11	−0.03	226	−0.03	0.00
Total	3395	−0.05	−0.01	2251	−0.07	−0.02	1144	−0.02	0.02

Equation 8: $r_t^i = \alpha^i + \sum_{k=1}^{K} \beta_k^i F_{k,i} + \varepsilon_{i,t}$

where r_t^i is the excess return (in excess of the risk-free rate) on hedge fund i for month t, α^i is the abnormal performance of hedge fund i over the regression time period, β_k^i is the factor loading of hedge fund i on factor k during the regression period, $F_{k,t}$ is the return for factor k for month t, and $\varepsilon_{i,t}$ is the error term. The main difference among those models is the selection of factors. Fung and Hsieh (2004) have developed a seven-factor model, which has shown strong explanatory power in variation of hedge fund performance. The factors are the S&P 500 return minus the risk-free rate, the Russul 2000 monthly total return minus the S&P 500 monthly total return, the change in the constant maturity yield of the 10-year Treasury, the change in the spread of Moody's Baa minus the 10-year Treasury, the bond PTFS, the currency PTFS, and the commodities PTFS, where PTFS denotes primitive trend following strategy. The estimated intercept $\hat{\alpha}^i$ is the alpha performance measure or the abnormal performance of hedge fund i over the regression time period.

In Table 4.8, we estimate Fung and Hsieh 7-factor alphas during the period from 1994 to 2008. Overall, the mean and median annualized alphas for all hedge funds are 10% and 5%, respectively. The mean and median annualized alphas for all fund of funds are 3% and 2%, respectively. Hedge funds outperform fund of funds measured by alpha. Furthermore, extant hedge funds have higher alphas (both the mean and median) than disappearing funds.

4.3. Measures of Hedge Fund Risk

In this section, we introduce several commonly used measures of hedge fund risk, including standard deviation, and beta estimated from factor models.

4.3.1. STANDARD DEVIATION

A common measure of hedge fund (total) risk is the standard deviation of the monthly returns.

Equation 9: $\sigma_i = \sqrt{\dfrac{1}{n-1}\sum (R_{i,t} - \bar{R}_i)^2}$

where σ_i represents the standard deviation of a hedge fund over a specific time period, n represents the number of observations (returns), $R_{i,t}$ is the monthly return of the hedge fund, and $\bar{R}_i$ represents the average return of the hedge fund over the specific time period.

Table 4.9 summarizes the standard deviation of hedge funds' monthly returns by investment categories. Overall, hedge funds have higher standard deviations than funds of funds. Across the investment categories, hedge funds with a focus on dedicated short bias, emerging markets, and Equity Long Only exhibit the highest standard deviations.

Table 4.8 **Mean and Median of Fung and Hsui 7-Factor Alpha (Annualized) by Fund Type and Investment Strategy**

	Panel A: Hedge Funds							
	Full Sample			*Extant Funds*			*Disappearing Funds*		
Strategy	Sample Size	Mean	Median	Sample Size	Mean	Median	Sample Size	Mean	Median
Capital Structure Arbitrage	25	0.08	0.05	2	0.00	0.00	23	0.09	0.05
Convertible Arbitrage	223	0.04	0.04	42	0.02	0.02	181	0.04	0.04
Distressed Securities	188	0.09	0.06	60	0.18	0.05	128	0.04	0.06
Emerging Markets	564	0.09	0.04	247	0.12	0.07	317	0.07	0.02
Equity Long Only	229	0.09	0.05	114	0.18	0.06	115	−0.01	0.01
Equity Long/Short	2557	0.12	0.05	1039	0.12	0.06	1518	0.12	0.04
Equity Market Neutral	358	0.04	0.03	124	0.10	0.05	234	0.01	0.02
Event Driven Multi-Strategy	260	0.08	0.06	113	0.10	0.05	147	0.07	0.06
Fixed Income	194	0.04	0.03	85	0.04	0.02	109	0.04	0.03
Fixed Income – MBS	97	0.19	0.06	31	0.15	0.04	66	0.21	0.06
Fixed Income Arbitrage	209	0.03	0.02	61	0.04	0.01	148	0.02	0.02
Global Macro	365	0.09	0.03	118	0.10	0.07	247	0.09	0.02
Market Timing	3	0.10	0.11	2	0.13	0.13	1	0.04	0.04
Merger Arbitrage	124	0.04	0.04	14	0.04	0.04	110	0.04	0.03
Multi-Strategy	367	0.13	0.05	227	0.16	0.05	140	0.10	0.05

(Continued)

Table 4.8 (Continued)

Panel A: Hedge Funds

Strategy	Full Sample Sample Size	Mean	Median	Extant Funds Sample Size	Mean	Median	Disappearing Funds Sample Size	Mean	Median
Option Arbitrage	46	0.17	0.06	25	0.05	0.06	21	0.32	0.05
Other Relative Value	33	0.24	0.07	15	0.46	0.09	18	0.05	0.07
Regulation D	18	0.16	0.13	3	0.27	0.15	15	0.14	0.12
Relative Value Multi-Strategy	106	0.00	0.04	46	−0.04	0.06	60	0.03	0.03
Sector	465	0.17	0.07	167	0.20	0.06	298	0.15	0.08
Short Bias	56	0.14	0.04	11	−0.01	0.03	45	0.17	0.05
Single Strategy	147	0.09	0.07	85	0.12	0.06	62	0.06	0.07
Total	6634	0.10	0.05	2631	0.12	0.06	4003	0.09	0.04

Panel B: Fund of Funds

Strategy	Full Sample Sample Size	Mean	Median	Extant Funds Sample Size	Mean	Median	Disappearing Funds Sample Size	Mean	Median
Conservative	31	−0.02	0.01	29	−0.02	0.01	2	−0.01	−0.01
Invest Funds in Parent Company	64	0.38	0.01	38	0.01	0.01	26	0.93	0.03
Market Neutral	162	0.02	0.01	105	0.02	0.00	57	0.01	0.02
Multi-Strategy	2426	0.02	0.02	1606	0.02	0.01	820	0.02	0.02
Opportunistic	57	0.02	0.02	44	0.02	0.02	13	0.03	0.02
Single Strategy	655	0.02	0.01	429	0.01	0.01	226	0.05	0.01
Total	3395	0.03	0.02	2251	0.02	0.01	1144	0.05	0.02

Table 4.9 **Mean and Median of Standard Deviation (of Monthly Returns) by Fund Type and Investment Strategy**

| | **Panel A: Hedge Funds** ||||||||
| | Full Sample ||| Extant Funds ||| Disappearing Funds |||
Strategy	Sample Size	Mean	Median	Sample Size	Mean	Median	Sample Size	Mean	Median
Capital Structure Arbitrage	25	0.02	0.09	2	0.01	0.01	23	0.02	0.01
Convertible Arbitrage	223	0.02	0.02	42	0.03	0.02	181	0.02	0.02
Distressed Securities	188	0.03	0.03	60	0.03	0.03	128	0.03	0.02
Emerging Markets	564	0.07	0.06	247	0.06	0.06	317	0.07	0.06
Equity Long Only	229	0.07	0.06	114	0.07	0.06	115	0.06	0.05
Equity Long/Short	2557	0.05	0.04	1039	0.04	0.04	1518	0.05	0.04
Equity Market Neutral	358	0.03	0.02	124	0.03	0.02	234	0.02	0.02
Event Driven Multi-Strategy	260	0.03	0.03	113	0.04	0.03	147	0.03	0.02
Fixed Income	194	0.02	0.02	85	0.03	0.02	109	0.02	0.02
Fixed Income – MBS	97	0.03	0.02	31	0.04	0.02	66	0.02	0.02
Fixed Income Arbitrage	209	0.03	0.02	61	0.03	0.03	148	0.02	0.02
Global Macro	365	0.05	0.04	118	0.05	0.04	247	0.04	0.03
Market Timing	3	0.03	0.03	2	0.02	0.02	1	0.03	0.03
Merger Arbitrage	124	0.02	0.01	14	0.01	0.01	110	0.02	0.02
Multi-Strategy	367	0.04	0.03	227	0.05	0.04	140	0.03	0.02

(Continued)

Table 4.9 (Continued)

Panel A: Hedge Funds

Strategy	Full Sample Sample Size	Mean	Median	Extant Funds Sample Size	Mean	Median	Disappearing Funds Sample Size	Mean	Median
Option Arbitrage	46	0.03	0.02	25	0.03	0.03	21	0.03	0.02
Other Relative Value	33	0.04	0.03	15	0.04	0.02	18	0.03	0.03
Regulation D	18	0.03	0.03	3	0.05	0.04	15	0.03	0.03
Relative Value Multi-trategy	106	0.02	0.02	46	0.02	0.02	60	0.02	0.02
Sector	465	0.07	0.06	167	0.07	0.05	298	0.08	0.06
Short Bias	56	0.07	0.06	11	0.06	0.05	45	0.07	0.06
Single Strategy	147	0.04	0.03	85	0.05	0.04	62	0.03	0.03
Total	6634	0.05	0.03	2631	0.05	0.04	4003	0.04	0.03

Panel B: Fund of Funds

Strategy	Full Sample Sample Size	Mean	Median	Extant Funds Sample Size	Mean	Median	Disappearing Funds Sample Size	Mean	Median
Conservative	31	0.03	0.02	29	0.03	0.02	2	0.01	0.01
Invest Funds in Parent Company	64	0.03	0.02	38	0.03	0.02	26	0.02	0.02
Market Neutral	162	0.03	0.02	105	0.03	0.03	57	0.02	0.01
Multi-Strategy	2426	0.03	0.02	1606	0.03	0.02	820	0.02	0.02
Opportunistic	57	0.04	0.03	44	0.04	0.03	13	0.02	0.02
Single Strategy	655	0.03	0.02	429	0.03	0.02	226	0.02	0.02
Total	3395	0.03	0.02	2251	0.03	0.02	1144	0.02	0.02

Table 4.10 **Mean and Median of Market Beta by Fund Type and Investment Strategy**

	Panel A: Hedge Funds								
	Full Sample			*Extant Funds*			*Disappearing Funds*		
Strategy	Sample Size	Mean	Median	Sample Size	Mean	Median	Sample Size	Mean	Median
Capital Structure Arbitrage	25	0.01	0.04	2	0.06	0.06	23	0.01	0.04
Convertible Arbitrage	223	0.13	0.05	42	0.15	0.10	181	0.13	0.03
Distressed Securities	188	0.33	0.18	60	0.16	0.24	128	0.42	0.15
Emerging Markets	564	0.62	0.53	247	0.55	0.50	317	0.68	0.55
Equity Long Only	229	0.83	0.72	114	0.86	0.69	115	0.80	0.77
Equity Long/Short	2557	0.35	0.25	1039	0.25	0.19	1518	0.42	0.30
Equity Market Neutral	358	0.04	−0.02	124	0.04	−0.02	234	0.04	0.00
Event Driven Multi-Strategy	260	0.26	0.22	113	0.15	0.22	147	0.35	0.22
Fixed Income	194	0.08	0.05	85	0.13	0.06	109	0.05	0.02
Fixed Income – MBS	97	−0.07	−0.02	31	0.08	0.10	66	−0.14	−0.06
Fixed Income Arbitrage	209	0.10	0.04	61	0.16	0.12	148	0.08	0.03
Global Macro	365	0.13	0.07	118	0.16	0.05	247	0.11	0.09
Market Timing	3	0.10	0.03	2	−0.10	−0.10	1	0.49	0.49
Merger Arbitrage	124	0.15	0.09	14	0.13	0.10	110	0.16	0.08
Multi-Strategy	367	0.24	0.11	227	0.30	0.13	140	0.14	0.08

(Continued)

Table 4.10 (Continued)

Panel A: Hedge Funds

Strategy	Full Sample Sample Size	Mean	Median	Extant Funds Sample Size	Mean	Median	Disappearing Funds Sample Size	Mean	Median
Option Arbitrage	46	0.20	0.07	25	−0.04	0.02	21	0.48	0.20
Other Relative Value	33	0.37	0.18	15	0.91	0.29	18	−0.08	0.12
Regulation D	18	0.06	0.04	3	0.14	0.20	15	0.04	0.02
Relative Value Multi-Strategy	106	0.27	0.06	46	0.48	0.06	60	0.10	0.05
Sector	465	0.61	0.42	167	0.51	0.39	298	0.66	0.46
Short Bias	56	−0.95	−0.82	11	−0.74	−0.88	45	−1.00	−0.81
Single Strategy	147	0.18	0.07	85	0.19	0.07	62	0.18	0.11
Total	6634	0.32	0.18	2631	0.29	0.18	4003	0.33	0.18

Panel B: Fund of Funds

Strategy	Full Sample Sample Size	Mean	Median	Extant Funds Sample Size	Mean	Median	Disappearing Funds Sample Size	Mean	Median
Conservative	31	0.37	0.14	29	0.39	0.15	2	0.11	−0.11
Invest Funds in Parent Company	64	0.55	0.16	38	0.20	0.12	26	1.07	0.21
Market Neutral	162	0.13	0.06	105	0.18	0.06	57	0.05	0.06
Multi-Strategy	2426	0.17	0.14	1606	0.18	0.14	820	0.15	0.13
Opportunistic	57	0.31	0.19	44	0.36	0.18	13	0.16	0.20
Single Strategy	655	0.26	0.15	429	0.25	0.14	226	0.28	0.18
Total	3395	0.20	0.14	2251	0.20	0.14	1144	0.19	0.13

4.3.2. FACTOR BETAS

The Fung and Hsieh (2004) 7-factor model also allows us to estimate the sensitivity of hedge fund returns relative to several risk factors such as market returns, size factor, credit spread factor, and others. We call these sensitivities factor betas. Here, our analysis will focus on the market beta, or the market risk of hedge fund returns. As shown in Table 4.10, the market betas of hedge funds partially reflect their investment focus. For instance, dedicated short bias hedge funds have negative betas; equity market neutral hedge funds have betas close to zero.

4.4. Conclusions

In this chapter, we introduce definitions of some key measures of hedge fund performance and risk profile. We discuss methods of computing these key measures and provide examples using data from CISDM, one of the major hedge fund databases. We compute these measures of return and risk for extant funds and disappearing funds, respectively, as well as by investment strategies, respectively. From the comparison across extant funds and disappearing funds and across investment strategies, we observe many systematic patterns.

Keywords

Annualized Returns
CISDM
Disappearing Funds
Excess Returns
Extant Funds
Factor Betas

Fung and Hsieh (2004) 7-factor alpha
Goetzmann et al. (2007) MPPM
Information Ratio
Sharpe Ratio
Standard Deviation
Treynor Ratio

Discussion Questions

Using hedge fund monthly return data for the period 2009 to 2012 from CISDM or other hedge fund databases, calculate:

1. Annualized returns
2. Excess returns
3. Sharpe Ratio
4. Treynor Ratio
5. Information Ratio
6. Goetzmann et al. (2007) MPPM
7. Fung and Hsieh (2004) 7-factor alpha
8. Standard Deviation of monthly return
9. Factor Betas

CHAPTER 5

Hedge Fund Forum Shopping

5.1. Introduction

This chapter provides an analysis of hedge fund strategies in the context of international differences in hedge fund regulation. Certain fund strategies have been characterized in the law and finance literature, as well as in popular media and public policy debates, as being inherently more risky and associated with more pronounced agency problems. For instance, managed futures, long/short, and event driven strategies might be associated with greater risk and agency problems than market neutral equity strategies and various arbitrage strategies. At issue, therefore, is whether funds engage in forum shopping to select jurisdictions that potentially offer greater scope for agency problems associated with hedge fund management. That is, law is a "product" (Romano, 1985), and the features of the hedge fund legal system can influence fund managers to engage in "jurisdiction shopping" or "choice of law" decision making.

The data examined in this chapter offer little or no support for the view that hedge fund managers pursuing riskier strategies or strategies with potentially more pronounced agency problems systematically select jurisdictions with less stringent regulations. For the most part, fund strategies are not systematically and statistically related to different regulations observed in different jurisdictions. In fact, to the extent that there is evidence of forum shopping, it is such that funds pursuing riskier strategies or strategies with greater potential agency problems select jurisdictions with more stringent regulations. We may infer from the evidence that forum shopping by fund managers in relation to fund strategic focus is not consistent with a "race to the bottom." Rather, hedge fund managers appear to select jurisdictions that are in the interests of fund investors in order to facilitate capital raising by the hedge fund.

Hedge funds have been the subject of media attention in the United States and around the world given the pronounced growth of the hedge fund sector in recent years and the comparative dearth of regulations faced by hedge fund managers. At the peak of the market prior to the financial crisis, some estimates suggested hedge fund managers managed more than US$2 trillion in hedge fund capital worldwide (Chapter 1; see also PricewaterhouseCoopers, 2007).[1] This amount, while not trivial, is small compared to the size of worldwide mutual fund capital, which some estimates placed at US$24.32 trillion at that time.[2]

Mutual fund investors are great in number and are comprised primarily of retail investors. Securities laws are thus designed to mitigate excessive risk taking and other behaviors of mutual fund managers that would be against the interests of retail investors. Hedge fund investors, by contrast, are usually much more limited in number and are deemed to be sophisticated investors (institutional and high net worth investors). This difference in the investor base creates a "gulf," so to speak, between the mutual fund and hedge fund industry. As a result of differing investor bases, hedge funds are able to take advantage of various exemptions in the laws and regulations, which were promulgated and implemented by some of the most sophisticated regulatory authorities in the world. By compromising on the extent to which their products or funds can be marketed to the public,[3] hedge funds are not prohibited from employing a variety of investment instruments and strategies, many of which would not be permitted to other funds such as mutual funds and private equity funds. Hedge funds, for example, may utilize derivative instruments; they may also short sell and leverage rather highly to achieve their investment goals. Commonly observed hedge fund strategies (i.e., the primary mandate of a hedge fund) include investments in distressed companies, commodity trading advisers/managed futures, short biased and small/micro capitalization ("micro cap") focused strategies, and many others that will be discussed here. Although hedge funds are able to use a multitude of investment strategies, many use similar ones. This behavior is termed as "herding" (Haigh et al., 2007).[4]

There are inevitably various agency problems associated with hedge fund management. While these agency problems were described in more detail in Chapter 2 of this book, here we briefly outline the extent to which potential agency problems may arise. First, in a more direct manner, hedge funds might pursue investment strategies and/or make financial reports that benefit the hedge fund managers at the expense of their investors. For example, hedge funds are much more likely to report marginally positive monthly returns than returns that are marginally negative, and this type of returns manipulation significantly aids capital raising efforts of hedge fund managers.[5] Second, in a more oblique manner, hedge funds'

---

[1] See also PriceWaterhouseCoopers, *The Regulation, Taxation and Distribution of Hedge Funds around the Globe,* June 2007, www.pwc.com/extweb/pwcpublications.nsf/docid/5D8AB75A01C274B985257 2FA0073A6C0/$File/under_the_spotlite.pdf.

[2] See Investment Company Factbook, www.ici.org/pdf/2011_factbook.pdf.

[3] In the United States and the United Kingdom, for example, hedge funds can only be distributed by private placements. See Chapter 1.

[4] Haigh et al. conclude that herding does exist among hedge funds and is similar in magnitude to such behavior in the private equity market.

[5] See Chapter 8. See also Bollen and Pool, (2006, 2008, and 2009).

investment strategies might be contrary to the interests of other investors or shareholders in portfolio companies in which hedge funds invest.[6] For example, hedge funds that acquire significant voting rights in a company may act in ways that bring about financial benefit solely for the fund (and therefore its investors) at the expense of the other company's shareholders and possibly more detrimentally at the expense of the fund investors' aim to promote industry.[7] Such active participation in portfolio companies by hedge funds has been labeled both in a flattering manner, as hedge fund activism, and more critically, as vulture fund activity.[8]

One concern shared by many regulators around the world is that the size of the hedge fund industry coupled with potential agency problems, activist (vulture) investment practices, and herding behavior, exacerbates financial instability. The hedge fund industry comprises more than US$2 trillion in capital under management in recent 2007 estimates.[9] Thus, this industry has significant ability to move markets. For example, in the week of August 6, 2007, hedge funds following long/short equity strategies experienced massive losses.[10] Empirical evidence on this event is suggestive of significant and growing systematic risk in the hedge fund industry (Boyson et al., 2010; see also Chapter 10).

As discussed in Chapters 1–3, hedge funds have been the subject of media attention in the United States and around the world, given the pronounced growth of the hedge fund sector in recent years and the comparative dearth of regulations faced by hedge fund managers. In Chapter 2 we provided an overview of the potential agency problems associated with managing a hedge fund and the associated rationales for hedge fund regulation. In Chapter 3 we provided an international comparison of hedge fund regulation. While hedge funds are hardly regulated in the United States, there are nevertheless jurisdictions outside this country with different and sometimes more onerous sets of regulatory requirements. Examples of international differences in hedge fund regulation include minimum capitalization requirements, restrictions on the location of key service providers, and different permissible distribution channels via private placements, banks, other

---

[6] Kahan and Rock (2007) provide many illustrative examples of such behavior.

[7] Hu and Black (2006) suggest the decoupling of economic interest from voting rights in order to deal with such possibly detrimental behavior by hedge funds.

[8] Kahan and Rock (2007) discuss hedge fund activism and its benefits and criticisms, concluding that such behavior does not warrant regulation.

[9] PricewaterhouseCoopers (2007), at page 2.

[10] Khandani and Lo (2007) discuss the causes and effects of the losses experienced by the quantitative long/short equity hedge funds. See also Getmansky et al. (2004), who analyzed the attrition rates of hedge funds across different investment styles and made recommendations to stabilize the market. For related media discussions of this period, see The Hedge Fund Quants of August, October 3, 2007, www.salon.com/tech/htww/2007/10/03/quants/index.html and What Happened to the Quants in August 2007?, October 2, 2007, www.nakedcapitalism.com/2007/10/what-happened-to-quants-in-august-2007.html.

regulated or non-regulated financial intermediaries, wrappers, investment managers, and fund distribution companies.

One argument consistently put forth against more onerous regulation of hedge funds is the threat of hedge funds moving from one jurisdiction to a less regulated one to avoid such onerous regulatory oversight. Hedge funds are free to forum shop by registering in many different countries around the world, subject to meeting the requirements of the particular jurisdiction (these requirements are summarized in Chapter 3). A central issue considered in this chapter is therefore whether hedge funds that are pursuing riskier strategies are in fact selecting jurisdictions that have less onerous regulation. If hedge funds pursuing risky investment strategies select jurisdictions with more onerous regulation, then we may infer that hedge fund managers perceive regulation to be informative to investors. By registering in jurisdictions with greater regulatory oversight, managers proactively mitigate potential agency conflicts associated with fund management, thus enhancing investor confidence. By gaining the investors' confidence through regulation, the hedge funds in return aim to raise more capital. On the other hand, if hedge fund managers pursuing riskier strategies select jurisdictions that have less onerous regulatory oversight, then we may worry that those international differences in hedge fund regulation facilitate a race to the bottom where fund managers' interests are served at the expense of their investors. Last, if hedge fund strategies do not vary by international differences in regulation, then we may infer that regulatory differences provide little or no information to a fund's investors.

The latter part of this chapter provides an empirical analysis of hedge fund strategies in the context of international differences in hedge fund regulation. The data examined encompass 1,845 funds registered in 24 countries around the world. The data offer scant support for the view that hedge fund managers pursuing riskier strategies or strategies with potentially more pronounced agency problems systematically select jurisdictions with less stringent regulations. For the most part, fund strategies are not systematically and statistically related to different regulations observed in different jurisdictions.[11] In fact, to the extent that there is evidence of forum shopping, it is for the most part suggestive that funds pursuing riskier strategies or strategies with greater potential agency problems select jurisdictions with more stringent regulations.[12] We may infer from the evidence that forum shopping by fund managers in relation to

---

[11] This finding is consistent with the evidence on US hedge fund registration presented in Brown et al. (2008).

[12] Consistent empirical evidence has been found in other unrelated contexts, such as in the seminal work on forum shopping in US corporate law by Romano (2005). Forum shopping has also been considered in the international context, and the evidence tends to be consistent in that there is not much evidence in support of a race to the bottom. For instance, an analysis of forum shopping in Canadian corporate law is provided in Cumming and MacIntosh (2000).

fund strategic focus is not consistent with a race to the bottom, where funds select jurisdictions with scant regulation such that regulators have incentives to offer limited regulation. Rather, the data suggest that hedge funds select heavily regulated jurisdictions that are in the fund investors' interests in order to facilitate capital raising by the hedge fund. The data examined, however, only offer imperfect proxies for agency problems associated with hedge fund management, and it is possible that the coarseness in the empirical measures do not pick up certain factors. Given these limitations, we interpret the evidence in light of the broader law and finance literature on hedge fund regulation and governance.

5.2. Hedge Fund Forum Shopping

This section considers whether hedge funds pursuing riskier strategies select jurisdictions that have less onerous regulation. We look at the average monthly return and standard deviation of returns to determine the riskiness of each strategy. In Section 5.3 we describe hedge fund strategies and relate different strategies to the extent to which risk and agency problems are more pronounced. In turn, we also conjecture hypotheses regarding fund strategies and forum shopping for different regulation, and describe the dataset used to test the hypotheses. Multivariate empirical tests are provided in Section 5.4. Limitations and extensions regarding the tests are acknowledged in Section 5.5. Thereafter concluding remarks follow in Section 5.6.

Hedge fund strategies are classified into different investment strategies. Funds report their primary strategies or investment focus to hedge fund data vendors such as the Center for International Securities and Derivatives Markets (CISDM), HedgeFund.Net, and TASS. The range of strategies recorded differs slightly across different data vendors. The strategies indicated in the HedgeFund.Net and CISDM datasets (which are described further below in Section 5.3) are indicated in Table 5.1. The range of strategies recorded in the HedgeFund.Net dataset is slightly broader than that found in CISDM.[13]

Hedge fund strategies in Table 5.1 are listed according to the frequency in which they are observed in the combined CISDM and HedgeFund.Net dataset. Additionally, each fund strategy presented shows the average monthly return and standard deviation of monthly returns over the period 2003 to 2005.

[13] The Center for International Securities and Derivatives Markets (CISDM) records styles for merger arbitrage, equity long/short, relative value multi-strategy, emerging markets, equity market neutral, multi-strategy, convertible arbitrage, global macro, fixed income, fixed income arbitrage, technology sector, event driven multi-strategy, distressed securities, option arbitrage, capital structure arbitrage, market timing, short bias, equity long only, Regulation D, other relative value, and other strategy. HedgeFund.Net records these styles, as well as the additional ones indicated in Table 5.1.

Table 5.1 **Hedge Fund Strategies**

Fund Strategy	# Funds	Average Monthly Return (%)	Average Standard Deviation of Returns (%)	Definition
Market Neutral Equity	512	1.17	2.90	An investment strategy that seeks to mitigate or avoid market risk in equity investments, such that there is minimal or zero correlation with fluctuations in the relevant set (as defined by the hedge fund) of equity investments.
Long/Short Equity	227	0.89	3.20	An investment strategy involving purchases of equity expected to increase in value and short sales of securities expected to decrease in value.
Multi-Strategy	169	0.94	2.11	A multi-faceted investment strategy (i.e., there is no specifically identified fund style).
CTA/Managed Futures	131	0.81	5.17	Commodity Trading Advisers (CTAs) operate managed futures, which are investment funds that take long and short positions in futures, options on futures, and government securities.
Emerging Markets	109	2.21	4.12	An investment strategy where the fund invests in emerging or developing regions of the world, often characterized by significant political risk and economic risk.
Technology Sector	104	1.35	3.74	A fund focused in technology sector-specific investments, such as Internet, semiconductors, hardware, software, etc.
Convertible Arbitrage	95	0.58	1.61	A market-neutral investment strategy that simultaneously involves the purchase of convertible securities and the short sale of the same issuer's common stock.
Fixed Income Arbitrage	94	0.72	1.28	An investment strategy that exploits inefficiencies in bond pricing.
Macro	73	0.91	4.64	A hedge used to eliminate the risk of a portfolio of assets, which implies taking a position in a single asset or multiple assets that offset the whole portfolio.
Distressed	67	1.47	2.04	Funds that invest in financially distressed companies.

(Continued)

Table 5.1 (Continued)

Fund Strategy	# Funds	Average Monthly Return (%)	Average Standard Deviation of Returns (%)	Definition
Merger/Risk Arbitrage	45	0.47	0.97	A minimal risk investment strategy where the stocks of two merging companies are simultaneously bought and sold at a profit. Risk relates to likelihood and timing of deal approval.
Event Driven	31	0.97	2.20	A fund strategy to invest in companies with special situations, including financial distress, mergers, and takeovers.
Value	22	1.04	3.30	An investment strategy focused on companies that are trading on values less than their intrinsic value.
Short Bias	19	−0.49	3.86	An investment strategy in which the fund manager takes more short positions than long positions.
Fixed Income (non-arbitrage)	18	0.80	1.45	Investments in fixed income securities beyond the realm of fixed income arbitrage strategies (defined earlier).
Options Strategies	17	0.55	2.44	Funds that focus investments in options.
Long Only	12	0.66	3.61	Funds that do not make short sale investments.
Finance Sector	11	1.06	1.97	Funds that focus investments in finance sector companies.
Small/Micro Cap	10	1.92	4.28	Small investee focus fund investments.
Regulation D	10	1.58	4.03	Of the U.S. Securities and Exchange Commission (SEC). Regulation D governs private placement exemptions for smaller companies raising debt or equity capital without registering their securities with the SEC.

Table 5.1 (Continued)

Fund Strategy	# Funds	Average Monthly Return (%)	Average Standard Deviation of Returns (%)	Definition
Health Care Sector	10	0.46	3.80	Funds focused in the health care sector.
Short-term Trading	8	0.50	1.74	Strategic trading for short term capital gains.
Statistical Arbitrage	8	0.51	1.32	A trading strategy focused on inefficient pricing of securities identified from statistical models.
Other Arbitrage	8	0.74	1.53	Funds that find inefficiency in the pricing of securities based on a variety of (non-specified) arbitrage techniques.
Market Timer	5	0.48	1.99	Funds that purchase or sell assets based on predicted future price movements.
Mortgages	5	0.92	0.79	Funds that focus their investments in the mortgage sector.
Energy Sector	4	2.18	4.32	Funds that focus investments in energy sector companies.
Country Specific	3	0.94	4.61	Funds that focus their investments within a certain country(ies).

This table defines the fund strategies.

Sources: www.hedgefund.net/def.php3, www.investopedia.com, and www.wikipedia.com. The number of funds in each strategy and the average monthly return and standard deviation for the period 2003–2005 are also presented.

These performance statistics provide a rough guide to risk and returns associated with different fund strategies.[14]

While it is not possible to perfectly classify different hedge fund strategies into different degrees of risk, it is possible to carry out a rather rough grouping of strategies into different risk profiles and potential agency problems with an analysis of average monthly returns and average standard deviation of returns. For example, strategies that involve risk-free arbitrage would, of course, be of minimal concern for either risk and/or agency problems.[15] The arbitrage strategies indicated in Table 5.1 include convertible arbitrage, fixed income arbitrage, merger/risk arbitrage, capital structure arbitrage, statistical arbitrage, and other arbitrage. Generally, the standard deviation of returns is lower for these arbitrage strategies relative to other non-arbitrage strategies. We may therefore infer that potential agency problems are less pronounced for these arbitrage strategies. For example, fixed-income arbitrage strategies have been described as analogous to steamrollers that pick up loose change on the street.[16]

For reasons identified in this section strategies for which agency problems may be more pronounced might include long/short equity, multi-strategy, commodity trading advisers/managed futures, emerging markets, technology sector, macro, event driven (in some classifications, event driven strategies encompass distressed securities, Regulation D, and high yield low grade fixed income securities),[17] short bias, small/micro cap, special situations,[18] energy sector and country specific. For example, long/short strategies have been associated with potential agency problems where the fund manager acts against the interests of the fund's investors,[19] and such strategies have been associated with massive volatility swings.[20] Funds pursuing small/micro cap strategies and distressed investments also are significantly relevant for exacerbated agency problems (Chapter 2).

While we do not seek to precisely identify the severity and scope of agency problems within each fund or class of funds for the purposes of this chapter, we can nevertheless determine whether fund managers pursuing different strategies, irrelevant of risk, tend to register their funds in different countries with different

---

[14] See Malkiel and Saha (2005), who provide similar information over the period from 1995 to 2003.

[15] In practice, arbitrage will involve an element of risk.

[16] See, e.g., Fixed-Income Arbitrage, www.investopedia.com/terms/f/fixedincomearbitrage.asp (indicating that large losses are nevertheless possible with fixed income arbitrage strategies).

[17] See Hedge Fund Styles, Lipper HedgeWorld's Education Center, www.hedgeworld.com/education/index.cgi?page=hedge_fund_styles (defining the categories of investment styles used by hedge fund managers).

[18] "Event driven" and "special situations" are arguably quite similar but are nevertheless two separate categories used by HedgeFund.Net and as such are maintained as separate categories herein.

[19] See note 10 and accompanying text, this chapter.

[20] Ibid.

sets of regulations identified in Table 5.1 and discussed earlier. As such, we may pose three alternative hypotheses about forum shopping:

> **Hypothesis 5.1**—Race to the Bottom: Hedge fund managers pursuing riskier strategies and strategies for which potential agency problems are more pronounced select jurisdictions that have less onerous regulatory oversight.
> **Hypothesis 5.2**—Neutrality: The relation between hedge fund strategies and hedge fund regulation is random.
> **Hypothesis 5.3**—Alignment of Interests: Hedge funds pursuing risky investment strategies select jurisdictions with more onerous regulation.

Next, we assess the empirical validity of these competing hypotheses. To the extent that we find evidence in support of Hypothesis 5.1, we may be concerned that international differences in hedge fund regulation facilitate a race to the bottom where fund managers' interests are served at the expense of their investors. In the alternative, if the data are consistent with Hypothesis 5.2 such that hedge fund strategies are invariant to international differences in regulation, then we may infer that regulatory differences provide little, if any, information regarding a fund manager's intentions with regards to potential agency problems. Finally, if we find evidence in support of Hypothesis 5.3, then we may infer that hedge fund managers perceive regulation to be informative to the funds' investors because fund managers signal their interest in mitigating potential agency conflicts associated with fund management by registering in a jurisdiction with greater regulatory oversight and thereby facilitating fund-raising efforts.

5.3. Data

The data used in this chapter comprise 1,845 funds. Data were used from two sources: (1) CISDM,[21] and (2) HedgeFund.Net (HFN) DataExport collected by Channel Capital Group Inc.[22] Similar data have been used in prior work.[23]

The number of fund strategies in each country of fund registration is indicated in Table 5.2. There are some patterns that are notable in this table. For example, a greater proportion of the funds pursuing emerging market strategies are registered in offshore centers such as the Bahamas, the Channel Islands, and the Cayman Islands.

---

[21] The Center for International Securities and Derivatives Markets, http://cisdm.som.umass.edu/.
[22] Hedgefund.net, www.hedgefund.net/.
[23] See also Chapter 6 where we use similar data to analyze the flow-performance relationship of hedge funds. We do not include fund of fund strategies in the dataset used in this chapter as such funds do not have an identifiable strategic focus. Of the fund of funds that were excluded from the data, we observe a majority registered in the United States.

Table 5.2 **Number of Hedge Funds using Different Strategies, by Country of Registration**

	Market-Neutral Equity	Long/Short Equity	Multi-Strategy	CTA/Managed Futures	Emerging Markets	Technology Sector
Australia	0	0	0	1	0	0
Austria	0	0	0	1	0	0
Bermuda	33	1	7	0	6	5
Brazil	0	1	0	0	4	0
Bahamas	3	0	1	0	7	0
British Virgin Islands	43	0	19	0	8	11
Canada	14	0	0	1	0	0
Switzerland	0	0	2	0	0	0
China	0	1	0	0	0	0
France	2	0	1	0	0	0
Channel Islands	0	0	0	0	3	0
Hong Kong	0	1	0	0	0	0
Ireland	12	0	0	4	0	0
Isle of Man	0	0	1	0	0	0
Japan	0	2	0	0	0	0
Cayman Islands	135	0	44	0	58	12
Luxembourg	4	0	2	0	0	0
Mauritius	1	0	0	0	1	0
Netherlands	0	0	0	0	0	0
Netherland Antilles	1	0	3	0	1	0
New Zealand	0	0	0	0	0	0
United Kingdom	2	11	1	1	0	0
United States	262	210	88	118	21	76
US Virgin Islands	0	0	0	5	0	0

Table 5.2   *(Continued)*

	Convertible Arbitrage	Fixed Income Arbitrage	Macro	Distressed	Merger/Risk Arbitrage	Event Driven	Other Less Common Fund Strategies
Australia	0	0	1	0	0	0	0
Austria	0	0	0	0	1	0	0
Bermuda	11	2	2	4	1	2	2
Brazil	0	0	1	0	0	0	0
Bahamas	0	3	2	0	2	0	1
British Virgin Islands	2	1	5	3	2	0	2
Canada	0	0	0	0	0	0	5
Switzerland	0	0	0	0	0	0	0
China	0	0	0	0	0	0	0
France	0	2	0	0	1	0	1
Channel Islands	0	0	0	0	0	0	1
Hong Kong	0	0	0	0	0	0	0
Ireland	3	0	2	0	3	0	0
Isle of Man	0	0	0	0	0	0	0
Japan	0	0	0	0	0	0	0
Cayman Islands	24	39	20	13	14	0	13
Luxembourg	1	2	0	0	0	0	0
Mauritius	0	0	0	0	0	0	0
Netherlands	0	0	0	1	0	0	0
Netherland Antilles	0	0	0	0	0	0	1
New Zealand	0	0	1	0	0	0	0
United Kingdom	0	0	1	0	0	0	0
United States	54	44	38	46	21	29	162
US Virgin Islands	0	1	0	0	0	0	0

This table presents the number of hedge funds using different strategies according to the country of registration. Fund strategies are as defined in Table 5.1.

While some patterns may already become apparent in Table 5.2, for the most part it is necessary and worthwhile to consider multivariate tests to ascertain patterns in fund registration relative to fund strategies. This exercise is provided next.

5.4. Multivariate Empirical Tests

Table 5.3, Panels A and B, provide empirical tests of the propensity of funds pursuing different strategies to select jurisdictions of registration based on their fund strategy. Panel A provides analyses with the use of the combined CISDM and HFN dataset, while Panel B provides analyses with the use of the HFN dataset alone.[24] We provide eight different regression models to assess the extent of jurisdiction shopping for minimum capitalization (Model 1), restrictions on location (Model 2), and different distribution channels (Models 3 to 8). In the regressions we include as control variables fund size and age, as well as dummy variables for their primary location of assets.[25]

Model (1a) and (1b) (for Panels A and B, respectively) provide an ordinary least squares regression of funds registering in jurisdictions with different minimum capitalization requirements. The data indicate very weak evidence of any jurisdiction shopping for fund strategies in relation to minimum capitalization in Models (1a) and (1b).[26] Model (1a) shows that Fixed Income Arbitrage funds are more likely to select jurisdictions with larger capital requirements. This is not surprising, as fixed income arbitrage strategies involve small gains on extremely large transactions.[27]

Models (1a) and (1b) show Market Timer funds tend to be registered in jurisdictions with lower minimum capitalization requirements. Some commentators have noted that market timing strategies may involve taking advantage of

---

[24] A limitation with the HedgeFund.Net dataset is that country of fund registration is not observable for many of the funds in the source data. The different data vendors also do not track all of the same fund types. As such, we show regression results below with and without the HedgeFund.Net dataset in Table 5.3, Panels A and B, to show robustness.

[25] Fund size is measured as of 2003, which is an imperfect control variable. We might measure fund size at the time of first registration, but size at that time would technically be at or close to zero. We control for fund size considering the possibility that funds expecting to raise more capital will tend to register in jurisdictions that have larger minimum capitalization. We do acknowledge that fund size will be in part endogenous to regulations in different countries; however, we do not have suitable instrumental variables to account for endogeneity. Excluding the fund size variable in any of the regressions does not materially impact the variables of interest pertaining to fund strategy and jurisdiction shopping.

[26] We also considered Tobit regressions to account for the fact that minimum capitalization cannot be bounded below by zero. Those regressions showed no significant relation between fund strategy and minimum capitalization.

[27] See note 16 and accompanying text, this chapter.

Table 5.3 Regression Analyses of Hedge Fund Forum Shopping

Panel A. Combined CISDM and HFN Data

	(1a)	(2a)	(3a)	(4a)
	Minimum Capitalization Requirements	Restrictions on the Location of Key Service Providers	Marketing via Private Placements	Marketing via Wrappers
Constant	380210.296***	0.296***	0.016	−0.057***
Hedge Fund Strategy				
Fixed Income Arbitrage	70454.269*	0.113	−0.038**	0.010
Merger/Risk Arbitrage	47740.678	0.150		0.050
Convertible Arbitrage	−3312.301	0.078		
Multi-Strategy	75605.281	0.041	−0.036***	0.024
Event Driven	−12643.066	0.241		
Short-term Trading	−11039.529			
Market-Neutral Equity	−18918.861	0.008	−0.003	0.010
Small/Micro Cap	−1872.101			
Short Bias	44861.133	0.039		
Long/Short Equity	−2457.890	−0.102		0.029*

(Continued)

Table 5.3 (Continued)

	(5a) Marketing via Banks	(6a) Marketing via Other Regulated Financial Institution	(7a) Marketing via Investment Managers	(8a) Marketing via Fund Distribution Companies
Constant	0.494***	−0.067***	0.466***	−0.069***
Technology Sector	−60895.931	−0.082*		
Emerging Markets	60490.056	0.232**		−0.001
Macro	145446.365	0.160		0.009
Capital Structure Arbitrage	43149.933			
CTA/Managed Futures	70527.075	0.239*		−0.001
Market Timer	−139038.931***			
Distressed Securities	−23136.145	−0.040		
Fund Characteristics				
Fund Size	0.00001*	1.06E-10***	0.00001	−5.63E-12
Fund Age	−488.661***	−0.0009***		−0.0001
Model Diagnostics				
Number of Observations	1845	1845	1845	1845
Number of Observations with Dependent Variable = 1	Not Applicable	612	1833	59

Loglikelihood Function	−25992.874	−749.307	−64.099	−233.041
Adjusted R² (Pseudo R² for Models 2–8)	0.110	0.361	0.117	0.108
F-Statistic (Chi-squared Statistic for Models 2–8)	25.38***	845.942***	16.572**	56.166***
Hedge Fund Strategy				
Fixed Income Arbitrage	0.051	0.0003	0.071	0.011
Merger/Risk Arbitrage	0.110	0.108	0.068	0.051
Convertible Arbitrage	0.063	0.036	−0.010	
Multi-Strategy	−0.015	0.002	−0.022	0.016
Event Driven	0.054		0.018	
Short-term Trading				
Market-Neutral Equity	−0.015	0.024	−0.063	0.006
Small/Micro Cap				
Short Bias	0.040		−0.011	
Long/Short Equity	0.052	0.001	0.025	0.005
Technology Sector	−0.129**		−0.144***	
Emerging Markets	0.082	0.008	0.188*	0.046
Macro	0.117	0.039	0.071	0.032

(Continued)

Table 5.3 (Continued)

	(5a) Marketing via Banks	(6a) Marketing via Other Regulated Financial Institution	(7a) Marketing via Investment Managers	(8a) Marketing via Fund Distribution Companies
Capital Structure Arbitrage				
CTA/Managed Futures	0.172	0.040		0.007
Market Timer			0.001	
Distressed Securities	−0.120**	−0.010	−0.105*	
Fund Characteristics				
Fund Size	2.74E-10***	1.10E-12	1.37E-10***	−5.71E-12
Fund Age	−0.002***	−0.0002**	−0.0014***	−0.00009
Model Diagnostics				
Number of Observations	1845	1845	1845	1845
Number of Observations with Dependent Variable = 1	640	73	633	49
Loglikelihood Function	−804.086	−286.646	−813.738	−215.631
Adjusted R^2 (Pseudo R^2 for Models 2–8)	0.325	0.067	0.314	0.046

	773.709***	41.328***	745.427***	21.139
F-Statistic (Chi-squared Statistic for Models 2–8)				
Panel B. CISDM Data Only				
Constant	410359.853***	0.540***	0.027	−0.096***
Hedge Fund Strategy				
Fixed Income Arbitrage	71212.581	0.091	−0.049**	0.043
Merger/Risk Arbitrage	25597.807	0.112		0.107
Convertible Arbitrage	−16830.136	0.061		
Multi-Strategy	15931.457	−0.007	−0.020	0.015
Market-Neutral Equity	−27607.358	−0.038	−0.004	0.029
Short Bias	41785.728	0.009		
Technology Sector	−78828.207	−0.205		
Emerging Markets	54200.932	0.211*		0.052
Macro	225534.869	0.143		0.080
Capital Structure Arbitrage	74264.175	0.248		
Market Timer	−180318.466***	−0.207		
Distressed Securities	−48694.995	−0.163		

(Continued)

Table 5.3 (Continued)

	(5b) Marketing via Banks	(6b) Marketing via Other Regulated Financial Institution	(7b) Marketing via Investment Managers	(8b) Marketing via Fund Distribution Companies
Fund Characteristics				
Fund Size	0.00001**	1.75E-10***		-2.59E-12
Fund Age	-515.783***	-0.001***	-2.17E-06	-1.86E-05
Model Diagnostics				
Number of Observations	1127	1127	1127	1127
Number of Observations with Dependent Variable = 1	Not Applicable	588	1118	28
Loglikelihood Function	-15787.576	-652.245	-48.276	-125.919
Adjusted R^2 (Pseudo R^2 for Models 2–8)	0.098	0.164	0.079	0.040
F-Statistic (Chi-squared Statistic for Models 2–8)	7.08***	255.732***	8.318	10.388
Hedge Fund Strategy				
Fixed Income Arbitrage	0.061	0.093	0.049	0.045
Merger/Risk Arbitrage	0.108	0.392	0.028	0.115

Constant	0.635	−0.123***	0.632***	−0.103***
Convertible Arbitrage	0.083	0.198	−0.046	
Multi-Strategy	−0.037	0.041	−0.085	0.017
Market-Neutral Equity	−0.016	0.103*	−0.118	0.032
Short Bias	0.071		−0.034	
Technology Sector	−0.192*		−0.263***	
Emerging Markets	0.115	0.162	0.190*	0.140
Macro	0.139	0.247	0.059	0.085
Capital Structure Arbitrage				
Market Timer				
Distressed Securities	−0.197*		−0.226**	
Fund Characteristics				
Fund Size	3.89E-10***	2.12E-12	1.98E-10***	−4.03E-12
Fund Age	−0.002***	−1.86E-04	−0.002***	−3.44E-05
Model Diagnostics				
Number of Observations	1127	1127	1127	1127
Number of Observations with Dependent Variable = 1	590	52	586	32

(Continued)

Table 5.3 (Continued)

	(5b)	(6b)	(7b)	(8b)
	Marketing via Banks	Marketing via Other Regulated Financial Institution	Marketing via Investment Managers	Marketing via Fund Distribution Companies
Loglikelihood Function	−645.732	−194.927	−661.944	−137.649
Adjusted R² (Pseudo R² for Models 2–8)	0.172	0.075	0.152	0.054
F-Statistic (Chi-squared Statistic for Models 2–8)	268.397***	31.619***	236.668***	15.724

Table 5.3, Panel A, presents logit regression analyses of the determinants of forum shopping for different rules for minimum capitalization, restrictions on location, and distribution channels in the HFN and CISDM datasets. Fund strategy variables are dummy variables equal to one where the fund's primary strategy is indicated, as per the fund strategies as defined in Table 5.1. All regression models in Panel A use dummy variables equal to 1 for the location of fund assets and a dummy variable equal to 1 for the HFN Dataset. Model (1a) includes but does not report (for reasons of space) the coefficient estimates for dummy variables equal to 1 for statistical arbitrage, value, Regulation D, fixed income (non-arbitrage), finance sector, long only, energy sector, country specific, options strategies and other arbitrage (all of these strategy variable estimates were statistically insignificant in Model 1a); Models (2a)–(8a) do not include any strategy variables not indicated; more parsimonious specifications were necessary in the logit models (2a)–(8a) due to collinearity and invariance with respect to the binary dependent variable. Fund size is excluded in Model (3a) to avoid collinearity problems. Marginal effects are reported and not the standard logit coefficients in order to highlight economic significance alongside statistical significance. Notations *, **, *** indicate that the results are statistically significant at the 10%, 5%, and 1% levels, respectively.

Table 5.3, Panel B, presents logit regression analyses of the determinants of forum shopping for different rules for minimum capitalization, restrictions on location and distribution channels in the CISDM dataset (excluding the HFN Dataset). Fund strategy variables are dummy variables equal to 1 where the fund's primary strategy is indicated, as per the fund strategies as defined in Table 5.1. All regression models in Panel B use dummy variables equal to 1 for the location of fund assets; there are no other non-reported variables in Table 5.3, Panel B. Fund size is excluded in Model (3a) to avoid collinearity problems. Marginal effects are reported and not the standard logit coefficients in order to highlight economic significance alongside statistical significance. Notations *, **, *** indicate that the results are statistically significant at the 10%, 5%, and 1% levels, respectively.

differences in market prices for funds that own assets in different parts of the world and differences in information after markets close at different points in time around the world and possibly trading strategies that are associated with manipulating closing prices.[28] While the evidence in Table 5.3 shows that Market Timer funds tend to select jurisdictions with lower capital requirements, we do note that our data comprise five funds with a primary market strategy of market timing; and of these, four are registered in the United States (where there are no minimum capitalization requirements for hedge funds) and one in Bermuda. Also, when we employ alternative estimation methods, we do not find evidence of a significant relation between market timing and minimum capitalization. It would thus be difficult to conclude from the evidence on a negative relation between market timing strategies and minimum capitalization in Table 5.3 that there is a "race to the bottom" along the lines of Hypothesis 5.1 outlined earlier.

Models (2a) and (2b) show some evidence that fund strategies are related to choice of jurisdiction in terms of restrictions on the location of key service providers. In particular, the data indicate at the 5% level of statistical significance that Emerging Markets funds are 23.2% more likely to register in countries with restrictions on the location of key service providers (Model (1a)). Model (1b) with the subset of CISDM data similarly only shows at the 10% level of significance that funds pursuing emerging market strategies are 21.1% more likely to register in countries with restrictions on the location of key service providers. If we may infer that emerging market strategies involve potentially more pronounced agency problems than other strategies, then the fact that these funds select jurisdictions that restrict location is consistent with Hypothesis 5.3 described in Section 5.2.

Consistent with the evidence on emerging markets and restrictions on location in support of Hypothesis 5.3, Table 5.3 Panel A, Model (2a) also shows at the 10% level of statistical significance that funds pursuing commodity trading advisers/managed futures strategies are 23.9% more likely to register in countries with restrictions on the location of key service providers. We had suggested earlier that commodity trading advisers/managed futures fund strategies involved potentially greater agency problems, and certainly this strategy is riskier than other strategies in terms of variance in returns (Table 5.1). As such, we would again infer that the data are consistent with Hypothesis 5.3 insofar as funds pursuing riskier strategies register in countries with more onerous regulations. We do note, however, that the positive association between commodity trading advisers/managed futures strategies is not statistically significant in Model (2a) with the subset of CISDM data only.

Model (2a) shows technology sector funds pursuing technology sector strategies are 8.2% less likely to register in jurisdictions that restrict the location of key

---

[28] See CNNMoney.com, Market Timing: A Weed that Won't Die, Aug. 26, 2005, http://money.cnn.com/2005/08/26/markets/hedge_timing/index.htm (reporting on a study that found that market timing strategies are still being used by some funds outside the United States).

service providers, and this evidence is significant at the 10% level in Model (2a) (although statistically insignificant in Model (2b)). Potentially a variety of reasons help explain why Technology Sector funds seek fewer location restrictions. One explanation is that these funds exhibit greater agency problems since information asymmetries are more pronounced with high-tech investments and, as such, there is greater scope for fund managers to pursue excessive risk-taking strategies. Another explanation is that these investments require greater geographical proximity to mitigate information asymmetries faced by the investee companies and the hedge fund's manager and key service providers, and any restrictions on location may in turn have a negative effect on the hedge fund value since better performing funds are more geographically proximate to their investee companies.[29] Overall, therefore, this is not conclusive evidence in support of Hypothesis 5.1.

It is noteworthy that there are very few significant strategy variable coefficients in Models (1a), (1b), (2a), and (2b). Hence, in terms of minimum capitalization and restrictions on location, the data tend to offer greatest support for Hypothesis 5.2 that fund strategies are largely invariant to fund regulation. Where coefficients are statistically significant, they tend to be more consistent with Hypothesis 5.3 and do not support the race to the bottom view of Hypothesis 5.1.

Models (3a) to (8b) analyze forum shopping for different marketing channels in relation to fund strategies. Funds pursuing fixed income arbitrage strategies are approximately 3.8% to 4.9% less likely to be registered in countries that offer distributions via private placements (Models (3a) and (3b)), and this evidence is statistically significant at the 5% level of significance. Distribution via private placements offers the potential of risk reduction to the investor since there is more room for negotiation. For example, ratchet clauses may be used alongside various covenants to protect the investors, and if necessary, prices may be discounted in cases of riskier strategies. Since fixed income arbitrage is a comparatively risk-free strategy it is not surprising that fixed income arbitrage is less commonly associated with private placement distribution jurisdictions. Model (3a) also indicates that multi-strategy funds are 3.6% less likely to be registered in jurisdictions that offer private placements; however, that evidence is not robust in the subsample of CISDM data in Table 5.3 Panel B for Model (3b).

Model (4a) indicates that funds pursuing long/short equity strategies are 2.9% more likely to be registered in jurisdictions that allow marketing via wrapper products. This might be suggestive of an exacerbated potential agency problem insofar as wrappers might facilitate distorted information distributed to investors with the combination of multiple products.[30] However, we note that this evidence is

---

[29] See, e.g., Coval and Moskowitz (1999) (discussing the bias in favor of investing close to home); Coval and Moskowitz (2001) positing that investors trade local securities at an information advantage resulting in fund managers earning substantial returns in local investments.

[30] See Chapters 2 and 3; see also Bollen and Pool (2006) (finding that misrepresenting strategy accounted for one of 53 SEC hedge fund litigation cases and allowing for more than one offense per case, misrepresenting strategy involved four of 80 offenses).

statistically significant at only the 10% level and not statistically significant in Model (4b) with the subsample of CISDM data only.

Models (5a) and (5b) show funds pursuing technology sector strategies and distressed securities funds are less likely to be distributed via banks. This evidence is statistically significant at the 5% level in Model (5a) and at the 10% level in Model (5b). In terms of the economic significance, technology sector funds are 12.9% and 19.2% less likely to be registered in bank distribution jurisdictions in Model (5a) and (5b), respectively. Distressed securities funds are 12.0% and 19.7% less likely to be registered in jurisdictions involving bank distributions in Models (5a) and (5b), respectively. As agency problems with technology sectors and distressed securities are more pronounced and as bank distributions tend to facilitate greater access to retail customers (albeit of typically more inflated wealth), this evidence supports Hypothesis 5.3 in that funds are less prone to register in countries if their strategies are in conflict with their potential investors' interests.

Similarly, there are no significant coefficients in Model (6a) for other regulated financial institutions, and Model (6b) shows that the market neutral equity strategy is the only significant coefficient for other regulated financial institutions. Market neutral equity funds are 10.3% more likely to register in countries that permit distributions via other regulated financial institutions. Overall, this is suggestive of the absence of forum shopping for other regulated financial institution distributions (in support of Hypothesis 5.2), and, in the alternative, to the extent that there is forum shopping, it is not in conflict with the interests with potential investors (in support of Hypothesis 5.3 and not Hypothesis 5.1).

Models (7a) and (7b) show funds pursuing emerging markets strategies are 18.8% Model (7a)–19.0% Model (7b) more likely to register in jurisdictions that offer marketing via investment managers. Investment managers are of interest to hedge funds that seek assistance for facilitating easier access to potential investors that have an interest in the particular strategy employed by the fund. The investment manager provides services for regular assessment of strategy and execution and also provides services for risk management reduction and reporting of the hedge fund. This makes the fund more attractive to its investors.[31] In view of the idiosyncrasies of emerging market hedge fund strategies, it is not surprising that it is more attractive for emerging market funds to seek jurisdictions that offer investment manager distribution channels so that the investment manager can help particular fund strategies match with suitable investors. In net, therefore, we may view this evidence of a positive association between emerging markets funds and distributions via investment managers as supportive of Hypothesis 5.3.

Models (7a) and (7b), however, also show that technology sector funds are 14.4% Model (7a) to 26.3% Model (7b) less likely to register in jurisdictions

---

[31] Zimmermann (2002) discussed the increase in services offered by third party investment managers to attract investors.

permitting distributions via investment managers. As well, distressed securities funds are 10.5% Model (7a) to 22.6% Model (7b) less likely to register in jurisdictions that permit distributions via investment managers. Fund managers typically require a performance fee of 20% of fund profits and an exclusivity arrangement.[32] It is possible that those terms are less suitable for hedge funds in the technology sectors and in distressed securities. As well, it is also possible that the client base of investment managers is less interested in technology focused funds and funds focused on distressed securities.

Finally, we note that there are no statistically significant relations between hedge fund strategies and registrations in jurisdictions that permit distributions via fund distribution companies. This is supportive of Hypothesis 5.2.

More generally, the comparative dearth of statistically significant coefficients in the eight models in Panels A and B of Table 5.3 can be considered supportive of Hypothesis 5.2. In other words, there is not much evidence of forum shopping in relation to fund strategies. Where we do observe forum shopping, the evidence is less consistent with the "race to the bottom" view expressed in Hypothesis 5.1 and more consistent with the alignment of interests view in Hypothesis 5.3.

5.5. Limitations and Extensions to Empirical Tests

The empirical evidence on forum shopping discussed here is limited in a few dimensions that are important to acknowledge. First, the measures used are coarse. We focus on broadly defined fund strategies as proxies for potential agency problems. More refined data that investigate the actual activities of the hedge fund manager might provide further insight into the issue of forum shopping.[33]

Second, the data in this chapter do not cover the universe of all hedge funds. Estimates suggest that there are possibly 10,000 funds worldwide and the data examined in this chapter cover 1,845 funds. We did show that the results are robust with the use of a sample that combines two datasets as well as with the use of only one of the two datasets. Additional data with more details on each fund could shed further light on this topic.

Third, the legal dimensions over which we measure forum shopping are coarse but broadly defined to enable comparisons across all of the countries represented in the data. More specific legal differences exist across the countries in the data, and further legal analyses could seek to identify factors that lead funds to select particular jurisdictions. For example, there are tax differences across countries that lead to differences in jurisdiction selection, particularly for comparing onshore funds and offshore funds. We note, however, that we do not believe that

---

[32] Zimmerman (2002), 13–14.

[33] To this end, further empirical work might consider differences in forum shopping among activist hedge funds. For work on hedge fund activism, see Brav et al. (2008a,b), Klein and Zur (2009), and Partnoy and Thomas (2007).

these differences distort the measures we study in our empirical tests since our focus is on legal dimensions that are available to select in both tax friendly and tax unfriendly jurisdictions. For example, restrictions on location exist in some offshore centers such as the Cayman Islands but not in others such as the Channel Islands (Table 5.1). Hence, while we do not believe these extraneous legal and tax factors influence our results and analyses, we do believe these issues offer avenues for investigation in future studies.

5.6. Concluding Remarks

The debate around hedge fund regulation in part involves the use of innovative investment strategies by hedge funds. On the one hand, these innovative hedge fund strategies provide various benefits to the financial systems involved, including providing crucial liquidity to markets, limiting price distortions and anomalies via arbitrage trading, and taking on risk across instruments and markets as hedge funds are able to change portfolio composition rather quickly. On the other hand, as active risk takers across instruments and markets, hedge funds may also exacerbate the risk of systemic failure, as their strategies involve multiple markets with as yet untested instrument links.[34]

Opponents of more stringent regulation believe that such beneficial hedge fund activities are facilitated within a "friendly" environment that allows freedom and discretion.[35] To curtail such freedom may just cause the players to leave for a friendlier playing field. To allow the players complete freedom, however, may enable them to run amok. Also, as more regulatory oversight would involve taking self-regulating functions away from hedge fund participants, this may encourage laxity with regard to investment decisions and risk management. The question now is not how to regulate the industry, but where to draw the boundaries for such regulation. If we assume that all hedge fund managers want complete freedom to do what they do best, then it follows that any extra regulatory oversight will cause them to forum shop. It also follows that they might forum shop in a "race to the bottom." We sought to determine in this chapter whether this is the case. We considered whether forum shopping exists across different hedge funds, applying different strategies. In view of the argument that hedge funds will forum shop at the threat of added regulation, we sought to determine how tolerant different hedge funds are to existing regulation.

We analyzed data from 1,845 funds registered in 24 countries. We concentrated on differences in hedge fund regulation across the 24 countries that fall within three primary categories: (1) minimum capital to operate as a hedge fund, (2) permissible marketing channels, and (3) restrictions on the location of key

---

[34] See note 10 for work showing exacerbated systemic risks.

[35] See Chapters 7 and 9 showing that hedge fund performance is hampered by more stringent regulation.

service providers. We considered the different strategies identified and characterized by the dataset providers, CISDM and HedgeFund.Net, to differentiate types of hedge funds. We also looked at the average monthly return and standard deviation of returns to determine the risk of each strategy. The data indicated scant evidence of hedge fund strategies that are systematically related to forum shopping for lower minimum capitalization requirements. We did find some evidence that fund strategies are related to choice of jurisdiction in terms of restrictions on the location of key service providers. However, the data showed that forum shopping was in line with the view that funds pursuing riskier strategies selected jurisdictions that restricted the location of key service providers. Similarly, with regard to availing themselves of different marketing channels, the data mostly indicated that where forum shopping exists, funds are less prone to register in countries whose strategies are in conflict with the interests of their potential investors. We may interpret this evidence as supporting the view that fund regulations are selected relative to a fund strategy in order to facilitate capital raising.

Overall, we did not find evidence of forum shopping in a "race to the bottom" due to international differences in hedge fund regulation and fund strategies. The data for the most part show scant evidence of forum shopping in relation to fund strategies. Where forum shopping exists, the evidence shows little support for the race to the bottom view. Instead, it supports the view that hedge funds select jurisdictions where strategies and regulations are aligned to suit investors' interests. We note that there have been no other studies of hedge fund forum shopping to date, and hence Section 5.5 of this chapter discussed possible caveats and extensions to the analysis provided in this chapter.

Keywords

Capital Structure Arbitrage
Choice of Law
Commodity Trading Advisors/
   Managed Futures
Convertible Arbitrage
Country Specific
Distressed
Emerging Markets
Energy Sector
Event Driven
Finance Sector
Fixed Income Arbitrage
Fixed Income (non-arbitrage)
Forum Shopping
Healthcare Sector

Hedge Fund Strategies
Jurisdiction Shopping
Long Only
Long/Short Equity
Macro
Market Neutral Equity
Market Timer
Mortgages
Merger/Risk Arbitrage
Multi-Strategy
Options Strategies
Other Arbitrage
Race to the Bottom
Race to the Top
Regulation D

Short Bias
Short-term Trading
Small/Micro Cap
Special Situations

Statistical Arbitrage
Technology Sector
Value

Discussion Questions

5.1. What hedge fund strategies are riskiest? Which ones are the least risky? Why?

5.2. What does it mean for a hedge fund to engage in forum shopping? What factors influence forum shopping among hedge funds?

5.3. Does empirical evidence on hedge fund forum shopping reflect a "race to the bottom" or a "race to the top"? How does this evidence compare with other contexts such as company choice of corporate law statutes?

5.4. What are the advantages and disadvantages to a hedge fund manager associated with selecting a jurisdiction that reflects a conflict of interest? And what are the advantages and disadvantages to a hedge fund manager associated with selecting a jurisdiction that reflects an alignment of interest? With whom are the fund managers' interests aligned or in conflict? How can you assess whether there is an alignment or conflict?

5.5. How are distribution channels, restrictions on the location of key service providers, and minimum capitalization related to hedge fund forum shopping? Explain, with reference to empirical evidence.

5.6. How do you think the Dodd-Frank Act, UCITS, and AIFMD might affect jurisdiction shopping over the coming years?

CHAPTER 6

Hedge Fund Capital Raising

6.1. Introduction

Hedge funds have attracted significant capital in recent years. As of 2005 they collectively managed more than a trillion US dollars of assets, while at the peak in the summer of 2008 some industry estimates suggested that the market even grew above US$2.5 trillion in assets (Ineichen and Silberstein, 2008, pp.16–17; see also Chapter 1). Many funds promise alphas of 5% or more, which collectively would amount to more than US$50 billion in excess returns in 2005 and more than US$125 billion in excess returns in 2008. Particularly in view of the recent market collapse, hedge funds may fall short of return promises made in the past. Further, regulators have expressed concern that hedge funds have significant potential to destabilize markets. Given regulatory mandates to protect investors and stabilize markets, it is not surprising that the significant flows of funds to and from hedge funds have attracted recent regulatory scrutiny.[1] How regulation influences hedge fund capital flows is a central issue considered by regulators and the question examined in this chapter. This question is important because it is central to the efficient allocation of capital in the hedge fund industry.

More specifically, in this chapter we empirically examine for the first time international evidence on how regulation influences the flow of funds to and from hedge funds. Perhaps most important, there are different distribution channels for hedge funds in different countries. Permissible distribution channels vary widely and may include banks, fund distribution companies, wrappers, private placements, investment managers, other regulated financial services institutions, and non-regulated financial intermediaries. Clearly, the permissible distribution channels may influence the flow-performance relationship as different distribution channels influence marketing, products, and the types of buyers and sell-

---

[1] www.sec.gov/news/speech/spch111704hjg.htm. For industry perspectives on hedge fund regulation, see, e.g., for example, www.hedgeco.net/hedge-fund-regulations.htm and www.hedgefundregulation.com/.

ers. For instance, wrappers involve tied selling and therefore capital flows do not depend merely on past performance of the fund but also on the companion securities. Furthermore, there are other regulations that may affect investor confidence and the flow of funds to and from hedge funds, such as restrictions on the location of key service providers,[2] and minimum capitalization requirements. As well, tax considerations may influence the flow of funds. The central importance of these hedge fund regulations to the flow of funds of investors is made clear in industry analyses such as that provided by PriceWaterhouseCoopers (2006).

In this chapter we use the Center for International Securities and Derivatives Markets (CISDM) dataset (described in Chapter 4) for hedge funds that are registered in 16 countries (listed in Section 6.3) around the world. We focus on the time period 2003–2005, for which data are available for a significant number of funds. The data indicate a very pronounced impact of hedge fund regulation on fund flows. First, the permissible distribution channels have a strong impact on the sensitivity of fund flows to past performance. Country-specific regulations that permit distribution channels in the form of wrappers mitigate the sensitivity of fund flows to past performance, while distribution channels via investment managers and fund distribution companies enhance flow-performance sensitivity. These findings are robust to different methods of measuring of past performance, as well as different methods of accounting for non-linearities in the flow-performance relation. Also, the evidence is robust to controls for share restrictions, as well as fund fees, fund age, country-GNP, and legal origin, among other control variables such as fund strategies and fund location of assets. As well, we explicitly show robustness to controls for selection effects using treatment regressions for the non-random decision of some funds to locate in an offshore jurisdiction.

Further, in this chapter we find evidence that other types of regulation apart from distribution channels influence fund flows. We empirically show that hedge funds registered in countries that have larger minimum capitalization requirements tend to have higher levels of inflows. This suggests that minimum capitalization enhances investor confidence in terms of greater stability with larger funds. This finding holds even after controlling for minimum investment amounts per transaction. We also empirically show that funds registered in countries that restrict the location of key service providers have lower levels of inflows. This latter result is consistent with the view that locational restrictions are perceived by investors to mitigate human resource quality, and this perceived reduction in human resource quality is more pronounced than any associated perceived improvement in regulatory oversight.

In addition to these regulatory impacts on fund flows and flow-performance relationship, two findings in this chapter are consistent with tax effects on hedge

---

[2] Key service providers include an audit/accounting firm, administrator, prime brokers, executing brokers, software and data providers, and marketing agents. See also note 4 and accompanying text, this chapter.

fund flows. First, offshore funds tend to have higher capital flows, and of course there are tax advantages associated with offshore funds. Second, we find pronounced seasonality effects in the data. Fund flows tend to be lower in later calendar months and higher in earlier calendar months, and as discussed further in this chapter, this seasonality pattern is consistent with tax incentives for timing investment flows. The seasonality effect documented in this chapter is a new finding in the context of hedge fund flows.[3]

As a complement to the law and finance analysis of hedge fund flows, in this chapter we also examine overall assets under management by the funds as of December 2005. We find regulatory factors influence hedge fund size in ways that are consistent with the evidence on the flow of funds. This suggests that the evidence on the flow of funds for 2003–2005 is not an artifact of the time period considered.

At a general level, this chapter contributes to the law and economics literature showing that regulation impacts firm value (e.g., Black and Khanna, 2007; Thompson, 2008) and curtails misreporting and other securities violations (e.g., Eisenberg and Macey, 2004; see also Cox and Thomas, 2005, 2006; Pritchard and Sale, 2005; Perino, 2006; Cox et al., 2008; and Choi et al., 2009, for related work). More specifically, we build on the growing literature on the flow-performance relationship in mutual funds (Chevalier and Ellison, 1997; Sirri and Tufano, 1998; Del Guercio and Tkac, 2002, 2008) and hedge funds (Agarwal et al., 2006; Bollen and Pool, 2008; Ding et al., 2007; Getmansky, 2005; Hodder and Jackwerth, 2007), as well as a growing literature on the law and finance of financial intermediaries, particularly for hedge funds (Brav et al., 2008a,b; Klein and Zur, 2009; Liang and Park, 2008; Verret, 2007, 2009). We add to this literature by considering how regulations from the country in which the fund is registered influence the flow of funds as well as the sensitivity of the flow of funds to changes in fund performance. The issue of hedge fund regulation has largely been overlooked in the hedge fund literature, despite the fact that most work on the topic involves international datasets and countries that have notable differences in regulation.

We note that the findings in this chapter on how regulation impacts fund flows are consistent with related work (Chapter 7) that shows hedge fund regulation in the form of restrictions on the location of key service providers and distributions wrappers tends to be associated with lower alphas, lower Sharpe ratios and manipulation proof performance measures, lower average monthly returns, higher management fees, and lower performance fees. Overall, the evidence is consistent with the view that observed differences in hedge fund regulation around the world not only affect performance but also impact the flow of funds into and out of hedge funds in relation to their performance. In effect, hedge fund regulation has the ability to influence capital flows and stability and in predictable ways.

---

[3] Seasonality has been documented in many other contexts apart from hedge funds; see, for example, Kamstra et al. (2005).

This chapter is organized as follows. Section 6.2 explains cross-country differences in hedge fund regulation and considers potential impacts on the flow-performance relation. Section 6.3 describes the data. Multivariate tests are provided in Section 6.4. Additional robustness checks not explicitly reported are discussed in Section 6.5. Conclusions and policy implications follow in Section 6.6.

6.2. Factors Influencing the Flow-Performance Relation

In this section we first discuss the new central hypotheses in this chapter pertaining to regulation and hedge fund flows. Thereafter, we briefly describe relevant control variables in the context of prior work on hedge fund flows.

6.2.1. HEDGE FUND REGULATION

Hedge funds are often formed as limited partnerships whereby the investors are considered limited partners and the hedge fund managers are general partners (Hammer et al., 2005). The limited partners are wealthy individuals and institutional investors. Compensation for hedge fund managers comprises a 1–2% fixed management fee based on hedge fund asset size and a 15–20% carried interest performance fee based on the profits (Hodder and Jackwerth, 2007). Funds face different degrees of regulatory oversight depending on the country in which they are registered, as summarized in Chapter 3.

A typical hedge fund delegates different functions to service providers of the hedge fund.[4] The most common service providers include prime brokers, administrators, and distributors. Prime brokers lend money, act as a counterparty to derivative contracts, lend securities in short sales, execute trades, and provide clearing, settlement, and custody services. Administrators issue and redeem interests and shares and calculate the net asset value (NAV) of the fund. Distributors are responsible for marketing the fund to potential investors. Practitioners warn against using low quality service providers: "beware of the potential downside of using third-tier service providers. Furthermore, it is hard to garner the confidence of investors when you do not employ a top notch support network."[5]

Outsourcing a hedge fund's functions minimizes risks of collusion among hedge fund participants to perpetuate fraud and also mitigates liability in the event the hedge fund participants are accused of improperly performing their management duties. A hedge fund's board of directors or trustees has a fiduciary duty to the investors to ensure that all parties involved in the fund can properly carry out their designated tasks. In some countries there are restrictions on the location of the hedge fund service providers, that they must be in the same

---

[4] See note 2, this chapter, for a list of different service providers.
[5] Source: .www.hedgefundlaunch.com/how-to-start-a-hedge-fund-part-1/

country where the fund is registered (see Chapter 3 for countries that restrict location; for additional details, see PriceWaterhouseCoopers, 2006). We would expect restrictions on location to reduce fund inflows if such restrictions limit the ability of a fund to freely contract with the service providers that are most likely to add value to the fund. Overall, this would reduce the attractiveness of funds in jurisdictions with restrictions on location, thereby shifting the intercept down in the flow-performance relationship, as depicted in Exhibit 6.1. We note as an alternative hypothesis that we might expect funds registered in jurisdictions that mandate restrictions on the location of key service providers to have higher fund inflows if the restrictions on location improve regulatory oversight and enhance investor confidence. These competing predictions are tested for the first time in the following sections of this chapter.

Some jurisdictions impose minimum capitalization requirements. Many countries do not do so because restrictions on minimum size may constrain a fund in terms of operating at an efficient operating scale and may give rise to inefficient allocation of fund manager time toward fund-raising and marketing as opposed to carrying out other functions that are in the best interests of the fund and its investors. Nevertheless, one rationale for minimum capitalization requirements is that higher levels might enhance investor confidence that hedge funds in the market are more stable or at least less likely to fail and thereby attract more capital. Further, while minimum capitalization levels are low (Chapter 3), we would nevertheless expect minimum capitalization to cut off the left tail of the distribution of flows, thereby increasing the mean level of capital flows. This effect is depicted in Exhibit 6.1.

Across countries there are different marketing channels through which funds attract investors. In the United States, hedge funds are not allowed to advertise, and they can avoid the public disclosure requirements of the US Securities Act of 1933 by claiming the status of a private placement.[6] Hedge funds are also exempt from the US Investment Company Act of 1940 (which regulates mutual funds) by having no more than 499 investors[7] with more than US$5 million in assets and by not making public offerings. Prior to February 2006, hedge funds in the United States were also exempt from any registration requirement (Brown et al., 2008 Thomas and Partnoy, 2007; Veret, 2007).

In other countries, unlike the United States, there are different avenues for marketing (not merely private placements). Permissible distribution channels vary widely in different countries and range from banks, fund distribution companies, wrappers, private placements, investment managers, other regulated financial services institutions, and non-regulated financial intermediaries. Clearly, the permissible distribution channels may influence the flow-performance relationship. Intuitively, one may conjecture based on related work in other contexts that permissible distribution channels via private placements will mitigate the flow-performance sensitivity as private placements are often associated with managerial entrenchment (Wu, 2004; Barclay et al., 2007). Also, one may expect

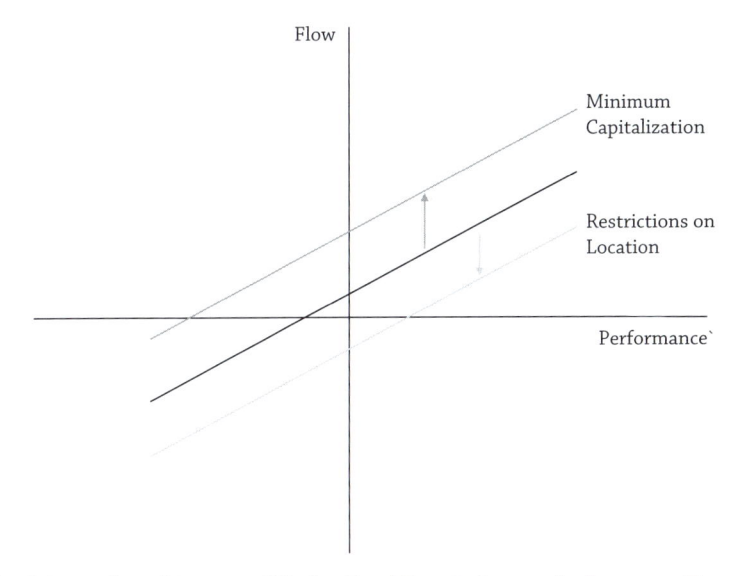

Exhibit 6.1. Predicted Impact of Hedge Fund Regulation on the Intercept Term in the Flow-Performance Relationship

NOTE: Minimum capitalization cuts off the left tail of the distribution and thereby gives rise to an increase in average flow levels. The predicted effect is positive, but small magnitude is expected due to low levels of minimal capitalization requirements. Restrictions on location discourage investors on average and thereby lower flow-performance levels on average.

distributions via wrappers to mitigate the flow-performance sensitivity due to the tied selling (Gerstein, 2006). Conversely, with investment managers and fund distribution companies, distributions are more aggressively marketed and expected to be associated with enhanced flow-performance sensitivity. These predictions are graphically illustrated in Exhibit 6.2.

6.2.2. CONTROL VARIABLES

Past performance is naturally the primary determinant of fund flows in both mutual funds and hedge funds. In the related literature there has been a variety of approaches to measuring past performance and controlling for non-linearities in the relationship between performance and fund flows. The earlier work originated in the context of mutual funds (Chevalier and Ellison, 1997; Sirri and Tufano, 1998). Using methods developed in this earlier work, Del Guercio and Tkac (2002) estimated the relation between asset flow and performance and showed the different investment patterns between pension fund and mutual

---

[6] In a private placement there must not be more than 35 "non-accredited" investors. A non-accredited investor is someone who has more than US$1 million in wealth or has earned more than US$200,000 in the previous two years.

[7] This restriction was previously set at 99 investors. For a further discussion, see, for example, http://faculty.fuqua.duke.edu/~charvey/Teaching/BA453_2001/SAM/SAM.htm.

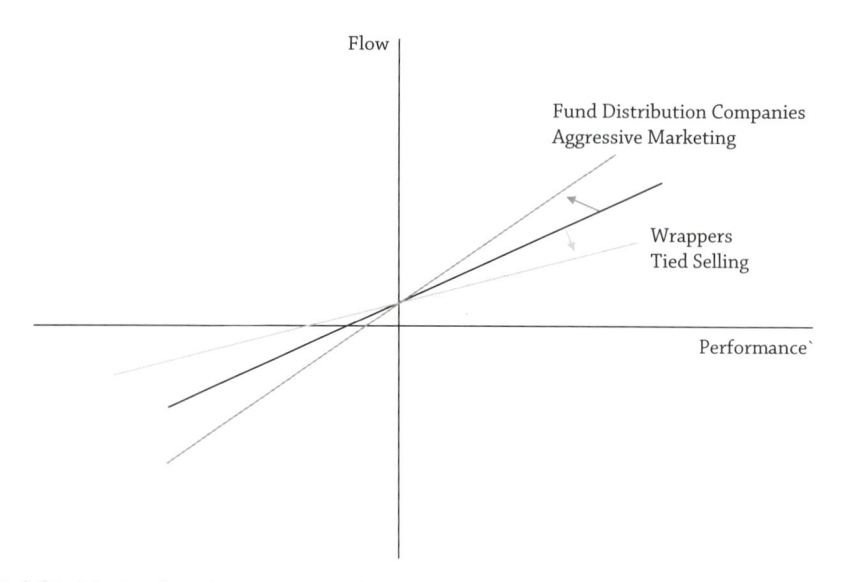

Exhibit 6.2. Predicted Impact of Hedge Fund Regulation on the Slope Term in the Flow-Performance Relationship

NOTE: Aggressive marketing channels such as via fund distribution companies strengthen the flow-performance relationship. Tied selling via wrappers mitigates the flow-performance relationship.

fund investors. They found that pension fund clients use more quantitatively sophisticated measures than do mutual fund investors. Pension clients punish poorly performing managers by withdrawing assets under management, while the mutual fund investors flock disproportionately to recent winners but do not withdraw assets from recent losers; in other words, the flow-performance relation is convex. Berk and Green (2004) found that flows for mutual funds increase for funds even if the fund does not outperform its benchmark and has no persistence in returns. Flows also react positively to the size of mutual funds, which have increasing returns to scale in returns up to a certain point. Chen et al. (2004) found that mainly due to issues of liquidity, hierarchical structures, and local stock selection, a fund's performance increases as its assets grow and then decreases as a fund becomes very large in general.

The flow-performance relation has been examined in the context of hedge funds in more recent studies given the availability of new industry data. Because hedge fund investors are quite different from mutual fund investors, fund flows may have a different relationship with the fund performance than the cases in mutual funds. Focusing on flows and their relationship to liquidation of funds, Getmansky (2005), shows that similar to mutual funds, the likelihood of a hedge fund being liquidated is decreased since investors are chasing individual fund performance. Agarwal and Naik (2004), Goetzmann et al. (2003), and Getmansky (2003) showed that there are decreasing returns to scale in the performance of hedge funds and explained their findings by the limited availability of assets that provide superior hedge fund returns.

Agarwal et al. (2004, 2006) controlled for additional factors such as managerial incentives and fees, size and age of funds, that ranked hedge funds based on non-risk adjusted return performance. They found that flows are positively associated with performance, which is different from the findings in Goetzmann et al. (2003). Similarly, Fung et al. (2008) showed that the alphas are associated with greater and steadier capital inflows of funds.

Convexity versus concavity of the flow-performance relationship has been debated in the hedge fund literature. Agarwal et al. (2004) found a convex relationship in hedge fund flow performance; Getmansky (2005) found a concave flow-performance relationship; and Baquero and Verbeek (2005) found a linear flow-performance relationship. The results depend on the database used, the time period analyzed, and the frequency of the sample. Ding et al. (2007) reconciles these conflicting findings by showing that hedge funds exhibit a convex flow-performance relation in the absence of share restrictions (similar to mutual funds), but exhibit a concave relation in the presence of restrictions. Further, live funds exhibit a concave flow-performance relation due to diseconomies of scale, but defunct funds display a convex relation due to the various reasons that they became defunct.

Next, we control for prior fund performance with various alternative measures of performance (such as returns and ranked performance) and use different methods to consider non-linearities, such as with the use of variables for the square of past performance as well as variables that measure tercile performance ranks (as in Ding et al., 2007). We do note some differences depending on the method employed, but this is not a central element of the research question. The findings pertaining to regulation are robust to these alternative methods to measure past performance and the different ways to study non-linearities.

We control for other fund specific factors that are important in hedge fund flows, including fixed fees, performance fees, and fund size. We also control for calendar effects and offshore registrations, which are important given tax factors in fund flows. Offshore centers are in fact tax havens. In terms of calendar effects, many funds face tax expenses at the end of the calendar year,[8] and the tax burden is incurred by all investors regardless of the time of year that they bought into the fund. Hence, it is less attractive to invest at the end of the year and more attractive to invest earlier in the year. While this is not a central aspect of the analysis of hedge fund regulation, the analysis of fund flows in relation to calendar effects is an important and new control variable.

Consistent with the broader law and finance literature (La Porta et al., 1998, 2002, 2006), we control for legal origin and gross national product (GNP) per capita. These controls are relevant to assess whether the hedge fund regulations we study are important over and above other country-specific factors.

Finally, we employ a number of dummy variables to control for the hedge fund strategies as well as the location of hedge fund assets. We use these variables in two related ways. First, we consider whether they have a direct impact on fund

---

[8] See, for example, www.greencompany.com/HedgeFunds/OffDocGTTTaxStrategies.shtml.

flows. Second, we use information on fund strategy and location of assets to assess the non-random probability that a fund will register in an offshore jurisdiction. Offshore domiciles are attractive to certain funds for tax reasons and ability to attract investors, among other things. These advantages vary to a significant degree depending on where the fund's assets are located and the particular investment strategy that the fund undertakes. Hence, as a robustness check to control for selection effects of fund location vis-à-vis regulation and fund flows, we use fund strategies and location of assets in two-step treatment regression methods that are described below.

6.3. Data

6.3.1. DATA SOURCE

In the empirical analysis, we use the Center for International Securities and Derivatives Markets (CISDM) data. CISDM has 21 different styles of hedge fund types. Of these styles the five most common are Equity Long/Short (38%), Emerging Markets (9%), Sector (8%), Global Macro (6%), and Equity Market Neutral (6%). Other useful information contained in the data is the inception date of the fund, the report date, management incentive fees, lockup period, and other information regarding terms and fee structure, investment strategy, and leverage.

We focus on fund flows in the sample period from January 2003 to December 2005. There are 729 hedge funds with monthly returns, assets under management, and other fund-specific information over this sample period. The focus on the narrow window enables us to observe fund flows for the same number of funds over this period. If we were to maintain a uniform set of funds over a longer period we would have more data points per fund but fewer funds and would not gain in terms of extra data points. An added advantage is that the hedge fund legislation in different countries considered was stable over this period and hence there is no concern that legislative changes were endogenous to fund flows (although there are important selection effects associated with choice of jurisdiction, and we explicitly deal with these selection effects below). The funds in the sample are registered in 16 countries (Austria, Bahamas, Bermuda, Brazil, British Virgin Islands, Canada, Cayman Islands, France, Guernsey, Ireland, Isle of Man, Luxembourg, Mauritius, Netherland Antilles, New Zealand, and the United States).

6.3.2. PERFORMANCE AND FLOW MEASURES

We measure flows as a proportion of Assets under Management (AUM) by the month t change in net AUM, adjusted for investment returns (Sirri and Tufano, 1998):

$$\text{Flow}_t = \frac{\text{AUM}_t - (1 + \text{return}_t)\text{AUM}_{t-1}}{\text{AUM}_{t-1}}$$

We consider alternative measures of performance to control for the effect of past performance on future returns. In the spirit of Sirri and Tufano (1998) and Ding et al. (2007), we use fractional rank as one measure of performance. First, the fractional rank is calculated for each fund in each period, from 0 to 1 based on the previous month's raw return. Then, the fractional terciles ranks are constructed as follows:

Bottom Tercile Rank: TRank.1 = min (1/3, FRank)
Middle Tercile Rank: TRank.2 = min (1/3, FRank-TRank.1)
Top Tercile Rank: TRank.3 = min (1/3, FRank-TRank1-TRank.2)

where FRank is the fractional ranks in each period.

The advantage of the fractional rank method is that it enables consideration of non-linearities in the flow-performance relationship.

As a robustness check we also use lagged raw monthly returns. We assess robustness by considering different lags, but focus on one and two month lags in reporting the results as these results are robust to consideration of additional lagged returns. We also considered non-linearities by including the squared values of lagged returns. We note that the use of raw returns with the CISDM database are consistent with that of related work using the same database over a different time period (e.g., Adams, 2007; Agrawal et al., 2007; Baghai-Wadji and Klocker, 2007; Cici et al., 2006). As discussed later in the chapter, the findings are consistent, but here we are focusing for the first time on international differences in regulation on fund flows.

6.3.3. SUMMARY STATISTICS

Table 6.1 formally defines each of the variables in the study and provides summary statistics for the period considered. The flow measure is from Siri and Tufano (1998) with the top 1% of flows winsorized to mitigate the influence of outliers (exactly as in Ding et al., 2007, although this winsorizing did not materially affect our results).[9] On average, flows have been positive to the funds in the data over the 2003–2005 period. Redemptions are permitted annually for 8.9% of the funds. The median fixed compensation fee is 1% and the median performance fee is 20%. Fund sizes range from US$10,000 to US$16.3 billion, and the median fund size is US$61 million. The median fund age is 77 months and 52.4% of the funds are registered in offshore jurisdictions. These summary statistics are consistent with those reported in other hedge fund datasets.

---

[9] Further, we considered robustness to sub-samples with a 36 month history, but did not find material differences, consistent with Baghai-Wadji and Klocker's (2007) observation that "the so-called multi-period sampling bias is negligibly small" (see also Fung and Hsieh, 2000, and Ackermann et al., 1999, for consistent findings).

Table 6.1 **Definition of Variables and Summary Statistics**

Variable	Definition	Mean	Median	Standard Deviation	Minimum	Maximum
Flow and Fund Performance						
Flow of Funds	Monthly flow of funds, with the top 1% of flows winsorized to control for outliers (as in Ding et al., 2007)	0.018	0.002	0.099	−0.298	0.537
Return Lagged 1 Month	Raw Monthly Return with 1-Month Lag	0.012	0.008	0.037	−0.307	0.990
Return Lagged 2 Months	Raw Monthly Return with 2-Month Lag	0.012	0.008	0.037	−0.307	0.990
Return Lagged 3 Months	Raw Monthly Return with 3-Month Lag	0.013	0.009	0.037	−0.307	0.990
Fractional Return Rank	Fractional Rank of Performance Lagged 1-Month	0.500	0.501	0.289	0.000	1.000
Bottom Tercile Fractional Rank	Bottom Tercile Fractional Rank of Lagged 1-Month Raw Return	0.278	0.333	0.096	0.000	0.333
Middle Tercile Fractional Rank	Middle Tercile Fractional Rank of Lagged 1-Month Raw Return	0.167	0.167	0.147	0.000	0.333
Top Tercile Fractional Rank	Top Tercile Fractional Rank of Lagged 1-Month Raw Return	0.055	0.000	0.096	0.000	0.333

Table 6.1 (Continued)

Variable	Definition	Mean	Median	Standard Deviation	Minimum	Maximum
Fund Characteristics						
Yearly Redemption	A dummy variable equal to 1 if capital redemptions are possible only on an annual basis	0.089	0	0.285	0.000	1
Management Fee	The fixed fee in percentages for management compensation	1.408	1	1.239	0.000	15
Performance Fee	The carried interest performance fee in percentages for management compensation	19.843	20	3.695	0.000	50
Assets under Management	The fund's assets in 2004 US$	$208,754,991	$61,000,000	$638,765,971	$10,000	$16,300,000,000
Minimum Investment	The minimum investment required for the fund in 2004 US$	$994,893	$500,000	$2,231,453	$0	$50,000,000
Onshore Dummy Variable	A dummy variable equal to 1 for onshore funds	0.524	1	0.499	0	1
Age	The fund's age in months from the date of formation to December 2005.	89.259	77.000	46.697	32.000	467.000

(Continued)

Table 6.1 (Continued)

Variable	Definition	Mean	Median	Standard Deviation	Minimum	Maximum
Fund Regulation						
Minimum Capitalization	The minimum capitalization required to operate as a hedge fund manager in 2004 US$	$217,738.312	0	$342,766.945	0.000	$6,750,000
Restrictions on Location of Key Service Providers	A dummy variable equal to 1 where the country imposes restrictions on the location of key service providers	0.494	0	0.49997198	0.000	1
Lagged 1-Month Return * Marketing Private Placements Dummy	A dummy variable equal to 1 where the country allows fund distribution via private placements	0.012	0.000	0.037	−0.307	0.990
Lagged 1-Month Return * Marketing via Wrappers Dummy	A dummy variable equal to 1 where the country allows fund distribution via wrappers	0.0004	0.008	0.007	−0.167	0.299
Lagged 1-Month Return * Marketing Funds Distribution Company Dummy	A dummy variable equal to 1 where the country allows fund distribution via fund distribution companies	0.0005	0.000	0.0074	−0.1672	0.2994

Table 6.1 (Continued)

Variable	Definition	Mean	Median	Standard Deviation	Minimum	Maximum
Lagged 1-Month Return * Marketing Investment Manager Dummy	A dummy variable equal to 1 where the country allows fund distribution via investment managers	0.006	0.000	0.024377887	−0.201	0.6227
Country GNP and Legal Origin						
GNP Per Capita	The country's GNP per capita, expressed in 2004 US$	$35,010.167	$36,000	$6,375.247	$8,100	$58,900
French Legal Origin	A dummy variable equal to 1 for French legal origin countries	0.023	0	0.150919616	0	1
German Legal Origin	A dummy variable equal to 1 for German legal origin countries	0.001	0	0.037012372	0	1

NOTE: This table defines the main variables used in the chapter. Summary statistics are also provided for each variable. The data are for the period January 2003–December 2005. The data comprise 729 funds from the CISDM database.

A correlation matrix is provided in Table 6.2. The correlation matrix indicates that funds with stronger lagged performance have higher capital flows. Month-to-month fund returns are positively correlated at 0.21, which suggests some degree of persistence with performance (although there are alternative interpretations of this serial correlation; see Getmansky et al., 2004). Funds with restrictions to yearly redemptions are negatively correlated with capital flows, while fixed fees and performance fees are positively correlated with capital flows. Minimum investment amounts per investment are positively correlated with capital flows. Larger funds and funds in offshore jurisdictions are negatively correlated with capital flows.

Table 6.2 shows that some of the explanatory variables of interest are significantly correlated, including, for instance, restrictions on location with other regulatory variables. In the next section we report the regression results with alternative sets of explanatory variables. The findings are robust to inclusion/exclusion of different right-hand-side variables. Details are discussed also.

6.4. Regression Analyses

The following regression is specified to investigate the determinants of fund flows:

$$Flow = \alpha + \beta_1 Performance + \beta_2 Characteristics + \beta_3 Regulation + \beta_4 Performance * Regulation + \varepsilon$$

where *Performance* is the performance measure that is the lagged raw returns in Table 6.3, Models 1–5, and the fractional rank in Table 6.4, Models 6–10. *Characteristics* are the fund specific variables including fund size, standard deviation of previous returns, onshore or offshore, minimum investment, capital redemption frequency, and management and incentive fee. The *Regulation* variables include the country specific variables including restrictions on the location of key service providers, minimum capital requirements, and various marketing channel restrictions (Chapter 3). Distribution regulations are modeled as interaction terms with lagged performance (lagged 1-month returns in Table 6.3 and the fractional rank in Model 5) to test their impact on sensitivity (the slope) of the flow-performance relationship. Restriction on the location key service providers and minimum capital requirements are modeled as regulations that impact the level of capital flows. Regulations that potentially affect the overall levels of flows are related to general investor confidence, while regulations that impact the ways in which hedge funds are distributed pertain to the sensitivity of the flow-performance relationship.

Various specifications are provided to show robustness. Models 1 and 6 make use of panel data methods with fund fixed effects.[10] Models 2–5 and 7–10 do not

Table 6.2 Correlation Matrix

		(1)	(2)	(3)	(4)	(5)	(6)	(7)	(8)	(9)	(10)	(11)	(12)	(13)	(14)	(15)	(16)	(17)	(18)	(19)	(20)	(21)	(22)
	Fund Performance																						
(1)	Flow of Funds	1.00																					
(2)	Return Lagged 1 Month	0.07	1.00																				
(3)	Return Lagged 2 Months	0.09	0.21	1.00																			
(4)	Fractional Rank	0.00	0.00	−0.01	1.00																		
(5)	Bottom Tercile Fractional Rank	0.00	0.00	0.00	0.78	1.00																	
(6)	Middle Tercile Fractional Rank	0.00	−0.01	−0.01	0.95	0.65	1.00																
(7)	Top Tercile Fractional Rank	0.00	0.00	−0.01	0.78	0.33	0.65	1.00															
	Fund Characteristics																						
(8)	Yearly Redemption	−0.01	0.03	0.03	−0.01	0.00	−0.01	−0.01	1.00														
(9)	Management Fee	0.03	0.00	0.00	0.01	0.01	0.01	0.01	−0.04	1.00													
(10)	Performance Fee	0.01	−0.02	−0.02	−0.01	−0.01	−0.01	0.00	0.11	0.11	1.00												
(11)	Log (Assets under Management)	−0.02	−0.03	−0.02	−0.01	0.00	−0.01	−0.02	0.03	0.05	−0.06	1.00											
(12)	Log (Minimum Investment)	0.03	−0.01	−0.01	−0.01	−0.01	−0.01	−0.01	0.00	−0.03	−0.03	0.36	1.00										
(13)	Onshore Dummy Variable	−0.03	0.01	0.01	−0.01	−0.01	−0.01	−0.01	0.15	−0.06	0.00	−0.17	0.02	1.00									
(14)	Log (Age)	−0.09	0.02	0.01	0.00	0.00	0.00	−0.01	0.13	−0.06	−0.16	0.09	0.01	0.12	1.00								
	Fund Regulation																						
(15)	Log (Minimum Capitalization)	0.02	−0.03	−0.02	0.02	0.01	0.02	0.01	−0.09	0.11	0.02	0.08	−0.01	−0.54	−0.07	1.00							
(16)	Restrictions on Location of Key Service Providers	0.02	−0.02	−0.02	0.02	0.01	0.02	0.02	−0.16	0.06	0.04	0.12	−0.02	−0.84	−0.13	0.57	1.00						
(17)	Marketing Private Placements Dummy	−0.01	0.01	0.01	0.02	0.01	0.02	0.01	0.02	0.02	−0.04	−0.30	−0.02	0.04	−0.05	0.01	0.07	1.00					
(18)	Marketing via Wrappers Dummy	0.01	0.00	0.00	0.00	0.00	0.00	0.00	−0.06	0.07	−0.03	−0.02	−0.03	0.01	−0.02	0.08	−0.16	0.01	1.00				
(19)	Marketing Funds Distribution Company Dummy	0.02	0.01	0.01	0.00	0.00	0.01	0.00	−0.06	0.06	−0.02	−0.02	−0.04	−0.01	−0.02	0.08	−0.14	0.01	0.96	1.00			
(20)	Marketing Investment Manager Dummy	0.03	−0.02	−0.02	0.02	0.01	0.02	0.02	−0.16	0.07	0.02	0.11	−0.01	−0.78	−0.15	0.58	0.89	0.07	0.16	0.17	1.00		
	Country GNP and Legal Origin																						
(21)	Log (GNP Per Capita)	−0.03	0.00	0.00	−0.03	−0.02	−0.03	−0.02	0.14	−0.06	−0.02	−0.02	0.04	0.65	0.01	−0.44	−0.76	−0.28	−0.11	−0.17	−0.71	1.00	
(22)	French Legal Origin	0.02	0.00	0.00	0.00	0.01	0.00	0.00	−0.05	−0.02	0.04	0.17	0.01	−0.09	0.12	−0.03	−0.03	−0.48	0.29	0.38	−0.03	−0.17	1.00
(23)	German Legal Origin	−0.01	−0.01	−0.01	0.01	0.00	0.00	0.00	−0.01	0.10	0.00	0.01	−0.02	−0.04	0.02	0.71	−0.04	0.00	0.21	0.20	−0.04	−0.02	−0.01

NOTE: This table presents correlations across the variables defined in Exhibit 6.3. Correlations greater than 0.01 and 0.02 in absolute value are significant at the 5% and 1% levels, respectively.

use fund fixed effects, but do include a large number of control variables, including but not limited to such as dummies for months and strategies. Models 2–3 and 7–8 use the full sample and different sets of right-hand-side variables to show robustness to concerns with collinearity. In Models 4 and 9 we show robustness by excluding onshore funds. Models 5 and 10 are two-step treatment regressions to show robustness to selection effects with the non-random decision to set up a fund offshore. We do not use the traditional approach, but use a modified selection effect approach that is consistent with that in other hedge fund work (most notably, see Baquero et al., 2005). Offshore funds are modeled on the basis that the decision depends on the fund's strategy and location of assets. The results are quite robust to models explicitly presented and otherwise;[11] alternative specifications not explicitly provided are available upon request from the authors and the results are quite robust.

Table 6.3 and Table 6.4 indicate that minimum capitalization requirements have a positive effect on the level of fund flows. This effect is statistically significant at the 5% level in Models 3, 4, and 8 and at the 1% level in Models 2, 5, and 7. The effect is significant at the 10% level in Model 10 and insignificant in Model 9. In terms of the economic significance, an increase in minimum capitalization of US$500,000 (as in the Virgin Islands compared to the Netherland Antilles, for example; see Chapter 3) gives rise to higher fund flows by 0.0078 per month. This is 21% of one standard deviation in fund flows, which is an economically significant effect. Overall, this suggests hedge fund investors' confidence is greater, and hence the level of capital flows is higher, for countries that have higher minimum capitalization requirements.

Unlike minimum capitalization rules that enhance the level of fund flows, Tables 6.3 and 6.4 indicate that restrictions on the location of key service providers have a negative effect on the level of fund flows. This effect is significant on at least the 10% level in ten models presented in Tables 6.3 and 6.4. The economic significance is such that fund flows are approximately 0.01 lower per month, which is roughly 27% of one standard deviation in fund flows. The data therefore indicate that locational restrictions lower investor confidence in fund quality, and

---

[10] The use of fund fixed effects is more stringent that the fixed effects regressions used in other work, in that the number of dummy variables (funds) is quite large; for example, panel methods in Ding et al. (2007), by contrast, use strategy or time fixed effects. Our results are robust to those other specifications.

[11] For instance, among other robustness checks, we considered the impact of survivorship bias by restricting the funds in the data based on their age. We also considered more parsimonious sets of right-hand-side variables (such as removal of some of the distribution variables), as well as other variables not reported herein (such as a variable for fund managers that run multiple funds). We note that in Chapter 5 we find little evidence of jurisdiction shopping among hedge funds, which suggests that we would not expect selection effects to be pronounced in the context considered herein. Nevertheless, we do present these robustness checks here.

Table 6.3 Regression Analyses: Fund Flows and Fund Raw Returns

Variable	Model (1): Full Sample Coefficient	t-statistic	Model (2): Full Sample Coefficient	t-statistic	Model (3): Full Sample Coefficient	t-statistic	Model (4): Excluding Onshore Funds Coefficient	t-statistic	Model (5a): Treatment Regression [1st Step] Co-efficient	t-statistic	Model (5b): Treatment Regression [2nd Step] Co-efficient	t-statistic
Constant	No		0.044	3.982***	0.035	1.364	0.030	1.301	1.127	23.246***	0.046	5.462***

Hedge Fund Regulation Variables

Log (Minimum Capitalization)					1.854E-08	3.424***	1.539E-08	2.541**			1.55E-08	3.045***
Restrictions on Location of Key Service Providers			−0.005	−1.724*	−0.009	−2.438**	−0.010	−1.771*			−0.016	−4.287***
Marketing Private Placement * 1-Month Prior Return			−0.361	−1.163	−0.247	−0.813	−0.429	−1.181			−0.509	−1.402
Marketing Via Wrappers * 1-Month Prior Return	−1.124	−2.489**	−0.172	−1.773*	−1.240	−3.056***	−1.234	−2.960***			−0.818	−2.656***

(Continued)

Table 6.3 (Continued)

Variable	Model (1): Full Sample Coefficient	t-statistic	Model (2): Full Sample Coefficient	t-statistic	Model (3): Full Sample Coefficient	t-statistic	Model (4): Excluding Onshore Funds Coefficient	t-statistic	Model (5a):Treatment Regression [1st Step] Co-efficient	t-statistic	Model (5b): Treatment Regression [2nd Step] Co-efficient	t-statistic
Marketing Fund Distribution Company* 1-Month Prior Return	0.112	2.847***			1.030	2.594***	0.967	2.401**			0.574	1.933*
Marketing Investment Manager* 1-Month Prior Return	0.955	2.165***			0.117	2.958***	0.196	2.158**			0.135	3.641***
Returns												
1-Month Prior Return	0.189	8.344***	0.661	2.129**	0.456	1.504	0.579	1.632			0.709	1.955*
(1-Month Prior Return)²	−0.452	−3.340***	−0.597	−4.289***	−0.613	−5.457***	−0.569	−4.263***			−0.596	−8.198***
2-Month Prior Return					0.242	11.359***	0.328	9.091***			0.226	11.038***

Table 6.3 (Continued)

Variable	Model (1): Full Sample Coefficient	t-statistic	Model (2): Full Sample Coefficient	t-statistic	Model (3): Full Sample Coefficient	t-statistic	Model (4): Excluding Onshore Funds Coefficient	t-statistic	Model (5a):Treatment Regression [1st Step] Coefficient	t-statistic	Model (5b): Treatment Regression [2nd Step] Coefficient	t-statistic
(2-Month Prior Return)[2]					-0.134	-1.193	-0.131	-1.373			-0.118	-1.661*
Fund Characteristics												
Yearly Redemption			0.003	1.523	0.004	1.974**	-0.002	-0.418			0.002	1.018
Management Fee			1.444E-03	3.190***	1.575E-03	3.515***	2.652E-03	3.514***			0.002	3.398***
Performance Fee			-2.666E-04	-1.794*	-2.142E-04	-1.454E+00	2.286E-05	9.200E-02			-0.0003	-1.837*
Log (Assets Under Management)	-2.388E-11	-7.612***	-5.101E-12	-5.625***	-3.939E-03	-7.602***	-5.963E-12	-4.726***			-5.00E-12	-4.425***
Log (Minimum Investment)					1.120E-09	3.547***	8.513E-10	2.527**			1.57E-09	5.216***
Onshore Fund Dummy			-0.004	-2.007**	-0.004	-1.907*						

(Continued)

Table 6.3 (Continued)

Variable	Model (1): Full Sample Coefficient	t-statistic	Model (2): Full Sample Coefficient	t-statistic	Model (3): Full Sample Coefficient	t-statistic	Model (4): Excluding Onshore Funds Coefficient	t-statistic	Model (5a): Treatment Regression [1st Step] Coefficient	t-statistic	Model (5b): Treatment Regression [2nd Step] Coefficient	t-statistic
Offhore (Treatment Regression)											0.014	3.277***
Log (Age)	−0.0002	−16.163***	−0.0002	−13.607***	−0.0002	−8.714***			−0.0002	−13.717***
Fund Fixed Effects?	Yes		No		No		No		No		No	
Dummy Variables for Primary Location of Assets?	No		Yes		Yes		Yes		Yes		No	
Dummy Variables for Primary Fund Strategy?	No		Yes		Yes		Yes		Yes		No	

Table 6.3 (Continued)

Variable	Model (1): Full Sample Coefficient	t-statistic	Model (2): Full Sample Coefficient	t-statistic	Model (3): Full Sample Coefficient	t-statistic	Model (4): Excluding Onshore Funds Coefficient	t-statistic	Model (5a): Treatment Regression [1st Step] Coefficient	t-statistic	Model (5b): Treatment Regression [2nd Step] Coefficient	t-statistic
Country GNP and Legal Origin												
GNP Per Capita			−4.215E-07	−2.302**	−2.296E-07	−1.274	−3.004E-07	−1.379			−3.85E-07	−2.278**
French Legal Origin			0.019	3.890***	0.016	3.504***	0.019	3.169***	0.471	7.472***	0.009	1.773*
German Legal Origin			−0.032	−1.528	−0.146	−3.491***	−0.138	−3.001***			−0.126	−3.276***
Calendar Effects Dummy Variables												
February	0.007	1.909*	0.008	1.955*	0.008	1.888*	0.012	1.871*			0.008	2.261**
March	0.003	0.828	0.004	1.042	0.006	1.428	0.009	1.459			0.006	1.720*
April	−0.0001	−0.034	0.001	0.347	0.002	0.440	0.003	0.503			0.001	0.315
May	0.003	0.881	0.005	1.216	0.008	2.091**	0.012	1.997**			0.008	2.430**
June	−0.004	−1.319	−0.004	−1.150	−0.0003	−0.065	−0.0002	−0.035			0.001	0.174
July	−0.008	−2.188**	−0.008	−1.987**	−0.007	−1.784*	−0.006	−1.065			−0.008	−2.443**
August	−0.0006	−0.189	0.0002	0.041	0.001	0.229	0.003	0.524			0.001	0.393
September	−0.009	−2.526*	−0.008	−2.205**	−0.006	−1.660	−0.006	−1.164			−0.006	−1.670*
October	−0.010	−2.720*	−0.010	−2.501**	−0.008	−2.091**	−0.011	−1.796*			−0.008	−2.203**

(Continued)

Table 6.3 (Continued)

	Model (1): Full Sample		Model (2): Full Sample		Model (3): Full Sample		Model (4): Excluding Onshore Funds		Model (5a):Treatment Regression [1st Step]		Model (5b): Treatment Regression [2nd Step]	
Variable	Coefficient	t-statistic	Coefficient	t-statistic	Coefficient	t-statistic	Coefficient	t-statistic	Co-efficient	t-statistic	Co-efficient	t-statistic
November	−0.003	−0.790	−0.002	−0.593	−0.002	−0.581	−2.834E-06	0.001			−0.001	−0.392
December	−0.011	−3.062***	−0.012	−2.970***	−0.008	−2.165**	−0.009	−1.573			−0.008	−2.264**
Lambda											−0.004	−1.600
Model Diagnostics												
Number of Observations	24726		24786		24786		11798		23050			
Adjusted R² (Pseudo R² for Model 5a Step 1)	0.109		0.029		0.040		0.041					
Loglikelihood	23630.14		22588.422		22732.281		9652.043					
F-Statistic (Chi Square for Model 5)	3.94***		17.45***		21.23***		11.16***		737.12***			
Akaike Information Statistic	−4.684		−1.819		−1.830		−1.628					

NOTE: This table presents OLS regression analyses of the determinants of fund flows for 2003–2005. Explanatory variables are as defined in Table 6.1. Dummy variables are included for the continents in which assets are primarily located and the funds' primary strategy (20 dummy variables in total). Models (1) – (3) present the full sample and different right-hand-side variable to check for collinearity problems. Model (4) shows robustness exclusion of the onshore funds. Models (5) shows a two-step regression whereby the first step is a logit regression on a dummy variable equal to one for offshore registrations, and the second step is a treatment sample selection regression given the results in the first step (using the treatreg function in stata). White's heteroscedastic consistent-covariance matrix estimator HCCME is used in all regressions.

Table 6.4 Regression Analyses: Fund Flows and Fund Rank Returns

Variable	Model (6): Full Sample Coefficient	t-statistic	Model (7): Full Sample Coefficient	t-statistic	Model (8): Full Sample Coefficient	t-statistic	Model (9): Excluding Onshore Funds Coefficient	t-statistic	Model (10a): Treatment Regression [1st Step] Coefficient	t-statistic	Model (10b): Treatment Regression [2nd Step] Coefficient	t-statistic
Constant	0.053	4.415***	0.052	4.415***	0.052	4.296***	0.063	2.644***	0.054	6.238	0.054	6.238***

Hedge Fund Regulation Variables

Log (Minimum Capitalization)					1.379E-08	2.461**	7.451E-09	1.117			1.670E-08	3.268***
Restrictions on Location of Key Service Providers	−0.006	−1.946*			−0.013	−3.226***	−0.014	−2.330**			−0.018	−4.707***
Marketing Private Placement * 1-Month Prior Return Rank	−0.035	−1.914*	−0.044		−0.044	−2.372**	−0.074	−3.254***			0.125	5.615***
Marketing Via Wrappers * 1-Month Prior Return Rank	0.0002	0.031	−0.083		−0.083	−2.407**	−0.092	−2.476**			−0.891	−2.882***

(Continued)

Table 6.4 (Continued)

Variable	Model (6): Full Sample Coefficient	Model (6): Full Sample t-statistic	Model (7): Full Sample Coefficient	Model (7): Full Sample t-statistic	Model (8): Full Sample Coefficient	Model (8): Full Sample t-statistic	Model (9): Excluding Onshore Funds Coefficient	Model (9): Excluding Onshore Funds t-statistic	Model (10a): Treatment Regression [1st Step] Coefficient	Model (10a): Treatment Regression [1st Step] t-statistic	Model (10b): Treatment Regression [2nd Step] Coefficient	Model (10b): Treatment Regression [2nd Step] t-statistic
Marketing Fund Distribution Company * 1-Month Prior Return Rank	0.030	2.473**			0.082	2.373**	0.076	2.138**			0.634	2.126**
Marketing Investment Manager * 1-Month Prior Return Rank	−0.0007	−0.158			0.005	1.202	0.024	3.290***			0.200	5.503***
Returns												
Fractional Rank			0.035	1.911*								
Bottom Tercile Fractional Rank	−0.006	−0.748			0.035	1.704*	0.056	2.131**			−0.007	−0.830
Middle Tercile Fractional Rank	−0.001	−0.139			0.042	2.100**	0.038	1.495			−0.002	−0.280

Table 6.4 (Continued)

Variable	Model (6): Full Sample Coefficient	t-statistic	Model (7): Full Sample Coefficient	t-statistic	Model (8): Full Sample Coefficient	t-statistic	Model (9): Excluding Onshore Funds Coefficient	t-statistic	Model (10a): Treatment Regression [1st Step] Coefficient	t-statistic	Model (10b): Treatment Regression [2nd Step] Coefficient	t-statistic
Top Tercile Fractional Rank	0.009	0.944			0.048	2.322**	0.068	2.503**			0.010	1.066
Fund Characteristics												
Yearly Redemption					0.004	2.049**	0.001	0.159			0.003	1.401
Management Fee			1.445E-03	3.168***	1.669E-03	3.646***	3.058E-03	3.940***			1.772E-03	3.449***
Performance Fee			−2.847E-04	−1.912*	−3.217E-04	−2.158**	−1.126E-04	−4.440E-01			−4.324E-04	−2.336**
Log (Assets under Management)	−2.499	−7.869***	−5.309E-12	−5.802***	−7.277E-12	−6.913***	−7.111E-12	−6.218***			−4.850E-12	−4.292***
Log (Minimum Investment)					1.441E-09	4.628***	9.267E-10	2.733***			1.580E-09	5.249***

(Continued)

Table 6.4 (Continued)

Variable	Model (6): Full Sample Coefficient	t-statistic	Model (7): Full Sample Coefficient	t-statistic	Model (8): Full Sample Coefficient	t-statistic	Model (9): Excluding Onshore Funds Coefficient	t-statistic	Model (10a): Treatment Regression [1st Step] Coefficient	t-statistic	Model (10b): Treatment Regression [2nd Step] Coefficient	t-statistic
Onshore Fund Dummy			−0.004	−1.679*	−0.004	−1.894*						
Offshore (Treatment Regression)											0.015	3.483***
Log (Age)	−1.986E-04	−15.798***	−1.932E-04	−15.196***	−1.935E-04	−8.163***			−1.996E-04	−13.671***		
Fund Fixed Effects?	Yes		No		No		No		No		No	
Dummy Variables for Primary Location of Assets?	No		Yes		Yes		Yes		Yes		No	
Dummy Variables for Primary Fund Strategy?	No		Yes		Yes		Yes		Yes		No	

Table 6.4 (Continued)

Variable	Model (6): Full Sample Coefficient	Model (6): Full Sample t-statistic	Model (7): Full Sample Coefficient	Model (7): Full Sample t-statistic	Model (8): Full Sample Coefficient	Model (8): Full Sample t-statistic	Model (9): Excluding Onshore Funds Coefficient	Model (9): Excluding Onshore Funds t-statistic	Model (10a): Treatment Regression [1st Step] Coefficient	Model (10a): Treatment Regression [1st Step] t-statistic	Model (10b): Treatment Regression [2nd Step] Coefficient	Model (10b): Treatment Regression [2nd Step] t-statistic
Country GNP and Legal Origin												
GNP Per Capita			-5.349E-07	-2.593***	-4.730E-07	-2.289**	-5.573E-07	-2.341**			0.011	2.115**
French Legal Origin			0.015	2.598***	0.010	1.870*	0.013	2.023**	0.471	7.472***	-0.138	-3.580***
German Legal Origin			-0.036	-1.76*	-0.127	-2.935***	-0.081	-1.590			0.000	-2.262**
Calendar Effects Dummy Variables												
February	0.005	1.419	0.005	1.304	0.005	1.319	0.011	1.759*			0.008	2.103**
March	0.002	0.468	0.002	0.591	0.002	0.559	0.007	1.163			0.003	0.974
April	-0.004	-1.073	-0.004	-0.896	-0.004	-0.921	-0.001	-0.212			-0.001	-0.295
May	-0.001	-0.281	-0.001	-0.134	-0.001	-0.160	0.003	0.512			0.003	0.892
June	-0.006	-1.757*	-0.006	-1.543	-0.006	-1.575	-0.007	-1.158			-0.004	-1.206

(Continued)

Table 6.4 (Continued)

	Model (6): Full Sample		Model (7): Full Sample		Model (8): Full Sample		Model (9): Excluding Onshore Funds		Model (10a): Treatment Regression [1st Step]		Model (10b): Treatment Regression [2nd Step]	
Variable	Coefficient	t-statistic	Coefficient	t-statistic	Coefficient	t-statistic	Coefficient	t-statistic	Coefficient	t-statistic	Coefficient	t-statistic
July	−0.009	−2.450**	−0.009	−2.242**	−0.009	−2.253**	−0.009	−1.456			−0.009	−2.709***
August	−0.003	−0.885	−0.0029	−0.752	−0.003	−0.780	−0.0005	−0.082			0.000	−0.103
September	−0.010	−2.917***	−0.010	−2.708***	−0.010	−2.741***	−0.010	−1.766*			−0.008	−2.458**
October	−0.010	−2.738***	−0.010	−2.562**	−0.010	−2.582**	−0.010	−1.755*			−0.010	−2.804***
November	−0.006	−1.591	−0.006	−1.509	−0.006	−1.511	−0.003	−0.457			−0.002	−0.709
December	−0.012	−3.142***	−0.012	−3.011***	−0.012	−3.016***	−0.012	−2.187**			−0.011	−3.143***
Lambda											−0.004	−1.800*
Model Diagnostics												
Number of Observations	24786		24786		24786		11798				23052	
Adjusted R² (Pseudo R² for Model 10a Step 1)	0.103		0.020		0.022		0.022					

Table 6.4 (Continued)

Variable	Model (6): Full Sample Coefficient	t-statistic	Model (7): Full Sample Coefficient	t-statistic	Model (8): Full Sample Coefficient	t-statistic	Model (9): Excluding Onshore Funds Coefficient	t-statistic	Model (10a): Treatment Regression [1st Step] Coefficient	t-statistic	Model (10b): Treatment Regression [2nd Step] Coefficient	t-statistic
Loglikelihood	23547.73		22472.368		22499.513		9533.464					
F-Statistic (Chi Square for Model 10)	3.70***		12.73***		12.05***		6.39***				526.28***	
Akaike Information Statistic	−4.678		−1.810		−1.811		−1.608					

NOTE: This table present OLS regression analyses of the determinants of fund flows for 2003–2005. Explanatory variables are as defined in Table 6.1 Dummy variables are included for the continents in which assets are primarily located and the funds' primary strategy (20 dummy variables in total). Models (1)–(3) present the full sample and different right-hand-side variable to check for collinearity problems. Model (4) shows robustness exclusion of the onshore funds. Models (5) shows a two-step regression whereby the first step is a logit regression on a dummy variable equal to 1 for offshore registrations, and the second step is a treatment sample selection regression given the results in the first step (using the treatreg function in stata). White's heteroscedastic consistent-covariance matrix estimator (HCCME) is used in all regressions.

there is no offsetting benefit in the perceived regulatory oversight associated with locational restrictions.

The models in Tables 6.3 and 6.4 indicate that distribution channels influence the sensitivity of the relation between fund flows and fund returns. At a general level, the flow-performance sensitivity is enhanced by distribution channels via fund distribution companies and investment managers and mitigated by distribution channels via wrappers. The statistical and economic significance of these effects depends on the particular specification. With past performance measured in terms of raw returns in Table 6.3, the interaction variable involving distributions via wrappers is negative and statistically significant in all five models. The economic significance in Model 2 is such that wrapper distributions are approximately 50% less sensitive to past returns. The economic significance is even more than 100% such that there is a complete reversal of signs relating past returns to future flows for wrappers. The interaction variable with wrappers is statistically insignificant in Table 6.4, Model 7, but significant in Models 8–10 at roughly the same magnitude as that in Models 3–5 in Table 6.4. Wrappers involve tied selling and therefore capital flows do not depend merely on past performance of the fund but also on the companion securities. That wrapper distributions mitigate flow-performance sensitivities is therefore an expected result.

The interaction variable involving private placements is insignificant in Table 6.3, negative and statistically significant in Models 7–9 in Table 6.4, but positive and significant in Model 10 with the use of treatment effects. These different results for private placements (only) are an outlier in that the results are not robust and depend on the model specification, unlike the other tests and findings herein. A negative and significant coefficient would be consistent with managerial entrenchment with private placements (Barclay et al., 2007; see also Wu, 2004, and Hertzel et al., 2002). Our differential results for private placements are perhaps representative of the literature on private placements which itself is not free from mixed findings (see Barclay et al., 2007 for a review).

Flow-performance sensitivities are significantly higher for distributions via fund distribution companies and for distributions via marketing investment managers in models in Tables 6.3 and 6.4 (the only insignificant coefficient is for investment managers in Models 6 and 8). This is expected, as these intermediaries aggressively promote past performance to potential investors. The economic significance is higher with fund distribution companies than with investment managers. Fund distribution companies enhance flow-performance sensitivities by more than 100%, while investment managers enhance flow-performance sensitivities by approximately 20%.

Note that we suppressed the variables for interactions with returns and distributions via banks and other financial institutions. When those variables are used, we generally find that they are insignificant or marginally significant and negative.

We report the results without these variables as they act more as a benchmark, and their inclusion would merely increase concerns over collinearity.

Overall, the data indicate regulation in the form of minimum capitalization, restrictions on location of key service providers, and differences in distribution channels have pronounced effects on the level of hedge fund flows and the flow-performance sensitivities. These findings are very robust to alternative specifications (with the sole exception of the results pertaining to private placements, as noted), as well as other country-specific control variables apart from country-specific hedge fund regulation (including variables for legal origin and GDP per capita).

Many of the control variables are statistically significant and briefly summarized as follows. Past raw returns are significantly positively related to performance at both one- and two-month lags in Table 6.3. The statistical significance of the one-month lagged return diminishes slightly below the 10% level in Models 3 and 4 with the use of additional explanatory variables. The negative coefficients for squared past performance in Table 6.3 suggest that the flow-performance relation is concave for hedge funds; however, we note that alternative methods to account for non-linearities gives rise to different inferences. For instance, the tercile rank specifications in Table 6.4 suggest a linear relation or slightly convex relation. As discussed above, there are differences in findings in terms of convexity and concavity in prior research. We do not extend this literature on concavity versus convexity in hedge fund flow-performance relations; rather, we do note that the findings regarding the influence of regulation such as fund distribution channels significantly affects the sensitivity of the flow-performance relation regardless of how non-linearities are modeled.

The data indicate fund flows are higher among funds with higher management fees and lower among funds with higher performance fees. One may have expected the opposite result as performance fees align the interests of investors and managers. One possible explanation for this result is that performance fees increase incentives for risk taking by fund managers.

The coefficient for yearly redemptions is positive and significant in Models 3 and 8, as would be expected since there are fewer opportunities to withdraw capital relative to other funds (but this effect is insignificant in the other models). We did consider modeling the yearly redemption dummy variable as an interaction term with prior returns, as well as a variable expressed in number of days, but the results for these alternative specifications for this variable were insignificant and did not materially affect the other coefficient estimates.

Older funds and funds with more capital experience lower levels of fund flows. This may suggest that there are diminishing returns to scale after funds reach a certain size. It may also merely reflect greater investor appetite for newer and smaller funds.

Finally, it is important to highlight two findings in Tables 6.3 and 6.4 that are consistent with tax effects on hedge fund flows. First, the variable for onshore funds is negative and significant in all specifications (Models 2–3 and 7–8; this variable is not used in Models 1, 4, 6 and 9 because onshore funds are excluded in Models 4 and 9, and Models 1 and 6 use fund fixed effects). Similarly, the treatment effect for offshore funds is positive and significant in Models 5 and 10. Onshore funds do not enjoy the tax benefits of offshore funds, and the flow measure is approximately 0.004 lower per month for onshore funds.

Second, it is quite noteworthy that there are pronounced seasonality effects in the data. Fund flows are approximately 0.01 higher in February and this effect is statistically significant in Models 1–5 Table 6.3 and in Models 9 and 10 in Table 6.4. This is interesting as the February flows are more pronounced than the effect for offshore funds, for example. By contrast, fund flows tend to be lower in later months in the calendar year, such as September, October, and December (but the statistical significance for some of the months depends on the specification. In view of the ongoing persistence of the January effect (Haug and Hirschey, 2006) this pattern of the flow of funds is at first thought surprising; however, it is consistent with tax effects associated with timing investment flows. Hedge fund investors typically share in the tax liability of the fund at year's end regardless of whether they were invested in the fund only at the year's end or throughout the entire year. Therefore, all else being equal, taxation skews capital flows away from funds at year's end and toward funds at the start of the year.

6.5. Additional Robustness Checks and Extensions

In order to complement the flow-performance regression analysis, we considered a number of additional robustness checks. One consideration is for other time periods and other countries. The analyses focus on 2003–2005, the period that has the largest number of funds in the CISDM data. Earlier time periods involve significantly fewer funds, and if we focus on the same set of funds over time, then this would lead to a reduction in the total number of observations considered. As well, it is more difficult to empirically control for factors that influence institutional investor interest in the asset class of hedge funds over a longer time period. Further, to the best of our knowledge, intra-country variations in hedge fund regulation have been limited prior to 2005. As such, we felt it is most prudent to focus the law and finance analysis of hedge fund capital flows on the 2003–2005 period. Further work could examine legal and regulatory changes and additional countries as more data are available in subsequent years.

We considered a variety of robustness checks, including selection effects for offshore jurisdictions. We considered other robustness checks, such as exclusion of offshore jurisdictions, and found the results to be robust. Additional specifications not presented here are available on request.

One robustness check we did report in an earlier draft was an analysis of overall fund size. We do not present this robustness check here, but it is available upon request. It was of interest to examine fund size as we may infer that if regulation affects the flow of funds in Tables 6.3 and 6.4, then we would expect the same regulation to be associated with fund size in terms of assets under management. We did not find evidence that would lead us to believe that the results in these tables are an artifact of the time period considered.

6.6. Conclusion

This chapter introduced a cross-country law and finance analysis of hedge fund capital flows. As identified by PriceWaterhouseCoopers (2006), the pronounced differences in hedge fund regulation across countries include differences in permissible distribution channels (private placements, wrappers, investment managers, fund distribution companies, banks, and other financial institutions), restrictions on the location of key service providers, minimum capitalization requirements, and taxation. Using the CISDM dataset with a focus on fund flows over 2003–2005, we found strong evidence that fund flows are more sensitive to past performance with permissible distributions via investment managers and fund distribution companies, and less sensitive to past performance with distributions via wrappers. The level of fund flows was negatively related to restrictions on location of key service providers and positively related to minimum capitalization requirements. We further found evidence that taxation impacts fund flows in terms of offshore funds attracting higher levels of fund flows, and in terms of calendar effects.

The evidence in this chapter suggests hedge fund regulation has an important role to play in influencing the size and stability of the hedge fund market. Future theoretical, legal, and policy research on hedge funds could more closely examine the design of regulations for efficient monitoring of fund activities and fund flows. Further hedge fund research could examine hedge fund tax strategies with other, more detailed datasets. As well, future research on fund flows could focus on aspects of regulation in the context of other financial intermediaries, including but not limited to international regulatory developments pertaining to in private equity funds and mutual funds.[12]

Keywords

Alpha
Calendar Effects

Concave
Convex

---

[12] For work on regulation and fund flows in private equity, see, for example, Gompers and Lerner (1998) and Cumming and Johan (2007, 2009). For regulation and mutual fund flows, see, for example, Choi and Kahan (2007).

Fixed Fees
Flow-Performance Relationship
Fractional Rank
Interaction Terms
Linear
Lockup Period
Offshore

Performance Fees
Raw Monthly Returns
Sharpe Ratio
Tercile Rank
Treatment Regression
Yearly Redemptions

Discussion Questions

6.1. What is the flow-performance relationship in funds management? Is the relationship between flow and performance concave, convex, or linear?

6.2. How do restrictions on location of key service providers, minimum capitalization, and different distribution channels affect the flow-performance relationship?

6.3. How do share restrictions, redemption periods, and lockup periods affect the flow-performance relationship?

6.4. Is the flow-performance relationship different for mutual funds, private equity funds, venture capital funds, and hedge funds? If there are any differences across these intermediaries, what are they and why do they exist?

6.5. Do calendar effects and/or taxation affect the flow-performance relationship for hedge funds? Why and how?

6.6. Do you expect that the Dodd-Frank Act, UCITS, and AIFMD would have an impact on the flow-performance relationship in years to come? Explain.

CHAPTER 7

Hedge Fund Performance and Compensation

7.1. Introduction

In the United States, hedge funds have been essentially an unregulated investment vehicle. By 2005 hedge funds collectively had accumulated over a trillion US dollars in assets; at their peak in the summer of 2008, industry estimates suggest the market grew to more than US$2.5 trillion in assets (Ineichen and Silberstein, 2008, pp.16–17). With over a trillion US dollars of capital under management and with 5% alphas sought/promised by most hedge funds, this implies that there needs to be at least an aggregate US$50 billion above systematic-risk justified return (and more than US$125 billion in excess returns in 2008). Given the implausibility of over US$50 billion being readily available for hedge fund investors and managers who aim to "beat the market," it seems highly likely that many hedge fund participants will be disappointed in the future. Further, the increasingly large pool of hedge fund capital under management has the potential to move other markets and impact financial stability. As a result, the tremendous growth of the hedge fund asset class and potential systemic risk has attracted regulatory attention from the US Securities and Exchange Commission (SEC).[1]

Hedge fund registration in the United States commenced only in 2006 (Partnoy and Thomas, 2007; Brav, Jian, Partnoy, and Thomas, 2008a,b). In other countries around the world, hedge funds face stricter regulations such as minimum capital requirements, marketing restrictions, and restrictions on retail investor participation, among other things. The growth of hedge funds worldwide has led regulators to reevaluate the suitability and effectiveness of their regulatory oversight (PriceWaterhouseCoopers, 2006, 2007). How has hedge fund regulation impacted hedge fund structure and performance?

The purpose of this study is to facilitate an understanding of the impact of hedge fund regulation on fund governance and performance. We measure fund

---

[1] www.sec.gov/news/speech/spch111704hjg.htm. For industry perspectives regarding hedge fund regulation, see www.hedgeco.net/hedge-fund-regulations.htm and www.hedgefundregulation.com/.

performance along a variety of different metrics including a multi-factor alpha (Fung and Hsieh, 2004), a manipulation-proof performance measure (MPPM) (Goetzmann, Ingersoll, Spiegel, and Welch, 2007) (as an alternative to the Sharpe ratio, which can be manipulated), and average monthly returns. With regard to fund structure, we focus on management and performance fees since hedge funds are best defined as a compensation scheme for a pool of money to be collectively managed and invested on behalf of the capital providers (Hodder and Jackwerth, 2007).[2]

In theory, there is an ambiguous correlation between hedge fund regulation and hedge fund structure and performance. On one hand, a lack of regulatory oversight may give rise to fund managers who disguise investment schemes and merely capture the fees. This view is consistent with theory and evidence in Bebchuk and Fried (2003), at least in other contexts, that the compensation structure is part of the agency problem rather than its solution. For instance, suppose there are two funds managed by the same group of fund managers. One has a strategy of shorting the Standard and Poor's 500 Index (S&P) while the other has a strategy of going long on the S&P.[3] The additional aspects of the hedge fund marketed to the hedge funds' investors hide the true nature of these hedge funds. In the end, half of the investors of these two hedge funds will lose, while the hedge fund managers reap the profits of the fixed management fees and carried interest performance fees of both hedge funds. The fund investors remain unaware of the scheme due to all of the "mumbo jumbo" of the marketing and promotional material of the hedge funds. Further, without regulatory oversight and/or hedge fund registration requirements, regulatory authorities would also be unaware. Hedge fund registration and oversight would curb this type of behavior thereby improving hedge fund structure and average performance.

Alternatively, regulatory oversight may hamper fund performance so that hedge fund managers and their investors lose freedom to contract and organize their resources in the way that they deem to be most efficient, thereby exacerbating agency problems. The most common forms of regulation in different countries around the world include restrictions on minimum hedge fund size; restrictions on the location of key service providers such as the administrator, custodian, investment adviser, auditors, legal and tax advisers, accountants, and consultants (as discussed in Section 7.2); and limitations on the main market channels for hedge fund distribution. Such restrictions may constrain the fund to an inefficient scale, give rise to inefficient choices of human resources associated with fund management, create barriers to entry, and limit investor participation most suited to the

---

[2] Hedge funds may further be categorized by their strategic focus, and in this chapter, we control for a variety of different strategies. For related work on fees in the mutual fund industry, see Khorana, Servaes, and Tufano (2009, 2005).

[3] This example was provided in a discussion at the DeGroote Microstructure Conference by Professor Larry Harris in November 2006 but does not necessarily reflect his views of the hedge fund industry.

particular hedge fund's strategy. If so, we would expect worse hedge fund performance and less efficient hedge fund structures (that do not as efficiently align the interests of investors and managers) in terms of higher management fees and lower performance fees.

These opposing views suggest that the interaction between hedge fund regulation and hedge fund structure and performance is theoretically ambiguous and subject to whatever effect one believes dominates in the marketplace. Therefore, the purpose of this chapter is to sort these issues out with an empirical analysis of pertinent data. In particular, we empirically examine the relationship between hedge fund performance (including Goetzmann et al., 2007), MPPMs, Fung and Hsieh (2004) multi-factor alphas, average monthly returns and the standard deviation of returns, hedge fund structure (fixed management fees and carried interest performance fees), and various aspects of hedge fund regulation (minimum capitalization, restrictions on the location of key service providers, and restrictions on marketing channels) with an international dataset of 3,782 hedge funds from 29 countries around the world (listed in Section 7.2). We demonstrate results for data spanning the years 1994–2005 and show robustness for the sub-sample over 2003–2005.

At a broad level, the data indicate that regulatory requirements in the form of restrictions on the location of key service providers and marketing channels that permit wrappers (securities that combine different products) are associated with lower alphas, lower average returns, and higher fixed fees. Related evidence confirms that restrictions on location are also negatively related to MPPMs, while wrapper distributions are significantly negatively related to performance fees. There is further evidence that the standard deviation of returns is lower among jurisdictions with restrictions on the location of key service providers and higher minimum capitalization requirements.

In particular, in jurisdictions with restrictions regarding the location of key service providers, monthly returns are approximately 0.3% lower, MPPMs are approximately 0.2% lower (the MPPM is the average monthly welfare of a power utility investor in the portfolio over our sample periods), and 7-factor alphas are approximately 0.1–0.5% lower. These effects are statistically significant and robust to alternative specifications including alternative control variables, different sample periods (both 2003–2005 and 1994–2005), exclusion of funds of funds, and instrumental variable framework correcting for the endogeneity of regulations.

There is fairly robust evidence that minimum capitalization restrictions lower the standard deviation of returns. The data indicate that an increase in required minimum capitalization for a hedge fund from US$1 to $2 million tends to be associated with a reduction in standard deviation of monthly returns by 0.02%. Minimum capitalization restrictions, however, are statistically unrelated to other aspects of fund performance.

The evidence indicates that jurisdictions with marketing via wrappers have lower monthly average returns by approximately 0.2% and 7-factor alphas

0.2–0.5% lower. These effects are economically large, ranging from 2.4% to 6.2% per year. Furthermore, wrapper distributions lower standard deviations of monthly returns by 0.9%. These effects are robust for the 1994–2005 period, but not for the 2003–2005 period.

Finally, there is evidence that jurisdictions permitting distributions via wrappers have lower performance fees by 0.43%. There is further evidence that jurisdictions with wrapper distributions and restrictions on the location of key service providers have higher fixed fees by 0.54% and 0.51%, respectively. Insofar as lower fixed fees and higher performance fees mitigate agency problems and better align the interests of fund managers and owners, this evidence is consistent with the related evidence demonstrating a negative association between performance and jurisdictions that permit distribution via wrappers and have restrictions on location.

The analyses build on a large and growing literature on hedge fund structure and performance (Ackermann, McEnally, and Ravenscraft, 1999; Brown, Goetzmann, and Ibbotson, 1999, 2001; Liang, 1999, 2000, 2003; Agarwal and Naik, 2000a,b, 2004; Edwards and Caglayan, 2001; Amin and Kat, 2003; Brown and Goetzmann, 2003; Brunnermeier and Nagel, 2004; Getmansky, Lo, and Makarov, 2004; Baquero, Horst, and Verbeek, 2005; Cremers, Martijn, and Nair, 2005; Getmansky, 2005; Gupta and Liang, 2005; Agarwal, Daniel, and Naik, 2006; Teo, 2009), as well as hedge fund activism (Brav et al., 2008a,b; Klein and Zur, 2009). The analyses are also related to analyses of hedge fund share restrictions (Aragon, 2007) and hedge fund registration (Brown, Goetzmann, Liang, and Schwartz, 2008). Prior evidence, however, has not considered a cross-country law and finance analysis of hedge fund regulation in relation to fund structure and performance in the spirit of La Porta, Lopez-de-Silanes, Shleifer, and Vishny (1998, 2002, and 2006). The analysis in this regard builds on evidence relating governance to hedge fund and mutual fund performance (Chevalier and Ellison, 1997; Elton, Gruber, and Blake, 2003; Cremers et al., 2005), and the structure of hedge funds and strategies (Fung and Hsieh, 1997, 2000, 2001; Goetzmann, Ingersoll, and Ross, 2003; Jorion, 2000; Ding, Getmansky, Liang, and Wermers, 2007.

This chapter is organized as follows. Section 7.2 briefly describes hedge fund regulation in the countries considered. Section 7.3 introduces the data. Multivariate analyses are presented in Section 7.4. Section 7.5 discusses limitations and future research. Policy implications and concluding remarks follow in Section 7.6.

7.2. Hedge Fund Regulation, Structure, and Performance

7.2.1. HEDGE FUND REGULATION

In the United States, hedge funds are formed as limited partnerships whereby the investors are considered limited partners and the hedge fund managers are general partners. The limited partners are wealthy individuals and institutional investors. Compensation for hedge fund managers comprises a 1–2% fixed management fee based on hedge fund asset size and a 15–20% carried interest performance fee based on the profits. Incentive fees align interests of hedge fund managers as general partners and the investors as limited liability partners who only retain their limited liability by not taking part in any aspect of the management of the fund. Hedge funds are not allowed to advertise in the United States. There is no restriction on the minimum size to operate as a hedge fund and no restrictions on the location of key service providers. Hedge funds in the United States can avoid the public disclosure requirements of the US Securities Act of 1933 by claiming the status of a private placement.[4] Hedge funds are also exempt from the US Investment Company Act of 1940 (which regulates mutual funds) by having no more than 499 investors with more than US$5 million in assets and by not making public offerings.[5] Prior to February 2006, hedge funds in the United States were also exempt from any registration requirement. Brown et al. (2008) analyzed the impact of this registration requirement and found favorable quality signals are possible with registration. Verret (2007) gave specific commentary regarding hedge fund regulation and presented a model of self-regulation as a major theme of the policy recommendation.

In other countries around the world, unlike the United States, there are minimum capital requirements for hedge fund managers to operate a hedge fund, as well as different avenues for marketing (not merely private placements) and restrictions on the location of key service providers (see Chapter 3) typically to be within the same jurisdiction. These regulations are summarized in Chapter 3 (see PriceWaterhouseCoopers, 2006, 2007, for an extended discussion for most of these countries).[6] The focus is on the regulations in place in two periods; the first is 2003–2005, which is a stable period for the regulations and countries in this study (Australia, Austria, British West Indies, Anguilla, Bahamas, Bermuda, Brazil, British Virgin Islands, Canada, Cayman Islands, Channel Islands, France, Germany, Gibraltar, Guernsey, Hong Kong, Ireland, Isle of Man, Italy, Jersey, Luxembourg, Malta, Mauritius, Netherlands, Netherlands Antilles, New Zealand, Sweden, Switzerland, the United States, and the United Kingdom). The second is

---

[4] In a private placement, there typically are not more than 35 "accredited" investors (an accredited investor is someone with more than US$1 million in wealth or who earned more than US$200,000 in the previous two years).

[5] Formerly, the maximum was 99; now, there is a maximum in the Investment Company Act or the rules thereunder, so the default maximum is the 500 person trigger under the Securities and Exchange Act (Thomas and Partnoy, 2007).

[6] The majority of countries and years are available in PriceWaterhouseCoopers (2006). For countries/years not available in PriceWaterhouseCoopers (2006), we obtained information regarding regulation on the hedge funds in a survey sent to selected funds. It is noteworthy that the broad regulatory categories we use have been stable over time (distribution channels, size, and restrictions on location are rarely modified restrictions), but there have been changes to other areas, particularly taxation.

the period 1994–2005; use of two periods enables our analysis to be consistent with previous studies on hedge fund returns.

A typical hedge fund does not have any employees, but instead delegates different functions to service providers of the hedge fund (Chapter 3). Outsourcing a hedge fund's functions minimizes the risk of collusion among hedge fund participants to perpetuate fraud and also mitigates liability in the event the hedge fund participants are accused of improperly performing their management duties. A hedge fund's board of directors or trustee has a fiduciary duty to the investors to ensure that all parties involved in the fund can properly carry out their designated tasks. At issue in this chapter is whether the form of regulatory oversight in each country provides an additional level of governance and an additional check so that fraud is not perpetuated. If regulatory oversight facilitates additional value-added governance, then we would expect hedge funds in those jurisdictions to have higher alphas, MPPMs, and average returns. In the alternative, one may infer that restrictions on minimum capital requirements for managers, restrictions on the location of key service providers, and limitations on the main market channels for hedge fund distribution constrain the fund to an inefficient scale, give rise to inefficient choice of human resources associated with hedge fund management, create barriers to entry, and limit investor participation most suited to the particular hedge fund's strategy.[7] Thus, we would expect hedge funds in those jurisdictions to have worse performance.

The most common service providers include prime brokers, administrators, and distributors (Chapter 3). Prime brokers lend money; act as counterparts to derivative contracts; lend securities in short sales; execute trades; and provide clearing, settlement, and custody services. Administrators issue and redeem interests and shares and calculate the net asset value (NAV) of the fund. Distributors are responsible for marketing the fund to potential investors. Restrictions on location of key service providers typically require the presence of a local agent (PriceWaterhouseCoopers, 2006, 2007). The local agent, however, may not be of sufficient scale and/or employ the individuals who are most suited to the effective operation, management, and governance of the fund (Wilson, 2007). Practitioners often warn against using low quality service providers (e.g., "beware of the potential downside of using third-tier service providers. Furthermore, it is hard to garner the confidence of investors when you do not employ a top notch support network").[8] The recent failure of hedge funds affiliated with Lehman Brothers,

---

[7] An alternative interpretation is as follows. It is possible that jurisdictions with more stringent hedge fund regulation also have more active regulators that monitor hedge fund manager activities. Klein and Zur (2009) find that activist hedge fund managers achieve their target returns by extracting cash from the investee firms from which they acquire at least a 5% stake by forcing increased investee debt capacity and higher dividends. If regulatory oversight curtails this type of activist investment, one may infer that it will also lower expected returns.

[8] Source: www.hedgefundlaunch.com/how-to-start-a-hedge-fund-part-1/. In other non-hedge fund contexts, service providers have been shown to be very important for performance (Butler, et al., 2007).

Bear Sterns, and Madoff has been attributable to low quality, unreliable service providers (Wilson, 2007). Service providers are vitally important because they provide due diligence services for the fund, provide research on counterparty risk, and generally facilitate the execution of the fund's activities.

A fund's relationship with its service providers involves substantial human capital and asset specificity. Local or lower cost service providers can save on fees by up to 20%, but such cost savings can drastically hurt fund performance due to the reduction in auditor timing and support, inaccurate auditing services, enhanced counterparty risk, slower execution, delayed custody services, and conflicts of interest in marketing the fund. Market sentiment for a fund is particularly vulnerable to rumors of a fund using low quality service providers (Wilson, 2007).

Hedge funds have a sponsor that is responsible for marketing the Sponsor Fund. To this end, it is noteworthy that a wrapper distribution channel has the potential to be associated with lower fund performance. Wrappers are securities whose returns tie together different financial products. In the case of wrappers, the sponsor distributes the offering materials for the sponsor fund as well as the disclosure materials for the affiliated wrapper products. There is a potential conflict of interest between the sponsor and the fund manager with respect to the disclosure of the wrapper relating to the fund manager (Gerstein, 2006). Wrapper constructions are often complex and incomprehensible for the average investor, thereby lowering the governance that hedge fund investors would otherwise provide. Empirical evidence confirms wrapper distributions are associated with a "flatter" or less sensitive flow-performance relationship (see Chapter 6); that is, investors are less likely to withdraw from poor performers and enter better performers. Wrapper distributions are likewise associated with more frequent misreporting of returns (see Chapter 8). Overall, we may expect that fund managers have greater latitude for opportunistic behavior under wrapper distributions. This conflict of interest can lead to a negative association between wrappers and fund performance.

In sum, we expect restrictions regarding the location of hedge fund key service providers and wrapper distributions to be associated with poorer hedge fund performance and less efficient hedge fund structures (that do not as efficiently align the interests of investors and managers) in terms of higher management fees and lower performance fees. These predictions are the focus of the ensuing empirical analyses herein.

7.2.2. HEDGE FUND LOCATION

Hedge fund location depends on economic conditions and the proximity to the fund's investors, taxation, and regulatory burdens. The country of domicile of the fund managers may influence fund location particularly in reference to countries with restrictions on the location of key service providers. Additionally, fund managers who expect better performance may locate in jurisdictions with fewer regulatory burdens and lower taxes. For instance, offshore locations such as the Bahamas, Bermuda, and the Cayman Islands have few regulatory burdens and minimal tax for funds and their investors; therefore, many fund managers might choose to register in those jurisdictions despite regulations such as restrictions on location. The absence of regulatory oversight in these countries would render it difficult for fund managers without a track record to raise capital from institutional investors, while more established fund managers with a track record are less likely to experience fund-raising difficulties depending on their fund strategy (see Chapter 5).

In the empirical analyses that follow, we consider econometric models that account for non-random selection of location. In particular, we provide instrumental variable estimates of location choice. We also consider two-step Heckman corrections and treatment regressions (as well as other specifications that exclude selected countries). We find that the results are quite robust to alternative statistical treatment of location choice.

7.2.3. HEDGE FUND PERFORMANCE MEASURES

This chapter uses Goetzmann et al.'s (2007) manipulation-proof performance measure (MPPM), Fung and Hsieh's (2004) multi-factor alpha, average monthly hedge fund returns, and standard deviation of average monthly returns over our sample periods to measure hedge fund performance. We consider a variety of performance measures to demonstrate robustness as there is little consensus regarding the appropriate performance measurement for hedge funds among academics and practitioners (Baghi-Wadji and Klocker, 2007). The results pertaining to regulation are nevertheless quite robust to specifications reported and otherwise; alternative specifications are available upon request.

The MPPM is analogous to the Sharpe ratio, originally called the "reward-to-variability" ratio, and has traditionally been one of the most popular measures for risk-adjusted performance. However, it is now widely known that Sharpe ratio and other reward-to-risk measures may be manipulated with option-like strategies (Goetzmann et al., 2007). This type of manipulation may reasonably be expected to be commonplace among hedge funds. Therefore, we use the recently proposed MPPM by Goetzmann et al. (2007) for the hedge fund industry to remove bias from the potential manipulation of the Sharpe ratio (and results using the Sharpe ratio in an earlier draft of the chapter were not materially different). The MPPM proposed by Goetzmann et al. (2007) is defined as follows:

$$\hat{\Theta} \equiv \frac{1}{(1-\rho)\Delta t}\ln(\frac{1}{T}\sum_{t=1}^{T}[(1+r_{ft})^{-1}(1+r_{ft}+x_{t})]^{1-\rho})$$

where r_{ft} and x_t is the per period (not annualized) risk-free rate and the excess return of the fund over period t. The parameter ρ is the relative risk aversion;

historically, this number ranges from 2 to 4 for the CRSP value-weighted market portfolio depending on the time and frequency of data used. The $\hat{\Theta}$ can be interpreted as the annualized continuously compounded excess return of the portfolio (Goetzmann et al., 2007). The MPPM is interpreted as the average per period welfare of a power utility investor in the portfolio over the time period in question. We found the regression results to be very robust to MPPMs for Risk Aversions 2, 3, and 4. We report MPPM values for Risk Aversion 3, and results for alternative risk aversion parameters are available upon request.

A second performance measure considered in this chapter is known as "alpha." Following the single factor models, a variety of multi-factor models have been developed and applied in the research of hedge funds (Fung and Hsieh, 1997, 2004; Getmansky et al., 2004; Lo, 2006). The multi-factor models could be expressed in a general form as follows:

$$r_t^i = \alpha^i + \sum_{k=1}^{K} \beta_k^i F_{k,i} + \varepsilon_{i,t}$$

where r_t^i is the excess return (in excess of the risk-free rate) on hedge fund i for month t, α^i is the abnormal performance of hedge fund i over the regression time period, β_k^i is the factor loading of hedge fund i on factor k during the regression period, $F_{k,t}$ is the return for factor k for month t, and $\varepsilon_{i,t}$ is the error term. The main difference among those models is the selection of factors. Fung and Hsieh (2004) have developed a 7-factor model, which has shown strong explanatory power in variation of hedge fund performance. The factors are the S&P 500 return minus the risk-free rate (SNPMRF), the Wilshire small cap minus the large cap return (SCMLC), the change in the constant maturity yield of the 10-year Treasury (BD10RET), the change in the spread of Moody's Baa minus the 10-year Treasury (BAAMTSY), the bond PTFS (PTFSBD), the currency PTFS (PTFSFX), and the commodities PTFS (PTFSCOM), where PTFS denotes primitive trend following strategy. The estimated intercept $\hat{\alpha}^i$ is the alpha performance measure or the abnormal performance of hedge fund i over the regression time period.

One challenge associated with multi-factor models is that they might be sensitive to alternative specifications and benchmarks (Agarwal and Naik, 2000a). We take the three-month LIBOR converted into a monthly rate as the risk-free rate. Alternative benchmarks were also considered and did not materially affect the results; these are available upon request. Additionally, it is important to note that the results in a prior version of this chapter made use of the single factor Jensen's alpha and demonstrated a consistent correlation between the regulation variables and the alphas as reported herein. Also, it is noteworthy that hedge funds have a variety of different strategies (the data, described in the next section, consider more than 20 strategies). We explicitly report results with strategy variables that are used to explain cross-sectional differences in hedge fund performance. Alternative approaches that account for strategy when estimating alphas and other performance metrics (such as grouping hedge funds into homogenous categories) did not materially influence the inferences drawn pertaining to legality and hedge fund performance.

7.2.4. OTHER FACTORS PERTINENT TO HEDGE FUND STRUCTURE AND PERFORMANCE

In the empirical analyses in the subsequent sections, we control for a variety of characteristics other than hedge fund regulation that may impact hedge fund performance. First, the quality of investor protection and enforcement differs across countries of different legal origin; therefore, we consider the law and finance legal origin variables in the different countries (as in La Porta et al., 1998, 2002, 2006). We also control for international differences in GNP per capita in the countries considered.

Second, we control for a variety of hedge fund characteristics including the frequency with which investors may withdraw capital, hedge fund size, hedge fund age, minimum investment amounts per investor, and performance and management fees. These control variables are used in ways consistent with prior work measuring hedge fund performance (Ackermann et al., 1999; Brown et al., 1999, 2001; Liang, 1999, 2000, 2003; Agarwal and Naik, 2000a,b, 2004; Edwards and Caglayan, 2001; Brown and Goetzmann, 2003; Brunnermeier and Nagel, 2004; Getmansky et al., 2004; Baquero et al., 2005; Cremers et al., 2005; Getmansky, 2005; Agarwal et al., 2006, 2008). Additionally, in the dataset considered (described immediately following), there are details regarding the primary fund strategy (24 different categories). In the multivariate empirical analyses, we indicate the robustness of the hedge fund regulation results to the inclusion/exclusion of all of these variables.

7.3. Data

7.3.1. DATA SOURCE

This chapter uses the dataset from the Center for International Securities and Derivatives Markets (CISDM), a commonly used dataset in the hedge fund literature (Bollen and Pool, 2009). The CISDM data comprise a total of 3,782 funds, both operating and defunct, over the 1994–2005 period (the same horizon studied by Bollen and Pool, 2009). Of these, 2,709 have performance statistics for 1994–2005, and 1,638 have performance statistics for 2003–2005. The total sample comprises funds registered in 29 different countries as enumerated in Sub-section 7.2.1. CISDM has data on funds from Israel and Panama; however, we could not locate reliable data regarding hedge fund regulations from those countries and so we dropped 35 funds from the sample. Summary statistics for the funds are provided in Table 7.1.

Table 7.1. Definition of Variables and Summary Statistics

Variable	Definition	Mean	Median	Standard Deviation	Minimum	Maximum	No. of Observations
Performance Variables							
Average Returns 1994–2005	Average Monthly Return, 1994–2005, adjusted for backdating (removing the first 18 months of the fund's reported returns)	0.009	0.008	0.009	−0.059	0.253	2,709
Average Returns 2003–2005	Average Monthly Return, 2003–2005, adjusted for backdating	0.010	0.008	0.008	−0.019	0.059	1,638
Standard Deviation of Returns 1994–2005	Average standard deviation of returns, 1994–2005, adjusted for backdating	0.038	0.027	0.044	0.001	1.505	2,709
Standard Deviation of Returns 2003–2005	Average standard deviation of returns, 2003–2005, adjusted for backdating	0.023	0.016	0.020	0.000	0.233	1,638
Manipulation Proof Performance Measure (MPPM) 1994–2005	Manipulation Proof Performance Measure (Goetzmann et al., 2007), 1994–2005, adjusted for backdating	0.002	0.003	0.011	−0.126	0.042	0.002
Manipulation Proof Performance Measure (MPPM) 20032005	Manipulation Proof Performance Measure (Goetzmann et al., 2007), 2003–2005, adjusted for backdating	0.007	0.006	0.007	−0.058	0.046	0.007

(Continued)

Table 7.1. (Continued)

Variable	Definition	Mean	Median	Standard Deviation	Minimum	Maximum	No. of Observations
Performance Variables							
Alpha 19942005	Alpha of Multi-factor Model (Fung and Hsieh, 2004), 1994–2005, adjusted for backdating	0.004	0.003	0.008	−0.066	0.176	2,709
Alpha 20032005	Alpha of Multi-factor Model (Fung and Hsieh, 2004), 2003–2005, adjusted for backdating	0.003	0.002	0.008	−0.044	0.064	1,638
Hedge Fund Regulation Variables							
Log Minimum Capitalization	The log of the minimum capitalization required to operate as a hedge fund manager in 2005 US$	6.216	0	6.369	0	15.725	3,747
Marketing Private Placement	A dummy variable equal to 1 where the country allows fund distribution via private placements	0.973	1	0.162	0	1	3,747
Marketing Bank	A dummy variable equal to 1 where the country allows fund distribution via banks	0.530	1	0.499	0	1	3,747
Marketing Fund Distribution Company	A dummy variable equal to 1 where the country allows fund distribution via fund distribution companies	0.048	0	0.213	0	1	3,747

Marketing Investment Manager	A dummy variable equal to 1 where the country allows fund distribution via investment managers	0.290	0.454	0	1	3,747
Marketing Via Wrappers	A dummy variable equal to 1 where the country allows fund distribution via wrappers	0.048	0.213	0	1	3,747
Marketing Other Regulated Financial Institution	A dummy variable equal to 1 where the country allows fund distribution via other regulated financial institutions	0.081	0.273	0	1	3,747
Marketing Non-Regulated Financial Institution	A dummy variable equal to 1 where the country allows fund distribution via other non-regulated financial institutions	0.027	0.161	0	1	3,747
Restrictions on Location of Key Service Providers	A dummy variable equal to 1 where the country imposes restrictions on the location of key service providers (Figure I)	0.514	0.500	0	1	3,747

Country GNP and Legal Origin

French Legal Origin	A dummy variable equal to 1 for French legal origin countries (La Porta et al., 1998)	0.030	0.170	0	1	3,747

(Continued)

Table 7.1. (Continued)

Variable	Definition	Mean	Median	Standard Deviation	Minimum	Maximum	No. of Observations
German Legal Origin	A dummy variable equal to 1 for German legal origin countries (La Porta et al., 1998)	0.005	0	0.067	0	1	3,747
Log GNP Per Capita	Log of the country's GNP per capita, expressed in 2004 US$	10.441	10.491	0.225	9.000	10.984	3,747
Fund Characteristics							
Yearly Capital Redemptions	A dummy variable equal to 1 if capital redemptions are possible only on an annual basis	0.092	0	0.289	0	1	3,782
Log Assets	The log of the fund's assets in millions of 2005 US$ as measured at the start date of the fund	12.707	15.104	6.286	0	22.575	3,782
Minimum Investment	The minimum investment required for the fund	2.22E+06	2.50E+05	8.26E+07	0	5.00E+09	3,700
Management Fee	The fixed fee in percentages for management compensation	1.324	1.2	0.701	0	15	3,721
Performance Fee	The carried interest performance fee in percentages for management compensation	17.241	20	6.024	0	50	3,642

Misreporting Fund	A dummy variable equal to 1 if the firm misreports monthly returns by reporting at least 50% of marginally negative returns as marginally positive (Bollen and Pool, 2009)	0.698	1	0.459	0	1	3,782
Master Feeder	A dummy variable equal to 1 if the fund is a master feeder structure	0.218	0	0.413	0	1	3,432
Number of Funds	The number of funds operated by the fund manager at the time of the fund's operations	3.534	2	5.240	1	46	3,782
Year of Fund Establishment	The year in which the fund was established	1997.540	1998	4.048	1967	2006	3,754

This table defines the main variables used in the chapter. Summary statistics are also provided for each variable. Data source: CISDM

Fung and Hsieh (2006) have demonstrated that only 3% of hedge funds appear in five of the major hedge fund databases (CISDM, TASS, EUR, MSCI, and HFN). The CISDM sample has 44.6% of the funds domiciled in the United States (and the combined CISDM/HFN sample has 68.1% of funds domiciled there), while the TASS sample reported in International Financial Services (2006) has 34% of funds domiciled in the United States. The CISDM sample has 50.1% of funds domiciled in offshore jurisdictions, while the TASS sample has 55%. The CISDM sample has 6.0% of the funds from the European Union, while the TASS sample has 9%. While we cannot say whether the CISDM sample is representative of the worldwide population of hedge funds, we nevertheless consider robustness to including/excluding different countries, such as those with and without US funds, to demonstrate robustness to different samples. We explicitly confirm the results are very robust to these different sub-samples and econometric methods.

7.3.2. POTENTIAL BIASES

Hedge fund databases may exhibit biased performance results through selection bias, survivorship bias, and backfilling bias. Selection bias is present when databases do not comprise the universe of hedge funds. As with other prior research using single country datasets, we cannot rule out selection bias. We nevertheless consider robustness of the results by excluding different countries, such as the United States, from the regression analyses. Survivorship bias is unlikely to be present due to the fact that we have defunct funds in our sample. Also, we consider the robustness of the results to the 1994–2005 period and the 2003–2005 subsample. Further, in an earlier draft, we considered different populations of funds based on strategies and years and found similar results (again, available upon request). Backfilling bias (funds start reporting to data vendors when they have successful returns in recent history) is likely mitigated by excluding the returns data for the first 18 months of returns data for each fund. Our results are robust to inclusion/exclusion of data with potential backfilling bias.

7.3.3. SUMMARY STATISTICS AND UNIVARIATE CORRELATIONS

Table 7.1 defines and summarizes the performance measures in the data for the January 1994–December 2005 and the January 2003–December 2005 periods, as well as the regulatory variables and variables for hedge fund characteristics. All returns calculations are expressed in decimals and on a monthly basis. The average hedge fund's alpha for 1994–2005 was 0.004 (median 0.003). MPPMs for 1994–2005 are largely left skewed, with significant outliers (seven very negative numbers for funds with almost –100% returns) associated with funds that almost failed in a given month and then failed shortly thereafter. After winsorizing the seven outliers, the average MPPM was 0.002 (median 0.003).

The average monthly return was 0.009 (median 0.008). The average hedge fund size was $29.113 million (median $3.628 million) in 2005 US$, measured as the first observation during our sample period. The median fund in our data started in 1998, and our sample consists of all continuing and defunct funds in CISDM. We considered robustness to excluding funds with longer life spans, and our results are extremely robust. The average fixed fee for the hedge funds was 1.32% (median 1.00%) and the average performance fee was 17.24% (median 20.00%). Additional hedge fund statistics, as well as minimum and maximum values, are presented in Table 7.1.

Table 7.2 provides a comparison of means and medians tests. Funds in jurisdictions without minimum capitalization restrictions have higher average and median returns, higher average and median standard deviation of returns, higher median MPPMs, higher average and median alphas, and lower average and median fixed fees. MPPMs are significantly negatively skewed due to the calculation with fund failures and have a high variance. This means the comparison of mean tests with MPPMs is insignificant (or possibly significant in the direction opposite that of the median test); therefore, we do not focus on the comparison of averages for MPPMs. Private placements are associated with higher average and median returns, higher median MPPMs, higher average and median alphas, lower median fixed fees, and higher average and median performance fees. Bank distributions are associated with lower average and median returns, lower average and median standard deviation of returns, lower median alphas, lower median MPPM, and higher average and median fixed fees. Fund distribution company distributions are associated with lower average and median returns, lower median standard deviation of returns, lower median MPPMs, lower average and median alphas, lower average and median fixed fees, and higher average and median performance fees. Wrapper distributions are associated with lower average and median returns, lower standard deviation of average and median returns, lower median MPPMs, lower average and median alphas, higher average and median fixed fees, and lower median performance fees. Distributions via other regulated financial intermediaries are associated with lower average and median returns, lower standard deviation of average and median returns, lower median MPPMs, lower average and median alphas, higher average and median fixed fees, and lower median performance fees. Distributions via non-regulated financial intermediaries are associated with lower median returns, lower median standard deviation of returns, lower median MPPMs, lower median alphas, and higher average and median fixed fees. Jurisdictions that restrict the location of key service providers are associated with lower average and median returns, lower standard deviation of average and median returns, lower median MPPMs, lower average and median alphas, and higher average management fees.

Table 7.3 provides univariate correlations across all of the variables enumerated in Table 7.1. Hedge funds in jurisdictions that restrict the location of key service

Table 7.2. Comparison of Means and Medians Tests

	Mean	Median	Standard Deviation	Minimum	Maximum	Number of Observations	Mean	Median	Standard Deviation	Minimum	Maximum	Number of Observations	Difference in Means (t-statistic)	Difference in Medians (Chi-Square)
	\multicolumn{6}{c}{No Minimum Capitalization}	\multicolumn{6}{c}{Minimum Capitalization >0}		
Average Returns, 1994–2005	0.009	0.008	0.008	−0.056	0.054	1,458	0.008	0.007	0.010	−0.059	0.253	1,284	3.735***	28.003***
Standard Deviation of Average Returns, 1994–2005	0.041	0.031	0.036	0.001	0.252	1,458	0.034	0.024	0.052	0.001	1.505	1,284	4.198***	39.592***
MPPM, 1994–2005	0.002	0.004	0.012	−0.126	0.033	1,456	0.002	0.003	0.010	−0.114	0.042	1,279	−0.796	5.605**
7-Factor Alpha, 1994–2005	0.004	0.004	0.008	−0.053	0.064	1,458	0.003	0.003	0.009	−0.066	0.176	1,284	2.723***	25.613***
Management Fee	1.233	1.000	0.770	0.000	15.000	1,446	1.421	1.500	0.776	0.000	15.000	1,201	−6.240***	178.420***
Performance Fee	19.222	20.000	4.568	0.000	50.000	1,446	19.352	20.000	4.275	0.000	50.000	1,179	−0.754	14.713***

	No Private Placements						Private Placements						
Average Returns, 1994–2005	0.006	0.006	0.005	−0.005	0.033	102	0.009	0.008	0.009	−0.059	0.253	2,640	−4.090***	27.506***
Standard Deviation of Average Returns, 1994–2005	0.032	0.024	0.029	0.001	0.131	102	0.038	0.027	0.044	0.001	1.505	2,640	−1.965**	16.200***
MPPM, 1994–2005	0.000	0.002	0.007	−0.030	0.019	102	0.002	0.003	0.011	−0.126	0.042	2,633	−1.916*	12.511***
7-Factor Alpha, 1994–2005	0.002	0.001	0.005	−0.015	0.026	102	0.004	0.003	0.009	−0.066	0.176	2,640	−4.121***	25.007***
Management Fee	1.283	1.000	0.716	0.120	4.800	59	1.319	1.000	0.780	0.000	15.000	2,588	−0.389	0.256
Performance Fee	17.814	20.000	6.407	0.000	33.000	59	19.314	20.000	4.379	0.000	50.000	2,566	−1.789*	16.869***
	No Bank Distributions						Bank Distributions						
Average Returns, 1994–2005	0.009	0.008	−0.041	0.054	1,355	0.008	0.007	0.010	−0.059	0.253	1,387	4.406***	31.867***

(Continued)

Table 7.2. (Continued)

	Mean	Median	Standard Deviation	Minimum	Maximum	Number of Observations	Mean	Median	Standard Deviation	Minimum	Maximum	Number of Observations	Difference in Means (t-statistic)	Difference in Medians (Chi-Square)
Standard Deviation of Average Returns, 1994–2005	0.042	0.032	0.036	0.001	0.252	1,355	0.034	0.024	0.050	0.001	1.505	1,387	4.480***	44.228***
MPPM, 1994–2005	0.002	0.004	0.012	−0.100	0.033	1,352	0.002	0.003	0.011	−0.126	0.042	1,383	−0.030	4.688**
7-Factor Alpha, 1994–2005	0.004	0.004	0.008	−0.066	0.064	1,355	0.003	0.003	0.009	−0.055	0.176	1,387	3.399***	31.867***
Management Fee	1.222	1.000	0.790	0.000	15.000	1,341	1.418	1.500	0.753	0.000	15.000	1,306	−6.519***	209.808***
Performance Fee	19.317	20.000	4.507	0.000	50.000	1,339	19.242	20.000	4.368	0.000	50.000	1,286	0.437	9.478***
	No Fund Distribution Company Distributions						*Fund Distribution Company Distributions*							
Average Returns, 1994–2005	0.009	0.008	0.009	−0.059	0.253	2,579	0.008	0.006	0.007	−0.005	0.035	163	1.476	20.213***

Standard Deviation of Average Returns, 1994–2005	0.038	0.027	0.045	0.001	1.505	2,579	0.032	0.021	0.031	0.001	0.179	163	2.490**	15.653***
MPPM, 1994–2005	0.002	0.003	0.011	y–0.126	0.042	2,572	0.002	0.003	0.010	–0.075	0.025	163	0.153	4.657**
7-Factor Alpha, 1994–2005	0.004	0.003	0.009	–0.066	0.176	2,579	0.003	0.002	0.007	–0.031	0.030	163	1.498	18.628***
Management Fee	1.310	1.000	0.780	0.000	15.000	2,561	1.557	1.500	0.674	0.000	4.800	86	–3.312***	32.084***
Performance Fee	19.281	20.000	4.461	0.000	50.000	2,543	19.268	20.000	3.695	10.000	30.000	82	0.029	14.282***

No Investment Manager Distributions | | | | | | | *Investment Manager Distributions* | | | | | | |

Average Returns, 1994–2005	0.009	0.008	0.008	–0.031	0.054	1,901	0.008	0.007	0.011	–0.059	0.253	841	–2.361**	17.028***
Standard Deviation of Average Returns, 1994–2005	0.039	0.028	0.035	0.001	0.260	1,901	0.036	0.025	0.060	0.001	1.505	841	–1.040	8.198***

(Continued)

Table 7.2. (Continued)

	Mean	Median	Standard Deviation	Minimum	Maximum	Number of Observations	Mean	Median	Standard Deviation	Minimum	Maximum	Number of Observations	Difference in Means (t-statistic)	Difference in Medians (Chi-Square)
MPPM, 1994–2005	0.002	0.004	0.011	−0.114	0.042	1,898	0.001	0.003	0.011	−0.126	0.025	837	0.915	5.560**
7-Factor Alpha, 1994–2005	0.004	0.004	0.008	−0.046	0.064	1,901	0.003	0.003	0.010	−0.066	0.176	841	−2.843***	14.361***
Management Fee	1.301	1.000	0.828	0.000	15.000	2,039	1.376	1.500	0.575	0.000	4.000	608	2.509**	29.785***
Performance Fee	19.431	20.000	4.124	0.000	50.000	2,022	18.773	20.000	5.332	0.000	50.000	603	−2.794***	4.716**
	No Wrapper Distributions						*Wrapper Distributions*							
Average Returns, 1994–2005	0.009	0.008	0.009	−0.059	0.253	2,579	0.007	0.006	0.006	−0.004	0.035	163	2.301**	23.576***
Standard Deviation of Average Returns, 1994–2005	0.039	0.027	0.045	0.001	1.505	2,579	0.031	0.020	0.031	0.001	0.179	163	3.024***	20.213***
MPPM, 1994–2005	0.002	0.003	0.011	−0.126	0.042	2,572	0.001	0.003	0.009	−0.075	0.025	163	0.374	5.466**

7-Factor Alpha, 1994–2005	0.004	0.003	0.009	−0.066	0.176	2,579	0.003	0.002	0.007	−0.031	0.030	163	2.151**	21.862***
Management Fee	1.311	1.000	0.781	0.000	15.000	2,560	1.550	1.500	0.663	0.000	4.800	87	−3.294***	33.161***
Performance Fee	19.304	20.000	4.415	0.000	50.000	2,542	18.554	20.000	5.092	0.000	30.000	83	1.325	9.593***

No Other Regulated Financial Intermediary Distributions   *Other Regulated Financial Intermediary Distributions*

Average Returns, 1994–2005	0.009	0.008	0.009	−0.059	0.253	2,514	0.007	0.006	0.006	−0.005	0.035	228	3.542***	34.520***
Standard Deviation of Average Returns, 1994–2005	0.039	0.028	0.045	0.001	1.505	2,514	0.030	0.019	0.030	0.001	0.179	228	4.232***	27.883***
MPPM, 1994–2005	0.002	0.003	0.011	−0.126	0.042	2,507	0.001	0.003	0.009	−0.075	0.025	228	0.637	10.227***
7-Factor Alpha, 1994–2005	0.004	0.003	0.009	−0.066	0.176	2,514	0.002	0.002	0.007	−0.031	0.030	228	3.568***	39.963***

(Continued)

Table 7.2. (Continued)

	\multicolumn{7}{c}{No Other Non-Regulated Financial Intermediary Distributions}	\multicolumn{7}{c}{Other Non-Regulated Financial Intermediary Distributions}	Difference in Means (t-statistic)	Difference in Medians (Chi-Square)
	Mean	Median	Standard Deviation	Minimum	Maximum	Number of Observations		Mean	Median	Standard Deviation	Minimum	Maximum	Number of Observations		
Management Fee	1.310	1.000	0.790	0.000	15.000	2,493		1.454	1.500	0.545	0.000	2.750	154	−3.089***	33.083***
Performance Fee	19.294	20.000	4.413	0.000	50.000	2,479		19.041	20.000	4.856	0.000	33.000	146	0.615	31.469***
Average Returns, 1994–2005	0.009	0.008	0.009	−0.059	0.253	2,640		0.008	0.007	0.007	−0.004	0.035	102	0.692	10.845***
Standard Deviation of Average Returns, 1994–2005	0.038	0.027	0.044	0.001	1.505	2,640		0.033	0.021	0.035	0.001	0.179	102	1.400	22.627***
MPPM, 1994–2005	0.002	0.003	0.011	−0.126	0.042	2,633		0.001	0.003	0.011	−0.075	0.025	102	0.665	0.729
7-Factor Alpha, 1994–2005	0.004	0.003	0.009	−0.066	0.176	2,640		0.003	0.002	0.008	−0.031	0.030	102	1.001	9.278***

	No Restrictions on Location						Restrictions on Location							
Average Returns, 1994–2005	0.009	0.008	−0.031	0.054	0.008	1,396	0.007	0.010	−0.059	0.253	1,346	3.853***	18.424***
Standard Deviation of Average Returns, 1994–2005	0.041	0.036	0.001	0.252	0.035	1,396	0.025	0.051	0.001	1.505	1,346	3.353***	23.364***
MPPM, 1994–2005	0.002	0.004	0.012	−0.100	0.033	1,394	0.002	0.011	−0.126	0.042	1,341	−0.418	1.437
7-Factor Alpha, 1994–2005	0.004	0.004	0.008	−0.046	0.064	1,396	0.003	0.009	−0.066	0.176	1,346	2.996***	14.655***
Management Fee	1.228	1.000	0.796	0.000	15.000	1,350	1.412	1.500	0.748	0.000	15.000	1,297	−6.141***	179.403***
Performance Fee	19.242	20.000	4.729	0.000	50.000	1,346	19.320	20.000	4.112	0.000	50.000	1,279	−0.448	1.708
Management Fee	1.316	1.000	0.783	0.000	15.000	2,597	1.420	1.500	0.485	0.000	2.250	50	−1.480	27.991***
Performance Fee	19.286	20.000	4.442	0.000	50.000	2,578	18.936	20.000	4.291	10.000	30.000	47	0.554	21.334***

This table presents a comparison of means and medians tests for differences in performance and fees for different regulatory conditions. The sample covers the 1994–2005 period. The fee tests are presented excluding fund of funds. The MPPM tests are presented with winsorized results (at the 95% level) in order to exclude extreme outliers in the left-hand tail. The fund performance data are presented for all funds as the results are robust to inclusion or exclusion of fund of funds. *, **, *** significant at the 10%, 5%, and 1% levels, respectively.

Table 7.3. Correlation Matrix

	(1)	(2)	(3)	(4)	(5)	(6)	(7)	(8)	(9)	(10)	(11)	(12)	(13)	(14)	(15)	(16)	(17)	(18)	(19)	(20)	(21)	(22)	(23)	(24)
1 Average Returns 1994–2005	1.00																							
2 Standard Deviation of Returns 1994–2005	0.54	1.00																						
3 Manipulation Proof Performance Measure 1994–2005	0.54	−0.31	1.00																					
4 Alpha 1994–2005	0.85	0.40	0.51	1.00																				
5 Log Minimum Capitalization	−0.06	−0.14	0.04	−0.01	1.00																			
6 Marketing Private Placement	0.08	0.07	0.03	0.06	−0.15	1.00																		
7 Marketing Bank	−0.11	−0.19	0.02	−0.07	0.78	−0.13	1.00																	
8 Marketing Fund Distribution Company	0.01	0.00	−0.01	0.01	0.09	0.01	0.14	1.00																
9 Marketing Investment Manager	−0.03	−0.05	0.00	−0.04	0.22	0.09	0.45	0.32	1.00															
10 Marketing Via Wrappers	−0.02	−0.02	−0.03	−0.03	0.09	−0.01	0.13	0.96	0.32	1.00														
11 Marketing Other Regulated Financial Institution	−0.07	−0.08	−0.04	−0.06	0.17	−0.53	0.25	0.62	0.12	0.60	1.00													
12 Marketing Non–Regulated Financial Institution	−0.02	−0.03	−0.04	−0.02	0.11	0.02	0.15	0.77	0.26	0.77	0.57	1.00												
13 Restrictions on Location of Key Service Providers	−0.07	−0.15	0.05	−0.03	0.75	0.15	0.83	−0.17	0.44	−0.19	−0.15	−0.17	1.00											
14 French Legal Origin	−0.05	−0.05	−0.01	−0.04	0.16	−0.88	0.10	0.13	−0.03	0.09	0.52	−0.03	−0.14	1.00										
15 German Legal Origin	0.04	0.04	0.02	0.05	0.04	−0.17	0.02	0.13	−0.02	0.13	−0.01	0.00	−0.03	0.00	1.00									
16 Log GNP Per Capita	−0.06	0.01	−0.08	−0.06	−0.61	−0.35	−0.45	−0.08	−0.60	−0.03	0.13	0.02	−0.70	0.23	−0.01	1.00								
17 Yearly Capital Redemptions	0.07	0.03	0.04	0.05	−0.21	0.05	−0.25	−0.07	−0.17	−0.07	−0.09	−0.05	−0.23	−0.06	−0.01	0.16	1.00							
18 Log Assets	0.00	0.06	−0.03	0.00	−0.07	0.07	−0.12	−0.02	−0.11	−0.01	−0.06	0.01	−0.12	−0.07	0.00	0.07	0.01	1.00						
19 Minimum Investment	−0.02	−0.03	0.00	−0.01	0.02	0.01	0.01	−0.02	−0.04	−0.02	−0.02	−0.01	0.01	−0.01	0.00	0.00	−0.01	0.02	1.00					
20 Management Fee	0.06	0.01	0.03	0.07	0.11	−0.01	0.12	0.10	0.09	0.10	0.05	0.04	0.10	0.02	0.12	−0.11	−0.07	−0.02	−0.01	1.00				
21 Performance Fee	0.13	0.23	0.00	0.14	−0.03	0.02	−0.06	−0.05	−0.12	−0.05	−0.07	−0.11	−0.04	0.00	0.01	0.04	0.02	0.15	−0.01	0.06	1.00			
22 Misreporting Fund	−0.13	−0.28	0.06	−0.09	0.05	0.00	0.06	0.03	0.07	0.03	0.02	0.04	0.04	0.01	−0.04	−0.04	0.02	0.00	0.03	0.02	−0.12	1.00		
23 Master Feeder	−0.11	−0.08	−0.04	−0.07	0.10	0.05	0.10	−0.06	0.01	−0.05	−0.09	−0.02	0.12	−0.06	−0.01	−0.06	−0.02	−0.04	0.05	0.04	0.11	0.01	1.00	
24 Number of Funds	−0.10	−0.12	−0.02	−0.12	0.16	−0.02	0.19	0.03	0.18	0.03	0.04	0.05	0.16	0.02	−0.01	−0.14	−0.08	−0.08	−0.01	0.01	−0.03	0.00	0.14	1.00
25 Year of Fund Establishment	−0.07	−0.20	0.14	−0.07	0.14	−0.06	0.16	0.04	−0.06	0.05	0.09	0.03	0.12	0.05	−0.01	0.01	−0.14	−0.09	0.01	0.04	−0.01	−0.05	0.10	0.06

This table presents correlations across the variables defined in Table 7.1. Correlations significant at the 5% level are highlighted in underline font providers have significantly lower average returns and lower standard deviations of returns (correlations are –0.07 and –0.15, respectively). Jurisdictions that restrict the location of key service providers are positively correlated with MPPMs at 0.05, but this is attributable to the outliers with MPPMs as discussed in conjunction with the comparison of means and medians tests in Table 7.2. Hedge funds with higher performance fees have significantly higher average returns, standard deviations of returns, and alphas (correlations are 0.13, 0.23, and 0.14, respectively). Table 7.3 also indicates high correlations across many of the variables; thus, we assess the robustness of the results to alternative specifications in the multivariate analyses.

7.4. Multivariate Analyses

The multivariate empirical tests are presented in Table 7.4 encompassing 15 regressions in three panels. Panels A and B consider, as dependent variables, the different performance (average monthly returns, standard deviation of monthly returns, MPPMs, and 7-factor alphas) measures over the 1994–2005 and 2003–2005 periods, respectively. Panel C considers the further robustness checks for the performance measures over 1994–2005, as well as the determinants of fixed fees and performance fees. The dependent variables in the MPPM regressions for the 1994–2005 period are winsorized at the 95% level due to outliers in the left tail, as discussed in Section 7.3. We include fund of funds in the Panel A and B regressions, but exclude them in the Panel C regressions. Results relating regulation to performance are invariant to including or excluding fund of funds, as regulations pertaining to funds also apply to fund of funds (PriceWaterhouseCoopers, 2006, 2007). We exclude fund of funds for regressions determining fees, as fee structures are materially different for fund of funds. The central focus of the following discussion is on the impact of regulation on hedge fund performance and structure. Robustness to inclusion/exclusion of control variables for legal origin, GNP per capita, and various hedge fund characteristics are also considered. As discussed further, alternative sets of explanatory variables, econometric methods, subsets of the data, and other information did not materially impact the results, and additional specifications not presented are available upon request.

In Models 5 and 10, we present the second step of a two-stage IV regression. The first step involves a logit regression on a dummy variable equal to 1 for restrictions on the location of key service providers and an OLS regression with the log of minimum capitalization. For these regressions, we include explanatory variables that include fund characteristics, legal origin, and more than two dozen explanatory variables for the fund's primary strategy, as well as explanatory variables for fund characteristics such as the number of funds and the year of first establishment of the funds in explaining jurisdiction choice. One important identifying

Table 7.4. Regression Analyses of Hedge Fund Performance and Compensation Structure

Panel A. Performance Measures 1994–2005

Variable	Model (1): Average Monthly Returns Coefficient	t-statistic	Model (2): Standard Deviation of Average Returns Coefficient	t-statistic	Model (3): MPPM Coefficient	t-statistic	Model (4): Fund Alpha Coefficient	t-statistic	Model (5): Fund Alpha (Hedge Fund Regulation Variables Endogenous) Coefficient	t-statistic
Constant	0.052	3.398**	0.237	3.884***	0.024	1.378	0.028	1.806*	0.026	0.610
Hedge Fund Regulation Variables										
Log Minimum Capitalization	−2.690E−06	−0.052	−4.385E−04	−2.401**	1.068E−04	1.399	2.11E−05	0.414	3.34E−05	0.147
Marketing Via Wrappers	−0.002	−1.935*	−0.009	−2.366**	0.001	0.329	−0.002	−1.852*		
Marketing Non-Regulated Financial Institution	0.002	1.178	0.010	1.721*	−0.003	−1.255	0.001	0.719		
Restrictions on Location of Key Service Providers	−0.003	−3.764***	−0.005	−2.315**	−0.002	−1.726*	−0.002	−3.086***	−0.002	−3.103***
Country GNP and Legal Origin										
French Legal Origin	−0.001	−1.285	0.001	0.326	−0.002	−1.146	−0.002	−1.515	−0.002	−0.657

German Legal Origin	0.011	6.291***	0.025	3.536***	0.009	3.295***	0.013	7.293***	0.013	6.762***
Log GNP Per Capita	−0.004	−2.965***	−0.018	−3.481***	−0.002	−1.354	−0.003	−1.761*	−0.002	−0.576

Fund Characteristics

Yearly Capital Redemptions	0.001	2.358**	0.000	−0.239	0.001	1.342	0.001	1.875*	0.001	2.445**
Log Assets	−8.051E-05	−2.439	−2.535E-04	−1.505	−4.776E-05	−1.609	−2.5E-05	−0.845	−4E-05	−1.388
Minimum Investment	8.295E-13	0.199	−4.234E-11	−1.099	8.525E-12	0.823	4.63E-12	0.679	4.34E-12	0.662
Management Fee	0.000	1.482	0.000	0.023	0.0002	0.349	0.001	1.846*	5.10E-04	1.736*
Performance Fee	−.959592D-05	−0.140	0.000	−0.418	0.0001	1.018	9.00E-05	1.533	8.00E-05	1.274
Misreporting Fund	−0.001	−1.792*	−0.009	−4.897***	0.001	1.392	−2.90E-04	−0.714	−3.40E-04	−0.762
Strategy Dummy Variables?	Yes		Yes		Yes		Yes		Yes	
Adjusted R^2	0.061		0.041		0.051		0.060		0.063	
F-Statistic	4.90***		12.68***		3.18***		3.79***		3.79***	

(Continued)

Table 7.4. (Continued)

Panel B. Performance Measures 2003–2005

	Model (1): Average Monthly Returns		Model (2): Standard Deviation of Average Returns		Model (3): MPPM		Model (4): Fund Alpha		Model (5): Fund Alpha (Hedge Fund Regulation Variables Endogenous)	
Variable	Coefficient	t-statistic	Coefficient	t-statistic	Coefficient	t-statistic	Coefficient	t-statistic	Coefficient	t-statistic
Constant	0.073	4.501***	0.139	4.521***	0.058	4.227***	0.052	2.808***	0.046	
Hedge Fund Regulation Variables										
Log Minimum Capitalization	−7.982E-05	−1.649*	−2.802E-04	−2.899***	−5.063E-05	−1.222	−3.031E-05	−0.566	−1.214E-05	−0.070
Marketing Via Wrappers	−0.001	−0.880	−0.004	−1.345	−2.500E-04	−0.210	−0.002	−1.580		
Marketing Non-Regulated Financial Institution	−0.001	−0.506	0.000	−0.042	−0.001	−0.815	0.002	0.880		
Restrictions on Location of Key Service Providers	−0.003	−4.139***	−0.004	−3.332***	−0.002	−3.147***	−0.001	−2.326**	−0.001	−2.275**

Country GNP and Legal Origin

French Legal Origin	0.000	−0.299	0.002	0.600	−0.001	−0.391	0.002	1.291	0.002	0.678
German Legal Origin	−0.002	−0.980	0.025	5.398***	−0.006	−2.926***	−0.013	−6.456***	−0.014	−7.035***
Log GNP Per Capita	−0.006	−3.865***	−0.011	−3.899***	−0.005	−3.681***	−0.005	−2.663***	−0.004	−1.162

Fund Characteristics

Yearly Capital Redemptions	0.001	2.109**	0.000	0.079	0.001	2.629***	2.700E-04	0.406	3.000E-04	0.449
Log Assets	−2.702E-05	−0.998	3.297E-05	0.610	−2.964E-05	−1.266	−3.248E-05	−1.321	−3.087E-05	−1.220
Minimum Investment	3.683E-12	1.813*	−1.341E-12	−0.092	4.073E-12	1.233	2.817E-12	0.542	2.627E-12	0.505
Management Fee	0.000	2.020**	0.002	1.835*	0.000	−0.034	2.300E-04	1.132	2.400E-04	1.192
Performance Fee	−.651385D-04	−2.291**	0.000	1.298	−8.333E-05	−2.757***	−6.000E-05	−1.879*	−6.000E-05	−1.896*
Misreporting Fund	−0.002	−3.733***	−0.007	−5.577***	−1.167E-03	−2.641***	−0.001	−1.604	−0.001	−1.743*

(Continued)

Table 7.4 (Continued)

Panel B. Performance Measures 2003–2005

Variable	Model (1): Average Monthly Returns Coefficient	t-statistic	Model (2): Standard Deviation of Average Returns Coefficient	t-statistic	Model (3): MPPM Coefficient	t-statistic	Model (4): Fund Alpha Coefficient	t-statistic	Model (5): Fund Alpha (Hedge Fund Regulation Variables Endogenous) Coefficient	t-statistic
Strategy Dummy Variables?	Yes		Yes		Yes		Yes		Yes	
Number of Observations	1435		1435		1478		1435		1431	
Adjusted R²	0.339		0.320		0.309		0.204		0.226	
F-Statistic	19.00***		17.57***		16.71***		9.99***		10.16***	

Panel C. Alphas 1994–2005, and Fixed Fees and Performance Fees Excluding Fund of Funds

Constant	0.028	1.353	0.043	1.634	0.033	1.219	−4.522	−10.270***	−3.734	−3.908***

Hedge Fund Regulation Variables

Marketing Bank			0.001	0.995	0.003	1.569				
Marketing Fund Distribution Companies			−0.001	−0.462						

Marketing Via Wrappers				−0.005	−2.384**	0.146	3.172***	−0.291	−1.861*
Marketing Other Financial Institution				−0.001	−0.720	0.073	2.690***	0.128	2.318**
Marketing Non-Regulated Financial Institution				0.005	1.318	−0.100	−1.463	0.220	1.555
Restrictions on Location of Key Service Providers	−0.002	−1.894*	−0.003	−1.852*	−0.005	−2.147**	0.076	4.181***	0.003	0.061

Country GNP and Legal Origin

French Legal Origin	−0.002	−1.250	−0.002	−1.429	0.005	1.872*	0.059	0.732	0.381	3.372***
German Legal Origin	0.011	6.555***	0.011	4.380***	0.023	4.645***	0.409	1.849*	0.621	2.542**
Log GNP Per Capita	−0.002	−1.244	−0.004	−1.579	−0.004	−1.594	0.044	1.196	0.141	1.784*

(Continued)

Table 7.4 (Continued)

Fund Characteristics

Panel C. Alphas 1994–2005, and Fixed Fees and Performance Fees Excluding Fund of Funds

Variable	Model (1): Average Monthly Returns Coefficient	t-statistic	Model (2): Standard Deviation of Average Returns Coefficient	t-statistic	Model (3): MPPM Coefficient	t-statistic	Model (4): Fund Alpha Coefficient	t-statistic	Model (5): Fund Alpha (Hedge Fund Regulation Variables Endogenous) Coefficient	t-statistic
Yearly Capital Redemptions	0.001	2.514**	0.002	2.537**	0.001	2.399**	−0.040	−2.331**	0.076	2.163**
Log Assets	−3.035E-05	−0.725	−2.83E-05	−0.687	−2.907E-05	−0.705	−2.543E-04	−0.335	1.595E-02	5.403***
Minimum Investment	.427196D-11	0.666	.449960D-11	0.696	.404473D-11	0.636				
Management Fee	4.100E-04	1.363	4.100E-04	1.362	4.100E-04	1.365				
Performance Fee	1.200E-04	1.221	1.200E-04	1.262	1.100E-04	1.212				
Misreporting Fund	−4.700E-04	−0.922	−4.900E-04	−0.974	−4.700E-04	−0.937	−0.006	−0.650	−0.001	−0.030
Strategy Dummy Variables?	Yes		Yes		Yes		Yes		Yes	

Number of Observations	1,837	1,837	1,837	2,601	2,541
Adjusted R²	0.052	0.053	0.057	0.100	0.052
F-Statistic	2.75***	2.63***	2.65***	7.69***	4.82***

This table presents OLS regression analyses of the determinants of the average monthly return, standard deviation of the average monthly return, MPPM or Manipulation Proof Performance Measure (Goetzmann et al., 2007), and the 7-factor fund alpha (Fung and Hsieh, 2004) for the cross-section of funds in the data. Explanatory variables are as defined in Table 7.1. Dummy variables are included for the funds' primary strategy (30 dummy variables in total). Panel A presents the results for performance measures using all CISDM data over the range 1994–2005 including defunct funds. Performance data are used for all available months. Model (3) winsorizes the left-hand-side variable at the 95% level, which results in removal of outliers in the left tail of the distribution. Panel B Models (6)–(10) include only funds with performance data from 2003–2005. Models (5) and (10) demonstrate the second step of a two-step regression. The first step involves a logit regression on a dummy variable equal to 1 for restrictions on location and an OLS regression for log (minimum capitalization). The second step uses the fitted values of those variables. Panel C, Models (11)–(13), presents results for 1994–2005 and demonstrates robustness of the determinants of the multi-factor alphas to different explanatory variables, as well as reporting results for the determinants of fixed fees (Model 14) and performance fees (Model 15). The logistic transformation is applied to the dependent variables in Models (14) and (15) so that the values are not bounded between zero and 1, and OLS can be applied without bias. Models (1)–(10) include fund of funds with dummy variables for fund of fund strategies, while Models (11)–(15) exclude funds of funds to illustrate robustness. White's (1980) HCCME is used in all regressions.

fund characteristic is the "master-feeder" structure.[9] A master-feeder structure allows funds to market a fund to both onshore and offshore investors, and, as such, it is possible that this structure explains, in part, jurisdiction choice, but will not necessarily be directly correlated with returns. Overall, the first step regressions model "hedge fund forum shopping" (hedge fund choice of law; Chapter 5). In Chapter 5 we rank the risks associated with different strategies and find some evidence of an alignment of interests between hedge fund managers and their investors in terms of jurisdiction choice. As considered in Chapter 5, there are three possibilities that give rise to a relationship between fund strategy and jurisdiction: (1) a race to the bottom (hedge fund managers pursuing riskier strategies and strategies for which potential agency problems are more pronounced select jurisdictions that have less onerous regulatory oversight),(2) neutrality (the association between hedge fund strategies and hedge fund regulation is random, and (3) an alignment of interests (hedge funds pursuing risky investment strategies select jurisdictions with more onerous regulation). Legal origin dummy variables are included to account for potential fund manager preferences for the legal system (La Porta et al., 1998; a dummy variable for the more flexible English legal system countries is suppressed to avoid collinearity). We had considered taxation variables, but tax benefits for different jurisdictions depend on fund strategies and characteristics and are not easily quantified into a few variables whereas fund strategies and asset location are intuitively related to hedge fund forum shopping (Chapter 5).

For a similar and comparable method to deal with endogeneity and selection, as reported in an earlier draft of the chapter, we considered two-step regressions in the spirit of Heckman (1976, 1979) with the first step selecting an offshore jurisdiction. Fund managers, in practice, typically register in the country in which they are domiciled or offshore (Wilson, 2007). By first running the logit regression as a non-random choice, we control for the non-random distribution of offshore registrants. Therefore, the two-step method is an improvement over an alternative approach of simply restricting the sample to the offshore subsample.[10] The results were extremely similar to those reported herein and are available upon request.

At a broad level, the data indicate regulatory requirements in the form of restrictions regarding the location of key service providers, and permissible distributions via wrappers are associated with lower manipulation proof performance measures, lower fund alphas, lower average monthly returns, and higher fixed fees. Wrapper distributions are significantly negatively related to performance

---

[9] We identify master-feeder funds using the method in Liang and Park (2008) where if there are both onshore and offshore funds with the same investment style managed by the same company, then these funds are identified as master-feeder funds.

[10] Heckman selection regressions, treatment regressions (using the treatreg function in Stata), and regressions with restricted subsample (such as excluding onshore funds or excluding US funds) all provided similar results to those reported.

fees. Also, the data show standard deviations of monthly returns are lower among jurisdictions with restrictions on the location of key service providers and higher minimum capitalization requirements. Specific details are summarized next.

7.4.1. RESTRICTIONS ON LOCATION

The data indicate that jurisdictions with restrictions on the location of key service providers (Chapter 3) have poorer performance results. Table 7.4, Panel A, indicates average monthly returns are lower by 0.003 (Model 1), MPPMs are lower by 0.002 (Model 3), and alphas are lower by 0.002 (Models 4 and 5) among jurisdictions that restrict location. These results are invariant to controls for endogeneity (Model 4 vs. Model 5). In other words, this is equivalent to a reduction in alpha by 2% per year, so the effect is not only statistically significant, but also economically large. We observe a similar effect for the sub-sample of data for 2003–2005 in Models 6, 8, 9, and 10. The results excluding fund of funds in Models 11–13 indicate monthly alphas are lower by 0.002, 0.003, and 0.005, respectively, in jurisdictions that restrict location. That is, the economic significance is largest in Model 13, where annualized alphas are lower by 6% per year.

Note that the standard deviation of monthly returns is lower by 0.005 (Model 2) and 0.004 (Model 7) for jurisdictions that restrict location, but that reduction is not sufficient to compensate for the reduction in returns, as MPPMs are lower with restrictions on location. The implication of the data is that a location restriction inefficiently constrains the human capital availed to a hedge fund, thereby leading to poorer performance. There is no net corporate governance benefit to a geographic proximity between a hedge fund's service providers and the hedge fund's regulatory body.

There is a positive and significant correlation between fixed management fees and restrictions on the location of key service providers. Fixed fees are 0.51% higher among jurisdictions that restrict location, which is economically significant given that Table 7.1 indicates the median fixed fee is 1.2% and the mean is 1.3%.[11] However, there is no statistically significant relationship between restrictions on location and performance fees.

7.4.2. MINIMUM CAPITALIZATION REQUIREMENTS

The data indicate some evidence that restrictions on minimum capitalization in a jurisdiction are associated with a reduction in the standard deviation of monthly returns. Table 7.4 confirms that an increase in required minimum capitalization for a hedge fund from US$1 to $2 million is associated with a reduction in standard deviation of monthly returns by 0.02–0.03% in Models 2 and 4.

---

[11] The economic significance for the OLS regressions in Table 7.4, Panel C, Models 14 and 15, can be calculated by transforming the regression $\ln(Y/(1-Y)) = X\beta$ to $Y = e^{X\beta}/(1 + e^{X\beta})$.

194   Hedge Fund Structure

The minimum capitalization restriction is generally insignificant in the other tables apart from its being marginally significant at the 10% level in Model 6 demonstrating that minimum capitalization lowers monthly returns for the sub-sample for 2003–2005. The economic significance is such that a raise in minimum capitalization from US$1 million to $2 million is associated with a lowering in monthly returns by 0.01% (or 0.12% per year). One limitation with regard to minimum capitalization (as indicated in Table 7.1) is that proxies are needed for some countries since the requirements are not exact. Note that minimum capitalization requirements appear binding on only a small portion of the sample (that is, some funds in countries without minimum capitalization are smaller than the minimum capitalization levels in other countries); nevertheless, it is possible that some funds face problems associated with achieving the minimum capitalization hurdle when they first start the fund.

7.4.3. PERMISSIBLE HEDGE FUND DISTRIBUTION CHANNELS

The data indicate that jurisdictions permitting distributions via wrappers show significantly lower average monthly returns by 0.002 in Model 1 and lower alphas by 0.002 in Model 4 and 0.005 in Model 13. These effects are economically large, ranging from 2.4% to 6.2% per year. This evidence is consistent with the conflicts of interest associated with wrappers, as discussed in detail in Sub-section 7.2.1. Note, however, that these effects are not robust to the restricted sample for 2003–2005 in Table 7.4, Panel B. We do observe that wrappers are also associated with lower standard deviations of monthly returns in Model 2 by 0.009, and there is no significant association between wrappers and MPPMs.

Wrapper distributions are associated with significantly higher fixed fees by 0.54% in Model 14. Also, wrapper distributions are associated with significantly lower performance fees by 0.43% in Model 15. In other words, fund managers appear able to extract higher fixed fees and require less performance based compensation when the fund is marketed in combination with other products.

There is evidence at the 10% level of significance that marketing via non-regulated financial institutions is associated with a higher standard deviation in returns in Model 2 by 0.010. That is, riskier unregulated distributions are associated with riskier actions by hedge fund managers. However, there is no significant association between non-regulated distributions and fund performance.

There is a positive relationship between fund alphas and private placements in Model 13 by 0.010 or 12.7% per year. This effect is significant regardless of inclusion or exclusion of the US sub-sample, which comprises a significant portion of the private placements. This result is consistent with the comparison tests in Table 7.2. As well, note that Models 14 and 15 demonstrate both higher fixed and higher performance fees associated with private placements and other financial institutions. Again, these results are robust to excluding the US sub-sample. The included variables for distribution channels were selected based on minimizing correlations with other variables as indicated in Table 7.3. When other distribution variables are included, the results tend to exhibit less statistical significance.

7.4.4. CONTROL VARIABLES

A number of the control variables are significant, such as legal origin variables. As in La Porta et al. (1998, 2002, 2006), a dummy variable for English legal origin is suppressed to avoid perfect collinearity. The results, however, vary depending on the time period (e.g., compare Panel A versus Panel B for German legal origin). We do not have a good explanation for these legal results. The data indicate hedge fund regulations are more consistently related to performance than legal origin.

There is evidence that hedge fund characteristics impact performance and structure. Share redemption restrictions at one year are rather consistently associated with better hedge fund performance, which can be attributed to greater flexibility in meeting liquidity requirements for investors. The relationship between performance fees and returns is not evidenced in our regressions, unlike Ackermann et al. (1999). For subsets of different fund strategies, we do see a correlation between performance fees and performance, but these sub-sets of the data do not materially affect our inferences between regulation and performance. Other variables were also considered, but not reported as they were insignificant or immaterial to the results pertaining to the regulatory variables of interest. Other specifications are available upon request.

7.5. Extensions and Future Research

This chapter introduced, for the first time, a cross-country law and financial analysis of the impact of hedge fund regulation on hedge fund performance. The data were based on 29 countries and focused on performance measures from January 1994 to December 2005, as well as January 2003 to December 2005. The data indicate that hedge fund regulations in the form of restrictions regarding the location of key service providers and marketing via wrapper distributions are negatively correlated to hedge fund performance and positively related to fixed fees. Wrapper distributions are also negatively related to performance fees.

One potential concern with the analysis of the relationship between hedge fund regulations and governance and performance relates to non-random location choice, as discussed in Section 7.4. We explicitly confirm the robustness of the results to endogeneity of forum shopping. Due to space restrictions, we exclude a number of robustness checks that are available upon request (and many of which were presented in an earlier draft). For instance, in separate regressions, we excluded onshore funds, offshore funds, and US funds from the sample. We also ran two-step regressions with Heckman-like selection effects for offshore registrants in the first step (e.g., using the treatreg function in Stata). Further, we considered excluding funds of different ages, such as excluding funds more than five years old. These regressions all produced results that were not materially different insofar as presenting hedge fund regulation impacts performance and fee structures.

A second potential concern is that tax differences for offshore versus onshore funds drive differences in performance. In specifications not presented, but available upon request, we demonstrate robustness to exclusion of offshore funds. Hence, the findings in this chapter are not likely attributable to tax differences.

A third potential concern is in respect to the robustness to alternative datasets. In this chapter, we have demonstrated robustness to different subsets of the CISDM dataset. We have considered robustness to the sub-set of onshore versus offshore funds and to the exclusion of US funds. We reported results that exclude the first 18 months of fund performance (for a possible backfilling bias). These and other robustness checks are available upon request.

Generalizations from the data are constrained to the markets and market conditions from which the data are drawn. The analyses focused on performance over 1994–2005 and over 2003–2005. It may be that hedge fund regulation plays a more favorable role on performance in times of market crashes, such as the 2008–2009 (current) financial meltdown. Hedge fund regulation may also play a more favorable role in other countries. Further research regarding other time periods and other countries is warranted. Further research could also investigate the interaction between hedge fund regulation and hedge fund activism (for US evidence, see Brav et al., 2008a,b, and Klein and Zur, 2009) and other similar forms of financial intermediation.

Finally, it is worth noting that we do not provide a normative evaluation about the desirability of regulations that give rise to lower performance measures for investors. Policy objectives may weight more heavily reductions in the standard deviation of returns than anything to do with performance, for example. Further research could assess governmental or societal objectives to appropriately consider suitable hedge fund regulations for different countries. The analysis has been confined to assessing the impact of fund regulation on risk-adjusted performance for investors and fund structure in terms of fixed and performance fees.

7.6. Concluding Remarks

This chapter empirically analyzed the impact of hedge fund regulation on fund structure and performance using a cross-country dataset of 3,782 hedge funds from 29 countries from January 1994 to December 2005. The focus of the analysis involved regulatory requirements in the form of minimum capitalization imposed on hedge fund managers, restrictions on the location of key service providers and permissible distribution channels in relation to hedge fund alphas, manipulation-proof performance measures (MPPMs), average monthly returns, fixed fees, and performance fees.

Restrictions on the location of a hedge fund's key service providers give rise to poorer performance in terms of lower MPPMs, lower alphas, lower average monthly returns, and higher fixed fees. Overall, hedge fund regulation, in terms of locational restrictions of key service providers, has hampered fund performance and distorted efficient fund compensation structures. We also found that distribution via wrappers was associated with lower performance results (albeit with some sensitivity to the time period considered), higher fixed fees, and lower performance fees, which may reflect conflicts of interest associated with the marketing and distribution of companion products. Nevertheless, we did see some evidence that distributions via wrappers, as well as minimum capital requirements and restrictions on location of key service providers, tend to be associated with lower standard deviations of returns. Hence, while hedge fund regulation tends to inhibit performance and incentive fees, it also has the potential to lower risks in the market. Therefore, the current evidence from hedge fund regulation does offer guidance for the ongoing policy debates regarding hedge fund regulation. Further research is warranted as more data and natural experiments arise with the likely upcoming changes in the regulatory environment around the world.

Keywords

7-Factor Alpha
Alpha
Backfilling Bias
Continuously Compounded Excess Return
Fixed Fees
Manipulation Proof Performance Measure

Net Asset Value
Performance Fees
Power Utility
Raw Returns
Relative Risk Aversion
Sharpe Ratio
Standard Deviation of Raw Returns
Value-Weighted Portfolio

Discussion Questions

7.1. If investors in hedge funds are aware of international differences in hedge fund regulation, how and why would regulation affect hedge fund performance?

7.2. What are the main types of hedge fund fees? How does hedge fund regulation affect fee structures?

7.3. What are the ways in which hedge fund performance can be assessed? What are the advantages and disadvantages associated with these different means of assessment?

7.4. How do hedge fund managers manipulate Sharpe ratios? How does the manipulation proof performance measure differ from a Sharpe ratio?

7.5. What are the 7 factors in the 7-factor alpha? Why are these factors potentially relevant in measuring hedge fund performance?

7.6. What types of hedge fund regulation are most pronounced for differences in fund performance: restrictions on location, distribution channels, or minimum capitalization? Why? Explain with reference to empirical evidence.

7.7 How do you expect hedge fund performance and fees will be influenced by the Dodd-Frank Act, UCITS, and AIFMD in coming years? Why?

CHAPTER 8

Hedge Fund Regulation and Misreported Returns

8.1. Introduction

The results were suspiciously smooth. Mr. Madoff barely ever suffered a down month, even in choppy markets.
  "The Madoff Affair: The Con of the Century"
  The Economist, December 18, 2008

The hedge fund industry has grown significantly in recent years. At the peak in the summer of 2008, industry estimates suggest the hedge fund market grew to more than US$2.5 trillion in assets (Ineichen and Silberstein, 2008, 16–17). Hedge funds have enjoyed comparatively scant regulation due to the fact that their investors are large institutional investors. However, growing concern over their size and ability to influence markets, combined with scandals of fraud such as the notorious Madoff affair, has led to increasing calls for hedge funds to be more heavily regulated.[1]

Hedge funds compete with each other to attract capital from institutional investors. Unlike mutual funds or pension funds, hedge funds are not required to report information publicly. Typically, funds report to a data vendor in order to attract new investors, maintain current investors, and raise capital (Fung and Hsieh, 1997, 2000, 2001, 2004; Fung et al., 2008). Fund managers have an incentive to report positive returns each month to attract investors. Recent evidence has shown that fund managers report monthly returns that are much more likely to be marginally positive than zero or marginally negative, and this evidence is best explained by the incentive to attract investors (Bollen and Pool, 2008, 2009).

In this chapter we address the issue of whether hedge fund regulation mitigates or exacerbates the tendency of fund managers to misreport returns.

---

[1] www.sec.gov/news/speech/spch111704hjg.htm. For industry perspectives on hedge fund regulation, see, for example, www.hedgeco.net/hedge-fund-regulations.htm and www.hedgefundregulation.com/.

While there have not been significant changes in regulation within a particular country to enable natural experiments on a country-by-country basis, there are nevertheless significant differences in hedge fund regulation across countries. By examining cross-country evidence on misreported returns, we can infer by holding other factors constant the impact of international differences on hedge fund regulation on the propensity to misreport returns. Further, we examine and calculate explicitly whether it pays to misreport.

The most salient differences in hedge fund regulation across countries are summarized by PriceWaterhouseCoopers (various years). There are marked international differences in permissible distribution channels, including distributions via private placements, wrappers, investment managers, fund distribution companies, banks, and other regulated and non-regulated institutional investors. One would expect different distribution channels to influence the propensity of a hedge fund manager to misreport returns when there are differences in the degree of monitoring of fund manager activities by the distributors. Some jurisdictions impose restrictions on the location of a fund's key service providers. These restrictions may influence the propensity to misreport where there are differences in governance provided by service providers. Other jurisdictions impose minimum capitalization requirements. Minimum capitalization requirements may influence the propensity of a fund manager to misreport in order to attract new investors and thereby maintain minimum requisite capital inflows.

We investigate these propositions with an international sample of hedge funds from the Center for International Securities and Derivatives Markets (CISDM) database. We find strong evidence that returns are misreported in the sense that returns are much more likely to be marginally positive than zero or marginally negative (consistent with Bollen and Pool, 2009, and Cassar and Gerakos, 2009). We extend the literature by empirically examining when hedge fund managers are more likely to misreport.

Most notably, there is a significant relation in the data between hedge fund regulation and misreporting, and the findings are robust to controls for selection effects, among other robustness checks. Returns in jurisdictions that permit distributions via wrappers are more likely to be misreported. Wrappers, by definition, are sold as tied products and appear to enable fund managers to avoid the same level of scrutiny as that provided via other distribution channels. This evidence is consistent with other work that shows wrappers have a "flatter" flow-performance relation (Cumming and Dai, 2009) and lower overall levels of performance (Cumming and Dai, 2010a). We find evidence that the sensitivity of wrappers to misreporting is stronger for funds without lockup provisions, which is intuitive as funds without a lockup risk losing capital allocations for poor performance each month and hence have a stronger incentive each month to report marginally positive as opposed to marginally negative returns. Also, we find some evidence that misreporting is less common among funds in jurisdictions with minimum capital requirements and restrictions on the location of key service providers. Minimum capitalization requirements prevent smaller, lower quality funds from entering; these funds might otherwise have had a pronounced incentive to misreport, and most jurisdictions that have minimum capitalization requirements likewise have restrictions on location. Further, we empirically show that misreporting significantly affects capital allocations. We find that wealth transfer, which is an estimate of the distorted capital allocation due to misreporting, is particularly large in jurisdictions permitting distributions via wrappers.

The evidence herein is in line with a growing literature on hedge funds returns and capital flows (Liang, 2000, 2003; Germansky, 2005; Agarwal et al., 2006, 2007; Ding et al., 2007; Hodder and Jackwerth, 2007; Teo, 2009; Bollen and Pool, 2008, 2009), as well as a growing literature on the law and finance of financial intermediaries, particularly for hedge funds (Burgstahler and Dichev, 1997; Healy and Palepu, 2001; Liang and Park, 2008; Brav et al., 2007; Brown et al., 2007; Thomas and Partnoy, 2007; Verret, 2007; Klein and Zur, 2009) and reporting quality related to accounting information (e.g., Bhattacharya et al., 2003; Ball and Shivakumar, 2005; Burgstahler et al., 2006). We add to this literature by considering how regulations from the country in which the fund is registered influence the reporting of monthly hedge fund returns.

The first part of this chapter (Section 8.2) discusses hedge fund regulation and the potential impact on misreporting returns. Section 8.3 introduces the data and provides summary statistics and comparison tests. Multivariate regressions are presented in Section 8.4. Section 8.5 reports the relation between misreporting and capital allocations. Section 8.6 discusses limitations and alternative explanations. Concluding remarks follow in Section 8.7.

8.2. Hedge Fund Misreported Returns and Regulation

In this chapter, we refer to "marginally positive" monthly hedge fund returns as those that are more likely to be "misreported returns" (i.e., it is more likely that they would otherwise have been zero or marginally negative), as fund managers have an incentive to misreport in order to attract more capital (Bollen and Pool, 2008, 2009). "Marginally positive returns" are referred to as "misreported returns" herein for ease of exposition herein. But note that marginally positive returns by themselves do not necessarily mean that the returns were in fact misreported. Rather, a series of marginally positive returns would warrant further investigation to determine whether the returns were being misreported. In practice, there is a returns discontinuity in that comparatively fewer hedge fund returns are reported as being zero or marginally negative relative to the frequency of returns reported as marginally positive (Bollen and Pool, 2009; see also Section 8.3).

In this section we conjecture that this type of returns discontinuity can be explained as a function of hedge fund regulation, as well as past performance, market returns, fund characteristics, country GDP and legal origin. The hypotheses are described immediately following. In this section we first discuss hedge fund regulation and the potential impact on misreporting behavior. Thereafter, we consider other factors that may influence the reporting of returns.

8.2.1. HEDGE FUND REGULATION

At issue in this chapter is whether the form of regulatory oversight in the countries enumerated in Table 3.1 provides an additional level of governance and an additional check that fraud is not perpetuated in the context of reporting returns. Hedge fund managers have a pronounced incentive and ability to misreport monthly returns as marginally positive in cases in which returns would otherwise be zero or marginally negative. It is comparatively more difficult to perpetually report monthly returns as positive when returns are otherwise significantly negative, as fraud would be more transparent or at least more difficult to hide. However, marginally negative returns are notably less attractive to investors and hedge fund managers have an incentive to manipulate monthly returns by reporting returns that are marginally positive when they would otherwise be zero or negative (Bollen and Pool, 2009). Hence, the focus is on the discontinuity in returns distributions from marginally negative to marginally positive levels.

If regulatory oversight in the form of minimum capitalization, restrictions on location, and restrictions on distribution channels facilitates additional value-added governance, then we would expect hedge funds in those jurisdictions to be less likely to misreport monthly returns. It is possible that minimum size restrictions eliminate lower quality funds from the market. Further, it is possible that restrictions on the location of key service providers centralize the regulatory oversight and better enable regulators to engage in surveillance of fund activities. Restrictions on distribution channels may afford superior investor protection and enable more effective regulatory oversight.

In the alternative, we may infer that restrictions on minimum capital requirements for managers increase incentives to manage earnings to maintain capital above minimum thresholds (Degeorge et al., 1999). Restrictions on the location of key service providers limit human resource choices and lower the quality of governance provided, thereby making it easier for fund managers to manipulate reported earnings each month. Further, restrictions on hedge fund distribution channels may limit the governance provided by those involved in the distribution channels. It is likely, for instance, that there is less governance provided by wrapper distributions where funds are sold in conjunction with other products (Gerstein, 2006). By contrast, investment managers and fund distribution companies might be more likely to provide active oversight and notice misreporting.

A typical hedge fund does not have any employees providing support services but instead delegates different functions to outsourced service providers of the hedge fund. Outsourcing a hedge fund's functions minimizes risks of collusion among hedge fund participants to perpetuate fraud and also mitigates liability in the event the hedge fund participants are accused of improperly performing their management duties. A hedge fund's board of directors or trustee has a fiduciary duty to the investors to ensure that all parties involved in the fund can properly carry out their designated tasks.

The most common service providers include prime brokers, administrators, and distributors. Prime brokers lend money, act as counterparty to derivative contracts, lend securities in short sales, execute trades, and provide clearing, settlement, and custody services. Administrators issue and redeem interests and shares and calculate the net asset value (NAV) of the fund. Distributors are responsible for marketing the fund to potential investors. Restrictions on location of key service providers are typically such that the presence of a local agent is required (PriceWaterhouseCoopers (PWC), various years). The local agent, however, may not be of sufficient scale and/or employ the individuals that are most suited to the effective operation, management, and governance of the fund (Wilson, 2007). Practitioners often warn against using low quality service providers; for example, "beware of the potential downside of using third-tier service providers. Furthermore, it is hard to garner the confidence of investors when you do not employ a top notch support network."[2] The recent failure of hedge funds affiliated with Lehman Brothers, Bear Sterns, and Madoff has been attributable to low quality, unreliable service providers.[3] Service providers are vitally important because they provide due diligence services for the fund, provide research on counterparty risk, and generally facilitate the execution of the fund's activities.

It is possible that misreporting by fund managers in ways that relate to regulations in a jurisdiction may vary depending on whether the fund has a lockup period for which investors are restricted from redeeming their capital contributions. Funds without a lockup risk have a pronounced incentive each month to report marginally positive as opposed to marginally negative returns due to the ongoing risk of withdrawal of capital by investors, and hence they may take advantage of distribution channels that facilitate misreporting such as wrappers.

We note that hedge funds may locate in jurisdictions other than the jurisdiction in which they are active or locate their assets. The common choice is for hedge funds to register in the jurisdiction in which they are based, or in an offshore jurisdiction. Offshore jurisdictions enable tax advantages that vary in scope and magnitude depending on the strategic focus of the fund. As well, the attractiveness of a hedge fund investment to investors for onshore versus offshore funds

---

[2] Source: www.hedgefundlaunch.com/how-to-start-a-hedge-fund-part-1/. In other non-hedge fund contexts, service providers have been shown to be very important for performance; see, for example, Butler et al., 2007).

[3] See http://richard-wilson.blogspot.com/2009/02/hedge-fund-service-provider-branding-pr.html; see also Wilson (2007).

depends on the strategic focus of the fund. In this chapter we assess the impact of offshore versus onshore funds in conjunction with the assessment of the relation between regulation and misreported returns. Likewise, we consider control for master-feeder funds and consider robustness to excluding master-feeder funds since there are cross-jurisdictional issues with regulations.[4] The various control variables considered are described in the next subsection.

8.2.2. CONTROL VARIABLES

Hedge fund returns may be misreported for reasons apart from fund regulation, and the multivariate analyses consider a variety of control variables to account for as many factors as possible. These control variables fall into the following categories: past fund performance, market returns, fund characteristics, country specific GDP per capita, and legal origin.

Past fund performance is a relevant control variable to assess fund returns because prior evidence has shown returns tend to be positively serially correlated (Getmansky et al., 2004; Baquero et al., 2005). Hence, marginally positive returns are more likely when past performance has been positive. Similarly, marginally positive returns are more likely when contemporaneous market returns have been higher (Bollen and Pool, 2009). As well, we might expect fund managers to behave differently under different market conditions. High market returns exacerbate the negative appearance of a negative fund return to a fund's potential investors and thereby increase the incentive to misreport marginally negative returns as being marginally positive.

Fund managers may simultaneously operate more than one hedge fund. Multiple funds allow fund managers to shift assets between funds to distort returns. Therefore, multiple funds better enable fund managers to misreport monthly fund returns and create marginally positive returns where they would otherwise be zero or negative. The ability to manipulate returns likewise

---

[4] Many fund managers employ a "master-feeder" structure that allow them to market a fund to both onshore and offshore investors. The manager typically set up one "master" company and two "feeders": one feeder for onshore investors and the other feeder for offshore investors. The two feeders share the same underlying asset portfolio and the investment decision is made at the master company level. If both feeders are tracked by a hedge fund database, typically they are treated as two separate funds. The master-feeder variable is used as a robustness check. Another important issue related to the "master-feeder" structure is that funds with such a structure may have different incentives to misreport monthly return than other funds without such a structure. Given that the two feeders of the master company share the same underlying asset portfolio, the fund manager may have less discretion to manipulate returns of the offshore feeder. Hence, for robustness we distinguish between funds operating as offshore feeders as part of a master-feeder structure and funds operating as stand-alone offshore funds. We identify master-feeder funds using the method in Liang and Park (2008), where if there exists both onshore and offshore funds with the same investment style managed by the same company, then these funds are identified as master-feeder funds.

depends on the strategies used by the funds; for example, some strategies such as multi-strategy funds afford greater flexibility to enable misreporting (Bollen and Pool, 2008, 2009).

A variety of other fund-specific factors also may influence misreporting behavior. For instance, funds with yearly redemptions are less liquid and investors are not free to withdraw funds when returns are negative on a month-to-month basis (Ding et al., 2007). This illiquidity may curb misreporting behavior. Fund managers who receive compensation in the form of higher performance fees may misreport more frequently. As well, because misreporting has the potential to attract more capital, fund managers who receive higher management fees (as a percentage of fund size) have a greater incentive to misreport returns (Hodder and Jackwerth, 2007). By contrast, larger funds and older funds with an established reputation might have less incentive to manipulate monthly returns as the reputation costs associated with being discovered for manipulating returns are larger.

Funds with larger minimum investment amounts may have a greater incentive to misreport returns to attract greater capital inflows. As well, it is possible that offshore funds will have a greater tendency to misreport if surveillance is less stringent, and taxation levels are significantly lower in than in onshore locations. Similarly, funds in civil law countries may be more inclined to misreport than English common law as regulatory oversight is generally weaker (La Porta et al., 1997, 1998, 2006). As in other law and finance studies relating to hedge funds (Cumming and Johan, 2007, 2008), we control for GDP per capita to separate country legal effects from differences in economic conditions. Also, in the empirical analyses we control for fund strategies and location of assets as well as calendar months with the use of numerous dummy variables.

8.3. Data

8.3.1. DATA SOURCE

In the empirical analysis, we use the Center for International Securities and Derivatives Markets (CISDM) data. CISDM has 28 different styles of hedge fund types. Of these styles, the five most common in terms of months of reported returns are multi-strategy (22.8%), equity long/short (18.2%), systematic (10.6%), single strategy (3.9%), and emerging markets (3.9%). Other useful information contained in the data is the inception date of the fund, the report date, management incentive fees, lockup period, and information regarding terms and fee structure, investment strategy, and leverage. The CISDM dataset has been used in related hedge fund studies, including but not limited to Bollen and Pool (2009).

We focus on fund flows in the sample period from January 1994 to December 2008 for funds registered in 48 countries around the world (Table 3.1). There are 8,641 hedge funds with monthly returns, assets under management, and other fund-specific information over this sample period. In an earlier version of this chapter we focused on a narrow window of 2003–2005 and 16 countries, which yielded similar results (available on request). As a robustness check, we also considered regression results below from all funds and all months in the CISDM dataset for the period 1994–2005 (the same time frame used by Bollen and Pool, 2009), and our findings were likewise very similar. Our regression results are extremely consistent for different time periods.

8.3.2. MISREPORTED HEDGE FUND RETURNS

Bollen and Pool (2009) show with the CISDM dataset over 1994–2005 that in the pooled distribution of monthly returns there seems to be a significant discontinuity around zero: marginally positive returns are much more frequently reported than zero and marginally negative ones. Bollen and Pool define marginally positive and marginally negative by minimizing the mean square error (MSE) using the Silverman (1986) approach and conclude the appropriate bin width is −0.0058 to +0.0058. In this chapter, we use this bin width as the starting point to focus the issue of what explains misreporting behavior.

We use the same CISDM dataset and focus on the years 1994–2008. We find extremely similar evidence of returns discontinuity in the histogram of returns as reported in Bollen and Pool (2009). We summarize this finding in Exhibit 8.1. The bin width −0.0058 to +0.0058 in Bollen and Pool (2009) is consistent with the returns discontinuity in the data.

Exhibit 8.1 shows a marked drop in probability of observing returns slightly below zero relative to returns slightly above zero with the sample of 543,923 monthly return observations. The objective in this chapter is to explain this monthly returns discontinuity around the levels −0.0058 to +0.0058. In the empirical analysis, we assess robustness to alternative bin widths and explicitly show the results for bin widths of −0.0048 to +0.0048 and −0.0068 to +0.0068. For each of these alternative bin widths, we define dummy variables equal to 1 for the (marginally) positive returns and dummy variables equal to zero for returns that are zero or (marginally) negative.

8.3.3. SUMMARY STATISTICS

Table 8.1 provides summary statistics for the variables in the chapter for the subsample of return observations that fall within −0.0058 to +0.0058. The average of the marginally positive returns dummy is 0.612, which means on the selected range (−0.0058, 0.0058) there were 61.2% return observations reported as marginally positive. On average, the monthly fund return with one month lag is 0.4%, while the average monthly return of the concurrent S&P 500 is 0.2%. Minimum capitalization ranges from $0 to $7.9 million. Among the funds in the sample, 55.5% are domiciled in a jurisdiction that restricts the location of key service providers, while 94.6% are through private placements, 42.7% are

Panel A. Bin width 0.0048

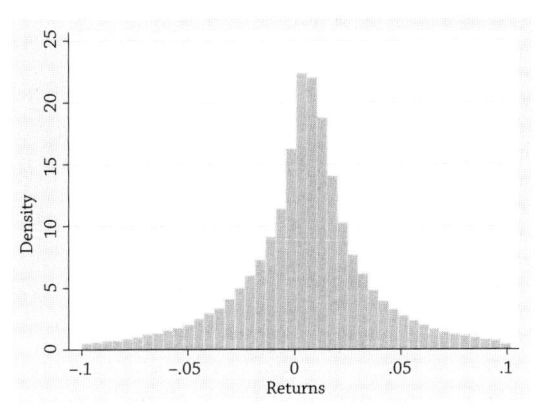

Panel B. Bin width 0.0058

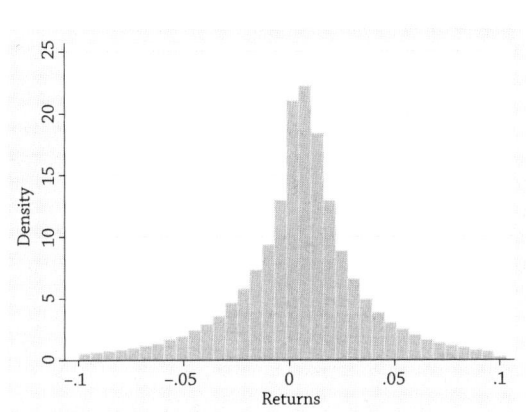

Panel C. Bin width 0.0068

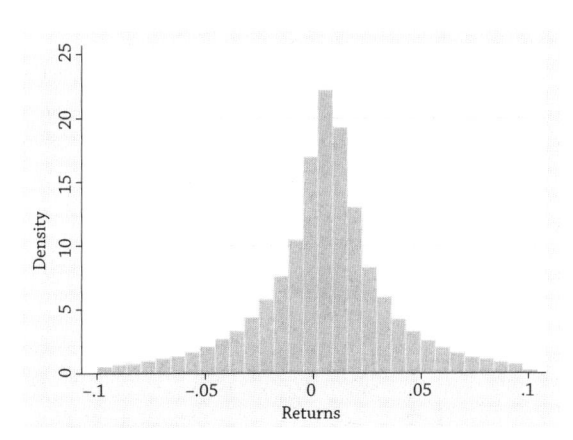

Exhibit 8.1. Discontinuity in Monthly Hedge Fund Returns around Zero

Exhibit 8.1 displays histograms of raw monthly returns for sample funds from CISDM. The number of observations is 24,786. Tails are omitted past 0.1 in order to highlight differences in marginally positive and marginally negative returns around zero.

Table 8.1. **Definition of Variables and Summary Statistics**

Variable	Definition	Mean	Median	Standard Deviation	Minimum	Maximum
Fund Performance						
Marginally Positive Return Dummy	A dummy variable equal to 1 for funds with monthly returns between 0 and 0.0058 and equal to zero for returns between −0.0058 and 0. This cutoff is selected based on Bollen and Pool (2009). (The sensitivity of this dummy variable to specifications at the 0.0048 and 0.0068 cutoff points is assessed in the regressions.)	0.612	1	0.487	0	1
Return Lagged 1 Month	Raw Monthly Return with One-Month Lag	0.004	0.004	0.041	−0.650	9.034
Return on S&P 500	Raw Monthly Return on S&P 500, a proxy for the market return	0.002	0.009	0.043	−0.168	0.097
Fund Regulation						
Minimum Capitalization	The minimum capitalization required to operate as a hedge fund manager in 2004 US$	$267,991	$45,517	$649,787	$0	$7,900,000
Restrictions on Location of Key Service Providers	A dummy variable equal to 1 where the country imposes restrictions on the location of key service providers.	0.555	1	0.497	0	1

Marketing Investment Manager Dummy	A dummy variable equal to 1 where the country allows fund distribution via investment managers	0.427	0	0.495	1
Marketing Funds Distribution Company Dummy	A dummy variable equal to 1 where the country allows fund distribution via fund distribution companies	0.068	0	0.252	1
Marketing Bank	A dummy variable equal to 1 where the country allows fund distribution via banks	0.592	1	0.491	1
Marketing via Wrappers Dummy	A dummy variable equal to 1 where the country allows fund distribution via wrappers	0.071	0	0.256	1
Marketing via Private Placements Dummy	A dummy variable equal to 1 where the country allows fund distribution via private placements	0.946	1	0.226	1
Marketing via Private Other Regulated Intermediary	A dummy variable equal to 1 where the country allows fund distribution via other regulated financial intermediary	0.121	0	0.327	1
Marketing via Non-Regulated Intermediary	A dummy variable equal to 1 where the country allows fund distribution via non-regulated financial intermediary	0.019	0	0.137	1
Fund Characteristics					
Fund Manager with Multiple Funds	A dummy variable equal to 1 if the fund is run by a fund manager running 2 or more funds	0.434	0	0.496	1

(Continued)

Table 8.1 (Continued)

Variable	Definition	Mean	Median	Standard Deviation	Minimum	Maximum
Yearly Redemption	A dummy variable equal to 1 if capital redemptions are possible only on an annual basis	0.053	0	0.225	0	1
Management Fee	The fixed fee in percentages for management compensation	1.440	1.500	0.709	0	15
Performance Fee	The carried interest performance fee in percentages for management compensation	15.400	20	6.890	0	50
Assets under Management	The fund's assets in 2004 US$	$335,079,058	$43,142,485	$2,397,239,470	$0	$86,553,523,384
Minimum Investment	The minimum investment required for the fund in 2004 US$	$2,603,486	$250,000	$73,932,392	$0	$5,000,000,000
Age	The fund's age in months from the date of formation to return report date	67.050	53.700	49.580	0	1314.830
Fund of Funds	A dummy variable equal to 1 if the fund is a fund of funds	0.349	0	0.477	0	1
Master-Feeder	A dummy variable equal to 1 if the fund is a master-feeder fund (an investment vehicle that pools its portfolio within another vehicle)	0.276	0	0.447	0	1

Lockup	A dummy variable equal to 1 if the fund has a lockup provision	0.412	0	0.492	1
Offshore	A dummy variable equal to 1 for offshore funds	0.438	0	0.496	1
Country GNP and Legal Origin					
GNP Per Capita	The country's GNP per capita, expressed in 2004 US	$38,653	$40,100	$9,186	$213,000

This table defines the main variables used in the chapter. Summary statistics are also provided for each variable. The data comprise 8,690 funds from 48 countries (Table 3.1) for the period January 1994– December 2008. In this table, fund returns outside the range of (−0.0058, 0.0058) are excluded.

associated with a distribution channel via investment managers, 6.8% via fund distribution companies, 59.2% through banks, 12.1% through other regulated financial intermediaries, 1.9% through non-regulated financial intermediaries, and 7.1% via wrappers.[5] It is notable that 43.4% of the observed returns are of funds that are operated by managers who simultaneously manage more than one fund. Only 5.3% of the observations are from funds that have annual capital redemptions. The median of management fee is 1.5%, while the median of carried-interest incentive fee is 20%. The assets under management of the funds range from $0 (funds that became defunct) to $86.6 billion, with an average of $335.1 million. Slightly more than half (56.2%) are onshore funds and the median age of funds is 54 months. These summary statistics are consistent with those reported in other hedge fund datasets. Note in our statistical and regression analyses we control for backfilling of returns by excluding the first 18 fund months from the sample since funds have a tendency to first report to data vendors once they have shown better performance.

Table 8.2 reports the results for comparison tests for proportions of marginally positive returns for the observations where returns are reported as marginally positive versus observations that were reported as zero or marginally negative. The comparison tests in Table 8.2 indicate that misreporting is less common among funds in jurisdictions with minimum capitalization requirements and restrictions on the location of key service providers. Marginally positive returns are more likely to be reported by funds registered in jurisdictions that prohibit banks, investment managers, and other regulated and non-regulated financial institutions distributions. Furthermore, funds in jurisdictions that permit distributions via fund distribution companies and wrappers are significantly more likely to misreport.

Table 8.3 reports the correlation coefficients for the main regulation variables of interest. Data in this table indicate that some of the explanatory variables of interest are highly significantly correlated, including minimum capitalization, restrictions on location of key service providers, and some of the distribution channels. In the next section we report the regression results with alternative sets of explanatory variables and assess robustness by excluding variables that are significantly correlated. The findings are robust to inclusion/exclusion of different right-hand-side variables. Details are discussed in the following section.

8.4. Regression Analyses

8.4.1. MODEL SPECIFICATIONS

In this section we report logit estimates of the probability that returns are reported as marginally positive, as opposed to zero or negative. We explicitly

---

[5] Oftentimes, multiple distribution channels are allowed in a specific jurisdiction. Therefore these statistics do not add up to 100%.

Table 8.2. **Comparison of Proportions of Marginally Positive Returns by Regulation**

	No Minimum Capitalization	Minimum Capitalization>0	Difference Tests
Proportion of Marginally Positive Returns (0, 0.0048)	60.62%	60.00%	0.070*
Proportion of Marginally Positive Returns (0, 0.0058)	61.62%	60.35%	0.024**
Proportion of Marginally Positive Returns (0, 0.0068)	62.31%	61.54%	0.007***
	No Private Placements	*Private Placements*	*Difference Tests*
Proportion of Marginally Positive Returns (0, 0.0048)	59.47%	60.77%	0.104
Proportion of Marginally Positive Returns (0, 0.0058)	61.00%	62.85%	0.246
Proportion of Marginally Positive Returns (0, 0.0068)	61.93%	62.55%	0.364
	No Bank Distributions	*Bank Distributions*	*Difference Tests*
Proportion of Marginally Positive Returns (0, 0.0048)	61.64%	60.06%	0.000***
Proportion of Marginally Positive Returns (0, 0.0058)	62.45%	61.36%	0.001***
Proportion of Marginally Positive Returns (0, 0.0068)	63.04%	62.15%	0.004***
	No Fund Distribution Company Distributions	*Fund Distribution Company Distributions*	*Difference Tests*
Proportion of Marginally Positive Returns (0, 0.0048)	60.61%	62.00%	0.051*
Proportion of Marginally Positive Returns (0, 0.0058)	61.70%	63.29%	0.014**
Proportion of Marginally Positive Returns (0, 0.0068)	62.43%	63.62%	0.049**

(Continued)

Table 8.2. *(Continued)*

	No Investment Manager Distributions	*Investment Manager Distributions*	*Difference Tests*
Proportion of Marginally Positive Returns (0, 0.0048)	61.14%	60.12%	0.006***
Proportion of Marginally Positive Returns (0, 0.0058)	62.14%	61.36%	0.019**
Proportion of Marginally Positive Returns (0, 0.0068)	62.93%	61.95%	0.001***

	No Wrapper Distributions	*Wrapper Distributions*	*Difference Tests*
Proportion of Marginally Positive Returns (0, 0.0048)	60.63%	61.69%	0.133
Proportion of Marginally Positive Returns (0, 0.0058)	61.70%	63.06%	0.036**
Proportion of Marginally Positive Returns (0, 0.0068)	62.44%	63.52%	0.069*

	No Other Regulated Financial Intermediary Distributions	*Other Regulated Financial Intermediary Distributions*	*Difference Tests*
Proportion of Marginally Positive Returns (0, 0.0048)	61.03%	58.31%	0.000***
Proportion of Marginally Positive Returns (0, 0.0058)	62.04%	60.07%	0.000***
Proportion of Marginally Positive Returns (0, 0.0068)	62.70%	61.18%	0.001***

	No Other Non-Regulated Financial Intermediary Distributions	*Other Non-Regulated Financial Intermediary Distributions*	*Difference Tests*
Proportion of Marginally Positive Returns (0, 0.0048)	60.78%	56.50%	0.001***
Proportion of Marginally Positive Returns (0, 0.0058)	61.86%	58.96%	0.016**
Proportion of Marginally Positive Returns (0, 0.0068)	62.54%	60.98%	0.160

Table 8.2. (Continued)

	No Restrictions on Location	Restrictions on Location	Difference Tests
Proportion of Marginally Positive Returns (0, 0.0048)	61.14%	60.35%	0.031**
Proportion of Marginally Positive Returns (0, 0.0058)	62.17%	61.51%	0.048**
Proportion of Marginally Positive Returns (0, 0.0068)	62.93%	62.18%	0.015**

This table presents the proportions of marginally positive returns in the subsamples of observations for which returns fall within the range −0.0048 to 0.0048, −0.0058 to 0.0058, and −0.0068 to 0.0068, respectively. The p-values for the differences in proportions are reported in the last column *, **, *** Significant at the 10%, 5%, and 1% level, respectively.

report six alternative models in Table 8.4 to assess robustness and discuss the results from other regressions considered but not explicitly reported. The first three models use a dependent variable as a dummy variable equal to 1 for positive returns between 0 and 0.0068 and zero for returns from −0.0068 and up to and equal to 0. The fourth model considers a bin width of 0.0048, while the fourth and fifth models consider a bin width of 0.0058. The 0.0058 level is the middle level reported for the regressions based on the summary statistics showing return discontinuity at that level and based on the prior work of Bollen and Pool (2009).

The explanatory variables in Table 8.4 include past performance, hedge fund regulations, fund characteristics, and country-specific GDP per capita and legal origin. The specific variables were defined in Table 8.1. Model 1 reports the 0.0068 cutoff for the subsample of funds, which gives the largest number of observations in the sample and focuses on a single hedge fund regulation variable for wrappers.[6] Model 2 adds additional explanatory dummy variables for different regulations, and Model 3 excludes master-feeder funds. Model 4 assesses the cutoff at 0.0048, while Models 5 and 6 assess the 0.0058 cutoff. Models 5 and 6 present the subsample of funds with a lockup. Model 6 considers a two-step model to account for selection effects associated with the non-random probability of returns being either marginally positive or negative (analogous to a Heckman, 1976, 1979,

---

[6] For Model 1 in Table 8.4 we present marginal effects to highlight economic significance, as well as variance inflation factors (VIFs) for the companion linear model (VIFs are technically not defined for logit models). As a general rule of thumb, VIFs above 5 present reasons to be very concerned with collinearity biasing the parameter estimate (some researchers use a more stringent cutoff for VIFs at 4). We do not present the VIFs for all coefficients for all six models, but we do show the average VIF for all models. Likewise, we present the Akaike Information Statistic (AIC) for all models.

Table 8.3. **Correlation Matrix**

	(1)	(2)	(3)	(4)	(5)	(6)	(7)	(8)	(9)	(10)
Fund Regulation										
(1) Log Minimum Capitalization	1.00									
(2) Restrictions on Location of Key Service Providers	0.69	1.00								
(3) Marketing via Wrappers	0.15	−0.14	1.00							
(4) Marketing via Banks	0.75	0.76	0.05	1.00						
(5) Marketing via Private Placements	−0.19	0.18	−0.12	−0.17	1.00					
(6) Marketing via Fund Distribution Companies	0.15	−0.13	0.96	0.06	−0.10	1.00				
(7) Marketing via Investment Managers	0.43	0.57	0.32	0.53	0.10	0.31	1.00			
(8) Marketing via Other Regulated financial Intermediaries	0.24	−0.13	0.46	0.30	−0.60	0.48	0.03	1.00		
(9) Marketing via Non-Regulated Financial Intermediaries	0.08	−0.14	0.49	0.12	0.02	0.50	0.16	0.37	1.00	
Country GNP and Legal Origin										
(10) Log GNP Per Capita	−0.14	−0.24	−0.08	0.07	−0.22	−0.07	−0.04	0.18	0.05	1.00
(11) English Legal Origin	−0.18	0.21	−0.31	−0.03	0.74	−0.32	0.06	−0.51	−0.02	−0.01

This table presents correlations across the hedge fund regulation and other country-level variables defined in Table 8.1. Correlations greater than 0.02 are statistically significant at the 5% level.

correction, but for a probit model binary dependent variable in the second step; see Greene, 2003). We do not use the traditional Heckman approach, but use a modified selection effect approach that is consistent with that in other hedge fund work (e.g., Baquero et al., 2005). Similarly, in an earlier version of this chapter we considered a two-step estimation whereby in the first step we considered the probability of registering offshore as a function of hedge fund strategies, the location of assets, and whether the fund manager managed more than one fund. We had considered alternative specifications that are not explicitly reported but available upon request.[7] The results presented in Table 8.4 highlight the main patterns observed in the data.

8.4.2. RESULTS

The evidence in Table 8.4 shows a strong impact of hedge fund regulation on the likelihood of observing (misreported) marginally positive returns. Most notably, permissible wrapper distributions exacerbate the likelihood of misreporting. This effect is statistically significant at the 10% level in Models 1, 3, and 6, at the 5% level in Models 2 and 5. The economic significance is such that wrapper distributions increase the likelihood of misreporting by 2.9% each month (Model 1). In Model 4, the economic significance is such that wrappers increase the propensity to misreport by 4.1% (this higher economic significance is largely due to exclusion of funds with lockups, even with the narrower bin width of the dependent variable). This higher economic significance is best attributed to the fact that funds without a lockup face an ongoing concern that investors will withdraw capital, and hence funds in jurisdictions that permit wrappers can take advantage of this distribution channel. Overall, this is very strong evidence that wrappers give rise to a greater propensity to misreport monthly returns. Wrappers weaken oversight from investors and hence reduce governance provided by investors. Similarly, it is noteworthy that there is consistent evidence showing that wrappers have a less sensitive flow-performance relation (Cumming and Dai, 2009) and lower returns on average (Cumming and Dai, 2010a).

Most of the other regulatory variables are statistically insignificant in the sample,[8] with a couple of exceptions. Model 4 shows that funds in jurisdictions that have restrictions on location are less likely to misreport, while Model 5 shows that funds with higher minimum capitalization are less likely to misreport. Note that in Models 2 and 3, if the bank variable is excluded, then minimum

---

[7] For example, we considered different sub-samples based on fund age to assess the possibility of survivorship bias, as well as different sub-samples with different countries. We also considered multi-step models that first considered the probability of setting up a fund with a certain structure. The results are quite robust.

[8] We do note that in an earlier version of this chapter (covering a shorter horizon between 2003 and 2005) we found that funds in jurisdictions that restricted location had a greater tendency to misreport; however, this effect is not observed in this extended sample.

Table 8.4. Regression Analyses of Marginally Positive Returns

	Model 1: Bin width 0.0068				Model 2: Bin Width 0.0068, Extra Explanatory Variables		Model 3: Bin Width 0.0068, Extra Explanatory Variables, No Master-Feeder		Model 4: Bin Width 0.0048		Model 5: No Funds with a Lockup, Bin Width 0.0058		Model 6: Bin width 0.0058, No funds with a Lockup			
													Step 1: Determinants of Returns within -0.0058 to +0.0058		Step 2: Determinants of Marginally Positive Returns	
	Coefficient	t-statistic	Marginal Effect	VIF	Coefficient	t-statistic	Coefficient	t-statistic	Coefficient	t-statistic	Coefficient	t-statistic	Coefficient	t-statistic	Coefficient	t-statistic
Constant	-0.384	-0.57			-0.420	-0.56	0.346	1.59	0.415	0.48	0.656	0.75	0.820	4.03***	0.447	0.96
Fund Performance																
Return Lagged 1 Month	2.300	4.71***	0.539	1.02	2.297	4.70***	0.470	3.41***	0.985	1.71*	1.716	2.51**	-0.562	-4.08***	1.137	3.09***
S&P 500	0.039	9.96***	0.009	1.08	0.039	9.96***	0.008	7.20***	0.022	4.76***	0.036	6.73***	0.003	1.83*	0.018	2.50**
Fund Regulation																
Log Minimum Capitalization					-0.006	-1.12	-0.001	-0.76	-0.004	-0.60	-0.009	-1.69*			-0.005	-1.56
Marketing via Wrappers	0.125	1.90*	0.029	1.24	0.154	2.16**	0.035	1.92*			0.173	2.11**			0.091	1.80*
Marketing via Banks					-0.104	-1.52	-0.024	-1.23								
Marketing via Private Placements					-0.071	-0.52	-0.023	-0.63			-0.024	-0.16			-0.014	-0.17
Marketing via Fund Distribution Companies									0.125	0.99						
Marketing via Investment Managers									-0.021	-0.38						

Marketing via Other Regulated financial Intermediaries								−0.106	−1.10				
Marketing via Non-Regulated Financial Intermediaries								−0.248	−1.41				
Restrictions on Location of Key Service Providers								−0.215	−1.97**				
Fund Characteristics													
Log Assets under Management	0.041	5.07***	0.010	1.13	0.044	5.39***	0.009	3.86***	0.046	4.92***	0.032	2.95***	0.023	6.80***	0.006	0.44
Yearly Redemption	−0.056	−0.88	−0.013	1.12	−0.064	−1.01	−0.034	−1.74*	−0.028	−0.36	0.129	0.84			0.069	0.83
Log Minimum Investment	−0.006	−1.07	−0.001	1.17	−0.006	−1.03	0.000	0.28	−0.011	−1.47	0.001	0.11			0.000	0.1
Performance Fee	0.005	1.87*	0.001	1.82	0.005	1.90*	0.001	1.10	0.005	1.57	0.004	0.92	−0.010	−7.78***	0.006	1.84*
Management Fee	0.004	0.14	0.001	1.2	0.008	0.27	−0.001	−0.08	−0.007	−0.19	0.042	1.06	−0.102	−9.29***	0.070	1.92*
Log Age	−0.034	−1.67*	−0.008	1.14	−0.039	−1.93*	−0.006	−0.94	−0.038	−1.55	−0.006	−0.21	−0.014	−1.61	0.003	0.21
Fund Manager with Multiple Funds	0.020	0.63	0.005	1.08	0.009	0.30	−0.017	−1.89*	0.013	0.35	0.006	0.12			0.004	0.16
Fund of Funds	−0.013	−0.25	−0.003	3.35	−0.016	−0.30	0.008	0.56	−0.115	−1.86*	−0.097	−1.22	0.038	1.57	−0.067	−1.54
Master-Feeder	0.004	0.13	0.001	1.13	−0.001	−0.03			−0.029	−0.82	0.037	0.83	−0.011	−0.84	0.025	1.05
Lockup	0.090	2.84***	0.021	1.3	0.079	2.46**	0.028	2.94***	0.075	1.97**						
Offshore	0.067	2.19**	0.016	1.25	0.213	3.48***	0.066	3.92***	0.316	3.27***	0.217	3.16***	0.044	3.31**	0.093	1.6
Fund Strategy Dummies?	Yes		Yes		Yes		Yes		Yes		Yes		Yes			

(Continued)

Table 8.4. (Continued)

	Model 1: Bin width 0.0068				Model 2: Bin Width 0.0068, Extra Explanatory Variables		Model 3: Bin Width 0.0068, Extra Explanatory Variables, No Master-Feeder		Model 4: Bin Width 0.0048		Model 5: No Funds with a Lockup, Bin Width 0.0058		Model 6: Bin width 0.0058, No funds with a Lockup			
													Step 1: Determinants of Returns within −0.0058 to +0.0058		Step 2: Determinants of Marginally Positive Returns	
	Coefficient	t-statistic	Marginal Effect	VIF	Coefficient	t-statistic	Coefficient	t-statistic	Coefficient	t-statistic	Coefficient	t-statistic	Coefficient	t-statistic	Coefficient	t-statistic
Month of Reporting Dummies?	Yes				Yes		Yes		Yes		Yes		Yes		Yes	
Country GNP and Legal Origin																
Log GNP Per Capita	0.026	0.42	0.006	1.12	0.037	0.55	0.013	0.69	−0.051	−0.64	−0.074	−0.95	−0.173	−9.40***	0.037	0.49
English Legal Origin	−0.045	−0.66	−0.010	1.31	−0.069	−0.69	−0.008	−0.26	−0.080	−0.81	−0.121	−1.00	0.061	2.65***	−0.091	−1.41
Model Diagnostics																
Number of Observations	23110				23110		14265		16123		11311		50026		11312	
AIC	30135.34				30133.33		18746.52		21429.03		15005.61		72092.48			
Chi-Square	598.48***				606.49***		368.73***		356.97***		287.39***		263.70***			
Loglikelihood	−15024.67				−15020.67		−9328.26		−10667.52		−7460.80		−35965.24			
Pseudo R2	0.02				0.02		0.02		0.02		0.02		0.02			
Mean (Linear) VIF	1.33				1.70		1.70		1.94		1.52		1.52			

This table presents logit regression analyses of the determinants of marginally positive monthly returns. Model 1 presents a base model with just the wrapper regulation variable to show results without potential collinearity. Model 2 includes extra regulation variables, while Model 3 excludes master-feeder funds. Models 4–6 consider the narrower bin widths as graphically illustrated in Exhibit 8.1. Models 5 and 6 exclude funds with a lockup. Model 6 presents a two-step Heckman conditional probit model where the first step considers whether the returns are in the marginally positive or marginally negative range, and then the second step regression is conditional on the first step. Variables are as defined in Table 8.1. Dummy variables are included in all models for the calendar months and the funds' primary strategy. *, **, *** indicates significance at the 10%, 5%, and 1% levels, respectively.

capitalization is significant at the 5% level (conversely, if minimum capitalization is excluded and banks included, the bank variable is negative and significant), and the other variables such as the wrapper variable are not materially different from what is shown in Table 8.4. Bank distributions and minimum capitalization are highly positively correlated (Table 8.3). Also, recall from Table 8.3 that there is a strong positive correlation between funds' minimum capitalization and restrictions on location, and as such it is difficult to include those variables in the same regression. These correlations give rise to alternative explanations: one interpretation of the results is that minimum capitalization restricts smaller funds with pronounced incentives to misreport. Another interpretation is that restrictions on location provide more oversight on reported returns from one month to the next; as such, managers are less likely to misreport.

In terms of the control variables in Table 8.4, it is noteworthy that misreporting is more likely among funds that have higher performance fees in Models 1, 2, and 6 (an increase in performance fees by 10% increases the probability of misreporting by 1%). Marginally positive returns are more likely when the return of the prior month is higher and when the S&P return is higher. A fund manager should have higher incentive to misreport returns when the market return is higher. The S&P 500 return may not be an appropriate benchmark depending on the investment style of the fund. Hence, as a further robustness check, we considered as a benchmark the average return of all hedge funds with the same investment style during the reporting month. Regardless, the main results of the regressions are consistent with either control.

Many of the other controls further indicate that positive monthly returns are not random. The data indicate misreporting is roughly 1.6% more common among offshore funds. Also, in terms of the monthly dummy variables, there is more pronounced misreporting in December by 6.1% (relative to January, and this effect is largest in December). Further, misreporting is 2.1% more common among funds that have a lockup. (Note that this latter result is a level effect, which is different from the issue of the size of the marginal effect (slope) noted above with wrappers.)

Finally, note as well that the data in Table 8.4 indicate that misreporting is less common among older funds in Models 1 and 2, and the effect of age is diminishing (modeled with logs): a fund that has been operating 20 years is 0.2% less likely to misreport than one that has been operating 10 years, while a fund that has been operating 10 years is 0.8% less likely to misreport than one that has been operating one year.[9] We also find evidence that larger funds are more likely to misreport, although this effect is not robust in Model 6 accounting for selection effects. The size effect is not due to collinearity with age (the correlation is 0.13). One explanation for this size effect is that larger funds have greater ability to

---

[9] Note as well that we do not include the first 18 months of data from any fund due to backfilling bias (funds first report to databases once they start showing strong performance).

smooth returns from more diverse investments. We note as well that in an earlier version of the chapter with a shorter time span we found evidence that fund managers who operated multiple funds were more likely to misreport, but that evidence is not observed in our extended sample presented here.

In sum, the evidence supports the view that distributions via wrappers offer weaker governance channels without monitoring discipline on hedge fund managers such that they may misreport monthly returns. This effect is more pronounced for funds that do not have a lockup where fund managers try to attract more capital and face concerns that capital may be freely taken out of the fund. Further, there is some evidence that minimum capitalization and restrictions on location of key service providers mitigate misreporting, but due to correlations across those variables it was more difficult to isolate the source of these effects.

8.5. Does Misreporting Pay?

To examine the economic significance of the regulatory impact on hedge fund misreported return, we estimated the distorted fund inflows or wealth transfer due to misreported returns under each regulatory regime. We borrowed the method used in Bollen and Pool (2009) to calculate wealth transfer for each misreporting fund. Specifically, we computed the percentage of returns in two 58-basis point bins bracketing zero for each fund. Funds with more small positives than small negatives are labeled "misreporting funds"; all other funds are labeled "non-misreporting funds." For misreporting funds, we then computed the difference between the actual cost incoming shareholders pay to obtain fund shares and the hypothetical fair cost if the returns were not misreported each month. The formula is as follows:

$$W_{it} = \frac{F_{i,t}}{NAV_{i,t}^R}(NAV_{i,t}^R - NAV_{i,t}^T)$$

where $F_{i,t}$ is fund inflow, $NAV_{i,t}^R$ is the actual net asset value, and $NAV_{i,t}^T$ is the hypothetical net asset value if the fund did not misreport the return. We assumed the true return was zero, then $NAV_{i,t}^T$ is equal to the actual net asset value of the fund in the previous month $NAV_{i,t-1}^R$. The advantage of this proxy is that we do not lose any observation. Furthermore, it provides a conservative estimate on the amount of wealth transfer due to misreported returns (which should be a larger number if the true return is negative).[10]

---

[10] We also conducted an assessment with the two methods used in Bollen and Pool (2009) that randomly draw negative returns from the fund's own past and its matched non-misreporting fund history as proxies for the true return. Many missing values were generated following either method. However, the general conclusion was the same as that reached with our method.

We reported both the aggregate amount and average amount of wealth transfer of misreporting funds conditional on regulation differences in Table 8.5. The amount of wealth transfer due to misreporting is certainly non-trivial, consistent with Bollen and Pool (2009). Furthermore, we found the impact of regulation on hedge fund misreported return was economically significant. For instance, the average amount of wealth transfer of misreporting funds in jurisdictions that permit banks and investment managers distributions, but prohibit distributions via wrappers and fund distribution companies was US$57,375, while the average wealth transfer of funds in jurisdictions that permit all the four distribution channels was US$736,597, more than 10 times the former.

8.6. Limitations and Alternative Explanations

Bollen and Pool (2009) noted that the pooled distribution of hedge fund returns may be due to (1) the skill of the manager to avoid losses, (2) non-linearities in underlying assets and strategies, or (3) database biases such as survivorship biases and backfilling. In effect, marginally positive returns are suspect of misreported returns. But one reason to interpret marginally positive returns as being misreported returns in conjunction with hedge fund regulation is that there is no economic reason for hedge fund regulation to be associated with managerial skill to avoid losses. On the contrary, Cumming and Dai (2010a) found that restrictions on location, minimum capitalization, and wrapper distributions were associated with lower skill and not higher skill in terms of numerous proxies for returns and performance measurement. A second reason is that our findings are robust to controlling for different asset strategies as well as subsets of the data for different asset classes. A third reason is that we have eliminated the first 18 months of data to avoid the possibility of backfilling bias (and our results are robust to controlling for or not controlling for the possibility of backfilling bias).

Overall, therefore, while the evidence is open to alternative interpretations, we do believe we have provided the most plausible interpretation of the data. We do hope that additional data and other regulations could be examined in further work as other regulatory changes appear across countries and more natural experiments are available for empirical scrutiny.

8.7. Conclusion

This chapter introduced a cross-country law and finance analysis of the impact of hedge funds on the reporting of returns. Consistent with Bollen and Pool (2009), we showed in Exhibit 8.1 of this chapter that the distribution of hedge fund returns close to zero is discontinuous. Hedge fund managers have an incentive

Table 8.5. **Wealth Transfer from Misreporting**

	Number of Funds	Aggregate Wealth Transfer	Wealth Transfer per Fund
Location			
Location Restriction	1658	$240,904,712	$145,298
No Location Restriction	991	$155,559,926	$156,973
Minimum Capitalization			
No Minimum Capitalization	941	$115,236,633	$122,462
(0,150000]	277	$24,008,367	$86,673
(150000,300000]	153	$59,719,949	$390,326
>300000	1365	$197,499,688	$144,688
Distribution Channel			
Private Placements Only	721	$84,747,775	$117,542
Private Placements/Banks	533	$88,593,695	$166,217
Private Placements/Investment Managers	69	$3,958,880	$57,375
Private Placements/Wrappers/Investment Managers/Fund Distribution Companies	44	$32,410,267	$736,597
Private Placements/Banks/Investment Managers	1140	$131,384,504	$115,250
Private Placements/Banks/Investment Managers/Other Regulated Financial Intermediation	47	$3,267,096	$69,513
Private Placements/Banks/Other Regulated Financial Intermediation	81	$8,173,548	$100,908
Private Placements/Banks/Investment Managers/Wrappers/Fund Distribution Companies/Other Regulated Financial Intermediations	107	$7,579,917	$70,840
Banks/Other Regulated Financial Intermediations	130	$27,552,510	$211,942

Table 8.5 (Continued)

	Number of Funds	Aggregate Wealth Transfer	Wealth Transfer per Fund
Distribution Channel			
Banks/Wrappers/investment Managers/Fund Distribution Companies/Other Regulated Financial Service Companies	31	$2,591,368	$83,593
Private Placements/Banks/ Investment Managers/ Wrappers/Fund Distribution Companies/Other Regulated Financial Intermediations/ Non-Regulated Financial Intermediations	75	$5,520,933	$73,612

This table presents the estimated wealth transfer of misreporting funds due to misreported returns under each regulatory regime. We estimated wealth transfer as $W_{it} = \frac{F_{i,t}}{NAV_{i,t}^R}(NAV_{i,t}^R - NAV_{i,t}^T)$, where $F_{i,t}$ is fund inflow, $NAV_{i,t}^R$ is the actual net asset value, and $NAV_{i,t}^T$ is the hypothetical net asset value if the fund did not misreport the return. We assumed the true return is zero, then $NAV_{i,t}^T$ is equal to the actual net asset value of the fund in the previous month $NAV_{i,t-1}^R$.

to misreport monthly returns that are zero or marginally negative returns as being marginally positive in order to attract investors and new investment.

We extended the literature in this chapter by analyzing when hedge fund returns are more likely to engage in this type of misreporting behavior. We found that hedge fund regulation plays a significant role in misreporting. Notably, we found that jurisdictions that permit wrapper distributions have a significantly higher propensity of misreporting. The positive association between wrappers and misreporting is stronger for funds that likewise do not have lockups, which is best explained by the fact that they face an ongoing possibility of investor capital withdrawals and have incentives to show positive returns each month.

In this chapter we also showed that misreporting influences capital flows, and we calculated the distorted capital allocation due to misreporting, or wealth transfer, associated with hedge fund regulations. We showed that restrictions on locations of key service providers increase distorted capital flows due to misreporting by funds with a lockup. For funds without a lockup, wealth transfer is mitigated by minimum capitalization requirements, while wrapper distributions exacerbated the wealth transfer.

The evidence in this chapter is consistent across a wide variety of robustness checks. Also, it is consistent with companion evidence that shows a relation between hedge fund regulation and performance, structure, and capital flows

(Cumming and Dai, 2009, 2010a). The evidence provides clear implications for guiding the ongoing policy debate on the efficient design of hedge fund regulations. Further research could investigate other aspects of hedge fund reporting, monitoring, and regulatory oversight.

Keywords

Assets under Management
Fund of Funds
Fund Manager with Multiple Funds
Illiquidity
Lockup Provision
Management Fee
Marginally Positive Returns
Marginally Negative Returns
Master-Feeder Funds
Minimum Capitalization
Misreported Returns
Misreporting Funds
Offshore Funds
Performance Fee
Restrictions on Distribution Channels
Restrictions on Location
Return Discontinuity
Wrappers
Yearly Redemption

Discussion Questions

1. What is misreporting? How can one empirically detect misreported returns?
2. What are the motivations of hedge fund managers to misreport returns? How does this agency problem potentially hurt benefits of hedge fund investors?
3. How do regulations such as minimum capitalization, restrictions on location, and restrictions on distribution channels affect misreporting behavior of hedge funds?
4. How are various fund characteristics (size, strategy, fund manager compensation, etc.) related to the misreporting behavior of hedge funds?
5. How does misreporting affect capital allocation? Discuss potential wealth transfer due to misreporting by hedge fund managers.
6. How do you think regulations such as the Dodd-Frank Act, UCITS, and AIFMD will affect hedge fund misreporting in the future?

CHAPTER 9

Regulatory Induced Performance Persistence

9.1. Introduction

> Hedge funds are concerned that compliance with reporting regulations proposed by the U.S. futures regulator last week will require too much time and money, creating an unnecessary cost burden for the industry.
>
> *Reuters,* January 31, 2011

This chapter examines the role of financial regulation on performance persistence in financial intermediaries. Prior work has shown that regulation can affect performance persistence of banks in cross-country evidence (Barth, Caprio, and Levine, 2002), but there is less evidence in other contexts and no evidence in the context of alternative investments. Herein we examine the specific empirical context of hedge funds. In view of recent proposals in Europe and the United States, among other countries, to increase regulation of hedge funds after the 2008 financial crisis, we believe it is important and worthwhile to examine financial regulation and performance persistence in hedge funds. Hedge fund regulation significantly differs across countries and in some cases also changes over time. There are key differences in permissible distribution channels, minimum capitalization requirements, and restrictions in the location of key service providers. We conjecture that such regulations strongly impact performance persistence.

Some types of hedge fund regulation clearly have the potential to mitigate performance persistence. First, restrictions on the location of key service providers potentially reduce persistence where such restrictions enable access to only inferior quality service providers. Second, minimum capitalization requirements mitigate the presence of low quality funds and thereby increase the likelihood of persistent performance. Third, distribution channels provide access to key institutional investors that facilitates capital flows as well as deal flows and networks to information, due diligence, and governance teams (and thereby better performance) (Clifford, 2008; Chou, Ng, and Wang, 2011). Distribution channels that mitigate a fund's presence to important investors are more likely to curtail performance persistence. Fourth, distribution channels that make investment performance opaque, such as wrapper distributions that by virtue tie financial products together, would mitigate the potential for performance persistence.

We examined these propositions using the Center for International Securities and Derivatives Markets (CISDM) data, an international dataset of hedge funds from 48 countries over the years 1994–2008 and for 8,641 funds. The CISDM dataset has been used in other recent work on hedge funds (e.g., Bollen and Pool, 2008, 2009). We merged the dataset with information on hedge fund regulation that significantly varies across countries and to a smaller degree also varies across time (PriceWaterhouseCoopers, various years). We focused our analysis on performance persistence across successive periods of 3-year alphas (and 1-year alphas as robustness) using panel data analyses and discussed robustness to alternative specifications.

Our findings indicate that hedge fund performance persistence depends to a nontrivial degree on hedge fund regulation. First, minimum capital requirements restrict lower quality funds from entering the market, so funds in jurisdictions with great minimum capital restrictions show greater performance persistence. Second, funds in jurisdictions that restrict the location of key service providers tend to have worse performance persistence. Service providers include a fund's administrator, custodian, investment adviser, auditors, legal and tax advisers, accountants, and consultants. It is very important for funds to have high-quality service providers, and there are even institutional investor guides to finding suitable service providers.[1] Restrictions on the location of a fund's service providers force the fund to make choices it might otherwise not have made, which in turn lower the likelihood of performance persistence. Third, we found evidence that permissible distribution channels such as wrappers (which combine different types of financial products) mitigate the strength of signals to attract higher quality investors that would enable performance persistence.

We carried out a number of robustness checks in the course of our analyses. For instance, we showed differences in the effect of regulation on persistence by fund quartile ranking. We also considered the robustness of our results to alternative econometric specifications of our tests, including but not limited to autoregressive specifications, as well as pooling and clustering standard errors by time period and fund. We further considered robustness to selection effects in terms of Heckman's (1976, 1979) selection for choice

[1] See, for example, www.iihedgefundguide.com/.

of offshore jurisdiction as well as funds that do and do not have consecutive years of performance persistence data, robustness to excluding certain countries, and robustness to selection for the probability that a fund has survived sufficiently long in the dataset to report multi-period returns. Our findings are quite robust and highlight the important role of financial regulation on performance persistence.

We note that our findings do not imply that funds seeking consistent top quartile returns can seek regulations that cause them always to be in the top quartile. Nevertheless, our findings do imply that some regulations are better able to facilitate persistence in the top quartile among fund managers with skill to obtain top quartile performance results. Similarly, our results also imply that lower quality funds are able to remain in the bottom quartiles without disappearing from the market where regulations make their persistent underperformance less transparent to institutional investors, such as jurisdictions that permit wrapper distributions.

Our work is related to the literature on hedge fund performance persistence, as well as other papers on hedge fund regulation. Performance persistence has been examined in other hedge fund contexts by Fung and Hseih (1997, 2000, 2001, 2004), Agarwal and Naik (2000a), Liang (2000, 2003), Koh et al. (2003), Baquero et al. (2005), Agarwal et al., (2006, 2007), Ding and Shawky (2007), Fung et al. (2007), Naik et al. (2007), Cassar and Gerakos (2009), Eling (2009), Teo (2009), Jagannathan et al. (2010), among others. Fund regulation and governance has been considered in the United States by Hu and Black (2007), Brown et al. (2008a), Verret (2008), Cassar and Gerakos (2009, 2011) and internationally by Cumming and Dai (2009, 2010a,b) and Cumming and Johan (2008). Prior work, however, has not examined the impact of regulation on performance persistence in the hedge fund context, or for that matter in any other similar context to the best of our knowledge.

Our findings have important implications for policy as well as other hedge fund research. Our findings show that hedge fund regulation has the ability to facilitate top quartile performance when it is structured properly, thereby benefiting investors. But hedge fund regulation can likewise facilitate consistently poor performance when it is improperly structured, thereby worsening investor welfare. Our findings are important for other academic work on hedge funds as we show, consistent with our other recent work on the topic (Cumming and Dai, 2009, 2010a,b), that hedge fund regulation is important to consider when using international hedge fund datasets in contexts related to fund structure and performance, particularly performance persistence.

This chapter is organized as follows. Hypotheses are presented in Section 9.2. The data and summary statistics are introduced in Section 9.3. Section 9.4 provides multivariate tests and discusses other extensions and robustness checks. Concluding remarks follow in the last section.

9.2. Hedge Fund Regulation and Performance Persistence

Hedge funds are typically formed as limited partnerships whereby the investors are considered limited partners and the hedge fund managers are general partners. The implementation of hedge fund investment strategies is facilitated by various external service providers, as depicted in Exhibit 3.2. Outsourcing a hedge fund's functions to service providers minimizes the risk of collusion among hedge fund participants to perpetuate fraud, and it also mitigates liability in the event the hedge fund participants are accused of improperly performing their management duties. A hedge fund's board of directors or board of trustees has a fiduciary duty to the investors to ensure that all parties involved in the fund can properly carry out their designated tasks. The hedge fund managers may have assisting them other investment and professional advisers such as lawyers, accountants, consultants, and tax and audit specialists. There are administrators who assist the fund managers in providing administrative and accounting services, including record keeping, independent valuation of investments, and meeting disclosure requirements. The registrar or transfer agent may assist the manager in processing subscriptions and redemptions and in maintaining the register of shareholders. Sometimes, depending on the structure of the fund and the manager, these duties may be carried out internally by the fund manager. The actual financing arrangements and execution of investments are carried out by prime brokers, which can be either securities firms or banks. Occasionally, the prime brokers decide to set up their own fund, and they therefore also become hedge fund managers. There is of course another service provider, the custodian that has custody over the fund assets.

In many countries around the world there are restrictions on the location of key service providers, requiring them to be within the same jurisdiction in which the fund is registered; there may also be minimum capital requirements for hedge fund managers to operate a hedge fund, as well as different avenues for marketing (not merely private placements).[2] These regulations are summarized for 2008 in Table 3.1 for 48 different countries (see PriceWaterhouseCoopers, various years, for an extended discussion for most of these countries). We make use of time varying changes in these regulations (albeit these regulations do not often change over time).[3]

[2] Hedge funds in the United States are distributed only as private placements. In a private placement, there typically are not more than 35 "accredited" investors, whereby an accredited investor is someone with more than US$1 million in wealth or who earned more than US$200,000 in the previous two years. Hedge funds are not allowed to advertise in the United States although this may soon change. There is no restriction on the minimum size to operate as a hedge fund, and no restriction on the location of key service providers. Prior to February 2006, hedge funds in the United States were also exempt from any registration requirement (Brown et al., 2008).

[3] The majority of countries and years are available in PriceWaterhouseCoopers (various years). For countries/years not available in PriceWaterhouseCoopers, we obtained information regarding regulation on the hedge funds in a survey sent to selected funds.

At issue in this chapter is whether different forms of regulatory oversight in different countries mitigate the presence of risky funds and facilitate additional value-added governance; if so, we would expect hedge funds in jurisdictions with such regulations to exhibit performance persistence. First, and perhaps most straightforward, minimum capitalization requirements mitigate the presence of low-quality funds and thereby increase the likelihood of persistent performance, especially among the most marginal and smaller funds in the bottom quartile.

Second, restrictions on the location of key service providers may constrain the fund to an inefficient scale, give rise to inefficient choice of human resources associated with hedge fund management, create barriers to entry, and limit investor participation most suited to the particular hedge fund's strategy (Wilson, 2007). The most common service providers include prime brokers, administrators, and distributors. Prime brokers lend money, act as counterparts to derivative contracts, lend securities in short sales, execute trades, and provide clearing, settlement, and custody services. Administrators issue and redeem interests and shares and calculate the net asset value (NAV) of the fund. Distributors are responsible for marketing the fund to potential investors. Restrictions on location of key service providers typically require the presence of a local agent (PriceWaterhouseCoopers, 2006, 2007). Service providers are vitally important because they provide due diligence services for the fund, provide research on counterparty risk and generally facilitate the execution of the fund's activities. A fund's relationship with its service providers involves substantial human capital and asset specificity. Lower cost service providers can save on fees, but such cost savings can drastically hurt fund performance due to the reduction in auditor timing and support, inaccurate auditing services, enhanced counterparty risk, slower execution, delayed custody services, and conflicts of interest in marketing the fund. Restrictions on the location of key service providers potentially reduce persistence where such restrictions enable access only to inferior quality service providers.

Third, there is an oft-repeated view in the hedge fund industry that fund distribution channels can facilitate performance persistence.[4] Distribution channels provide access to key institutional investors that facilitates capital flows as well as deal flow and networks to information, due diligence, and governance teams. Therefore, distribution channels that promote a fund's presence to key institutional investors will facilitate performance persistence.

Fourth, distribution channels that make fund performance more opaque have the potential to be associated with lower fund performance. Wrappers—that is, securities whose returns tie together different financial products—bear a potential conflict of interest between the sponsor and the fund manager with respect to the disclosure of the wrapper relating to the fund manager (Gerstein, 2006).

---

[4] Mark Cobley, "Threadneedle: 'We are worth a second look'," 01 November 2010, http://www.efinancialnews.com.

Wrapper constructions are often complex and incomprehensible for the average investor, thereby lowering the governance that hedge fund investors would otherwise provide. Empirical evidence confirms that wrapper distributions are associated with a "flatter" or less sensitive flow-performance relationship (Cumming and Dai, 2009); that is, investors in hedge funds distributed through wrappers are less likely to withdraw from poorly performing hedge funds to enter better performing hedge funds. Wrapper distributions are likewise associated with more frequent misreporting of returns (Cumming and Dai, 2010b) and worse overall performance (Cumming and Dai, 2010a). Overall, we may expect a negative association between distribution channels that make fund performance more opaque and fund performance persistence.

In sum, we expect restrictions regarding the location of hedge fund key service providers, minimum capital restrictions, and permissible distribution channels all to affect fund performance persistence, as stated in the four testable hypotheses.

Hypothesis 9.1. *Minimum capital restrictions increase the probability of performance persistence.*

Hypothesis 9.2. *Restrictions on the location of key service providers decrease the probability of performance persistence.*

Hypothesis 9.3. *Distribution channels that promote a fund's presence to institutional investors, such as distribution by banks, fund distribution companies, and other regulated financial services institutions, will increase the probability of performance persistence.*

Hypothesis 9.4. *Distribution channels that make fund performance more opaque, such as wrappers, and distributions directly through investment managers themselves without certification of external agents, will decrease the probability of performance persistence.*

The differences in hedge fund regulation around the world are summarized in Table 3.1 (these regulations are summarized for 2008, the most recent year in our dataset). Table 3.1 likewise presents information on other country differences, legal origin, GDP per capita, and the number of hedge funds by country in the CISDM dataset. The CISDM dataset is described further in the next section, along with summary statistics and comparison tests.

9.3. Data

9.3.1. DATA SOURCE

In the empirical analysis, we used CISDM data, as we have done in the previous chapters. We focused on fund flows in the sample period from January 1994 to December 2008 for funds registered in 48 countries around the world (Table 3.1).

Table 9.1 Definitions of Variables and Summary Statistics

Variable	Definition	Mean	Median	Standard Deviation	Minimum	Maximum
Fund Performance						
3-year Alpha	3-year alpha is estimated using Fung and Hseih (2004) 7-factor model for every 3-year return data (99% winsorized). The first 18 months of returns are eliminated for each fund due to the possibility of backfilling.	0.310	0.278	1.212	−4.158	4.728
1-year Alpha	1-year alpha is estimated using Fung and Hseih (2004) 7-factor model for every 1-year return data (99% winsorized). The first 18 months of returns are eliminated for each fund due to the possibility of backfilling.	0.125	0.140	1.830	−6.520	6.616
Fund Regulation						
Minimum Capitalization	The minimum capitalization required to operate as a hedge fund manager in 2004 US$.	$249,057	$45,517	$464,840	$0	$6,750,000
Restrictions on Location of Key Service Providers	A dummy variable equal to 1 where the country imposes restrictions on the location of key service providers.	0.527	1	0.499	0	1
Marketing Investment Manager Dummy	A dummy variable equal to 1 where the country allows fund distribution via investment managers.	0.288	0	0.453	0	1

(Continued)

Table 9.1 (Continued)

Variable	Definition	Mean	Median	Standard Deviation	Minimum	Maximum
Marketing Funds Distribution Company Dummy	A dummy variable equal to 1 where the country allows fund distribution via fund distribution companies.	0.054	0	0.226	0	1
Marketing Bank	A dummy variable equal to 1 where the country allows fund distribution via banks.	0.554	1	0.497	0	1
Marketing via Wrappers Dummy	A dummy variable equal to 1 where the country allows fund distribution via wrappers.	0.056	0	0.229	0	1
Marketing via Private Placements Dummy	A dummy variable equal to 1 where the country allows fund distribution via private placements.	0.952	1	0.214	0	1
Marketing via Private Other Regulated Intermediary	A dummy variable equal to 1 where the country allows fund distribution via other regulated financial intermediary.	0.100	0	0.300	0	1
Marketing via Non-Regulated Intermediary	A dummy variable equal to 1 where the country allows fund distribution via non-regulated financial intermediary.	0.020	0	0.141	0	1
Fund Characteristics						
Fund Manager with Multiple Funds	A dummy variable equal to 1 if the fund is run by a fund manager running 2 or more funds.	0.395	0	0.489	0	1

Annual Redemption	A dummy variable equal to 1 if capital redemptions are possible only on an annual basis.	0.058	0	0.234	0	1
Assets under Management	The fund's assets in millions of 2004 US$.	111.000	$20	705.000	$0	$23,700
Minimum Investment	The minimum investment required for the fund in millions of 2004 US$.	2.000	$0.25	63.500	$0.00	$5,000.00
Master-Feeder	A dummy variable equal to 1 if the fund is a master-feeder fund (an investment vehicle that pools its portfolio within another vehicle).	0.186	0	0.389	0	1
Misreporting Fund	A dummy variable equal to 1 if the fund report returns fall within 0, (0.0058) more than 50% of the time (following Bollen and Pool, 2009).	0.625	1	0.484	0	1
Country GNP and Legal Origin						
GNP per Capita	The country's GNP per capita, expressed in 2004 US$.	$36,547	$38,500	$7,112	$0	$71,400
English Origin	A dummy variable equal to 1 for English legal origin countries (La Porta et al., 1998).	0.923	1	0.266	0	1

This table defines the main variables used in the book. Summary statistics are also provided for each variable. The data are for the period January 1994–December 2008.

There are 8,641 hedge funds with monthly returns, assets under management, and other fund-specific information over this sample period, which includes live and defunct hedge funds, regardless of the reason for defunctness. Therefore, we do not have survivorship bias due to defunct funds in our sample. Note in our statistical and regression analyses we control for backfilling of returns by excluding the first 18 fund months from the sample since funds have a tendency to first report to data vendors once they have shown better performance. Further, to estimate 3-year alpha, we requested that funds have at least 36 observations. Our sample includes 2,073 (3-year alpha) and 4,038 (1-year alpha) hedge funds. We merge the dataset with information on hedge fund regulation that significantly varies across countries and to a smaller degree also varies across time (PriceWaterhouseCoopers, various years).

9.3.2. SUMMARY STATISTICS

Table 9.1 defines and summarizes the performance measures in the data for the January 1994–December 2008 period, as well as the regulatory variables and variables for hedge fund characteristics. The 3-year alpha is estimated using the Fung and Hsieh (2004) 7-factor model for every instance of 3-year return data, winsorized at the 99% level due to the outliers. The average 3-year alpha (1-year alpha) is 0.310 (0.125), with a median at 0.278 (0.140). Minimum capitalization ranges from US$0 to $6.75 million. Among the funds in the sample, 52.7% are domiciled in a jurisdiction that restricts the location of key service providers, while 95.2% are associated with a distribution channel via private placement, 28.8% via investment managers, 5.4% via fund distribution companies, 55.4% through banks, and 5.6% via the way of wrappers.[5] About 39.5% of the funds are simultaneously managed by fund managers that manage more than one fund. Only 5.8% of the observations are from funds that have annual capital redemptions. About 18.6% of the funds are structured as master-feeder funds, which are investment vehicles that pool their portfolios within another vehicle. It is notable that about 62.5% of the funds are misreporting funds, which, according to Bollen and Pool (2009) and Cumming and Dai (2010b), are those funds that frequently (more than 50% of the time) report returns falling (0, 0.0058). The assets under management of the funds range from US$0 (funds that became defunct) to $23.7 billion, with an average of $111 million. These summary statistics are consistent with those reported in other hedge fund datasets.

In Table 9.2, we grouped our sample into quartiles based on the rank of their 3-year alpha during the benchmark period. The bottom (top) quartile represents the worst (best) performers during the benchmark period. We then tabulated the proportion of the funds that remained in the same rank (quartile) during the

---

[5] Oftentimes, multiple distribution channels are allowed in a specific jurisdiction. Therefore these statistics do not add up to 100%.

subsequent 3-year period. However, we noted that this only provides unconditional evidence as we did not control for regulation variables and fund characteristics. Therefore, these results present only preliminary evidence. We show, in general, unconditional on regulation and fund characteristics, that the top performers exhibited greater performance persistence, or a notably higher proportion of funds remained in the top quartile in the subsequent 3-year period. Further, overall, funds in jurisdictions with minimum capitalization exhibited greater performance persistence, while funds in jurisdictions with restrictions on locations and permitting distributions via investment manager exhibited smaller performance persistence. Moreover, we found that different regulations have distinctive effects on the performance persistence of poorly performing funds and better performing ones. For instance, we observed greater performance persistence among poorly performing funds (the last two quartiles based on performance during the benchmark period) in jurisdictions with minimum capitalization requirements and permitting distributions via banks, fund distribution companies, wrappers, and other regulated financial intermediaries. On the other hand, the better performing funds were more likely to stay in the same rank in jurisdictions with no minimum capitalization requirement and not permitting distributions via private placement and banks, investment managers, and other regulated financial intermediaries.

The data in Table 9.2 also suggest that performance persistence is conditional on various fund characteristics. Overall, master-feeder funds and multi-funds showed smaller performance persistence. Further, the association was dependent on the previous performance of the funds. For example, for funds in the bottom two quartiles, annual redemption was associated with weaker performance persistence. In contrast, it was associated with greater performance persistence for funds in the top two quartiles. Master-feeder funds exhibited significantly smaller performance persistence in both the bottom and top quartiles. Further, multi-funds showed greater performance persistence in the middle two quartiles, and smaller persistence in the bottom quartile. Moreover, we found that misreporting funds in the middle two quartiles showed greater performance persistence than non-misreporting funds. On the contrary, among the top quartile and the bottom quartile, non-misreporting funds exhibited better performance.

9.4. Multivariate Tests

9.4.1 REGRESSION MODELS

Our multivariate tests assessed performance persistence by examining the relationship between current 3-year Fung and Hseih (2004) 7-factor alphas and prior 3-year alphas (lagged 3 years so that there was no overlap in measurement. Our dataset was structured as a panel that has 2,073 funds with performance statistics with at least two successive periods of 3-year alphas over the years 1994–2008. One limiting factor was the requirement of a rather long return series

Table 9.2. **Comparison Tests**

	No Minimum Capitalization	Minimum Capitalization>0	Difference Tests
All	33.08%	34.92%	0.004***
Bottom Quartile	27.58%	38.81%	0.000***
2nd Quartile	30.50%	33.85%	0.009***
3rd Quartile	33.81%	29.32%	0.000***
Top Quartile	38.31%	36.97%	0.295

	No Restrictions on Location	Restrictions on Location	Difference Tests
All	34.05%	32.87%	0.097*
Bottom Quartile	27.20%	25.86%	0.354
2nd Quartile	33.68%	34.46%	0.626
3rd Quartile	33.60%	31.79%	0.186
Top Quartile	39.69%	38.61%	0.449

	No Private Placements	Private Placements	Difference Tests
All	37.83%	33.30%	0.014**
Bottom Quartile	23.53%	26.68%	0.342
2nd Quartile	49.03%	33.15%	0.000***
3rd Quartile	25.90%	32.91%	0.118
Top Quartile	46.82%	38.99%	0.076*

	No Bank Distributions	Bank Distributions	Difference Tests
All	33.77%	33.18%	0.409
Bottom Quartile	27.41%	25.73%	0.247
2nd Quartile	32.04%	35.60%	0.011**
3rd Quartile	33.87%	31.51%	0.084*
Top Quartile	39.43%	38.93%	0.724

Table 9.2. (Continued)

	No Fund Distribution Company Distributions	Fund Distribution Company Distributions	Difference Tests
All	33.42%	34.55%	0.490
Bottom Quartile	26.62%	24.76%	0.556
2nd Quartile	33.66%	39.52%	0.041**
3rd Quartile	33.00%	26.52%	0.069*
Top Quartile	38.95%	44.90%	0.095*

	No Investment Manager Distributions	Investment Manager Distributions	Difference Tests
All	34.01%	32.18%	0.019**
Bottom Quartile	27.76%	23.53%	0.008***
2nd Quartile	33.85%	34.40%	0.712
3rd Quartile	32.86%	32.49%	0.791
Top Quartile	40.06%	36.81%	0.045***

	No Wrapper Distributions	Wrapper Distributions	Difference Tests
All	33.48%	33.41%	0.962
Bottom Quartile	26.67%	23.94%	0.381
2nd Quartile	33.63%	39.80%	0.028**
3rd Quartile	32.97%	27.55%	0.113
Top Quartile	39.19%	39.50%	0.93

	No Other Regulated Financial Intermediary Distributions	Other Regulated Financial Intermediary Distributions	Difference Tests
All	33.46%	33.69%	0.854
Bottom Quartile	26.88%	23.14%	0.125
2nd Quartile	32.98%	41.96%	0.000***
3rd Quartile	33.31%	24.23%	0.001***
Top Quartile	39.07%	41.28%	0.462

(Continued)

Table 9.2. (Continued)

	No Other Non-Regulated Financial Intermediary Distributions	Other Non-Regulated Financial Intermediary Distributions	Difference Tests
All	33.44%	35.63%	0.412
Bottom Quartile	26.63%	20.59%	0.264
2nd Quartile	33.91%	38.79%	0.273
3rd Quartile	32.79%	30.00%	0.622
Top Quartile	39.03%	51.52%	0.039**

	Not Annual Redemption	Annual Redemption	Difference Tests
All	34.06%	35.76%	0.166
Bottom Quartile	35.36%	28.87%	0.062*
2nd Quartile	33.17%	24.24%	0.000***
3rd Quartile	30.25%	41.79%	0.000***
Top Quartile	37.36%	40.12%	0.226

	Not Master-Feeder Fund	Master-Feeder Fund	Difference Tests
All	33.88%	31.14%	0.002***
Bottom Quartile	31.63%	23.09%	0.000***
2nd Quartile	32.68%	34.49%	0.284
3rd Quartile	31.06%	31.99%	0.574
Top Quartile	39.52%	33.33%	0.002***

	Not Multi-Funds	Multi-Funds	Difference Tests
All	34.72%	33.38%	0.036**
Bottom Quartile	41.65%	23.12%	0.000***
2nd Quartile	30.67%	34.95%	0.001***
3rd Quartile	27.23%	36.71%	0.000***
Top Quartile	37.77%	37.29%	0.717

Table 9.2. (Continued)

	Non-Misreporting Funds	Misreporting Funds	Difference Tests
All	32.85%	34.88%	0.000***
Bottom Quartile	37.79%	33.10%	0.000***
2nd Quartile	24.28%	35.53%	0.000***
3rd Quartile	22.14%	34.85%	0.000***
Top Quartile	40.14%	35.81%	0.001***

We grouped our sample into quartiles based on the rank of their 3-year alpha during the benchmark period. The bottom (top) quartile includes the worst (best) performers during the benchmark period. We then tabulated the proportion of the funds that remained in the same rank (quartile) during the subsequent 3-year period conditional on the regulation variables and fund characteristics. The 2-tailed p-values for the differences in proportions are reported in the last column. *, **, *** denote significance at the 10%, 5%, and 1% level, respectively.

of six consecutive years. To determine whether our results held if we included more hedge funds in the analyses, we conducted a further calculation that included the 1-year alpha in addition to the 3-year alpha.[6] This reduced the required time span and consequently increased our sample size to 4,038. To test whether our results were prone to a conditioning bias, we also calculated "1-year alpha," and compared the results with those from the "3-year alpha." Overall, we found that (1) statistical significance (not surprisingly) increases, but more important, (2) the signs of the significant coefficients did not change. Therefore, we found no evidence of a conditioning bias in our results, and we thus believe strongly that our results are representative. The basic structure of our regression equation is

(1) 7-factor alpha = β_0 + β_1 Lag(7-factor alpha) + β_2 Lag(7-factor alpha) * Minimum Capitalization + β_3 Lag(7-factor alpha) * Restrictions on Location + β_4 Lag(7-factor alpha) * Private Placement + β_5 Lag(7-factor alpha) * Investment Manager + β_6 Lag(7-factor alpha) * Fund Distribution Company + β_7 Lag(7-factor alpha) * Bank + β_8 Lag(7-factor alpha) * Wrapper + β_9 Lag(7-factor alpha) * Other Regulated Financial Intermediary + β_{10} Lag(7-factor alpha) * Non-Regulated Financial Intermediary + $\Sigma_i \gamma_i$ Control Variable$_i$ + ε

Positive coefficients on β_2 to β_{10} imply performance persistence attributable to regulation as historical alphas interacted with regulatory structures positively

---

[6] We thank the anonymous referee for pointing this out.

predict future alphas and the β_1 coefficient is the sole determinant of the degree of return persistence that cannot be explained by hedge fund regulation. By contrast, insignificant coefficients on β_2 to β_{10} imply no evidence of performance persistence. Negative and significant coefficients for β_1, β_2, β_3, and β_4 imply the funds have negative performance persistence or substantial luck in achieving performance outcomes from one period to the next. The regression estimates for equation (1) appear in Sub-section 9.4.2.

As a robustness check, we present in Sub-section 9.4.2 regressions with relative quartile rankings of funds, as specified in equation (2):

(2) *7-factor alpha quartile ranking = β_0 + β_1 Lag(7-factor alpha ranking) + β_2 Lag(7-factor alpha ranking) * Minimum Capitalization + β_3 Lag(7-factor alpha ranking) * Restrictions on Location + β_4 Lag(7-factor alpha ranking) * Private Placement + β_5 Lag(7-factor alpha ranking) * Investment Manager + β_6 Lag(7-factor alpha ranking) * Fund Distribution Company + β_7 Lag(7-factor alpha ranking) * Bank + β_8 Lag(7-factor alpha ranking) * Wrapper + β_9 Lag(7-factor alpha ranking) * Other Regulated Financial Intermediary + β_{10} Lag(7-factor alpha ranking) * Non-Regulated Financial Intermediary + $\Sigma_i \gamma_i$ Control Variable$_i$ + ε*

The coefficients in regression (2) have the same interpretation as in equation (1), with the exception that the variables are based on relative rankings and not the absolute values of alpha as in equation (1). Also, equation (2) is estimated with ordered logit techniques, while equation (1) is estimated with panel data methods for continuous dependent variables.

As a further robustness check, we present in Sub-section 9.4.2 regressions with treatment sample selection regressions (similar to Heckman, 1976, 1979). These regressions have two steps. The first step (equation (3a)) is a binary logit regression for selecting an offshore registration, and the second step (equation (3b)) models the persistence in alpha conditional on selecting an offshore registration. We assess robustness in equation (3b) to the use of 7-factor alphas and relative quartile rankings of 7-factor alphas.

(3a) *Offshore = β_0 + β_1 Fund Regulation Variables + β_2 Fund Strategy Variables + β_3 Variables for Fund Characteristics (such as Size) + ε*

(3b) *7-factor alpha quartile ranking = β_0 + β_1 Lag(7-factor alpha ranking) + β_2 Lag(7-factor alpha ranking) * Minimum Capitalization + β_3 Lag(7-factor alpha ranking) * Restrictions on Location + β_4 Lag(7-factor alpha ranking) * Private Placement + β_5 Lag(7-factor alpha ranking) * Investment Manager + β_6 Lag(7-factor alpha ranking) * Fund Distribution Company + β_7 Lag(7-factor alpha ranking) * Bank + β_8 Lag(7-factor alpha ranking) * Wrapper + β_9 Lag(7-factor alpha ranking) * Other Regulated Financial Intermediary + β_{10} Lag(7-factor alpha ranking) * Non-Regulated Financial Intermediary + $\Sigma_i \gamma_i$ Control Variable$_i$ + β_{11} Offshore + ε | (step 3a)*

Of course, there are several ways to specify these two-step regressions. We use strategy variables to identify choice of offshore versus onshore, consistent with Cumming and Dai (2009, 2010a,b) and Cumming and Johan (2008). In addition, we use various fund regulation dummy variables. The results for the second step estimates are invariant to different possible specifications of the first-step regressions. Also, as discussed next, the main results of interest are invariant to modeling selection and various other specification issues.

9.4.2. REGRESSION RESULTS

Table 9.3 presents the regression results for equation (1) with four Panels (A and B are related to 3-year-alphas and A' and B' to 1-year-alphas) and 11 regression models in total. Panel A (A') of Exhibit 9.3 shows five alternative regression models based on the full sample of all funds in the dataset. Models (1)–(3) use panel methods with an AR(1) specification to account for the fact that there is autocorrelation in the error terms. Different independent variables are used in Models (1)–(3). Model (4) uses the panel method without the AR(1) correction. Models (5) and (6) use a pooled regression and cluster the standard errors by period and fund (based on Petersen, 2009). Model (6) is presented to show the benchmark results without regulatory variables (which shows performance persistence). Panel B (B') uses the full sample of all funds but breaks the data into four quartiles based on the fund's lagged 7-factor alphas for the regression models.

Table 9.3 provides strong statistical support for Hypothesis 9.1 for a positive association between minimum capitalization and performance persistence. The effect is statistically significant in Models (1)–(4) in Panel A (A') and in Model (11) in Panel B (B'). However, the effect is not economically large. To see the size of the effect, consider a 1-standard deviation change in alpha from the mean for hedge funds that operate in jurisdictions with US$1 million minimum capitalization versus hedge funds that operate in jurisdictions with US$5 million minimum capitalization. The data indicate that for the larger US$5 million minimum capitalization jurisdictions, prior lagged 3-year alphas (1-year alphas) are more closely related to future alphas by only 0.003 (0.004) or 0.3% (0.4%). This small economic significance is perhaps not surprising, as hedge funds themselves are very large while minimum capitalization restrictions across countries are comparatively small, thereby keeping only the smallest of the marginal funds. In Panel B (B') in Model (11) for the sub-set of bottom quartile funds we provide evidence that size of the effect is very similar to that reports in Panel A (A'). For other quartiles considered in Panel B (B'), the effect for minimum capitalization is not significant (and hence not included in the regressions), which is intuitive since minimum capitalization levels are quite small (Table 9.1) and hence impact only the most marginally operating funds.

Table 9.3 provides strong statistical and economic support for Hypothesis 9.2 for restrictions on the location of key service providers. The effect is statistically significant in Panel A (A') for all models. To see the size of the effect, consider a 1-standard deviation difference in alpha from the mean for hedge funds that

Table 9.3. **Multivariate Regressions**

Panel A. All Funds, Full Sample, 3-Year Alpha

	(1) Panel, AR(1)		(2) Panel, AR(1)		(3) Panel, AR(1)		(4) Panel		(5) Pooled, 2-Way Clustering		(6) Pooled, 2-Way Clustering	
	Co-efficient	p-value	Co-efficient	p-value	Co-efficient	p-value	Co-efficient	p-value	Co-efficient	p-value	Co-efficient	p-value
3-Year Lagged Alpha	0.030	0.479	0.028	0.462	0.033	0.045	0.038	0.625	0.045	0.038	0.072	0.016**
3-Year Lagged Alpha *Minimum Capitalization	0.003	0.020**	0.003	0.042**	0.001	0.004	0.199	0.003***	0.004	0.199		
3-Year Lagged Alpha *Restrictions on Location	-0.047	0.008***	-0.041	0.019**			-0.059	0.001***	-0.069	0.085*		
3-Year Lagged Alpha *Private Placement	-0.055	0.194	-0.054	0.154	-0.057	0.132	-0.049	0.251				
3-Year Lagged Alpha *Investment Manager					-0.061	0.000***						
3-Year Lagged Alpha *Fund Distribution Company			0.008	0.768								

3-Year Lagged Alpha *Bank					0.043	0.112		
3-Year Lagged Alpha *Wrapper	−0.018	0.596					−0.018	0.588	−0.035	0.64
3-Year Lagged Alpha *Other Regulated Financial Intermediary	0.005	0.865					0.014	0.634	−0.049	0.379
3-Year Lagged Alpha *Non-Regulated Financial Intermediary	−0.021	0.676					−0.075	0.130	0.085	0.421
3-Year Lagged Alpha *Multiple Funds	0.460	0.000***	0.460	0.000***	0.460	0.000***	0.464	0.000***	0.438	0.000***
3-Year Lagged Alpha *Master Feeder	0.370	0.000***	0.370	0.000***	0.369	0.000***	0.357	0.000***	0.389	0.000***
3-Year Lagged Alpha *Annual Redemption	0.389	0.000***	0.389	0.000***	0.388	0.000***	0.403	0.000***	0.337	0.000***

(Continued)

Table 9.3. (Continued)

Panel A. All Funds, Full Sample, 3-Year Alpha

	(1) Panel, AR(1)		(2) Panel, AR(1)		(3) Panel, AR(1)		(4) Panel		(5) Pooled, 2-Way Clustering		(6) Pooled, 2-Way Clustering	
	Co-efficient	p-value	Co-efficient	p-value	Co-efficient	p-value	Co-efficient	p-value	Co-efficient	p-value	Co-efficient	p-value
3-Year Lagged Alpha	0.738	0.000***	0.738	0.000***	0.738	0.000***	0.734	0.000***	0.730	0.000***		
*Misreporting Fund												
Log Assets under Management	−0.014	0.000***	−0.014	0.014	−0.015	0.012**	−0.013	0.012**	−0.014	0.092*	−0.024	0.202
Log GDP per Capita	−0.026	0.466	−0.026	0.476	−0.026	0.461	−0.023	0.548	−0.053	0.322	−0.604	0.695
English Legal Origin	−0.050	0.247	−0.051	0.240	−0.052	0.225	−0.045	0.333	−0.047	0.229	−0.086	0.108
Constant	0.633	0.107	0.629	0.110	0.644	0.101	0.585	0.166	0.834	0.164	1.452	0.447
Strategy Dummy Variables?	Yes		Yes		Yes		Yes		Yes		Yes	
Estimated Autocorrelation Coefficient	0.391		0.392		0.392		Not Applicable		Not Applicable		Not Applicable	
N	12,597		12,597		12,597		12,597		12,597		12,597	
Adjusted R2	0.6131		0.6131		0.6138		0.6118		0.6200		0.072	

Panel A': All Funds, Full Sample, 1-Year Alpha

	(1) Panel, AR(1)		(2) Panel, AR(1)		(3) Panel, AR(1)		(4) Panel		(5) Pooled, 2-Way Clustering		(6) Pooled, 2-Way Clustering	
	Co-efficient	p-value	Co-efficient	p-value	Co-efficient	p-value	Co-efficient	p-value	Co-efficient	p-value	Co-efficient	p-value
1-Year Lagged Alpha	0.072	0.000***	0.072	0.000***	0.072	0.000***	0.097	0.000***	0.175	0.000***	0.309	0.000***
1-Year Lagged Alpha * Minimum Capitalization	0.004	0.004***	0.003	0.010***	0.003	0.042**	0.005	0.001***	0.004	0.206		
1-Year Lagged Alpha *restrictions on location	−0.053	0.003***	−0.046	0.007***			−0.062	0.000***	−0.099	0.017**		
1-Year Lagged Alpha *Private Placement	−0.041	0.000***	−0.042	0.000***	−0.039	0.000***	−0.062	0.000***				
1-Year Lagged Alpha *Investment Manager					−0.051	0.000***						
1-Year Lagged Alpha *Fund Distribution Company			0.002	0.948								

(Continued)

Table 9.3. (Continued)

Panel A': All Funds, Full Sample, 1-Year Alpha

	(1) Panel, AR(1) Co-efficient	(1) p-value	(2) Panel, AR(1) Co-efficient	(2) p-value	(3) Panel, AR(1) Co-efficient	(3) p-value	(4) Panel Co-efficient	(4) p-value	(5) Pooled, 2-Way Clustering Co-efficient	(5) p-value	(6) Pooled, 2-Way Clustering Co-efficient	(6) p-value
1-Year Lagged Alpha *Bank					0.016	0.363						
1-Year Lagged Alpha *Wrapper	−0.018	0.596					−0.015	0.653	−0.058	0.397		
1-Year Lagged Alpha *Other Regulated Financial Intermediary	0.003	0.912					0.004	0.888	−0.050	0.327		
1-Year Lagged Alpha *Non-Regulated Financial Intermediary	−0.029	0.554					−0.073	0.128	0.053	0.613		
1-Year Lagged Alpha *Multiple Funds	0.460	0.000***	0.460	0.000***	0.460	0.000***	0.460	0.000***	0.421	0.000***		

1-Year Lagged Alpha *Master Feeder	0.367	0.000***	0.367	0.000***	0.366	0.000***	0.354	0.000***	0.374	0.000***
1-Year Lagged Alpha *Annual Redemption	0.379	0.000***	0.379	0.000***	0.378	0.000***	0.388	0.000***	0.309	0.000***
1-Year Lagged Alpha *Misreporting Fund	0.731	0.000***	0.731	0.000***	0.732	0.000***	0.725	0.000***	0.698	0.000***
Log Assets under Management	−0.011	0.041**	−0.012	0.038**	−0.012	0.035**	−0.011	0.071*	−0.007	0.358	−0.013	0.223
Log GDP per Capita	−0.023	0.507	−0.023	0.504	−0.021	0.544	−0.020	0.585	−0.057	0.255	−0.049	0.206
English Legal Origin	−0.050	0.229	−0.051	0.219	−0.053	0.194	−0.042	0.336	−0.044	0.225	0.018	0.629
Constant	0.5230	0.596	0.535	0.156	0.518	0.168	0.478	0.228	0.786	0.180	0.942	0.084*
Strategy Dummy Variables?	Yes		Yes		Yes		Yes		Yes		Yes
Estimated Autocorrelation Coefficient	0.390		0.390		0.390		Not Applicable		Not Applicable		Not Applicable
N	17,258		17,258		17,258		17,258		17,258		17,258
Adjusted R2	0.6281		0.6280		0.6287		0.6294		0.6200		0.1420

(Continued)

Table 9.3. (Continued)

Panel B. Full Sample by Quartiles, 3-Year Alpha

	(7) 1st Quartile (Top)		(8) 2nd Quartile		(9) 3rd Quartile		(10) 4th Quartile (Bottom)		(11) 4th Quartile (Bottom)	
	Coefficient	p-value	Coefficient	p-value	Coefficient	p-value	Coefficient	p-value	Coefficient	p-value
3-Year Lagged Alpha	−0.013	0.262	0.005	0.109	−0.002	0.326	0.001	0.932	0.003	0.800
3-Year Lagged Alpha * Minimum Capitalization									0.004	0.087*
3-Year Lagged Alpha *Restrictions on Location	−0.041	0.015**	−0.006	0.212	0.000	0.830	−0.016	0.427	−0.061	0.058*
3-Year Lagged Alpha *Wrapper	−0.157	0.000***	−0.016	0.160	−0.004	0.490	0.154	0.026*		
3-Year Lagged Alpha *Multiple Funds	0.301	0.000***	0.144	0.000***	0.324	0.000***	0.357	0.000***	0.358	0.000***
3-Year Lagged Alpha *Master Feeder	0.231	0.000***	0.111	0.000***	0.221	0.000***	0.451	0.000***	0.452	0.000***
3-Year Lagged Alpha *Annual Redemption	0.218	0.000***	0.140	0.000***	0.176	0.000***	0.542	0.000***	0.539	0.000***
3-Year Lagged Alpha *Misreporting Fund	0.530	0.000***	0.321	0.000***	0.734	0.000***	0.591	0.000***	0.592	0.000***
Log Assets under Management	−0.064	0.000***	0.001	0.628	−0.001	0.143	0.039	0.000***	0.039	0.000***

Log GDP per Capita	−0.062	0.453	−0.028	0.018	−0.004	0.521	−0.008	0.878	−0.010	0.839
English Legal Origin	−0.222	0.044	−0.010	0.425	−0.013	0.016	−0.035	0.647	−0.041	0.598
Constant	2.519	0.003***	0.658	0.000***	0.101	0.133	−0.850	0.122	−0.806	0.142
Strategy Dummy Variables?	Yes		Yes		Yes		Yes		Yes	
Estimated Autocorrelation Coefficient	0.295		0.369		0.358		0.285		0.284	
N	3,004		3,621		3,508		2,464		2,464	
Adjusted R2	0.306		0.243		0.7554		0.4503		0.4516	

Panel B': Full Sample by Quartiles, 1-Year Alpha

	(7) 1st Quartile (Top)		(8) 2nd Quartile		(9) 3rd Quartile		(10) 4th Quartile (Bottom)		(11) 4th Quartile (Bottom)	
	Coefficient	p-value	Coefficient	p-value	Coefficient	p-value	Coefficient	p-value	Coefficient	p-value
1-Year Lagged Alpha	0.080	0.000***	0.003	0.094*	0.006	0.074*	0.049	0.000***	0.047	0.000***
1-Year Lagged Alpha * Minimum Capitalization									0.009	0.000***
1-Year Lagged Alpha *Restrictions on Location	−0.042	0.009***	−0.003	0.116	−0.003	0.435	−0.067	0.000***	−0.026	0.347
1-Year Lagged Alpha *Wrapper	−0.123	0.071*	−0.007	0.237	−0.013	0.238	0.177	0.000***		

(Continued)

Table 9.3. (Continued)

Panel B': Full Sample by Quartiles, 1-Year Alpha

	(7) 1st Quartile (Top)		(8) 2nd Quartile		(9) 3rd Quartile		(10) 4th Quartile (Bottom)		(11) 4th Quartile (Bottom)	
	Coefficient	p-value	Coefficient	p-value	Coefficient	p-value	Coefficient	p-value	Coefficient	p-value
1-Year Lagged Alpha *Multiple Funds	0.363	0.000***	0.324	0.000***	0.142	0.000***	0.290	0.000***	0.287	0.000***
1-Year Lagged Alpha *Master Feeder	0.441	0.000***	0.221	0.000***	0.110	0.000***	0.232	0.000***	0.231	0.000***
1-Year Lagged Alpha *Annual Redemption	0.524	0.000***	0.173	0.000***	0.140	0.000***	0.207	0.000***	0.206	0.000***
1-Year Lagged Alpha *Misreporting Fund	0.584	0.000***	0.734	0.000***	0.319	0.000***	0.517	0.000***	0.516	0.000***
Log Assets under Management	0.041	0.000***	-0.001	0.199	0.001	0.638	-0.059	0.000***	-0.059	0.000***
Log GDP per Capita	-0.011	0.827	-0.005	0.456	-0.027	0.024**	-0.079	0.321	-0.068	0.392
English Legal Origin	-0.041	0.593	-0.013	0.014**	-0.010	0.430	-0.199	0.065	-0.224	0.038**
Constant	-0.871	0.108	0.104	0.120	0.644	0.000***	2.587	0.002***	2.488	0.003***

Strategy Dummy Variables?	Yes	Yes	Yes	Yes
Estimated Autocorrelation Coefficient	0.282	0.369	0.368	0.277	0.284
N	4,782	4,730	4,177	3,569	3,569
Adjusted R2	0.463	0.243	0.244	0.3223	0.4516

This table presents Panel AR(1) (by years and funds) estimates of performance persistence, alongside Panel estimates without AR(1) specifications, and Pooled Regressions with errors clustered by both time and fund. Panel A considers the full sample of all funds, while Panel B considers sub-sample based on quartile rankings. The dependent variable for panel A and B (A' and B') is the 3-year alpha (1-year alpha) for each fund for each year (winsorized at 99%). Explanatory variables include the 3 [1]-year alpha (lagged by 3 [1] years), the interaction between lagged alpha and fund regulation variables (minimum capitalization, restrictions on location, and distribution channels for investment manager, fund distribution company, and wrappers), the interaction between lagged alpha and fund characteristics (fund managers who operate multiple funds, master-feeder funds, funds with annual redemptions), log of assets under management, and country factors that include GDP per capita and a dummy variable for English legal origin. Twenty-seven dummy variables are included for different strategies in the CISDM database (one is excluded to avoid collinearity, and a constant is included in all regressions). Variables are as defined in Table 9.1. Select variables excluded in different regression to check for collinearity. Regressions are presented for the full sample, as well as the different quartiles of performance (based on 2006–2008 performance). Data source: CISDM. Sample period: 1994–2008. *, **, *** Significant at the 10%, 5%, and 1% levels, respectively.

operate in a jurisdiction with restrictions on location versus funds that do not operate in a jurisdiction with restrictions on location. The data indicate that for the jurisdiction with restrictions on the location of key service providers, prior lagged 3-year alphas (1-year alphas) are less closely related to future alphas by 4.7% (5.3%). Further, note that the effect of restrictions on location is negative and significant in Panel B (B') for Model (7) (for the top quartile funds) and in Model (11) (for the bottom quartile funds). The effect is robust only for the top quartile funds for 1-year-alphas as shown with Model (7) in Panel B'. Hence, the impact of restrictions on location is more detrimental to top quartile funds.

The data show no statistical support for Hypothesis 9.3. The coefficients for Bank interacted with lagged alpha and Other Regulated Financial Intermediary interacted with lagged alpha are positive but insignificant.

The data indicate mixed statistical support for Hypothesis 9.4 for distribution channels that make fund performance more opaque in Table 9.3. In Panel A (A'), the coefficient for Investment Managers interacted with lagged alpha is negative and significant and also for Private Placements interacted with lagged alpha in Panel A', but the other coefficients are insignificant. In Panel B (B'), there is stronger support for a negative association with wrappers and performance persistence in Model (7) for top quartile funds. To see the size of the effect, consider a 1-standard deviation difference in alpha from the mean for hedge funds that operate in a jurisdiction with wrapper distributions versus funds that do not operate in a jurisdiction with wrapper distributions. The data indicate that for the jurisdiction with wrapper distributions, prior lagged 3-year alphas are less closely related to future alphas by about 15.7% (Model 7) for the top quartile, but more closely related to future alphas by 15.4% for funds in the bottom quartile (Model 10) (the effect is insignificant for the other quartiles). Simply put, wrappers hurt performance persistence for top quartile funds, but for bottom quartile funds, wrappers enable persistently bad performance. The data thus provide very strong support for Hypothesis 9.4 for wrappers.

The control variables for misreporting funds, multi-funds, master-feeder funds, and funds with annual redemptions are all positive and statistically significant as well as economically large. The regressions in Table 9.4 are presented for winsorized alphas at the 99% level. When we winsorized at the 95%, these results were not as significant or as large. Therefore, we considered and explicitly show robustness with an alternative approach with the use of quartile ranks.

The regressions for relative quartile rankings (equation (2)) are presented in Table 9.4. The results are consistent with those in Table 9.3 in that they show very strong support for Hypotheses 1 and 2. Furthermore, the statistical and economic significance of the effects for minimum capitalization and restrictions on location are very similar for Table 9.5 as they are for Table 9.3. We note, however, that there is less consistent support for Hypothesis 9.3 and 9.4 in terms of the effects on performance from distribution channels. Further, note in Table 9.4 that the control variables for misreporting funds, multi-funds, master-feeder funds, and funds with annual redemptions are not as statistically and/or as economically large as in Table 9.3, as the modeling takes away any possible outliers with the specification equation (2) for Table 9.4.

Table 9.4. **Ranking Regressions**

Panel A: 3-Year Alpha Quartile Ranking

	(12) Panel, AR(1)		(13) Ordered Logit				
	Coefficient	p-value	Coefficient	p-value	Marginal Effects for Top Quartile	Marginal Effects for 2nd Quartile	Marginal Effects for 3rd Quartile	Marginal Effects for Bottom Quartile
3-Year Lagged Alpha Quartile Rank	0.033	0.525	0.226	0.030**	0.040	0.016	-0.022	-0.034
3-Year Lagged Alpha Rank * Minimum Capitalization	0.003	0.038**	0.006	0.019**	0.001	0.0004	-0.001	-0.001
3-Year Lagged Alpha Rank *Restrictions on Location	-0.056	0.070*	-0.143	0.028**	-0.025	-0.010	0.014	0.021
3-Year Lagged Alpha Rank *Private Placement	-0.080	0.116	-0.095	0.346	-0.017	-0.007	0.009	0.014
3-Year Lagged Alpha Rank *Investment Manager	0.031	0.038**	0.067	0.015**	0.012	0.005	-0.007	-0.010
3-Year Lagged Alpha Rank *Fund Distribution Company	0.039	0.547	-0.046	0.780	-0.008	-0.003	0.005	0.007
3-Year Lagged Alpha Rank *Bank	-0.019	0.428	-0.003	0.948	-0.001	-0.0002	0.0003	0.0005

(Continued)

Table 9.4. (Continued)

Panel A: 3-Year Alpha Quartile Ranking

	(12) Panel, AR(1)			(13) Ordered Logit				
	Coefficient	p-value	Coefficient	p-value	Marginal Effects for Top Quartile	Marginal Effects for 2nd Quartile	Marginal Effects for 3rd Quartile	Marginal Effects for Bottom Quartile
3-Year Lagged Alpha Rank *Wrapper	−0.062	0.292	0.004	0.978	0.001	0.0003	−0.0004	−0.001
3-Year Lagged Alpha Rank *Other Regulated Financial Intermediary	−0.079	0.006***	−0.135	0.024**	−0.024	−0.010	0.013	0.020
3-Year Lagged Alpha Rank *Non-Regulated Financial Intermediary	0.035	0.518	−0.014	0.886	−0.003	−0.001	0.001	0.002
3-Year Lagged Alpha *Multiple Funds	0.020	0.027**	0.033	0.043**	0.006	0.002	−0.003	−0.005
3-Year Lagged Alpha Rank *Master Feeder	0.002	0.843	−0.006	0.761	−0.001	−0.0004	0.001	0.001
3-Year Lagged Alpha Rank *Annual Redemption	0.038	0.014**	0.060	0.029**	0.011	0.004	−0.006	−0.009
3-Year Lagged Alpha Rank *Misreporting Fund	0.011	0.257	0.004	0.857	0.001	0.0003	−0.0004	−0.001

Log Assets under Management	−0.013	0.120	−0.017	0.244	−0.003	−0.001	0.002	0.003
Log GDP per Capita	−0.075	0.219	−0.244	0.133	−0.043	−0.017	0.024	0.037
English Legal Origin	0.221	0.010**	0.356	0.014**	0.058	0.031	−0.030	−0.059
Constant	3.484	0.000***						
Strategy Dummy Variables?	Yes				Yes			
Estimated Autocorrelation Coefficient	0.339				Not Applicable			
N	12597				12,597			
Adjusted R2 (Pseudo R2 for Ordered Logit)	0.0394				0.0211			

Panel B: 1-Year Alpha Quartile Ranking

	(12) Panel, AR(1)				(13) Ordered Logit			
	Coefficient	p-value	Coefficient	p-value	Marginal Effects for Top Quartile	Marginal Effects for 2nd Quartile	Marginal Effects for 3rd Quartile	Marginal Effects for Bottom Quartile
1-Year Lagged Alpha Quartile Rank	−0.006	0.586	−0.010	0.707	0.001	0.001	−0.001	−0.002
1-Year Lagged Alpha Rank * Minimum Capitalization	0.003	0.044**	0.007	0.022**	0.001	0.001	0.001	0.001

(Continued)

Table 9.4. (Continued)

Panel B: 1-Year Alpha Quartile Ranking

	(12) Panel, AR(1)		(13) Ordered Logit				
	Coefficient	p-value	Coefficient	p-value	Marginal Effects for Top Quartile	Marginal Effects for 2nd Quartile	Marginal Effects for 3rd Quartile	Marginal Effects for Bottom Quartile
1-Year Lagged Alpha Rank *Restrictions on Location	−0.085	0.022**	−0.184	0.010***	−0.027	−0.019	0.013	0.032
1-Year Lagged Alpha Rank *Private Placement	−0.041	0.005***	−0.113	0.001***	−0.017	−0.011	0.008	0.020
1-Year Lagged Alpha Rank *Investment Manager	0.038	0.024**	0.076	0.017**	0.011	0.008	0.006	0.013
1-Year Lagged Alpha Rank *Fund Distribution Company	−0.024	0.713	−0.205	0.247	0.030	0.021	−0.015	−0.036
1-Year Lagged Alpha Rank *Bank	0.003	0.922	0.027	0.628	−0.004	−0.003	0.002	0.005
1-Year Lagged Alpha Rank *Wrapper	−0.014	0.819	0.120	0.472	−0.018	−0.012	0.009	0.021
1-Year Lagged Alpha Rank *Other Regulated Financial Intermediary	−0.086	0.003***	−0.081	0.201	0.012	0.008	−0.006	−0.014
1-Year Lagged Alpha Rank *Non-Regulated Financial Intermediary	−0.012	0.850	−0.104	0.373	0.015	0.011	−0.008	−0.018
1-Year Lagged Alpha *Multiple Funds	0.014	0.163	0.027	0.158	−0.004	−0.003	0.002	0.005

1-Year Lagged Alpha Rank *Master Feeder	0.009		−0.007		0.758	0.001	0.001	−0.001
1-Year Lagged Alpha Rank *Annual Redemption	0.046	0.008***	0.066		0.032**	−0.010	−0.007	0.005	0.012
1-Year Lagged Alpha Rank *Misreporting Fund	0.009		0.012		0.620	−0.002	−0.001	0.001	0.002
Log Assets under Management	−0.009		−0.013		0.442	0.002	0.001	−0.001	−0.002
Log GDP per Capita	−0.168	0.049**	−0.264		0.082*	0.039	0.027	−0.019	−0.046
English Legal Origin	0.229	0.007***	0.243		0.110	−0.038	−0.022	0.021	0.040
Constant	4.416	0.000***							
Strategy Dummy Variables?	Yes						Yes		
Estimated Autocorrelation Coefficient	0.296						Not Applicable		
N	17258						17,258		
Adjusted R2 (Pseudo R2 for Ordered Logit)	0.0468						0.0235		

This table presents Panel AR(1) panel (by years and funds) estimates of performance persistence with a quartile ranking dependent variable in Model (12), alongside ordered logit estimates of the quartile ranking without an AR(1) specification in Model (13). In panel A [B] the dependent variable is the 3-year alpha quartile ranking [1-year alpha quartile ranking] for each fund for each year. Explanatory variables include the 3-year alpha quartile ranking [1-year alpha quartile ranking] (lagged by 3 [1] years), the interaction between lagged alpha rankings and fund regulation variables (minimum capitalization, restrictions on location, and distribution channels for investment manager, fund distribution company and wrappers), the interaction between lagged alpha and fund characteristics (fund managers that operate multiple funds, master feeder funds, funds with annual redemptions), log of assets under management, and country factors that include GDP per capita and a dummy variable for English legal origin. Twenty-seven dummy variables are included for different strategies in the CISDM database (one is excluded to avoid collinearity, and a constant is included in all regressions). Ordered logit estimates are presented for clustering by fund. Regression results, particularly for the fund regulation variable of interest, are not affected by collinearity and/or clustering. Data source: CISDM. Sample period: 1994–2008. *, **, *** significant at the 10%, 5%, and 1% levels, respectively.

Table 9.5. Two-Step Treatment Sample Selection Regressions for Offshore Registrants

	(14) Treatment Sample Selection Regression for Quartiles				(15) Treatment Sample Selection Regression for Quartiles			
	(a) Dependent Variable: Offshore		(b) Persistence Regression		(a) Dependent Variable: Offshore		(b) Persistence Regression	
	Coefficient	p-value	Coefficient	p-value	Coefficient	p-value	Coefficient	p-value
3-Year Lagged Alpha Quartile Rank (Alpha for (24))			0.121	0.002***			0.093	0.028
3-Year Lagged Alpha Rank (Alpha for (24))*Minimum Capitalization			0.003	0.002***			0.005	0.001***
3-Year Lagged Alpha Rank (Alpha for (24))*restrictions on location			−0.039	0.055*			−0.065	0.000***
3-Year Lagged Alpha Rank (Alpha for (24))*Private Placement			−0.035	0.329			−0.045	0.281
3-Year Lagged Alpha Rank (Alpha for (24))*Wrapper			0.023	0.351			−0.0295	0.371
3-Year Lagged Alpha Rank (Alpha for (24))*Other Regulated Financial Intermediary			−0.133	0.000***			−0.057	0.042**
3-Year Lagged Alpha Rank (Alpha for (24))*Non-Regulated Financial Intermediary			0.125	0.005***			0.151	0.002***
3-Year Lagged Alpha (Alpha for (24))*Multiple Funds			0.018	0.006***			0.454	0.000***
3-Year Lagged Alpha Rank (Alpha for (24))*Master Feeder			−0.009	0.291			0.381	0.000***

3-Year Lagged Alpha Rank (Alpha for (24))*Annual Redemption			0.048	0.000***	0.333	0.000***
3-Year Lagged Alpha Rank (Alpha for (24))*Misreporting Fund			0.000	0.993	0.7316	0.000***
Misreporting Fund	0.050	0.278				
					0.2780	
Log Assets under Management	0.118	0.000***	−0.013	0.033**	0.050	
Log GDP per Capita	−0.861	0.000***	−0.135	0.004***	0.118	0.000***
English Legal Origin	−0.417	0.000***	0.087	0.189	−0.861	0.001***
Offshore			−0.008	0.881	−0.417	0.000***
					−0.003	0.863
Strategy Dummy Variables?	Yes		No		Yes	No
Fund Regulation Dummy Variables for Distributions and Restrictions on Location?	Yes		No		Yes	No
Constant	4.490	0.000***	3.871	0.000***	4.490	0.000***
Lambda		0.089**				1.298
						−0.016
N	12597		12597		12597	

This table presents treatment regressions of performance persistence based on a quartile ranking dependent variable in Model (14) and the continuous alpha dependent variable in Model (15). The dependent variable in the step (a) regressions is a dummy variable for offshore registrants. The dependent variable in step (b) of Model (14) is the 3-year alpha quartile ranking for each fund for each year and in Model (15) is the actual 3-year alpha. Explanatory variables include the 3-year alpha quartile ranking (lagged by 3 years), the interaction between lagged alpha rankings and fund regulation variables (minimum capitalization, restrictions on location, and distribution channels for investment manager, fund distribution company, and wrappers), the interaction between lagged alpha and fund characteristics (fund managers who operate multiple funds, master-feeder funds, funds with annual redemptions), log of assets under management, and country factors that include GDP per capita and a dummy variable for English legal origin. Twenty-seven dummy variables are included for different strategies in the CISDM database (one is excluded to avoid collinearity, and a constant is included in all regressions). Regressions are presented for the full sample. Regression results, particularly for the fund regulation variable of interest, are not affected by collinearity. Data source: CISDM. Sample period: 1994–2008. *, **, *** significant at the 10%, 5%, and 1% levels, respectively.

Table 9.4 presents regression estimates of equation (3) for sample selection for non-random jurisdiction choice. Regardless of the first step-sample selection model and/or the use of 7-factor alphas or relative rankings of 7-factor alphas, the data again provide strong support for the proposition that minimum capitalization facilitates performance persistence (Hypothesis 9.1) while restrictions on location mitigate performance persistence (Hypothesis 9.2). The statistical and economic significance is very similar to the results presented in Tables 9.3 and 9.4. As before, however, there is mixed support for Hypothesis 9.3 and 9.4 in terms of the effect of distribution channels.

Overall, the data herein strongly support the predictions that minimum capitalization facilitates performance persistence, particularly for bottom quartile funds. These findings are consistent with other work that shows that minimum capitalization reduces the left tail of performance figures and hence raises average performance levels (Cumming and Dai, 2010a) and increases flows to funds (Cumming and Dai, 2009). Furthermore, the data show that restrictions on location of key service providers mitigate performance persistence, particularly for top quartile funds. This evidence is consistent with other work that shows that restrictions on location mitigate average levels of fund performance (Cumming and Dai, 2010a) and lower capital flows to funds (Cumming and Dai, 2009). Also, there is evidence in the data presented here of less performance persistence among top quartile funds for wrapper distributions, but also evidence of more performance persistence among bottom quartile funds for wrapper distributions. Again, this evidence is consistent with other work that shows wrapper distributions are associated with lower levels of fund performance (Cumming and Dai, 2010a) and flatter or less sensitive flow-performance relationships (Cumming and Dai, 2009). The contribution here is unique by showing that performance persistence among intermediaries is affected by regulation, which is important for hedge fund managers and regulators alike, as well as other types of investors and intermediaries.

9.4.3. ADDITIONAL ROBUSTNESS CHECKS

We carried out a number of other robustness checks in the course of our analyses but do not explicitly present the regressions for reasons of conciseness. We briefly discuss these results here. We considered differences in the effect of regulation on persistence by whether the fund persistently misreports or smooths returns. We considered two-step models for funds that do and do not have consecutive years of performance persistence data. We considered various other control variables that are available in hedge fund datasets in other specifications not reported but available on request. We further considered robustness to selection effects in terms of Heckman (1976, 1979) selection for choice of other jurisdictions, robustness to excluding certain countries, and robustness to selection for the probability that a fund has survived sufficiently long in the dataset to report multi-period returns. Our findings are quite robust and highlight the important role of financial regulation on performance persistence, particularly in support of Hypotheses 1 and 2 as discussed.

9.5. Conclusions

This chapter proposed the idea that performance persistence can either be enhanced or mitigated by financial regulation. We tested this idea in the context of the hedge fund industry with data from 48 countries spanning the years 1994–2008. International and time-series differences in hedge fund regulation exist for minimum capitalization requirements, restrictions on the location of key service providers, and permissible distribution channels. Overall, the data provide support for the idea that minimum capitalization enhances performance persistence, while restrictions on location mitigate performance persistence. As well, we found some evidence consistent with the view that wrapper distributions are associated with lower performance persistence in ways that differ significantly depending on the quartile ranking of the fund. We did not find evidence that distribution channels that promote a fund's presence to institutional investors increase performance persistence. Our findings are robust to different econon.etric specifications, controlling for potential selection effects and alternative measures of performance (alpha and quartile rankings).

Future work in coming years could consider newly proposed hedge fund regulation in Europe and the United States as regulators contemplate regulatory changes in the aftermath of the financial crisis. Also, future work could consider the impact of regulation on performance persistence and aspects of financial intermediation in other contexts outside the hedge fund industry.

Keywords

Binary Logit Regression
Performance Persistence
Distribution Channels
Funds with Annual Redemption
Key Service Provider
Master-Feeder Funds

Minimum Capitalization
Misreporting Funds
Offshore Registration
Private Placement
Selection Effect
Wrappers

Discussion Questions

1. What is performance persistence? Why is performance persistence relevant to fund managers, investors, and/or regulators?
2. Why is minimum capital restriction likely to increase the probability of performance persistence? Is this empirically supported?

3. Why is restriction on the location of key service providers likely to decrease the probability of performance persistence? Is this empirically supported?
4. Why are distribution channels that promote a fund's presence to institutional investors, such as distribution by banks, fund distribution companies, and other regulated financial services institutions, likely to increase the probability of performance persistence? Is this empirically supported?
5. Why are distribution channels that make fund performance more opaque, such as wrappers, and distributions directly through investment managers themselves without certification of external agents likely to decrease the probability of performance persistence? Is this empirically supported?
6. What are the major implications for policy makers of the relationship between performance persistence and hedge fund regulation documented in this chapter?

CHAPTER 10

Hedge Fund Liquidation and Hedge Fund Influence on the General Market

10.1. Introduction

One of the most vibrant parts of the financial market over the last decade has been the hedge fund industry. As unregulated and opaque investment partnerships that engage in a variety of active investment strategies, the return/risk profile of a hedge fund differs in important ways from that for more traditional investments, and such differences may have potentially significant implications for systematic risk.

Systematic risk is usually taken to mean the risk of a broad-based breakdown in the financial system, often realized as a series of correlated defaults among financial institutions that occur over a short period of time and are typically caused by a single major event. For instance, in August 1998, the Long Term Capital Management (LTCM) and many other fixed income hedge funds suffered catastrophic losses within a few weeks after the Russian government defaulted on its debt, which created significant stress on the global financial system and several major financial institutions. Since the collapse of LTCM in 1998, it has become clear that hedge fund failure can be a significant source of systematic risk.

However, as part of the shadow banking system, hedge funds lie outside the oversight of the Federal Reserve, the Office of the Controller of the Currency, the SEC, the Commodity Futures Trading Commission (CFTC), and the Treasury. Without access to necessary data about the hedge fund industry, it is impossible to determine definitively what its contribution is to systematic risk, hence, impossible to monitor and manage its systematic risk.

In Section 10.2, we study the survival of hedge funds. By analyzing what causes the failure of hedge funds, we may develop a better understanding of the risks in the hedge fund industry. In Section 10.3, we discuss the relation between hedge funds and systematic risk in the recent financial crisis. In Section 10.4, we discuss ways we can improve hedge fund regulation to better manage systematic risk in the future.

10.2. Hedge Fund Liquidation

10.2.1. THE ANNUAL DISTRIBUTION OF NEW ENTRIES, EXITS, AND ATTRITION RATES

To develop a sense of hedge fund entries and exits in the CISDM database, in Table 10.1 we report annual frequency counts of funds in the database at the start of each year, funds entering during the year, funds exiting during the year, and total funds at the end of each year during the period from 1994 to 2008. The attrition rates are defined as the ratio of funds exiting in a given year to the sum of the number of existing funds at the start of the year and the new entries in a given year. As shown in Table 10.1, a total of 1,877 hedge funds were liquidated in 2008, which is a historical high. This represents an attrition rate of about 25%.

10.2.2. HEDGE FUND LIQUIDATION AND FUND CHARACTERISTICS

To estimate the influence of various hedge fund characteristics on the likelihood of failure, in Table 10.2, we report the results (hazard ratios) of the COX Proportional Hazard Regressions. Our sample consists of 9,876 funds, both extant funds and disappearing funds, both funds of funds and hedge funds. Our dependent variable is the age of the fund. The failure event is disappearing from the CISDM database. A hazard ratio less (more) than 1 indicates that the fund is less (more) likely to fail. The explanatory variables include a dummy variable that indicates whether the fund is a hedge fund or fund of fund, the natural logarithm of assets under management, annual excess return, standard deviation of excess return, and other performance measures such as information ratio and MPPM. The method and process of estimating these return and risk measures are discussed in detail in Chapter 4. We further control the investment strategies of hedge funds in relevant specifications.

In specification (1), we first examined whether funds of funds are more likely to survive than hedge funds as they are generally regarded as better diversified. We found a hazard ratio of 0.518, significant at the 1% confidence level. This result supports the notion that funds of funds are less likely to fail than hedge funds on average. In specifications (2) to (4), we examined what affects the survival of hedge funds. We included various performance measures and controlled for both the size of assets under management and the fixed effect of hedge funds investment strategies. We showed that larger funds and funds with better performance are more likely to survive.

In specification (5), we further controlled for regulatory variables such as requirements for minimum capital, restrictions on key service provider location, distribution channels permitted, and legal origin. We did not find that requirement for minimum capital, restrictions on key service provider location, and

Table 10.1. **Annual Frequency Counts of Entries and Exits Out of the CISDM Database (1994–2008)**

Year	Existing Funds	New Entries	New Exits	Total Funds	Attrition Rate (%)
1994	1418	532	35	1915	1.79%
1995	1915	478	148	2245	6.18%
1996	2245	610	198	2657	6.94%
1997	2657	649	348	2958	10.53%
1998	2958	604	450	3112	12.63%
1999	3112	666	440	3338	11.65%
2000	3338	622	396	3564	10.00%
2001	3564	759	414	3909	9.58%
2002	3909	847	376	4380	7.91%
2003	4380	950	388	4942	7.28%
2004	4942	1178	469	5651	7.66%
2005	5651	1189	458	6382	6.70%
2006	6382	1095	653	6824	8.73%
2007	6824	960	748	7036	9.61%
2008	7036	494	1877	5653	24.93%

Table 10.2. **COX Proportional Hazards Regressions**

	(1)	(2)	(3)	(4)	(5)
FOF	0.518*** (0.0176)				
Annual excess return		0.201*** (0.0272)			0.220*** (0.0299)
Standard deviation of excess return		0.613 (0.3146)			1.225 (0.6011)
Information Ratio			0.800*** (0.0486)		

(Continued)

Table 10.2. (Continued)

	(1)	(2)	(3)	(4)	(5)
MPPM				0.985*** (0.0058)	
Ln (AUM)		0.803*** (0.0069)	0.799*** (0.0066)	0.797*** (0.0065)	0.796*** (0.0071)
Ln(Minimum Capital)					1.042 (0.0415)
Restrictions on Key Service Provider Location					0.746 (0.4223)
Wrappers					1.211 (0.6427)
Banks					0.534 (0.4956)
Fund Distribution Companies					1.028 (0.5099)
Private Placements					0.882 (0.6267)
English					1.594** (0.3677)
French					1.248*** (0.0505)
German					1.054 (0.1077)
Investment Strategy		Yes	Yes	Yes	Yes
Observations	9876	5885	5885	5885	5885
Log Likelihood	−41772.01	−27860.33	−27860.33	−27933.78	−26782.63
LR Chi2	418.97	874.30	874.32	727.43	902.89
Prob > Chi2	0.000	0.000	0.000	0.000	0.000

distribution channels significantly affected the failure of hedge funds (and this evidence is consistent with the view that survivorship bias is not an explanation for the performance persistence results we observed in Chapter 9). However, legal origin seems to have some effect on the survival of hedge funds. For instance, we showed that hedge funds with domiciles in English and French legal origins are more likely to fail.

10.3. Hedge Fund and the 2008 Financial Crisis

10.3.1. GROWTH OF ASSETS AND LEVERAGE IN THE HEDGE FUND INDUSTRY

Unlike banks, which are highly regulated entities, with specific capital adequacy requirements and leverage and risk constraints, hedge funds and their investors are less constrained. The dynamic and competitive nature of hedge funds implies that hedge fund investors will shift their assets tactically and quickly, moving into markets when profit opportunities arise and moving out when those opportunities have been depleted. Although such tactics benefit hedge fund investors, they can also cause market dislocation in crowded markets with participants who are not fully aware of or prepared for the crowdedeness of their investments. For instance, the responsiveness of hedge fund investors to underperformance is well known, and these rapid changes in risk capital can lead to wild market gyrations as we experienced in the 2008 financial crisis (Khandani and Lo, 2007, 2008). To develop a sense of the scale of such a gyration, consider the growth of hedge fund assets from 1990 to 2008 as shown in Exhibit 10.1. and Table 10.3 and note the sharp decline in assets and leverage in 2008.

10.3.2. INDIRECT EVIDENCE OF THE LEVEL OF SYSTEMIC RISK IN THE HEDGE FUND INDUSTRY

As early as 2004, Chan et al. (2004) presented indirect evidence that the level of systemic risk in the hedge fund industry had increased; in particular, they concluded with the following summary:

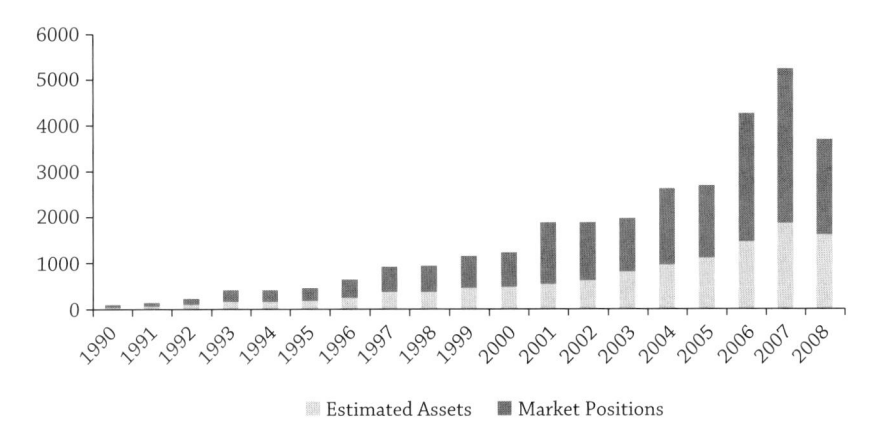

Exhibit 10.1. Growth of Assets (Billions of US$) and Leverage in the Hedge Fund Industry from 1990 to 2008

Source: Reproduced based on figure 3 in Lo (2008).

Table 10.3. **Distribution of Assets and Leverage in the Hedge Fund Industry from 1990 to 2008**

Year	Estimated Assets	Market Positions	Leverage
1990	38	95	2.50
1991	58	145	2.50
1992	95	238	2.51
1993	167	418	2.50
1994	167	418	2.50
1995	185	463	2.50
1996	256	640	2.50
1997	367	918	2.50
1998	374	935	2.50
1999	456	1140	2.50
2000	490	1225	2.50
2001	539	1887	3.50
2002	625	1877	3.00
2003	820	1968	2.40
2004	972	2620	2.70
2005	1105	2674	2.42
2006	1464	4247	2.90
2007	1868	5231	2.80
2008	1600	3680	2.30

1. The hedge fund industry has grown tremendously over the last few years, fueled by the demand for higher returns in the face of stock market declines and mounting pension fund liabilities. These massive fund inflows have had a material impact on hedge fund returns and risks in recent years, as evidenced by changes in correlations, reduced performance, increased illiquidity, and the large number of hedge funds launched and closed.
2. The banking sector is exposed to hedge fund risks, especially smaller institutions, but the largest banks are also exposed through proprietary trading activities, credit arrangements and structured products, and prime brokerage services.

3. The risks facing hedge funds are non-linear and more complex than those facing traditional asset classes. Because of the dynamic nature of hedge fund investment strategies and the impact of fund flows on leverage and performance, hedge fund risk models require more sophisticated analytics and more sophisticated users.
4. The aggregate level of distress in the hedge fund sector is increasing. This, coupled with the recent uptrend in the weighted autocorrelation, implies that systemic risk is increasing.

Chan et al. (2006, 2007) extended these tentative conclusions with additional data and analytics and they uncovered more indirect evidence for increasing levels of systematic risk. In the first half of 2007, the blow-up of two Bear Stearns credit strategies funds, the sale of Sowood Capital Management's portfolio to Citadel after losses exceeding 50%, and mounting problems at Countrywide Financial—the largest home lender in United States—set the stage for further turmoil in fixed income and credit markets during the month of August 2007.

10.3.3. THE INCREASING CORRELATION AND CONNECTEDNESS IN THE HEDGE FUND INDUSTRY

Much progress has been made in the recent literature in explaining liquidity risk and credit risk, but the complex network of creditor/obligator relationships, revolving credit agreements, and other financial interconnections is still largely unmapped. A number of recent advances in the theory of networks are used to analyze the degree of connectedness and the vulnerability of the financial system. For instance, Khandani and Lo (2007) calculated the changes in the absolute values of correlations between hedge fund indexes over time to measure the change in the degree of "connectedness" in the hedge fund industry. Exhibit 10.2. displays the absolute values of correlations among hedge fund indexes over two sub-periods, April 1994 to December 2000 and January 2001 to June 2007. Thicker lines represent absolute correlations greater than 50%, thinner lines represent absolute correlations between 25% and 50%, and no connecting lines correspond to correlations less than 25%. A comparison of the two sub-periods shows that the various indexes in the hedge fund industry have clearly become more closely connected.

Another significant indicator for the increased connectedness in the hedge fund industry is that in the more recent period, the Multi-Strategy category has become significantly highly correlated with almost every other index, which is a symptom of large influx of assets into the hedge fund industry.

The increase in correlations among hedge fund returns can be attributed to at least two potential sources: increased exposure of hedge funds to standard factors such as S&P 500, the US 10-year Treasury bond, and the US Dollar Index,

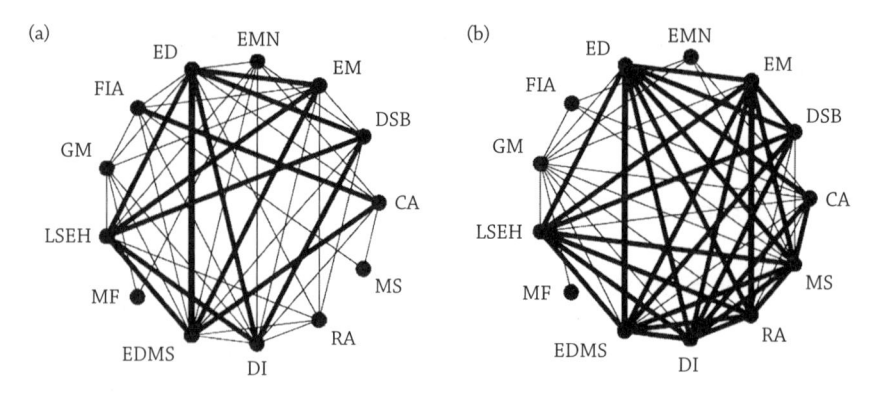

Exhibit 10.2. Network Diagrams

Network diagrams of correlations among 13 CS/Tremont hedge fund indexes over two sub-periods: (a) April 1994 to December 2000 (excluding the month of August 1998) and (b) January 2001 to June 2007. Thicker lines represent absolute correlations greater than 50%, thinner lines represent absolute correlations between 25% and 50%, and no connecting lines correspond to correlations less than 25%. CA: Convertible Arbitrage, DSB: Dedicated Short Bias, EM: Emerging Markets, EMN: Equity Market Neutral, ED: Event Driven, FIA: Fixed Income Arbitrage, GM: Global Macro, LSEH: Long/Short Equity Hedge, MF: Managed Futures, EDMS: Event Driven Multi-Strategy, DI: Distressed Index, RA: Risk Arbitrage, and MS: Multi-Strategy. (Source: Khandani and Lo, 2007).

and increased linkage due to more complex channels such as liquidity and credit relationships through multi-strategy funds and proprietary trading desks. Although we cannot distinguish between these two sources given the lack of more data, the increasing correlations and connectedness in the hedge fund industry imply the potential for systemwide shocks in the industry.

Boyson et al. (2010) provided empirical evidence for this view. They studied contagion—correlation over and above that expected from economic fundamentals—and found strong evidence of worse return contagion across hedge fund styles for the period from 1990 to 2008. In the theoretical model of Brunnermeier and Pedersen (2009), shocks to asset liquidity can lead to funding constraints that force hedge funds to reduce their leverage. As a result of this deleveraging, asset liquidity worsens, which leads to further deleveraging. Alternatively, a shock to funding liquidity leads to deleveraging, which reduces asset liquidity. These spirals affect all assets for which hedge funds are the marginal investors, not only the assets affected directly by the initial shock. Boyson et al. (2010) empirically showed that large adverse shocks to asset and hedge fund liquidity strongly increase the probability of contagion. Specifically, large adverse shocks to credit spreads, the TED spread (the difference between the three-month London Interbank Offered Rate [LIBOR] and the three-month US Treasury bill interest rate), prime broker and bank stock prices, stock market liquidity, and hedge fund flow are associated with a significant increase in the probability of hedge fund contagion.

The network of the global financial system is considerably more complex, involving many different types of organizations (banks, hedge funds, prime brokers, investors, regulators, etc.) and different types of relationships among these organizations. A number of recent studies have applied the mathematic theory of networks to financial markets; nevertheless, there are virtually no data with which to calibrate such models.

10.4. Implications for Hedge Fund Regulation Reform

Systematic risk is a public good (or public "bad"). Everyone in the global economy benefits from a stable, liquid, and reliable financial market, but no single individual is willing to pay for this public good. Hence, government can play a positive role in addressing this market failure. As for now, hedge funds lie outside the oversight of the Federal Reserve, the Office of the Controller of the Currency, the SEC, the CFTC, and the Treasury. The recent growth of the hedge fund industry and hedge funds' increasing contribution to the systematic risk has significantly reduced the ability of these regulatory institutions to maintain the same level of financial market safety as before. Several regulatory reforms are proposed with the aim that regulations can adapt to the changing market conditions and can more effectively monitor and control systematic risk.

10.4.1. INFORMATION TRANSPARENCY

Hedge funds are among the most secretive of financial institutions. Without access to necessary data about the hedge fund industry, no one can definitively measure what their contribution to systematic risk is and it is difficult to regulate or to monitor and control its systematic risk. As Lo pointed out in his written testimony to the US House of Representatives, "the need for additional data from all parts of the shadow banking system is a pre-requisite for regulatory reform in the hedge-fund industry." He proposes that hedge funds with more than US$1 billion in gross notional exposures be required to provide regulatory authorities such as the Federal Reserve or the SEC with the following information on a regular, timely, and confidential basis:

- Assets under management
- Leverage
- Portfolio holdings
- List of credit counterparties
- List of investors

However, the value of hedge funds is highly dependent on the performance of investment strategies. It is unreasonable to force hedge funds to give up the confidentiality of this key information. A compromise could be for regulators to collect this information from prime brokers that service hedge funds in an aggregated, redacted, and anonymously coded format (Lo, 2008) or even to request prime brokers to compute certain pre-specified risk measures periodically and report to regulators. This approach is operationally more efficient, and the proprietary aspects of the hedge funds' strategies are protected.

10.4.2. INVESTOR PROTECTION AND RISK MANAGEMENT

The recent debates among regulators and legislators have centered around the registration of hedge funds under the Investment Advisor Act of 1940 with the aim of providing more investor protections. However, registration does not directly address the systematic risk that hedge funds pose to the global financial system. Currently, no regulatory agency has a mandate to monitor, much less manage, such risks in the hedge fund sector. Lo (2008) proposes creating a "Capital Markets Safety Board" (CMSB). This board will be dedicated to investigating, reporting, and archiving the crises in the financial industry. In addition, the CMSB should also be tasked with the responsibility of obtaining and maintaining information from the shadow banking system—hedge funds, private partnerships, sovereign wealth funds, and others—and integrating this information with that of other regulatory agencies. Furthermore, the CMSB would be responsible for communicating its analysis to the public in a timely fashion. If one single agency was responsible for managing data related to systemic risk and creating high-level risk analytics such as a network map of the financial system, estimates of illiquidity exposure, leverage, and asset flows, the repository of data would be far easier to access and analyze.

10.4.3. FAIR-VALUE ACCOUNTING

Recently, the Financial Accounting Standards Board (FASB) Statement No. 157 Fair-Value Accounting was blamed for the 2008 financial crisis. Fair-value accounting requires firms to value their assets and liabilities at fair market value, not historical cost. During the crisis, as the market value of assets declined, fair-value accounting forced many firms to write down their assets. Some people argue that this triggered defaults and insolvencies and proposed suspending fair-value accounting. For instance, Plantin, Sapra, and Shin (2008) argued that during periods when liquidity is very low, a forced liquidation of an asset by one firm can depress the market price of that asset, which affects the value of another firm if it holds the same asset and is required to mark that asset to the market. In other words, fair-value accounting increases the correlation among assets of many firms and may lead to a "death spiral" in which liquidations cause deterioration of collateral that leads to more liquidations, and so on. Other recent studies (for example, Allen and Carletti, 2008; Easley and O'Hara, 2008; and Sapra, 2008) argue that during liquidity crises, market prices are not as meaningful as they are during normal times; hence, marking securities to market may not always yield the same information content.

As a general principle, the more transparency is provided to the market, the more efficient are the prices it produces and the more effectively will the market allocate capital and other limited resources. A permanent suspension of fair-value accounting will lead to significant reduction in market transparency. A direct consequence would be that market participants will lose significant transparency regarding the true value of assets and liabilities and will price securities accordingly. Borrowing cost will consequently increase and liquidity will be reduced.

Although it is commonly recognized that neither historical cost accounting nor fair-value accounting can be appropriate for all circumstances, no consensus has yet emerged regarding which alternative to mark-to-market pricing is best. Lo (2008) proposed a separate "risk balance sheet" with the observation that accounting methods are designed to yield information about value, not about risk. In the risk balance sheet (as shown in Exhibit 10.3), the variances of assets and liabilities instead of their values are reported. Since assets are always equal to liabilities, the variances of assets must always equal the variance of liabilities. The variance of both total assets and total liabilities is given by the sum of the

Assets	Liabilities
A_1	L_1
A_2	L_2
...	...
A_N	L_M
V	V

⬇

Assets	Liabilities
$\text{Var}[A_1]$	$\text{Var}[L_1]$
$\text{Var}[A_2]$	$\text{Var}[L_2]$
...	...
$\text{Var}[A_N]$	$\text{Var}[L_M]$
$\text{Cov}[A_i, A_j], i \neq j$	$\text{Cov}[L_i, L_j], i \neq j$
$\text{Var}[V]$	$\text{Var}[V]$

Exhibit 10.3. The Risk Balance Sheet

The Risk Balance Sheet, defined as the risk decomposition of a firm's market value balance sheet. (*Source*: Lo (2008))

variances of the individual assets and liabilities, plus their pairwise covariances. This challenge requires regulators, accountants, and financial experts to collaborate to develop a completely new set of accounting principles focusing on risk management.

10.5. Conclusions

In this chapter, we discussed the liquidation of hedge funds, the contribution of the hedge fund industry to systematic risk, and the role of hedge funds in the 2008 financial crisis as well as implications for future regulatory reform. The number of hedge funds that were liquidated reached a historical high in 2008. In general, funds of funds are more likely than hedge funds to survive. Better performances contribute to higher probability of survival; so does larger size. Anecdotal evidence shows that the hedge fund industry is playing an increasingly important role in the global financial system given its increased size, leverage, and connectedness with other parties. A more precise and direct measure of systematic risk is necessary for us to better understand and monitor systematic risk. This requires greater information transparency in the hedge fund industry. We expect certain regulations to be established to facilitate such disclosure without hurting the performance of hedge funds. We also expect government to play a greater role in monitoring and managing the systematic risk of the hedge fund industry and the whole shadow banking industry.

Keywords

Attrition Rates
Correlation and Connectedness in the
  Hedge Fund Industry
Fair-Value Accounting
Financial Interconnection
Growth of Assets and Leverage in the
  Hedge Fund Industry

Hedge Fund
  Liquidation
Information
  Transparency
Risk Balance Sheet
Shadow Banking System
Systematic Risk

Discussion Questions

1. What is systematic risk?
2. What are the patterns of the relationship between fund characteristics (e.g., size, performance, risk) and the probability of survival?
3. Why and how does the hedge fund industry contribute to the systematic risk of the global financial system?
4. How would you evaluate the role of the hedge fund industry in the 2008 financial crisis?

5. What could be the role of government in monitoring and managing systematic risk?
6. Some hedge funds argue that information on strategies, holdings, and positions are the key determinants for the success of hedge funds and therefore have to be kept confidential. Hence, too much disclosure will damage the value of hedge funds. What is your view on this?
7. What is fair-value accounting?
8. Some argue that fair-value accounting exacerbated (to some extent) the 2008 financial crisis; therefore, we should abandon it and go back to historical cost-based accounting. Do you agree? Why?

CHAPTER 11

Conclusion

In this book we examined the agency problems in hedge fund management and the role of regulation in mitigating such agency problems. We showed that where a fund is located results in significant differences in hedge fund regulation pertaining to restrictions on the location of key service providers, permissible distribution channels, and minimum size requirements. We showed that hedge fund forum shopping (Chapter 5), capital flows (Chapter 6), performance (Chapter 7), fixed management fees and carried interest performance fees (Chapter 7), misreporting (Chapter 8), and performance persistence (Chapter 9) all were affected by these differences in hedge fund regulation across countries and over time. In addition, in Chapter 3 we reviewed other recent changes in hedge fund regulation in the United States (Dodd-Frank) and Europe (UCITS and AIFMD). With the passage of time there will be more data to analyze these new regulatory developments with reference to datasets and empirical tests similar to those presented in this book.

More specifically, in Chapter 2 of this book, we provided an overview of the potential agency problems associated with managing a hedge fund and associated rationales for hedge fund regulation. In Chapter 3 we also provided examples of international differences in hedge fund regulation including minimum capitalization requirements, restrictions on the location of key service providers, and different permissible distribution channels via private placements, banks, other regulated or non-regulated financial intermediaries, wrappers, investment managers, and fund distribution companies.

If it is assumed that all hedge fund managers want complete freedom to do what they do best, then it follows that any extra regulatory oversight will cause them to forum shop. And it also follows that they might forum shop in a "race to the bottom." In Chapter 5 we sought to determine whether this is the case. We considered whether forum shopping exists across different hedge funds applying different strategies. Chapter 5 provided an empirical analysis of hedge fund strategies, structure, fund flows, performance, and misreporting behavior in the context of international differences in hedge fund regulation. The data offer little support for the view that hedge fund managers pursuing riskier strategies or strategies with potentially more pronounced agency problems systematically select jurisdictions with less stringent regulations. Rather, the data suggest that hedge funds select jurisdictions that are in the fund investors' interests in order to facilitate capital raising by the hedge fund.

We then showed that hedge fund regulation has an important role to play in influencing the size and stability of the hedge fund market. In Chapter 6, we showed that the level of fund flows was negatively related to restrictions on location of key service providers and positively related to minimum capitalization requirements. This suggests that minimum capitalization enhances investor confidence in terms of greater stability with larger funds. This finding holds even after controlling for minimum investment amounts per transaction. Hedge funds registered in countries that restrict the location of key service providers have lower levels of inflows. This result is consistent with the view that locational restrictions are perceived by investors to mitigate human resource quality, and this perceived reduction in human resource quality is more pronounced than any associated perceived improvement in regulatory oversight.

In Chapter 7 we explained the different ways to measure hedge fund performance, including raw returns, alphas, Sharpe ratios, and manipulation proof performance measures. The data in Chapter 7 highlighted the fact that restrictions on the location of key service providers and wrapper distributions are associated with worse performance measures and lower performance fees. Fund risk as measured by the standard deviations of monthly returns is lower among jurisdictions with restrictions on the location of key service providers and higher minimum capitalization requirements.

Data and empirical tests in Chapter 8 were used to analyze hedge fund misreporting to their institutional investors. Chapter 8 shows strong evidence of a significant relation between hedge fund regulation and misreporting. The data highlighted a positive association between wrappers and misreporting, particularly for funds that do not have a lockup provision. Also, we presented evidence that misreporting is less common among funds in jurisdictions with minimum capitalization requirements and restrictions on the location of key service providers. Moreover, we showed how misreporting significantly affects capital allocation, and we calculated the wealth transfer effects of misreporting and related this wealth transfer to differences in hedge fund regulation.

In Chapter 9 of this book we presented evidence consistent with the view that minimum capital restrictions restrict lower quality funds and hence increase the likelihood of performance persistence. As well, restrictions on location of key service providers restrict human capital choices and tend to mitigate performance persistence. Finally, distribution channels, which make fund performance more opaque, decrease the likelihood of performance persistence. We showed differences in the effect of regulation on persistence by fund quartile ranking.

The debate around hedge fund regulation in part involves the use of innovative investment strategies by hedge funds, coupled with the significant and growing systematic risk in the hedge fund industry (Chapter 10). On the one hand, these innovative hedge fund strategies provide various benefits to the financial systems involved including providing crucial liquidity to markets, limiting price distortions and anomalies via arbitrage trading, and taking on risk across instruments and markets as they are able to change portfolio composition rather quickly. On the other hand, as active risk takers across instruments and markets, hedge funds may also exacerbate the risk of systemic failure as their strategies involve multiple markets with as yet untested instrument links.

Opponents of more stringent hedge fund regulation believe that such beneficial hedge fund activities are facilitated within a "friendly" environment that allows freedom and discretion. To curtail such freedom may just cause the players to leave for a much friendlier playing field so to speak. To allow the players complete freedom, however, may just enable them to run amok. Regulation and oversight may be so heavy handed that hedge funds and managers will move their operations to more accommodating, less regulated jurisdictions. Also, as more regulatory oversight will involve taking away the self-regulating functions from hedge fund participants, this may encourage laxity with regard to investment decisions and risk management. The question now is not how to regulate the industry but where to draw the line between under- and over-regulation.

The empirical evidence in this book provides guidance to students, academics, practitioners, and policy makers as to appropriate forms of regulation with reference to existing empirical data and existing international differences in hedge fund regulation. We believe the evidence on the interaction between hedge fund regulations and fund structure, governance, and performance herein shows that evidence-based policy assessment has an important role for appropriately guiding future policy making in the hedge fund industry around the world.

REFERENCES

Ackermann, C., R. McEnally, and D. Ravenscraft. 1999. "The Performance of Hedge Funds: Risk, Return and Incentives." *Journal of Finance* **54**(3), 833–874.

Adams, B. D. 2007. "The Effect of Investor Flows on Hedge Fund Manager Performance and the Decision to Invest." Working Paper, Princeton University.

Admati, A. R., and P. Pfleiderer. 1997. "Does It All Add Up? Benchmarks and the Compensation of Active Portfolio Managers." *Journal of Business* **70**, 323–350.

Aitken, M., and A. Siow. 2003. "Ranking Equity Markets on the Basis of Market Efficiency and Integrity." In H. Skeete, ed., *Hewlett-Packard Handbook of World Stock, Derivative and Commodity Exchanges*. Dublin: Mondo Visione, pp. xliv–lv.

Agarwal, V., and N.Y. Naik. 2000a. "Multi-Period Performance Persistence Analysis of Hedge Funds." *Journal of Financial and Quantitative Analysis* **35**(3), 327–342.

Agarwal, V., and N.Y. Naik. 2000b. "On Taking the Alternative Route: Risks, Rewards and Performance Persistence of Hedge Funds." *Journal of Alternative Investments* **2**(4), 6–23.

Agarwal, V., and N.Y. Naik. 2004. "Risks and Portfolio Decisions Involving Hedge Funds." *Review of Financial Studies* **17**(1), 63–98.

Agarwal, V., N. Daniel, and N.Y. Naik. 2006. "Flows, Performance, and Managerial Incentives in the Hedge Fund Industry." Working Paper, London Business School.

Agarwal, V., N. Daniel, and N.Y. Naik. 2007. *"Why Is Santa So Kind to Hedge Funds? The December Return Puzzle!"* Working Paper, Georgia State University.

Agarwal, V., N. Daniel, and N. Naik. 2009. "Role of Managerial Incentives and Discretion in Hedge Fund Performance." *Journal of Finance* **64**, 2221–2256.

Allen, F., and E. Carletti. 2008. "Mark-to-Market Accounting and Liquidity Pricing." *Journal of Accounting and Economics* **45**, 358–378.

Amin, G. S., and H. M. Kat. 2003. "Hedge Fund Performance 1990–2000: Do the 'Money Machines' Really Add Value?" *Journal of Financial and Quantitative Analysis* **38**(2), 251–274.

Aragon, G. O. 2007. "Share Restrictions and Asset Pricing: Evidence from the Hedge Fund Industry." *Journal of Financial Economics* **83**(1), 33–58.

Avgouleas, E. 2005. *The Mechanics of Regulation of Market Abuse*. Oxford: Oxford University Press.

Baghai-Wadji, R., and S. Klocker. 2007. "Performance and Style Shifts in the Hedge Fund Industry." Working Paper, London Business School.

Ball, R., and L. Shivakumar. 2005. "Earnings Quality in U.K. Private Firms Comparative Loss Recognition Timeliness." *Journal of Accounting and Economics* **39**, 83–128.

Baquero, G., J. T. Horst, and M. Verbeek. 2005. "Survival, Look-Ahead Bias, and Persistence in Hedge Fund Performance." *Journal of Financial and Quantitative Analysis* **40**(3), 493–517.

Barclay, M., C. G. Holderness, and D. P. Sheehan. 2007. "Private Placements and Managerial Entrenchment." *Journal of Corporate Finance* **13**, 461.

Barth, J. R., G. Caprio, and R. Levine. 2002. "Financial Regulation and Performance: Cross-Country Evidence." In *Banking, Financial Integration, and International Crises,* Vol. 3, pp. 113–142. Santiago: Central Bank of Chile.

Basak, S., A. Pavlova, and A. Shapiro. 2007. "Optimal Asset Allocation and Risk Shifting in Money Management." *Review of Financial Studies* **20**, 1583–1621.

Bebchuk, L. A., and J. M. Fried. 2003. "Executive Compensation as an Agency Problem." *Journal of Economic Perspectives* **17**, 71–92.

Berk, J. B., and R. C. Green. 2004. "Mutual Fund Flows and Performance in Rational Markets." *Journal of Political Economy* **112**, 1269–1295.

Berkowitz, M. K., and Y. Kotowitz. 1993. "Incentives and Efficiency in the Market for Management Services: A Study of Canadian Mutual Funds." *Canadian Journal of Economics* **26**, 850–866.

Bhattacharya, U., H. Daouk, and M. Welker. 2003. "The World Price of Earnings Opacity." *Accounting Review* **78**, 641–678.

Black, B. S., and V. S. Khanna. 2007. "Can Corporate Governance Reforms Increase Firm Market Values? Event Study Evidence from India." *Journal of Empirical Legal Studies* **4**, 749–796.

Bollen, N. P. B., and V. K. Pool. 2006. "A Screen for Fraudulent Return Smoothing in the Hedge Fund Industry." Working Paper, SSRN eLibrary.

Bollen, N. P. B., and V. K. Pool. 2008. "Conditional Return Smoothing in the Hedge Fund Industry." *Journal of Financial and Quantitative Analysis* **43**, 267–298.

Bollen, N. P. B., and V. K. Pool. 2009. "Do Hedge Fund Managers Misreport Returns? Evidence from the Pooled Distribution." *Journal of Finance*, **64**, 2257–2288.

Bollen, N. P. B., and V. K. Pool. 2012. "Suspicious Patterns in Hedge Fund Returns and the Risk of Fraud." *Review of Financial Studies*, forthcoming.

Boyson, N. 2010. "Another Look at Career Concerns: A Study of Hedge Fund Managers." *Journal of Empirical Finance*, forthcoming.

Boyson, N. M., C. W. Stachel, and R. M. Stulz. 2010. "Hedge Fund Contagion and Liquidity Shocks." *Journal of Finance* **55**, 1789–1816.

Brav, A., W. Jiang, F. Partnoy, and R. Thomas. 2008a. "Hedge Fund Activism, Governance and Firm Performance." *Journal of Finance* **63**, 1729–1775.

Brav, A., W. Jiang, F. Partnoy, and R. Thomas. 2008b. "The Returns to Hedge Fund Activism." *Financial Analysts Journal* **64**, 45–61.

Brown, S., T. Fraser, and B. Liang. 2008a. "Hedge Fund Due Diligence: A Source of Alpha in a Hedge Fund Portfolio Strategy." *Journal of Investment Management* **6**, 23–33.

Brown, S. J., and W. N. Goetzmann. 2003. "Hedge Funds with Style." *Journal of Portfolio Management* **29**(2), 101–112.

Brown, S. J., W. N. Goetzmann, and R. G. Ibbotson. 1999. "Offshore Hedge Funds: Survival and Performance 1989–1995." *Journal of Business* **72**(1), 91–117.

Brown, S. J., W. N. Goetzmann, B. Liang, and C. Schwarz. 2008. "Lessons from Hedge Fund Registration." *Journal of Finance* **63**, 2785–2815.

Brown, S., W. Goetzmann, B. Liang, and C. Schwarz. 2009. "Estimating Operational Risk for Hedge Funds: The o-Score." *Financial Analysts Journal* **65**, 43–53.

Brown, S. J., W. N. Goetzmann, and J. Park. 2001. "Careers and Survival: Competition and Risk in the Hedge Fund and CTA Industry." *Journal of Finance* **56**(5), 1869–1886.

Brown, K., W. Harlow, and L. Starks. 1996. "Of Tournaments and Temptations: An Analysis of Managerial Incentives in the Mutual Fund Industry." *Journal of Finance* **51**, 85–110.

Brunnermeier, M. K., and S. Nagel. 2004. "Hedge Funds and the Technology Bubble." *Journal of Finance* **59**(5), 2013–2040.

Brunnermeier, Markus, and Lasse H. Pedersen. 2009. "Market Liquidity and Funding Liquidity." *Review of Financial Studies*, **22**, 2201–2238.

Burgstahler, D., and I. Dichev. 1997. "Earnings Management to Avoid Earnings Decreases and Losses." *Journal of Accounting and Economics* **24**, 99–126.

Burgstahler, D., L. Hail, and C. Leuz. 2006. "The Importance of Reporting Incentives: Earnings Management in European Private and Public Firms." *Accounting Review*, **81**, 983–1016.

Busse, J. A. 2001. "Another Look at Mutual Fund Tournaments." *Journal of Financial and Quantitative Analysis* **36**, 53–73.

Campos, R. 2006. Speech by SEC Commissioner: Remarks before the SIA Hedge Funds and Alternative Investments Conference, New York, NY, June 14.

Carhart, M. M., Kaniel, R., Musto, D. K., and Reed, A. V. 2002. "Leaning for the Tape: Evidence of Gaming Behavior in Equity Mutual Funds." *Journal of Finance* **57**(2), 661 – 693.

Cassar, G., and J. Gerakos. 2009. "Determinants of Hedge Fund Internal Controls and Fees." *Accounting Review*, **85**, 1887–1919.

Chan, N., M. Getmansky, S. Haas, and A. Lo. 2004. *"Systematic Risk and Hedge Funds."* Conference Paper, NBER Conference on the Risks of Financial Institutions, Woodstock, VT.

Chan, N., M. Getmansky, S. Haas, and A. Lo. 2006. "Do Hedge Funds Increase Systemic Risk?" *Federal Reserve Bank of Atlanta Economic Review* **Q4**, 49–80.

Chen, J. S., H. G. Hong, M. Huang, and J. D. Kubik. 2004. "Does Fund Size Erode Mutual Fund Performance? The Role of Liquidity and Organization." *American Economic Review* **95**(5), 1276–1302.

Chevalier, J., and G. Ellison. 1997a. "Risk Taking by Mutual Funds as a Response to Incentives." *Journal of Political Economy* **105**, 1167–1200.

Chevalier, J. and G. Ellison. 1997b. "Career Concerns of Mutual Fund Managers." *Quarterly Journal of Economics* **114**, 389–432.

Choi, S. J., K. K. Nelson, and A. C. Pritchard. 2009. "The Screening Effect of the Private Securities Litigation Reform Act." *Journal of Empirical Legal Studies* **6**, 35–68.

Chou, J., L. Ng, and Q. Wang. 2011. "Are Better Governed Funds Better Monitors?" *Journal of Corporate Finance*, forthcoming.

Cici, G., S. Gibson, and R. Moussawi. 2006. "Side-by-Side Management Relationships with Hedge Funds." Working Paper, Wharton.

Clifford, C. P. 2008. "Value Creation or Destruction? Hedge Funds as Shareholder Activists." *Journal of Corporate Finance* **14**, 323–336.

Comerton-Forde, C., and J. Rydge. 2006. "Market Integrity and Surveillance Effort." *Journal of Financial Services Research* **29**, 149–172.

Cox, J. D., R. Thomas, and L. Bai. 2008. "There Are Plaintiffs and . . . There Are Plaintiffs: An Empirical Analysis of Securities Class Action Settlements." *Vanderbilt Law Review*, **61**, 3550–3386.

Cremers, K., J. Martijn, and V. Nair. 2005. "Governance Mechanisms and Equity Prices." *Journal of Finance* **60**(6), 2859–2875.

Cumming, D., and N. Dai. 2009. "Capital Flows and Hedge Fund Regulation." *Journal of Empirical Legal Studies* **6**, 848–873.

Cumming, D., and N. Dai. 2010a. "A Law and Finance Analysis of Hedge Funds." *Financial Management* **39**, 997–1026.

Cumming, D., and N. Dai. 2010b. "Hedge Fund Regulation and Misreported Returns." *European Financial Management* **16**, 829–867.

Cumming, D. J., M. Humphrey-Jenner, and E. Wu. 2012. "Exchange Trading Rules, Governance, and the Trading Location of Cross-Listed Stocks." Working Paper, York University.

Cumming, D. J., G. Imad'Eddine, and A. Schwienbacher. 2012a. "Harmonized Regulatory Standards, International Distribution of Investment Funds and the Recent Financial Crisis." *European Journal of Finance* **18**(3–4), 261–292.

Cumming, D. J., G. Imad'Eddine, and A. Schwienbacher. 2012b. "Legality and the Spread of Voluntary Investor Protection." http://ssrn.com/abstract=1990477.

Cumming, D., and N. Dai. 2009. "Capital Flows and Hedge Fund Regulation." *Journal of Empirical Legal Studies* **6**, 848–873.

Cumming, D., and N. Dai. 2010a. "A Law and Finance Analysis of Hedge Funds." *Financial Management* **39**, 997–1026.

Cumming, D. J., and N. Dai. 2010b. "Hedge Fund Regulation and Misreported Returns." *European Financial Management* **16**, 829–867

Cumming, D., and S. A. Johan. 2007. "Regulatory Harmonization and the Development of Private Equity Markets." *Journal of Banking and Finance* **31**, 3218–3250.

Cumming, D., and S. Johan. 2008. "Hedge Fund Forum Shopping." *University of Pennsylvania Journal of Business and Employment Law* **10**, 783–831.

Cumming, D. J., and S. Johan. 2008. "Global Market Surveillance." *American Law and Economics Review* **10**, 454–506.

Cumming, D., and S. A. Johan. 2009. *Venture Capital and Private Equity Contracting: An International Perspective.* San Diego: Elsevier Science Academic Press.

Cumming, D. J., S. A. Johan, and D. Li. 2011. "Exchange Trading Rules and Stock Market Liquidity." *Journal of Financial Economics* **99**(3), 651–671.

Cumming, D. J., and D. Li. 2011. "Runup of Acquirer Stock in Public and Private Acquisitions." *Corporate Governance: An International Review* **19**(3), 210–239.

Cumming, D., and J. MacIntosh. 2000. "The Role of Interjurisdictional Competition in Shaping Canadian Corporate Law." *International Review of Law and Economics*, **20**, 141.

Cumming, D. J., F. Zhan, and M. Aitken. 2012. "Exchange Trading Rules, Surveillance, and Insider Trading." Working Paper, York University.

Degeorge, F., J. Patel, and R. Zeckhauser. 1999. "Earnings Management to Exceed Thresholds." *Journal of Business* **72**, 1–33.

Del Guercio, D., and P. A. Tkac. 2002. "The Determinants of the Flow of Funds of Managed Portfolios: Mutual Funds versus Pension Funds." *Journal of Financial and Quantitative Analysis* **37**, 523–557.

Del Guercio, D., and P. A. Tkac. 2008. "Star Power: The Effect of Morningstar Ratings on Mutual Fund Flow." *Journal of Financial and Quantitative Analysis* **43**, 907–936.

Dimmock, S., and W. Gerken. 2009. "Finding Bernie Madoff: Detecting Fraud by Investment Managers. Working Paper, SSRN eLibrary.

Ding, B., M. Getmansky, B. Liang, and R. Wermers. 2007. "Market Volatility, Investor Flows, and the Structure of Hedge Fund Markets." Working Paper, University of Massachusetts.

Ding, B., and H. A. Shawky. 2007. "The Performance of Hedge Fund Strategies and the Asymmetry of Return Distributions." *European Financial Management* **13**, 309–331.

Donaldson, W. H. 2003. Testimony Concerning Investor Protection Implications of Hedge Funds by Chairman, US Securities and Exchange Commission, before the Senate Committee on Banking, Housing and Urban Affairs, April 10, 2003. www.sec.gov/news/testimony/2006/ts072506cc.htm.

Easley, D., and M. O'Hara. 2008. "Liquidity and Valuation in an Uncertain World." Working paper, SSRN eLibrary.

Edelen, Roger M., Richard B. Evans, and Gregory B. Kadlec. 2011. "Disclosure and Agency Conflict in Delegated Investment Management: Evidence from Mutual Fund Commission Bundling." *Journal of Financial Economics,* forthcoming.

Edwards, F. R., and M. O. Caglayan. 2001. "Hedge Fund Performance and Manager Skill." *Journal of Futures Markets* **21**(11), 1003–1028.

Eisenberg, T., and J. R. Macey. 2004. "Was Arthur Andersen Different? An Empirical Examination of Major Accounting Firm Audits of Large Clients." *Journal of Empirical Legal Studies* **1**, 263–300.

Eling, M. 2009. "Does Hedge Fund Performance Persist? Overview and New Empirical Evidence." *European Financial Management* **15**, 362–401.

Elton, E. J., M. J. Gruber, and C. R. Blake. 2003. "Incentive Fees and Mutual Funds." *Journal of Finance* **58**(2), 779–804.

Fink, S. 2005 "The Distribution of Hedge Funds to Mass Affluent Investors." *Alternative Investment Management Association Journal* (September). www.aima.org/uploads/Fink68.pdf.

Fleischer, V. 2008. "Two and Twenty: Taxing Partnership Profits in Private Equity Funds." *New York University Law Review* **83**, 1–55.

Fotak, Veljko, Bernardo Bortolotti, and William Megginson. 2008. "The Financial Impact of Sovereign Wealth Fund Investments in Listed Companies." Unpublished paper, University of Oklahoma.

Fung, W., and D. A. Hsieh. 1997. "Empirical Characteristics of Dynamic Trading Strategies: The Case of Hedge Funds." *Review of Financial Studies* **10**(2), 275–302.

Fung, W., and D. Hsieh. 1999. "A Primer on Hedge Funds." *Journal of Empirical Finance* **6**, 309–331.

Fung, W., and D. A. Hsieh. 2000. "Performance Characteristics of Hedge Funds and CTA Funds: Natural Versus Spurious Biases." *Journal of Financial and Quantitative Analysis* **35**(3), 291–307.

Fung, W., and D. A. Hsieh. 2001. "The Risk in Hedge Fund Strategies: Theory and Evidence from Trend Followers." *Review of Financial Studies* **14**(2), 313–341.

Fung, W., and D. A. Hsieh. 2004. "Hedge Fund Benchmarks: A Risk Based Approach." *Financial Analyst Journal* **60**, 65–80.

Fung, W., and D. A. Hsieh. 2006. "Hedge Funds: An Industry in Its Adolescence." *Federal Reserve Bank of Atlanta Economic Review* (Fourth Quarter) 1–34.

Fung, W., D. A. Hsieh, N. Naik, and T. Ramadorai. 2008. "Hedge Funds: Performance, Risk, and Capital Formation." *Journal of Finance*, **63**, 1777–1803.

Garbaravicius, T., and F. Diereck. 2005. "Hedge Funds and Their Implications for Financial Stability." European Central Bank Occasional Paper Series No 34, 6.

Gaspar, M., M. Massa, and P. Matos. 2006. "Favoritism in Mutual Fund Families? Evidence on Strategic Cross-Fund Subsidization." *Journal of Finance* **61**, 73–104.

Gerstein, K. S. 2006. "Hedge Fund Distribution: Regulatory Hot Buttons." Presentation at SRZ Greenwich Private Investment Funds Seminar, May 2006.

Getmansky, M. 2005. "The Life Cycle of Hedge Funds: Fund Flows, Size and Performance." Working Paper, University of Massachusetts.

Getmansky, M., A. W. Lo, and I. Makarov. 2004. "An Econometric Model of Serial Correlation and Illiquidity in Hedge Fund Returns." *Journal of Financial Economics* **74**(3), 529–609.

Getmansky, M., A.W. Lo, and S. X. Mei. 2004. "Sifting through the Wreckage: Lessons from Recent Hedge Fund Liquidations." *Journal of Investment Management* **2**(4), Fourth Quarter, 6–38.

Goetzmann, W. N., J. E. Ingersoll, and S.A. Ross. 2003. "High-water Marks and Hedge Fund Management Contracts." *Journal of Finance* **58**(4), 1685–1717.

Goetzmann, W. N., J. E. Ingersoll, M. I. Spiegel, and I. Welch. 2007. "Portfolio Performance Manipulation and Manipulation-Proof Performance Measures." *Review of Financial Studies* **20**(5), 1503–1546.

Golec, J., and L. T. Starks. 2004. "Performance Fee Contract Change and Mutual Fund Risk." *Journal of Financial Economics* **73**, 93–118.

Goldschmid, H. J. 2004. Speech by SEC Commissioner. "Should Hedge Funds Be Regulated?" November 17, 2004. www.sec.gov/news/speech/spch111704hjg.htm.

Goriaev, A. P., T. E. Nijman, and B. J. M. Werker. 2001, *"The Dynamics of the Impact of Past Performance on Mutual Fund Flows."* Working Paper, Tilburg University.

Greene, W. H. 2003. *Econometric Analysis*. 5th ed. Upper Saddle River, NJ: Prentice Hall.

Gregoriou, G. N., and Gueyie, J. P. 2003. "Risk-Adjusted Performance of Funds of Hedge Funds Using a Modified Sharpe Ratio." *Journal of Wealth Management* **6**, 77–83.

Grinblatt, M., and S. Titman. 1989. "Adverse Risk Incentives and the Design of Performance-Based Contracts." *Management Science* **35**, 807–822.

Gupta, A., and B. Liang. 2005. "Do Hedge Funds Have Enough Capital? A Value-at-Risk Approach." *Journal of Financial Economics* **77**(1), 219–253.

Haigh, M. S., N. E. Boyd, and B. Buyuksahin. 2007. "Herding among Large Speculative Traders in Futures Markets." Working Paper. http://ssrn.com/abstract=981752.

Hammer, D. J., C. S. Reiser, G. W. Haynes, N. J. Koren, A. J. Caldwell, J. J. Frolik, C. E. Mickelson, B. H. Sacks, J. F. Milani, and H. E. Dunn. 2005. *U.S. Regulation of Hedge Funds*. Chicago: American Bar Association.

Harris, L. 2002. *Trading and Exchanges: Market Microstructure for Practitioners*. Oxford: Oxford University Press.

Harris, F. H. deB., M. A. Aitken, R. M. Cook, and T. H. McInish. 2008. "Market Design and Execution Costs for Matched Securities Worldwide." *Institutional Investor's Guide to Global Liquidity*, Vol. **2**. Goldman Sachs.

Haug, M., and M. Hirschey. 2006. "The January Effect." *Financial Analysts Journal* **62**, 78–88.

Healy, P., and K. Palepu, 2001. "Information Asymmetry, Corporate Disclosure, and the Capital Markets: A Review of the Empirical Disclosure Literature," *Journal of Accounting and Economics* **31**, 405–440.

Heckman, J. 1976. "The Common Structure of Statistical Models of Truncation, Sample Selection, and Limited Dependent Variables and a Simple Estimator for Such Models." *Annals of Economic and Social Measurement* **5**, 475–492.

Heckman, J. 1979 "Sample Selection Bias as a Specification Error." *Econometrica* **47**, 153–161.

Hertzel, M., M. Lemmon, J. S. Linck, and L. Rees. 2002. "Long-Run Performance Following Private Placements of Equity." *Journal of Finance* **57**(6), 2595–2617.

Hirsch, E. D., J. F. Kett, and J.Trefil. 2002. *The New Dictionary of Cultural Literacy*. 3rd ed. Boston: Houghton Mifflin.

Hodder, J. E., and J. C. Jackwerth. 2007. "Incentive Contracts and Hedge Fund Management." *Journal of Financial and Quantitative Analysis* **42**, 811–826.

House Committee on Banking and Financial Services. 1999. *Hedge Funds, Leverage, and the Lessons of Long-Term Capital Management: Report of the President's Working Group on Capital Markets* (April).

Hu, H., and B. Black. 2006. "Empty Voting and Hidden (Morphable) Ownership: Taxonomy, Implications, and Reforms." *Business Lawyer* **61**(3), 1011.

Hu, H. T. C., and B. Black. 2007. "Hedge Funds, Insiders, and the Decoupling of Economic and Voting Ownership: Empty Voting and Hidden (Morphable) Ownership." *Journal of Corporate Finance* **13**, 343–367.

Huddart, Steven. 1999. "Reputation and Performance Fee Effects on Portfolio Choice by Investment Advisers." *Journal of Financial Markets* **2**, 227–271.

Ineichen, A., and K. Silberstein. 2008. "AIMA's Roadmap to Hedge Funds." Alternative Investment Management Association. www.aima.org/download.cfm/docid/6133E854–63FF-46-FC-95347B445AE4ECFC.

Jackson, H. E., and M.J. Roe. 2009. "Public and Private Enforcement of Securities Laws: Resource-based Evidence." *Journal of Financial Economics* **93**, 207–238.

Jagannathan, R., A. Malakhov, and D. Novikov. 2010. "Do Hot Hands Exist among Hedge Fund Managers? An Empirical Evaluation." *Journal of Finance* **65**, 217–255.

Jensen, M. 1968. "The Performance of Mutual Funds in the Period 1945–1968." *Journal of Finance* **23** (2), 389–416.

Jensen, Michael C., and William H. Meckling. 1976. "Theory of the Firm: Managerial Behavior, Agency Costs and Ownership Structure." *Journal of Financial Economics* **3**, 305–360.

Jorion, P. 2000. "Risk Management Lessons from Long-Term Capital Management." *European Financial Management* **6**, 277–300.

Kacperczyk, M., C. Sialm, and L. Zheng. 2008. "Unobserved Actions of Mutual Funds." *Review of Financial Studies* **21**, 2379–2416.

Kahan, M., and E. B. Rock. 2007."Hedge Funds in Corporate Governance and Corporate Control." *University of Pennsylvania Law Review* **155**, 1021.

Kamstra, M. J., L. A. Kramer, and M. D. Levi. 2003. "Winter Blues: Seasonal Affective Disorder (SAD) and Stock Market Returns." *American Economic Review* **93**, 324–343.

Kao, D.-L. 2002. "Battle for Alphas: Hedge Funds versus Long-Only Portfolios." *Financial Analysts Journal* **58** (March/April), 16–36.

Khandani, Amir E., and Andrew W. Lo. 2007. "What Happened to the Quants in August 2007?" *Journal of Investment Management* **5**(4), 29–78.

Khandani, A., and A. Lo. 2008. "What Happened to the Quants in August 2007? Evidence from Factors and Transactions Data." NBER Working Paper No. 14465.

Klein, A., and E. Zur. 2009. "Entrepreneurial Shareholder Activism: Hedge Funds and Other Private Investors." *Journal of Finance* **64**, 187–229.

Koh F., W. T. H. Koh, and M. Teo. 2003. "Asian Hedge Funds: Return Persistence, Style and Fund Characteristics." Working Paper, Singapore Management University.

Lakonishok, Josef, Andrei Shleifer, Richard Thaler, and Robert Vishny. 1991. "Window Dressing by Pension Fund Managers." *American Economic Review Papers and Proceedings* **81**, 227–231.

La Porta, R., F. Lopez-de-Silanes, A. Shleifer, and R. Vishny. 1998. "Law and Finance." *Journal of Political Economy* **106**, 1113–1155.

La Porta, R., F. Lopez-de-Silanes, A. Shleifer, and R. Vishny. 2002. "Investor Protection and Corporate Valuation." *Journal of Finance* **57**, 1147–1170.

La Porta, R., F. Lopez-de-Silanes, A. Shleifer, and R. Vishny. 2006. "What Works in Securities Laws?" *Journal of Finance* **61**, 1–32.

Leondis, A. 2010. "U.S. Millionaires' Ranks Rose 16% in 2009." March 9. *BusinessWeek*. www.businessweek.com.

Liang, B. 1999. "On the Performance of Hedge Funds." *Financial Analysts Journal* **55**, 72–85.

Liang, B. 2000. "Hedge Funds: The Living and the Dead." *Journal of Financial and Quantitative Analysis* **35**, 309–326.

Liang, B. 2003. "The Accuracy of Hedge Fund Returns." *Journal of Portfolio Management* **29**, 111–122.

Liang, B., and H. Park. 2008. "Share Restrictions, Liquidity Premium, and Offshore Hedge Funds." Working Paper, University of Massachusetts, Amherst.

Lo, A. 2006. "Where Do Alphas Come From? A New Measure of the Value of Active Investment Management." Working Paper, Massachusetts Institute of Technology.

Lo, A. 2008. *Hedge Funds: An Analytic Perspective*. Princeton, NJ: Princeton University Press.

Lynch, Anthony, and David Musto. 2003. "How Investors Interpret Past Fund Returns." *Journal of Finance* **58**, 2033–2058.

Mackintosh, J. 2008. "Hedge Funds Agree to Greater Disclosure." *Financial Times,* January 22, 2008.

Meier, Iwan, and Ernst Schaumburg. 2004. "Do Funds Window Dress? Evidence for U.S. Equity Mutual Funds." Unpublished manuscript, Northwestern University.

Merrick, J. J. Jr., N.Y. Naik, and P. K. Yadav. 2005. "Strategic Trading Behavior and Price Distortion in a Manipulated Market: Anatomy of a Squeeze." *Journal of Financial Economics* **77**, 171–218.

Modigliani, Franco, and Gerald A. Pogue. 1975. "Alternative Investment Performance Fee Arrangements and Implications for SEC Regulatory Policy." *Bell Journal of Economics* **6**, 127–160.

Naik, N. Y., T. Ramadoria, and M. Stromqvist. 2007. "Capacity Constraints and Hedge Fund Strategy Returns." *European Financial Management* **13**, 239–256.

Partnoy, F., and R. S. Thomas. 2007. "Gap Filling, Hedge Funds, and Financial Innovation." In Y. Fuchita and R. E. Litan, eds., *Brookings-Nomura Papers on Financial Services*. Washington, D.C.: Brookings Institution Press.

Peter, A., and M. D. Kinsman. 2007. "SEC Quest to Regulate Hedge Funds Hits Speed Bump." *Graziadio Business Review* **10**(1). http://gbr.pepperdine.edu/2010/08/sec-quest-to-regulate-hedge-funds-hits-speed-bump/#_edn15.

Petersen, M. A. 2009. "Estimating Standard Errors in Finance Panel Data Sets: Comparing Approaches." *Review of Financial Studies* **22**, 435–480.

Perino, M. A. 2006. "Law, Ideology, and Strategy in Judicial Decision Making: Evidence from Securities Fraud Actions." *Journal of Empirical Legal Studies* **3**, 497–524.

Plantin, G., H. Sapra, and H. Shin. 2008. Marking-to-Market: Panacea or Pandora's Box? *Journal of Accounting Research* **46**, 435–460.

PriceWaterhouseCoopers [PWC], various years. *The Regulation, Taxation and Distribution of Hedge Funds*. London: PriceWaterhouseCoopers.

Pritchard, A. C., and H. A. Sale. 2005. "What Counts as Fraud? An Empirical Study of Motions to Dismiss under Private Securities Litigation Reform Act." *Journal of Empirical Legal Studies* **2**, 125–149.

Romano, R., 1985. "Law as a Product: Some Pieces of the Incorporation Puzzle." *Journal of Law, Economics and Organization*, **1**, 225.

Sapra, H. 2008. "Do Accounting Measurement Regimes Matter? A Discussion of Mark-to-Market Accounting and Liquidity Pricing." *Journal of Accounting and Economics* **45**, 379–387.

Sias, R., and L.T. Starks. 1997. "Institutions and Individuals at the Turn-of-the-Year." *Journal of Finance* **52**, 1543–1562.

Silverman, B. W. 1986. *Density Estimation for Statistics and Data Analysis*. New York: Chapman and Hall.

Sirri, E., and P. Tufano. 1998. "Costly Search and Mutual Fund Flows." *Journal of Finance* **53**, 1589–1622.

Sharpe, W. F. 1966. "Mutual Fund Performance." *Journal of Business* **39** (1), 119–138.

Starks, L. T. 1987. "Performance Incentive Fees: An Agency Theoretic Approach." *Journal of Financial and Quantitative Analysis* **22**, 17–32.

Teo, M. 2009. "The Geography of Hedge Funds." *Review of Financial Studies* **22**, 3531–3561.

Thomas, R. S., and F. Partnoy. 2007. "Gap Filling, Hedge Funds, and Financial Innovation." In Y. Fuchita and R. E. Litan, eds., *Brookings-Nomura Papers on Financial Services*. Washington, DC: Brookings Institution Press.

Thompson, R. B., 2008. "Globally Integrated Corporations as 'Good for the Country': The Impact of Soft Law." Vanderbilt Public Law Research Paper No. 08-35.

Verret, J. W. 2007. "Dr. Jones and the Raiders of Lost Capital: Hedge Fund Regulation, Part II." *Delaware Journal of Corporate Law* **32**, 799–841.

Verret, J. W. 2009. "Economics Makes Strange Bedfellows: Pensions, Trusts, and Hedge Funds in an Era of Financial Re-Intermediation." *University of Pennsylvania Journal of Business and Employment Law* **10**, 63–88.

White, H. 1980. "A Heteroskedasticity-Consistent Covariance Matrix Estimator and a Direct Test for Heteroskedasticity." *Econometrica* **48**, 817–838.

Wilson, R. 2007. *Hedge Fund Blog Book*. http://hedgefundgroup.org/Hedge-Fund-Book.pdf.

Wu, Y. L. 2004. "The Choice of Equity-Selling Mechanisms,." *Journal of Financial Economics* **74**, 93–119.

Zitzewitz, E. 2003. "Who Cares about Shareholders? Arbitrage-Proofing Mutual Funds." *Journal of Law, Economics, and Organization*, **19**, 245–280.

Zitzewitz, E. 2006. "How Widespread Was Late Trading in Mutual Funds?" *American Economic Review* **96**, 284–289.

INDEX

accountants, 228
activism, hedge fund, 16, 96, 160, 162n7
activist investors, 10
administrators, 3–4, 125, 162, 228, 230, 231
   AIFMD and, 62
   misreported returns and, 203
advisers
   commodity trading, 1, 24, 99t, 115
   legal, 228
   private exemption, 56
   registration of, 56–57
   tax, 228
age, of fund, 106, 123, 129, 131, 138n11, 166, 212, 217n7, 221
agency. *See also* broker-agency conflict
   costs, 15–16, 22, 26
   relationship, 21
agency problems, 37, 95, 278
   compensation structures and, 158
   in delegated portfolio management, 22–26
   evidence of, 22–24
   fee structures and, 28
   full picture of investment and, 29–30
   in hedge fund management, 13, 15, 26–35
   internal and external conflicts, 33t–34t
   investor base and, 27–28
   leverage and, 30–31
   mechanisms designed to alleviate, 24–26
   mitigating, 31–35
   principal-agent problem, 21–22
   proprietary investment and, 28
   regulatory oversight lacking and, 29
   strategies and, 30–31, 98, 102
agents, 21. *See also* principal-agent problem
   local, 162, 203
   transfer, 4, 230
AIFMD. *See* Alternative Investment Fund Managers Directive
alignment of interests hypothesis, 103, 115, 116, 117, 118, 192

alpha, 165–66, 194, 196–97, 279. *See also* 1-year alpha; 7-Factor Alpha; 3-year alphas
   changes in, 243
   lagged, 253
   multi-factor, 71, 158, 159, 164–65
   performance and structure impacted by regulation and, 184t–191t
   returns, 13, 129
   single factor, 165
Alternative Investment Fund Managers Directive (AIFMD), 61–62, 67, 278
analysis process, 7t
annual distribution, 266
annualized returns average, 71
   by fund type and investment strategy, 72t–73t
appointed parties, to operate hedge fund, 4f
arbitrage strategies. *See also specific types*
   capital structure, 98n13, 102
   convertible, 102
   event driven merger, 10–11
   fixed income, 106
   merger/risk, 98n13, 102
   statistical, 102, 112
assets, 1, 223. *See also* net asset value
   custody of client, 58, 230
   distribution of, 1990–2008, 270t
   growth of, 1990–2008, 55, 157, 269, 269f
   influx, 271
   portfolio, 204n4
   shocks, 272
   source of, by country, directly and indirectly, 15f
   variances in, 275
asset classes, 6t
   capital under management by, 14f
assets under management, 266
   return to scale and, 7t
asymmetric performance fee contracts, 24
attrition rates, 266
auditors, 32, 228
   timing and support, 46, 163, 231

Index

backfilling bias, 172, 223, 236
banks, 155, 230. *See also* shadow banking
  distribution via, 45, 152–53
  marketing and regression analyses of forum shopping, 108t–114t
  risk exposed to, 270
bargaining power, 44
benchmark, 6t
bias
  backfilling, 172, 223, 236
  conditioning, 241
  data, 172
  selection, 172
  short, 95, 98n13, 102
  survivorship, 172, 223, 236, 268
bids-asks, 64
  layering of, 65
binary logit regression, 242
bin width, 206, 207f
board of directors, 125, 162, 203, 230
bonus contract, 25
Born, Brooksley, 38
bottom quartile funds, 228, 236, 243, 262
  wrappers and, 254
brokers, 66. *See also* prime brokers
broker-agency conflict, 62
  rules, 66
brokerage ownership, 63
build indices, 62
business conflict, 27, 28, 30

calendar effects, 129
Campos, Roel, 30
capital flow. *See* flows, of funds
Capital Markets Safety Board (CMSB), 274
capital raising, 95, 122–25. *See also* flows, of funds; flow-performance relationship
  data, 130–36
  regression analyses, 136, 138–54
  summary statistics, 131, 132t–135t, 136
  variables defined, 132t–135t, 137t
capital structure, 34t
  arbitrage, 98n13, 102
capital under management
  by asset class, 14f
  number of hedge funds by year and, 15f
capital worldwide, 1, 95
career concerns, 25–26, 32
carried interest fee, 3, 16, 54, 158–59, 161, 278
Center for International Securities and Derivatives Markets (CISDM), 93, 98, 98n13, 123. *See also* investment strategies, CISDM categories
  annualized returns, 71, 72t–73t
  database, 11, 39, 69, 130, 166, 172, 205, 228, 232
  entries and exits in, 266, 267t
  excess returns and, 74, 75t–76t
  forum shopping data from, 103
  information ratio and, 82t–83t
  market beta and, 91t–92t
  MPPM and, 84t–85t
  number of funds in, 70t–71t
  7-Factor Alpha and, 87t–88t
  sharp ratio and, 77t–78t
  standard deviation and, 89t–90t
  Treynor ratio and, 80t–81t
CFTC. *See* Commodity Futures Trading Commission
Chan, N. M., 269–71
Channel Capital Group Inc., 103
characteristics, hedge fund, 13, 18, 27, 43, 136, 166, 195
  failure and, 266
  flows and, 133t, 141t, 147t
  forum shopping and, 108t, 110t, 112t, 113t
  liquidation and, 266, 268
  misreported returns and, 202, 204
  performance persistence and, 236, 237, 241
  variables defined, 170t–171t
Chinese Walls, 31, 63
"choice of law" decision making, 94. *See also* forum shopping
churning, 64
CISDM. *See* Center for International Securities and Derivatives Markets
client
  custody of assets, 58, 230
  investor and, 56
  know-your-, rule, 66
  manager-, relationship, 26
  precedence, 63
  qualified, 57
CMSB. *See* Capital Markets Safety Board
Commodity Futures Trading Commission (CFTC), 265
commodity trading advisers/managed futures, 1, 24, 99t, 115
compensation, 7t, 25, 125, 161
  incentive-based, 59
  management, 18
  mutual fund, 24
compensation structure, 158. *See also* performance and structure, regulation impacting
  option-like, 28, 32
concave flow-performance relationship, 129, 153
conditioning bias, 241
conflicts
  broker-agency, 62, 66
  business, 27, 28, 30
  from fees, 28
  from investor base, 27–28
  legal, 27, 28, 30
  leverage and, 30–31
  proprietary investment, 28
  regulatory oversight lacking and, 29
  strategies and, 30–31
conflicts of interest, 31, 44, 96–97, 194
  internal and external, 32, 33t–34t, 35

risk and, 35
sponsor and manager, 231–32
strategies and, 16
connectedness
of global financial system, 272–73
in industry, 271–73
network diagrams, 272f
constraints, 7t
leverage, 9
consultants, 228
contagion, 272
convertible arbitrage, 102
convex flow-performance relationship, 129
corners, in market activity, 64
correlations, 6t
of flow-performance variables, 137t
in industry, 271–73
of misreported returns variables, 216t
of performance and structure variables, 173, 182t, 183
cost
accounting, 275
agency, 15–16, 22, 26
country specific, 9, 102, 136
GDP, 204, 215
covered financial institutions, 59
Cox, Christopher, 37, 55
COX Proportional Hazard Regression, 266, 267t–268t
credit
agreements, 271
risk, 271
creditor/obligator relationship, 271
cross hedge, 9
cross subsidization, 24
custodian, 4, 228
custody, of client assets, 58, 230

databases, hedge fund, 69. *See also* Center for International Securities and Derivatives Markets; HedgeFund.Net; TASS; *specific databases*
death spiral, 274
delegated portfolio management, 21
agency problems in, 22–26
depository, AIFMD and, 62
derivative, 64
instruments, 1, 9, 31, 95
short-selling, 30
direct hedge, 9
directional hedge fund strategies, 11
directive, 61n8. *See also* Market Abuse Directive; Markets in Financial Instruments Directive; Undertakings for Collective Investment in Transferable Securities Directive
disclosure
Dodd-Frank Act and, 58–59
false, 65
requirements, 26, 31, 35
voluntary, 37

distressed securities funds, 95, 98n13, 102, 117–18
distribution, 136
annual, 266
of assets, 1990–2008, 270t
via banks, 45, 152–53
fund flows and, 152
of leverage, 1990–2008, 270t
private placement, 116
tax barriers to, 53t–54t
distribution channels, 19, 279. *See also* wrapper distribution; *specific channels*
failure and, 268
flow-performance relation and, 153
forum shopping for, 106
misreported returns and, 200, 202, 223
multiple, 236n5
performance and structure impacted by, 194–95, 196–97
performance persistence and, 227–29, 231, 254, 263
permissible, 39, 40t–43t, 44–45, 122, 126, 278
distribution companies, 152, 155, 202
marketing and regression analyses of forum shopping, 108t–114t
distributor, 4, 125, 162, 231
misreported returns and, 203
Dodd-Frank Act of 2010, 32, 55, 67, 278
disclosure and, 58–59
U.S. regulation and, 56–59
domination and control, 64
due diligence exercise, 27
durations, 6t
dynamic hedge, 10

economic significance, 117, 138, 152, 193, 194, 215n6
of misreported returns, 222–23
of regulation, 222, 254
wrapper distribution and, 217
economies of scale, 5t
The Economist, 37, 38, 199
emerging markets funds, 115
emerging market strategies, 117
empty voting, 31
endowment fund, 27
energy sector, 9, 102, 114
EU. *See* European Union
Eurekahedge Database, 11, 60
Europe, 278
regulation in, 59–62
European Union (EU), 59
event driven hedge fund strategies, 10, 94, 98n13, 102
event driven merger arbitrage hedge fund strategies, 10–11
excess returns average (annualized), 74
by fund type and investment strategy, 75t–76t
exchange trading rules, 62–65
financial markets impacted by, 66–67

execution of investment, 230
exits, 266
explicit incentives, 24–25

facilities, 30
factor betas, 93
failure, hedge fund, 265, 273
　characteristics and, 266
　distribution channels and, 268
fair-value accounting, 274–76
false appearance, 65
false disclosure rules, 65
FASB. *See* Financial Accounting Standards Board
Federal Reserve
　information provided for, 273
　outside oversight of, 265
feeder company, 12. *See also* master-feeder hedge fund structure
fees, 5*t*. *See also* performance fee
　carried interest, 3, 16, 54, 158–59, 161, 278
　conflicts from, 28
　fixed, 3, 129, 197, 278
　highwatermark, 12–13
　incentives, 130, 161
　management, 12, 13, 158, 161, 163
　manager structures, 28
　mutual funds, 12–13
　private equity funds, 12–13
　risk, 24–25
　structures, 2–3, 28
　2 and 20 model, 2–3
fiduciary duty, 13, 27, 28, 125, 162, 203, 230
Financial Accounting Standards Board (FASB), 274
financial crisis (2008), 37–38, 227, 274, 276
　regulations prior to, 39–46
　systematic risk in, 265, 269–73
financial instability, 1, 96
financial institutions, 152–53, 155. *See also specific types*
　covered, 59
　international, 16–17
　large covered, 59
　marketing and regression analyses of forum shopping, 108*t*–114*t*
financial interconnections, 271
financial intermediation, 3*f*, 227, 262
　regulation and, 38*f*
financial regulators, 2
financing arrangements, 230
fixed effects, 138n10, 266
fixed fee, 3, 129, 197, 278
fixed income
　arbitrage funds, 106
　non-arbitrage, 102
flows, of funds, 278
　characteristics and, 133*t*, 141*t*, 147*t*
　distribution and, 152
　jurisdiction selection and, 130
　leverage and, 271

liquidation and, 128
measures of, 130–31
minimum capitalization and, 123, 138, 155
misreported returns and, 225
performance and, 271
performance persistence and, 232, 236
regression analyses for, 139*t*–144*t*, 145*t*–151*t*
regulation and, 122–25
restrictions on location and, 123, 138, 155
taxation and, 123–24, 153–54, 155
flow-performance relationship, 25, 122–23. *See also specific types*
　concave, 129, 153
　control variables, 127–30
　convex, 129
　correlation of variables matrix, 137*t*
　distribution channels and, 153
　factors influencing, 125–30
　flatter, 232
　intercept term impacts, 127*f*
　linear, 129
　minimum capitalization and, 136, 153
　mutual funds and, 127–28
　non-linearity in, 131
　pension funds and, 127–28
　regression analyses and, 154
　regulation and, 125–27, 127*f*, 128*f*, 153
　restrictions on location of service providers and, 136, 153
　slope term impacts, 128*f*
　summary statistics, 131, 132*t*–135*t*, 136
　variables defined, 132*t*–135*t*, 137*t*
　wrappers and, 127, 217
forum shopping, 17, 36, 97, 97n12, 98–102, 195, 278–79
　data, 103–6
　empirical evidence limitations, 118–19
　hypotheses about, 103
　minimum capitalization and, 106, 116, 119–20
　multivariate empirical tests, 106–18
　regression analyses of, 107*t*–114*t*
　restrictions on location of service providers and, 106, 115–16, 119–20
　strategies and, 118, 120, 192
fractional rank, 131
fraud, 162, 202
freedom, 280
front-running, 63
functions, of hedge fund
　appointed parties to operate, 4*f*
　delegation of, 3, 125, 162, 202–3, 230
fund of funds, 69, 69n1, 103n23, 183
　annualized returns and, 73*t*
　in CISDM, 71*t*
　excess returns average and, 76*t*
　information ratio and, 83*t*
　market beta and, 92*t*
　MPPM and, 85*t*

7-Factor Alpha and, 88*t*
Sharpe ratio and, 78*t*
standard deviation and, 90*t*
survival and, 266
taxation by country, 47*t*–52*t*
Treynor ratio and, 81*t*
Fung, W., 79, 86, 164–65

GDP. *See* gross domestic product
general partners, 125, 160–61, 230
GNP. *See* gross national product
Goetzmann, W. N., 79, 164–65
Goh, Bryan, 60
Goldstein, Phillip, 55–56
governance, 280
 regulation and, 19–20, 157–60
 value-added, 162, 202, 231
Greenspan, Alan, 38
gross domestic product (GDP), 202, 205
 country specific, 204, 215
 misreported returns and, 204
gross national product (GNP), 123, 129, 166, 183
 variables defined, 169*t*–170*t*
growth, 1, 94, 96
 of assets, 55, 157, 269, 269*f*
 industry, 270, 273
 of leverage, 269*f*

hazard ratios, 266, 267*t*–268*t*
HedgeFund.Net (HFN), 98
 DataExport, 103
 limitations with, 106n24
"Hedge Fund Rule," 55–56
herding, 95
HFN. *See* HedgeFund.Net
Highly Leveraged Institutions, 2
high net worth individuals, 2, 27
highwatermark fees, 12–13
highwatermark provision, 32
Hsieh, D., 79, 86, 164–65
Hypothesis 5.1. *See* race to the bottom
Hypothesis 5.2. *See* neutrality hypothesis
Hypothesis 5.3. *See* alignment of interests hypothesis

illegal activity, 11
illiquidity, 29, 205
implicit incentives, 25
 asymmetry of, 26
incentives, 22
 based compensation restrictions, 59
 explicit, 24–25
 fees, 130, 161
 implicit, 25–26
 mechanisms, 21
 to misreport returns, 199, 202, 205, 223, 225
 performance, 32
 risk taking and, 23, 25–26

incentive-fee fund risk, 24–25
inception date, 130
indexes, 271
information
 asymmetries, 15–16, 116
 material non-public, 63
 misreported, 18–19
 transparency, 273–74, 276
information ratio, 74, 79
 by fund type and investment strategy, 82*t*–83*t*
insider trading, 62–63
institutional investors, 2, 27, 199
 attracting, 18
 service provider quality guides, 228
insurance policies, 45
internal control system, 32
international institutions, 16–17
Investment Advisers Act of 1940, 11, 55, 274
Investment Company Act (1940), 2, 11, 55, 126, 161n5
 Section 3(c)(1), 8
Investment Company Institute, 1
investment managers. *See* managers, investment
investment policy, 5*t*
investment strategies, CISDM categories, 69, 70*t*–71*t*, 98
 annualized returns by, 72*t*–73*t*
 excess returns average by, 75*t*–76*t*
 information ratio by, 82*t*–83*t*
 market beta by, 91*t*–92*t*
 MPPM by, 84*t*–85*t*
 7-Factor Alpha by, 87*t*–88*t*
 Sharpe ratio by, 77*t*–78*t*
 standard deviation by, 89*t*–90*t*
 Treynor ratio by, 80*t*–81*t*
investors, 22, 95, 230. *See also specific types*
 accredited, 57, 161n4
 activist, 10
 age average, 27
 attracting, 202
 certifications, 57–58
 characteristics, 18, 46
 client and, 56
 confidence, 123, 126, 279
 foreign, 54
 non-accredited, 127n6
 number of, 44
 protection, 166, 274
 responsiveness to underperformance, 269
 types, 262
investor base, 2, 5*t*, 8, 95. *See also specific types*
 conflicts from, 27–28
issues relevant to study, of hedge funds, 14–20

Jones, Alfred Winslow, 13–14
jurisdiction selection, 17–18, 36, 94, 138n10. *See also* forum shopping
 fund flows and, 130
 restrictions on location and, 125–26

key service providers. *See* service providers
know-your-client rule, 66

large covered financial institutions, 59
legal adviser, 228
legal conflict, 27, 28, 30
legal origin, 166, 195, 268
   misreported returns and, 202, 204
   variables defined, 169*t*–170*t*
legal structure, 5*t*, 16–17
leverage, 6*t*, 9–11
   AIFMD and, 61
   conflict potentials from, 30–31
   distribution of, 1990–2008, 270*t*
   fund flows and, 271
   growth of, 1990–2008, 269*f*
   in industry, 269
   reduce, 272
   UCITS and, 60
Leveraged Investment Funds, 2
liabilities, 125, 162, 163, 230, 270, 274
   partners, 161
   tax, 154
   variances in, 275
limited partnership, 125, 160–61, 230
linear flow-performance relationship, 129
linkage, 272
liquidation, 128, 276
   fund characteristics and, 266, 268
liquidity, 5*t*, 8, 44, 271
   AIFMD and, 61
   crisis, 274
   flow funds and, 128
   lack of, 29–30
   low, 274
   misreported returns and, 205
   shocks to, 272
   UCITS and, 60
Lo, A., 273, 275
local agent, 162, 203
location choice, 163–64. *See also* restrictions on location, of service providers
lockup periods, 8, 130, 203, 279
long-short hedge fund strategies, 10, 96, 102, 116
Long Term Capital Management (LTCM), 26, 38, 265
LTCM. *See* Long Term Capital Management

M&A. *See* mergers and acquisitions
macro-financial outcomes, 19–20
MAD. *See* Market Abuse Directive
Madoff affair, 199
managed futures, 1, 24, 99*t*, 115
management, 3, 5, 17, 278
   agency problems in, 13, 15, 26–35
   assets under, 7*t*, 266
   capital under, 14*f*, 15*f*
   compensation, 18
   fee, 12, 13, 158, 161, 163

   risk, 6*t*, 61, 117, 274
   style, 4, 5*t*
   style drift, 31
managers, hedge fund, 22, 230. *See also* assets under management; misreported returns
   agency problems and, 13, 15, 26–35
   conflicts of interest with sponsor, 231–32
   duties, 13
   fee structures for, 28
   fired, 32
   information misreported and, 18–19
   investor base conflicts and, 27
   jurisdiction selection and, 94
   multiple fund, 204–5, 212, 222, 254
   proprietary investment conflicts and, 28
   returns reported, 13
   risk taking and, 23–24
   skill, 11
   taxation and, 16, 47*t*–52*t*
managers, investment, 45, 117, 155, 202
   marketing and regression analyses of forum shopping, 108*t*–114*t*
manager-client relationship, 26
manipulation-proof performance measure (MPPM), 79, 158, 164–65, 196–97
   by fund type and investment strategy, 84*t*–85*t*
   performance and structure impacted by regulation and, 184*t*–191*t*
marginal effects, 215n6
marginally negative returns, 202, 206, 212, 215
marginally positive returns, 201, 206, 212, 215, 217, 222, 223
   random, 221
   regression analyses of, 218*t*–220*t*
   regulation and comparison of proportions of, 213*t*–215*t*
market
   beta, by fund type and investment strategy, 91*t*–92*t*
   corners in activity of, 64
   dislocation, 269
   efficiency, 62
   emerging, 117
   failure, 273
   integrity, 62
   participants, 62n13
   squeezes in activity of, 64
   stabilization, 122, 157
   timer funds, 106, 115
   timing, 24
Market Abuse Directive (MAD), 66
marketing channels, 67, 108*t*–114*t*, 116, 119–20, 163. *See also specific channels*
   performance and structure impacted by, 159–60
   performance persistence and, 230
   U.S., 126, 161
market manipulation, 62
   rules, 63–65
Market Manipulation Rules Index, 65

market neutral hedge fund strategy, 10, 10f, 117
market prices, 64, 115
    liquidity crisis and, 274
Markets in Financial Instruments Directive (MiFiD), 66
marking the close, 64
marking the open, 64
master company, 12
master-feeder hedge fund structure, 12, 12f, 192, 192n9, 204, 204n4, 236
    performance persistence and, 254
mean square error (MSE), 206
media attention, 94–95, 96
merger/risk arbitrage, 98n13, 102
mergers and acquisitions (M&A), 30
micro cap
    capitalization, 95, 102
    investments, 31
MiFiD. See Markets in Financial Instruments Directive
mini-manipulations, 64
minimum capitalization, 8, 39, 40t–43t, 44, 115, 278, 279
    flow-performance relation and, 136, 153
    forum shopping for, 106, 116, 119–20
    fund flow and, 123, 138, 155
    misreported returns and, 200–201, 202, 205, 217, 221, 223, 225
    performance and structure impacted by, 159, 161, 193–94, 196–97
    performance persistence and, 227–29, 230, 231, 243, 254, 262, 263
    quality of funds and, 228
    regression analyses of forum shopping and, 107t
    requirements, 126
    restrictions, 19
misappropriation, 29
misreported returns, 163, 278, 279. See also marginally positive returns
    administrators and, 203
    characteristics and, 202, 204
    comparison of proportions by regulation, 213t–215t
    control variables, 204–5
    correlation of variables matrix, 216t
    data on regulation and, 205–6, 212
    discontinuity in returns around zero and, 207f
    distribution channels and, 200, 203, 223
    economic significance of, 222–23
    flow of funds, 225
    incentive, 199, 202, 205, 223, 225
    legal origin and, 202, 204
    liquidity and, 205
    minimum capitalization and, 200–201, 202, 205, 217, 221, 223, 225
    past performance and, 201–2, 204
    performance persistence and, 254

regression analyses, 212–22
regression analyses of marginally positive returns, 218t–220t
regulation and, 199–205, 208t–211t, 217, 221–22, 223, 225–26
research limitations, 223
restrictions on location of service providers and, 200, 202, 217, 221, 223
results of study, 217, 221–22
summary statistics, 206, 208t–211t, 212
variables defined, 208t–211t
wealth transfer and, 224t–225t
wrapper distribution and, 200–201, 217, 222, 223, 225
misreporting funds, 222–23
    performance persistence and, 236
monitoring, 35
    mechanisms, 21
MPPM. See manipulation-proof performance measure
MSE. See mean square error
multi-factor alpha, 71, 158, 159, 164–65
multi-factor models, 79, 86, 165–66
multi-fund, 204–5, 212, 222
    performance persistence and, 254
multi-strategy funds, 98n13, 102, 116, 271–72
mutual funds, 5, 6t–7t, 8
    compensation for, 24
    cross subsidization and, 24
    fees, 12–13
    flow-performance relation and, 127–28
    investors, 95
    manager, 13
    market timing and, 24
    proprietary investment and, 12–13
    regulatory oversight and, 11–12
    risk taking and, 23–24
    strategies and leverage, 9–11
    window dressing and, 22
    worldwide capital, 1, 95

net asset value (NAV), 162, 203, 222, 231
network diagrams, 272f
neutrality hypothesis, 103, 116, 117, 118, 192
new entries, 266
non-misreporting funds, 222–23
    performance persistence and, 236
nonproblem funds, 33t, 34t

obligator/creditor relationship, 271
Office of the Controller of the Currency, 265
offshore funds, 11, 124, 129, 138, 164, 192, 192n9, 204n4
    misreported returns and, 205
    onshore versus, 203–4, 243
    selection effects for, 154, 195
    taxation, 196, 203
    two-step treatment sample selection regressions, 260t–261t

1-year alpha, 241
  full sample, 247*t*–249*t*
  quartile ranking, 257*t*–259*t*
  by quartiles, 251*t*–253*t*
onshore funds, 11, 124, 129, 138, 154, 164, 192, 192n9, 204n4
  misreported returns and, 205
  offshore *versus*, 203–4, 243
  taxation, 196
operational risk, 32–33, 35
option-like compensation structure, 28, 32
orders, 65
ownership/capital structure, 34*t*

painting the tape, 65
parking manipulation, 65
partial hedges, 9
past performance, 127, 152
  misreported returns and, 201–2, 204
pension funds
  flow-performance relation and, 127–28
  window dressing and, 22
perfect hedge, 9
performance, 18, 136, 278, 280. *See also* flow-performance relationship; past performance
  fund flows and, 271
  incentives, 32
  measures of, 71–86, 130–31, 158, 164–66
  opaque, 254
  persistence, 19–20
  poor, 163
  regulation and, 19–20
  value and, 273
  variables defined, 167*t*–168*t*
performance and structure, regulation impacting, 157–58, 162
  comparison of means and medians tests, 174*t*–181*t*
  control variables, 195
  correlation of variables matrix, 173, 182*t*, 183
  data biases, 172
  data source, 166, 172
  data summarized, 193–94
  distribution channels and, 194–95, 196–97
  factors pertinent to, 166
  location and, 163–64
  measures, 164–66
  minimum capitalization and, 159, 161, 193–94, 196–97
  multivariate analyses, 183, 192–95
  regression analyses of, 184*t*–191*t*
  summary statistics, 167*t*–171*t*, 172–73
  variables defined, 167*t*–171*t*
  wrapper distribution and, 159, 160, 163, 192–93, 194–95
performance fee, 12, 14, 129, 158, 161, 197, 278. *See also* carried interest fee
  asymmetric, 24
  low, 163
  misreported returns and, 221
  returns and, 195
  schedules, 25
  symmetric, 24
performance persistence, 268, 278, 279
  fund flows and, 232, 236
  hypotheses, 232, 243, 254, 262
  minimum capitalization and, 227–29, 230, 231, 243, 254, 262, 263
  regression equation, 241–42
  robustness check on, 228, 262–63
  strategy variables for, 243
  treatment regression of, 260*t*–261*t*
  wrapper distribution and, 231–32, 262, 263
performance persistence, and regulation, 227–29, 230–32, 254, 263
  comparison tests, 238*t*–241*t*
  data, 232, 236–37
  multivariate regressions, 244*t*–253*t*
  multivariate tests, 236–63
  ranking regressions, 255*t*–259*t*
  regression models, 236, 241–43
  regression results, 243, 254, 262
  sources of data, 232, 236
  summary statistics, 233*t*–235*t*, 236–37
  variables defined, 233*t*–235*t*
personnel, 7*t*
Phillip Goldstein et al. v. SEC, 56
pooled investment vehicles, 8
poorly performing funds, 232, 237
portfolio, 3. *See also* delegated portfolio management
  assets, 204n4
  companies, 16
potential loss, 44
pre-arranged trade, 64
price. *See also* market prices
  entry and exit, 7*t*
  manipulation rules, 63–64
pricing, 8, 44
  lack of, 29–30
prime brokers, 4, 28, 125, 162, 230, 274
  misreported returns and, 203
principal-agent problem, 21–22, 32, 66
principals, 21
private adviser exemption, 56
private equity funds, 1, 5, 6*t*–7*t*, 8
  fees, 12–13
  manager, 13
  proprietary investment and, 12–13
  regulatory oversight and, 11–12
  strategies and leverage, 9–11
  taxation and, 54
private placement, 44, 127n6, 152, 155, 161n4, 194, 230n2, 254
  distribution, 116
  regression analyses of forum shopping and, 107*t*
  status, 126, 161

Index   297

problem funds, 33, 33t, 34t, 35
proprietary investment, 12–13
  conflicts from, 28
pump and dump schemes, 63

quartiles, 254. *See also* bottom quartile funds; top quartile funds
  based on rank of 3-year alpha, 238t–241t
  1-year alpha ranking, 257t–259t
  1-year alphas by, 251t–253t
  7-factor alpha rankings, 242
  3-year alphas by, 250t–251t
  3-year alphas ranking, 255t–257t

race to the bottom, 97, 98, 27 ,–79
  hypothesis, 103, 115, 116, 117, 118, 192
ramping/gouging, 63
rank returns, 152
  regression analyses for, 145t–151t
raw returns, 152, 279
  regression analyses for, 139t–144t
registrar, 4, 230
registration, 160, 192
  of advisers, 56–57
  under Investment Advisers Act, 55
  offshore/onshore, 11, 129, 154
  regulation and, 17–18
  requirements, 126, 158, 161
  strategies by country of, 104t–105t
  strategies relative to, 106
  systematic risk and, 274
  in U.S., 157
regression analyses
  capital raising, 136, 138–54
  flow-performance relationship and, 154
  of forum shopping, 107t–114t
  fund flows and fund rank returns, 145t–151t
  fund flows and fund raw returns, 139t–144t
  marginally positive returns, 218t–220t
  misreporting returns and regulation, 212–22
  of performance and structure impacted by regulation, 184t–191t
regulation, 7t, 26, 119–20, 136, 253. *See also* distribution channels; forum shopping; minimum capitalization; performance and structure, regulation impacting; performance persistence, and regulation; restrictions on location, of service providers; *specific regulations*
  D, 98n13, 114
  data on misreported returns, 205–6, 212
  Dodd-Frank Act and, 56–59
  economic significance, 222, 254
  in Europe, 59–62
  financial intermediation and, 38f
  flow-performance relation and, 125–27, 127f, 128f, 153
  fund flows and, 122–25
  fund governance impacted by, 19–20, 157–60
  Goldstein and, 55–56
  of hedge fund by country, 40t–43t
  improving, 265
  international differences in, 16–17, 39, 40t–43t, 67, 96–97, 131, 155, 200, 227, 232, 263, 278–80
  intra-country variations in, 154
  marginally positive return proportions by, 213t–215t
  market participants and, 62n13
  misreported returns, comparison of proportions by, 213t–215t
  misreported returns and, 199–205, 208t–211t, 217, 221–22, 223, 225–26
  performance and, 19–20
  prior to financial crisis, 39–46
  reform, 273–76
  registration and, 17–18
  regression analyses of misreporting returns and, 212–22
  restrictions on location and, 125–26
  role of, 278
  SEC and, 55
  structure and, 19–20
  time varying changes, 230, 263
  tolerance of, 119–20
  trading activity and, 62–67
  U.S., 2, 37–38, 55–59, 157, 160–63
  variables, 168t–169t, 266, 268
regulatory oversight, 11–12, 36, 162n7
  conflict from lack of, 29
  UCITS and, 60
  value-added governance and, 162, 231
report date, 130
reputation, 25–26
  hedge fund, 46
  service providers, 46
restrictions on location, of service providers, 19, 39, 40t–43t, 45–46, 278, 279
  flow funds and, 123, 138, 155
  flow-performance relation and, 136, 153
  forum shopping and, 106, 115–16, 119–20
  jurisdiction selection and, 125–26
  misreported returns and, 200, 202, 217, 221, 223
  performance and structure impacted by, 159, 161, 162, 192–93, 196–97
  performance persistence and, 227–29, 230, 231, 243, 254, 262, 263
  regression analyses of forum shopping and, 107t
  regulation and, 125–26
retail investors, 59, 95
  unsophisticated, 45
returns, 202. *See also* annualized returns average; excess returns average; marginally negative returns; marginally positive returns; misreported returns; rank returns; raw returns; standard deviation, of returns

returns (*Cont.*)
  alpha, 13, 129
  manipulation, 16, 95
  performance fee and, 195
  reported, 13
  targets, 5*t*
returns, monthly average, 99*t*–101*t*, 120, 158, 164
  discontinuity, 206
  discontinuity around zero, 207*f*
  performance and structure impacted by regulation and, 184*t*–191*t*, 196–97
return to scale, 7*t*
reward-to-variability ratio, 164
risk, 9, 98n13, 102. *See also* systematic risk; systemic risk
  balance sheet, 275, 275*f*
  banks exposed to, 270
  conflicts of interest and, 35
  credit, 271
  incentive-fee funds and, 24–25
  measures of, 86, 89–93
  non-linear, 271
  operational, 32–33, 35
  strategies and, 17, 94, 98
risk management, 6*t*, 117, 274
  AIFMD and, 61
risk taking, 24
  implicit incentives and, 23, 25–26
Rubin, Robert, 38

screening, 35
seasonality effect, 124, 154
SEC. *See* Securities and Exchange Commission
securities, 6*t*. *See also* distressed securities funds
  firm, 230
Securities Act of 1933, 11, 126
Securities and Exchange Commission (SEC), 11, 24, 25, 30, 32, 157, 161n5
  adviser registration and, 56–57
  Form ADV, 33, 33*t*–34*t*, 35, 35n1, 57
  information provided for, 273
  outside oversight of, 265
  regulation and, 55
  reporting requirements, 57, 58
  rule-making authority, 58
  Staff Report (2003), 55–56
Securities Exchange Act of 1933, 11
selection bias, 172
selection effects, 19, 215, 217, 221, 228, 262, 263
  with non-random decision, 138
  for offshore funds, 154, 195
  treatment regression and, 123
self-regulation, 119, 161, 280
sensitivities factor betas, 93
service providers, 125. *See also* restrictions on location, of service providers; *specific types*
  guides to, 228
  key, 39*f*
  misreported returns and, 203

quality, 162–63, 203, 227, 231, 279
reputation, 46
7-factor alpha, 79, 86, 93, 165–66, 236
  by fund type and investment strategy, 87*t*–88*t*
  quartile rankings of, 242
shadow banking, 265, 273
share restrictions, 160
Sharpe ratio, 74, 164, 279
  by fund type and investment strategy, 77*t*–78*t*
shocks, 272
short biased strategies, 95, 98n13, 102
short-selling, 30, 61
single factor alpha, 165
single-strategy fund, 47*t*–52*t*
size, hedge fund, 13–14, 106, 106n25, 129, 154–55, 157, 166, 199, 279. *See also* minimum capitalization
size effect, 221–22
small/micro cap capitalization, 95, 102
Sophisticated Alternative Investment Vehicles, 2
sophisticated investor, 27, 95
speed, 7*t*
sponsor, 163
  conflicts of interest with manager, 231–32
  fund, 163
spoofing manipulation rules, 65
squeezes, in market activity, 64
Stability Oversight Council, 58–59
standard deviation, of returns, 86, 99*t*–101*t*, 102, 120, 159, 164
  by fund type and investment strategy (monthly returns), 89*t*–90*t*
  performance and structure impacted by regulation and, 184*t*–191*t*
standard factors exposure, 271–72
static hedge, 10
statistical arbitrage, 102, 112
stock exchanges, 62
strategies, hedge fund, 1, 3, 6*t*, 9–11, 95, 99*t*–101*t*, 278. *See also* investment strategies; CISDM categories; *specific strategies*
  agency problems and, 30–31, 98, 102
  benefits of, 119–20
  classifications, 102
  conflict of interest and, 16
  conflict potentials from, 30–31
  by country of registration, 104*t*–105*t*
  forum shopping in relation to, 118, 120, 192
  off-setting, 31
  registration relative to, 106
  risk and, 17, 94, 98
  structure and, 160
  UCITS and, 60
  variables for performance persistence, 243
structure, of hedge funds, 2–13, 158, 278, 280. *See also* performance and structure, regulation impacting

efficiency, 162, 163
  regulation and, 19–20
  strategies and, 160
  top quartile, 228
Summers, Larry, 38
support services, 30
survival, of hedge fund, 265, 266
  determinants of, 19
survivorship, 138n10
  bias, 172, 223, 236, 268
switches, 65
symmetric performance fee contracts, 24
systematic risk, 1, 273, 276, 279
  financial crisis and, 265, 269–73
  registration and, 274
systemic risk, 37
  indirect evidence of, 269–71
systemwide shocks, 272

TASS, 98, 172
tax adviser, 228
taxation
  barriers to distribution of hedge funds, 53t–54t
  by country, 47t–52t
  fund flow and, 123–24, 153–54, 155
  international differences in, 46
  liabilities, 154
  managers and, 16, 47t–52t
  offshore funds, 196, 203
  onshore funds, 196
  private equity funds and, 54
  venture capital funds and, 54
technology sector funds, 115–16, 117–18
tercile rank, 129, 153
3-year alphas, 236
  full sample, 244t–246t
  quartile ranking, 255t–257t
  by quartiles, 250t–251t
  quartiles based on rank of, 238t–241t
Tobit regressions, 106n26
top quartile funds, 229, 236, 262
  structure and, 228
  wrappers and, 254
trading
  activity and regulations, 62–67
  commodity advisers, 1, 24, 99t, 115
  exchange, 62–67
  insider, 62–63
  pre-arranged, 64
  wash, 64–65
traditional investment funds, hedge funds versus, 4, 5t, 6t–7t
transfer agent, 4, 230
transparency, 8, 26, 275
  Dodd-Frank Act and, 58–59
  information, 273–74, 276
  lack of, 29–30
  seeking, 44

UCITS and, 60
Treasury, 265
treatment regression, 123, 130, 138
  of performance persistence, 260t–261t
  selection effects and, 123
Treynor ratio, 74, 79
  by fund type and investment strategy, 80t–81t
trustees, 125, 162, 203, 230
2 and 20 fee model, 2–3

UCITS. *See* Undertakings for Collective Investment in Transferable Securities Directive
UK. *See* United Kingdom
underperformance, 269
Undertakings for Collective Investment in Transferable Securities Directive (UCITS), 38, 59–60, 278
United Kingdom (UK), 1
  financial regulators in, 2
  voluntary disclosure standards, 37
United States (U.S.), 1, 278
  Dodd-Frank Act and, 56–59
  marketing channels, 126, 161
  net worth of investor families, 27
  registration, 157
  regulations, 2, 37–38, 55–59, 157, 160–63

valuation, 8, 44
  AIFMD and, 61
  independent, 29–30
value, 98n13, 116. *See also* net asset value
  performance and, 273
value-added governance, 162, 202, 231
variance inflation factors (VIF), 215n6
venture capital funds, 5, 6t–7t
  taxation and, 54
VIF. *See* variance inflation factors
Volcker Rule, 58
volume manipulation rules, 64–65
voluntary reporting, 13
voting rights, 31, 96
vulture fund activity, 16, 96

Wall Street Journal, 37
warehousing, 65
wash trading, 64–65
wealth transfer, 201, 223, 225
  misreporting and, 224t–225t
window dressing, 22–23
winsorization, 71n2
wrappers, 152, 155, 163, 279
  construction, 232
  flow-performance relation and, 127, 217
  products, 45, 116–17
  quartiles and, 254
wrapper distribution
  economic significance and, 217

wrapper distribution (*Cont.*)
  misreported returns and, 200–201, 217, 222, 223, 225
  performance and structure impacted by, 159, 160, 163, 192–93, 194–95
  performance persistence and, 231–32, 262, 263
wrapper marketing, 123

regression analyses of forum shopping and, 107*t*

yearly redemption, 153, 205
  performance persistence and, 254

zero reports, 206, 207*f*, 212, 215